Florida A&M University, Tallahassee
Florida Atlantic University, Boca Raton
Florida Gulf Coast University, Ft. Myers
Florida International University, Miami
Florida State University, Tallahassee
University of Central Florida, Orlando
University of Florida, Gainesville
University of North Florida, Jacksonville
University of South Florida, Tampa
University of West Florida, Pensacola

Maximum Insight

Selected Columns by

Bill Maxwell

University Press of Florida

GAINESVILLE · TALLAHASSEE · TAMPA · BOCA RATON

PENSACOLA · ORLANDO · MIAMI · JACKSONVILLE · FT. MYERS

06 05 04 03 02 01   6 5 4 3 2 1

Library of Congress Cataloging-in-Publication Data
Maxwell, Bill, 1945–
Maximum insight : selected columns / by Bill Maxwell.
p. cm.
ISBN 0-8130-2436-6 (acid-free paper)
1. African Americans—Florida—Social conditions. 2. Florida—Race
relations. 3. Florida—Social conditions. 4. Florida—Environmental
conditions. 5. United States—Race relations. 6. African Americans—
Social conditions—1975– . 7. United States—Social conditions—1980– .
8. Maxwell, Bill, 1945– —Political and social views. 9. Maxwell, Bill,
1945– . 10. African American journalists—Florida—Biography. I. Title.

F320.N4 M39 2001
305.896'0730759—dc21   2001034786

The University Press of Florida is the scholarly publishing agency
for the State University System of Florida, comprising Florida A&M
University, Florida Atlantic University, Florida Gulf Coast University,
Florida International University, Florida State University, University of
Central Florida, University of Florida, University of North Florida,
University of South Florida, and University of West Florida.

University Press of Florida
15 Northwest 15th Street
Gainesville, FL 32611–2079
http://www.upf.com

This book is dedicated to Iris Rose Hart,

the consummate editor

Contents

Foreword

I remember the first time I heard Bill Maxwell speak in public. It was in the fall of 1997 at the *St. Petersburg Times* Reading Festival. I was sitting with several hundred others in a large circular chapel at Eckerd College, where Maxwell was about to introduce the famous New York City columnist and author Jimmy Breslin.

I sat up high behind the lectern, where I could not see the speaker's face but had a good view of the audience across the chapel. It was overwhelmingly white, in both skin tone and hair color.

Up to the lectern stepped one of the few African-Americans in the room. He was middle-aged and had broad shoulders, the body of a rugged old marine or aging pugilist.

"Good afternoon," he said in a shy, deep voice, "I'm Bill Maxwell from the *St. Petersburg Times*."

That simple introduction produced a hearty burst of applause—warmer, as it turned out, than anything his more famous Big Apple counterpart would inspire that day. His audience was expressing its appreciation for one of the most distinctive and independent voices in American journalism. It is a voice that can inspire and infuriate, especially when Bill Maxwell writes about race. But it is a voice that must not be ignored, especially if we Americans hope to create in this next century something that looks vaguely like a multiracial, multiethnic democracy.

His liberal credentials are impeccable. Maxwell writes and speaks with passion in favor of affirmative action, preserving the environment, civil liberties, and social justice for immigrants and migrant farmworkers. He runs a writing program for young minority students. And on issues of race, he has written with enormous power about the routine indignities that black Americans—including Maxwell himself—face. He does not ignore or deny the historical or contemporary victimization of African-American citizens by white people.

But here's the rub: he is impatient with those who do not proceed boldly toward self-sufficiency, and he refuses to accept white racism as an excuse for black criminality, incivility, disrespect, or other forms of misbehavior. In criticizing some aspects of African-American culture, Maxwell has violated one of that culture's most enduring standards, which is not to hang out dirty laundry in public.

Surely, the argument goes, enough white journalists exist out there writing about young African-American males in negative ways. Must we abide a "brother" writer who follows the same path? Is he trying to please white readers? Does his criticism mask self-hatred?

Because Maxwell is not a joiner, his work has been rejected, and he has been ostracized by parts of the community from which he sprang. He has been the object of threats. And he has been lumped—foolishly—with a so-called new vanguard of conservative black thinkers, including that all-purpose bête noire, Clarence Thomas.

Such critics ignore the powerful forces that forged within Bill Maxwell his independent spirit. A proud and stubborn south Florida native, Maxwell was raised in a migrant farming family. At 19 years of age, he marched with Dr. King across the Edmund Pettus Bridge in Selma, Alabama, and was gassed and beaten by white deputies. During the Vietnam era, he served in the U.S. Marines. His schooling led him from Bethune-Cookman College to the University of Chicago, where a lifelong love of literature was punctuated with a master's degree in English. Maxwell is, all at once, a Floridian, a social activist, a teacher, a journalist, and a man of letters.

The combination reveals itself in this collection of columns, which could not come to us at a better time. The general reader will be impressed by Bill Maxwell's range and passion. The student and teacher will find models of style and analysis worthy of study and debate. And those Americans ready for a real conversation about race will find all the stimulus we need to get our juices flowing.

Roy Peter Clark

Preface

As an African-American columnist for the *St. Petersburg Times*, one of the nation's largest dailies, I feel a special responsibility to be more than the average newspaperman. I feel the need to cast light on subjects that most of society would prefer to leave in the dark. I intentionally look for those areas most of us only whisper about in our homes—those that reveal our humanity.

How many of us, for example, speak truthfully about race, about the historical, ugly enmity between white and black people? Most journalists I know, especially whites, would rather avoid the subject altogether because to discuss it means exposing oneself to the wrath of a public that made up its mind about race and race matters long ago. Many of my African-American colleagues routinely tackle race, but they, too, would rather write about something else.

Frankly, I also would rather not write about race. Sometimes, the process is almost too painful to bear.

Since I have been given a venue from which to voice my opinion, however, I feel obligated to explore race and other issues that make most of us uncomfortable. Indeed, my main interest lies in the zones of emotion and thought that define who we are—if only we have the courage to confront ourselves, to discover new answers, to deconstruct the easy postulates that have guided our thinking, our private conduct, and our relations with others unlike ourselves.

Again, I see myself as more than a newspaper columnist and an editorial writer. I also view myself as a social critic. As the late Christopher Lasch stated in a 1994 interview with the *Journal of American History*, social criticism is unlike columns and editorials in that it is "more deeply informed by a study of history, literature, philosophy, and the social sciences. It is less concerned with public policy, strictly speaking, or with day-to-day commentary on party politics or administrative detail. A social critic tries to catch the general drift of the times, to show how a particular incident or policy or a distinctive configuration of sentiments holds up a mirror to society, revealing patterns that otherwise might go undetected. But a social critic, unlike a scholar of the purest type, also takes sides, passes judgment."

For me, then, the editorial and the column provide the literary form for my social commentary. And passing judgment on a host of issues—farmworkers' affairs, discrimination against black farmers, religious intolerance, homophobia, public education, literacy, Florida's environment—is central to my work, especially as an African-American. For the black male, who naturally lacks real power in America, whose voice is often muted by selective exposure and selective retention, the column offers a unique entrée into mainstream discourse. I have long known that the black voice outside mainstream discourse is no voice at all. Once inside the mainstream, the black writer has a duty to take risks, to take unpopular positions, to be the iconoclast. Needless to say, though, he or she also must be a voice of reason and moderation when the rest of society loses its way.

But walking into controversy and generating debate are not enough to validate the work of the black writer. Even winning the argument is not enough. The black columnist must try to find the truth, no matter how painful. By truth, I mean more than reporting what is actual or making sure that what we write conforms to reality and fact. I also mean discovering and interpreting the root causes of our cultural and social crises. I also mean offering viable solutions to the problems that drive wedges among the various groups. Truth-seeking and truth-telling demand the courage to be condemned by readers. The thin-skinned will not be able to withstand the venom in those nasty letters to the editor.

The black writer's most agonizing task—and duty—is being dispassionate about the foibles and self-destructive behavior of African-Americans. Much of my writing comments on negative behavior among blacks. The wrath of blacks toward black writers who criticize their own is virtually unmatched between other writers and the groups to which they belong. The black writer is seen as a member of a "family" of victims and the dispossessed. Family members do not criticize their kin, their brethren. To do so is to betray the faith and, of course, to give ammunition to the enemy, the white bigots who are irredeemably hostile toward the very existence of black people in U.S. society.

I comment on black self-immolation as often as I comment on white racism. Why? Because I believe that such exposure, the very act of acknowledging our faults, strengthens black people. For example, blacks are better off when permitted to discuss openly the discrimination along skin-tone lines that has kept light-skinned and dark-skinned blacks separated ever since slave owners produced the first mulattoes. Untold numbers of black relationships have been destroyed—or never got off the ground—because of skin tone. But few blacks openly discuss this well-kept secret. Little does the rest of society know that light-skinned and dark-skinned blacks often have relations that are as hateful and strained as those between blacks and whites.

Many black writers pretend that they are writers first and black second. I do not. I was black before I became a writer, and my skin color is more than a reflection of my soul. It is my soul. It is Bill Maxwell, the black columnist. It shapes my views and influences my reactions to events and ideas.

So in addition to examining the self-destructive side of black culture, the black writer should affirm the beauty and authenticity of blackness, which takes courage in our increasingly conservative culture, a culture that views blacks with contempt, that sees us as whining beneficiaries of so-called preferential treatment. Here, the black writer must stand up to the thinking, the rhetoric, and the acts that diminish blacks and further divide the nation.

The black writer, especially a newspaper columnist who enjoys broad readership, must define who black people are in relation to a society that generally despises them. For me, no human issue in the United States is more important than the precarious condition of the black male. He has been dubbed an endangered species for good reason. Part of my job is to show the reader the essence of the black male in all of its complexity.

What is the essence of being a black male in America, a nation that has criminalized black male masculinity, that perceives us as dangerous, exotic outsiders? The black columnist must use his insight to illuminate this problem for others. The whole world, especially America, has much to learn from the black male. A main problem, obviously, is the dearth of black writers, especially males, willing to open their veins and let the secrets, frustrations, and ideas flow.

But someone must write about the black male condition. How else can whites understand that their vision of themselves and their world is in large measure intricately tied to their perceptions of black males? Another of my tasks, then, is to show white people that their existence is the black male's existence, that their whiteness is what it is because of African-American blackness.

Affirmative action, for example—seen by many whites as a program giving pathetic, unqualified blacks, especially males, a leg up over qualified white males—is as much of a way to help blacks as it is a painless way for white people to redeem their race for centuries of inhumanity against an entire class of citizens. Seen in this way, affirmative action is not a black or a white program. Whites need to know that affirmative action is an American program, a buffer, a neutral place where right and wrong intersect for the purpose of moral healing and establishing long-overdue fairness.

Further, my job is to show that blacks are a redacted class crying out for affirmation, and I also must let whites see that blacks, males in particular, have been reduced to being shadowy lines, blurred or invisible characters, and abbreviated images beneath the pitch-black ink on the page. As a result of such diminution, our faces have no definition, and, therefore, we all look alike. Our voices are barely audible, and, therefore, we all sound the same. Society knows that we are there—or that we have been there. No one can touch us, however. Few want to touch us. We have been driven back.

White Americans need to know all of this. The black writer can help them come to terms with the nation's legacy of racism and the nation's need to understand that the problems of black people should be the concern of every American.

I do not intend to leave the impression that all of the columns collected here are about race matters. They are not. All of them do, however, reflect the Weltanschauung of a black man in Florida, a state with a diverse population, where various ethnicities clash, where resurgent bigotry and Republicanism have left blacks more marginalized than they have been in a generation. I hope that these selections deepen readers' appreciation and understanding of the newspaper column as social criticism and of the role of the black writer as an interpreter of the forces that define a diverse America. The black writer in me wants to help people of all races sincerely engage the difficult and often painful task of thinking through the complex issues of whiteness and blackness.

Acknowledgments

When you are a professional curmudgeon—an irascible opinion writer—
you make many enemies. So when your publisher asks you to write acknowl-
edgments for a collection of your opinions, you suddenly wonder who to
thank for helping you forge such a dubious career. After all, who in his or her
right mind wants to be associated with an ill-tempered fellow who apparently goes out of his way to offend others?

Alas, such is the plight of a newspaper opinion columnist. For the last 15
years, I have written a syndicated column that has sparked controversy
among readers who want matters to be agreeable and tidy. And during these
years, many people, including relatives, friends, colleagues, employers, and
strangers, have aided me in developing my craft and have provided safe
harbor when I fell into the bottomless pit of self-doubt—that moment when
a columnist mistrusts his own opinion or on those bleak mornings when a
dumb mistake appears in bold print for millions to read.

The introduction to this book was originally published in *Forum: The
Magazine of the Florida Humanities Council*, in its summer 1999 issue, under
the title "Parallel Lives: Bill Maxwell, Angry Young Man." I am happy to be
able to reprint an edited version here. I also wish to thank the *St. Petersburg
Times* not only for allowing me to work out of its offices but for the use of the
photos contained in this book (with the exception of my childhood ones, of
course).

These are the wonderful people who nurtured me along the way:

My parents, Jeanette Wise Maxwell and Willie Wise.

From many walks of life: Harriet Abram, Mike Abram, Gloria Brown
Anderson, Caryn Baird, Andy Barnes, Kitty Bennett, Lennie Bennett, Rob-
ert Bentley, Lillie Mae Bentley, Arthur Berger, Gloria Bonaparte, Sharon
Bond, Neil Brown, Tony Burns, Les Carson, Charles Cherry, Angela
Clifford, Beverly Coyle, Carol Craig, Ron Cunningham, Buddy Davis,
Kim Davis, CeCe DeWolf, Letitia Dobosy, Martin Dyckman, Jon East,

Bob Enns, Robert Friedman, Bob Fryer, Phil Gailey, Dude Glover, Kathy Green, Archie Gresham, John Griffith, Eileen Gudat, Margo Hammond, Deb Harvey, Iris Rose Hart, George Hatcher, Grace Hatcher, Ann Henderson, John Hill, Charli Holtz, Norma Homan, Sid Homan, Constance Howard, Anna Hubbard, Ann Hull, Bernard Irving, Steve Jackson, Laura Jones, Kurt Kent, Karen Kisten, Jeff Klinkenberg, Eric Lacker, Charlene Lawson, Gretchen Letterman, Mary Little, Judith Lombard, Alzeda Maxwell, Benjamin Maxwell, Anastasia Maxwell, Elizabeth Maxwell, Jeannie Maxwell, Maree Maxwell, Phyllis McEwen, Robert McKee, Bill McKeen, Robin Mitchell, Hubert Mizell, Barbara Moch, John Moran, Jean Mull, Tim Nickens, Laura Oldanie, Betty Owen, Mary Jane Park, Benton Patterson, Gene Patterson, Acenett Peters, Bobby Popler, Sam Puckett, Jack Reed, Eric Reno, Diane Roberts, Ned Rosenheim, Bob Rosenthal, Lois Sessems, Jonathan Shaw, Wilbert Sippio, Karen Sitren, Barbara Sloan, Marion Speight, Thurman Stanback, Gigi Stengard, Chip Stout, Paul Tash, Leonard Tipton, Gina Vivinetto, Deborah Hardin Wagner, Jamie Watson, Gloria Weinberg, Sally Ann Welford, Josephine Wesley, Ed Weston, Charlie Wise, Helen Wise, Barbara Wise, Sharon Wynne, John Young, and Erma Young-Certain.

The people who contributed to the making of this book: John Ames, Jay Black, Deidre Bryan, Stephanie Chariello, Roy Peter Clark, Susan Fernandez, Corinna Greene, Larry Leshan, Sam Riley, Brad Rogers, and Nicole Sorenson.

And finally, the staff of the Florida Humanities Council, the staff of Bok Tower Gardens, the members of the Role Models Foundation, and all the loyal readers of my column.

Introduction

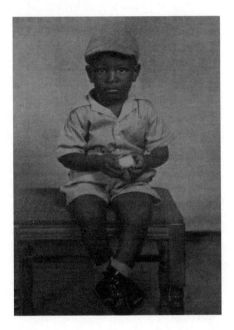

I was born in Ft. Lauderdale on October 16, 1945, in the city's all-Negro hospital. Negro babies could not be delivered in the white hospitals. My parents were farmworkers who labored long and hard but could not regularly make ends meet. When I was 18 months old, Broward County's pole bean crop was devastated by heavy rains, and my parents had to "go up the road" to find work. En route to Exmore, Virginia, where they would work in potatoes, they left me in Crescent City with my father's mother and stepfather, Lillie Mae and Robert Albert Dunlap; there I lived much of my childhood until I went away to college in 1963.

Crescent City, between Palatka and DeLand on U.S. Highway 17, is on the eastern rim of the Ocala National Forest, less than 40 miles inland from the Atlantic Ocean. It is next to Lake Stella, tiny Lake Argenta, and Crescent Lake.

Crescent City was not a utopia. It seemed, however—and I am speaking only of the Negro communities because I rarely had close contact with local whites—a black version of paradise in my early years, where black children, mostly boys, roamed the woodlands and fields barefoot without a care, where black girls in gingham dresses skipped rope under live oak, magnolia, and camphor trees. And back then, citrus, fern, and pulpwood provided jobs for most Negroes who wanted to work, at least seasonally. The eccentric could eke out a living pulling deer tongue and Spanish moss, pulling and selling gopher tortoises.

My grandparents' house was a green-shingled, three-bedroom, shotgun-style structure with a matching two-hole outhouse across the dirt road. On three acres of sandy soil near Lake Argenta, we grew all of our vegetables and fruits. We had no cows or hogs, but our chickens laid enough eggs for five families.

Religion—the real fear of a living God who, at will, intervenes in earthly matters—anchored the lives of the adults. My grandfather was a presiding elder in the House of God, Church of the Living God, the Pillar Ground of Truth Without Controversy—a black Pentecostal, or Holiness, denomination. He was also the pastor of three congregations: one in St. Augustine, one in Palatka, and one in Crescent City. He routinely conducted or participated in tent revivals throughout north central Florida and the Panhandle. I accompanied him on these trips when my grandmother had to work or was "too plumb tired" to travel, as she would say.

Things were different beyond the boundaries of our communities, however. One of the most violent events of my early childhood involving white people occurred when I was 10 years old and went with my grandfather to a three-day tent revival in Lake City. Pilgrims came from several nearby counties. On the second afternoon of the gathering, a group of boys and I walked to a store in a black neighborhood. I bought my usual: a frosty bottle of Nehi grape soda, a bag of salted peanuts, and a giant dill pickle. Returning to the tent, we roughhoused, played the dozens, and fantasized about pretty girls as we approached the railroad tracks.

Out of nowhere, a Ford pickup roared toward us. We could hear the horn blasting and the rebel yells. Three white teenage boys sat in the cab, and five or six others rode in the bed. We knew what was coming because, although we came from different regions of the state, we had seen this potentially deadly game before.

We were about to be "nigger-knocked."

As the adults in our lives had taught us, we ran in different directions to confuse our attackers. I had been nigger-knocked a year earlier on my newspaper route in Crescent City. I was pedaling my bicycle along Union Avenue and was preparing to toss a copy of the *Palatka Daily News* into a yard when a woody carrying three white boys approached. The passenger in the backseat hit me in the face with a balloon full of urine.

On that day in Lake City, I knew immediately that I had doomed myself by looking back. A boy in the truck bed held a leather belt in the air, the silver buckle twirling above his head. Suddenly, I saw the buckle descend, and, just as suddenly, everything went black. Pain ripped through my face. Cupping my nose, I smelled my own blood and felt it pouring into my palms, then between my fingers. I thought that I would pass out and that I had lost both eyes. After several of my companions returned to help, I was surprised that I could see.

My nose had been broken, and the gash was deep enough to reveal bone. My friends helped me back to the tent, where the standing-room-only crowd was "shouting" (a spiritual dance) to the syncopated sounds of drums, a piano, and dozens of tambourines.

My grandfather, who was in the makeshift pulpit with several other preachers, saw me and ran toward me. The eyes of the crowd followed. I stood in the aisle holding the bridge of my nose.

The front of my starched white shirt was covered with my blood. The wife of the local minister, with whom we were staying, took me to her house, flushed my wound with antiseptic, bandaged it, and gave me one of her husband's shirts. That night, my grandfather drove me to the black doctor in Gainesville.

That incident made me fully aware of our estrangement. In fact, white people were a mystery to us in Crescent City. They were strangers. We would see them downtown or catch a glimpse of them driving their cars and trucks. Some of us took orders from them at work. But we rarely saw their faces up close.

The early morning sun was blazing hot as my grandfather and I drove to the Putnam County Courthouse in Palatka. I was excited because I was about to start the paperwork for getting a restricted driver's license. I had stayed up all night, dreaming of driving my grandparents' 1949 Chevrolet, of showing off in front of the girls at Middleton High School in Crescent City, of wearing exotic cologne and holding my wrist dangerously loose over the steering wheel as I had seen my father and other men do around women. And, of course, I dreamed of owning a fast, sporty coupe.

The year was 1959, and I was a few months away from being old enough to drive legally.

My grandfather and I climbed the courthouse stairs, moving aside at the door to let three white women pass. At the counter, a clerk, an older white woman with eyes that instinctively looked through black people without seeing their humanity, gave me a form to fill out. My grandfather sat in the chair beneath the ceiling fan, his hat resting awkwardly on his lap. An armed sheriff's deputy, a tall white man with a ruddy face and hairy arms, stood beside me. Leaning on the counter, he chatted with the woman, studied me from head to toe, and glanced over at my grandfather. The room was hot, and I was nervous.

When the woman asked if I had a pen, I said, "No, I don't." I had no idea that those three simple words had violated two centuries of strict tradition and had exposed me to the oath that required a white man to protect the honor of a white woman—especially if he imagined that her honor had been trampled on by a Negro.

As I reached for the pen that she was handing me, the deputy grabbed my left shoulder, spun me around to face him, shoved my back against the wall, and pressed his forearm against my chest.

"You say, 'Yes, ma'am,' and 'No, ma'am' to a white lady, you little nigger," he said in a low, deliberate tone, his breath smelling of tobacco.

Never will I forget the way he said "nigger" and the rage in his eyes. Over the years, I have relived this incident, assessing my reaction to it at the time and measuring its long-term effect on who I have become. Doubtless, it was a watershed in the life of a proud 14-year-old black kid, a happy teenager who saw himself quickly growing into manhood. Now, I look back and marvel that—given the racial customs of that time, when white men believed that they had a God-given right to do anything they pleased to Negroes—I was lucky to have escaped physically unharmed.

Weighing about 190 pounds and standing nearly six feet, I stiff-armed the deputy in the face. I caught him off balance, and he went back, stumbling to hold himself up.

"Keep your hands off me!" I shouted.

Unaccountably, I was unafraid, only insulted and angry. He grabbed the edge of the counter and balanced himself. I looked into his eyes, knowing that he wanted to shoot me. Perhaps I imagined the hesitant downward movement of his hand for his pistol. But I did not imagine the heat of bigotry in his eyes, the heavy burden of his being of the "superior race."

As I stared at him, he looked away, turned to my grandfather, and said, "Git this little trouble-making nigger out of here. He thinks he's Martin Luther King or somebody."

"Don't call me a nigger!" I shouted, moving toward him.

By now, my grandfather, a gentle man infused with the serenity of the deeply devout, was trembling. Jumping to his feet, he pulled me down the hallway and out of the building. Terror was in his eyes as we passed the Confederate Heroes monument on the front lawn. In the car, he did not look at me, nor did he speak to me. We drove the 26 miles back to Crescent City in silence.

When he died four years ago, we still had not discussed that day. I can only guess at his reason for never talking about it. But I know what it did to me. It introduced into my young consciousness a sense of personal vulnerability and mortality. Until then, I had been like other children: I believed that I was invincible and would live forever. But on that day, there I stood, in that muggy courthouse, facing a man who wanted to annihilate me, who could have annihilated me with the squeeze of a finger.

Why would he have done so?

Because my skin was black. Because I forgot the lay of the land and stepped out of my "place" when I did not say "ma'am" to a white woman. Even at that young age, I understood that my fate was in the hands of a total stranger, a white man—an adult—who despised me—a young boy—for no logical reason. I clearly understood that life in the South was unfair, that being a Negro in northeast Florida was a high-risk game of minimizing physical assaults.

Even more, though, I walked away from that courthouse with an altered psyche and a diminished sense of self—conditions that I would spend subsequent years trying to repair. Indeed, the courthouse encounter was a turning point for me, but it was also the fulcrum in my growth, the point of support from which I now can appreciate the wholeness of my life. In other words, all events that occurred before that day in Palatka prepared me for surviving it.

Crescent City was not an openly brutal place. In many ways, beyond what I have said already, it was a good place, better than most other towns I later visited as a farmworker on the nation's East Coast and throughout the Southeast. In Crescent City, the separation of the races was taken for granted on both sides. Black people bowed and scraped. Whites felt superior and benevolently endured our presence. Their neglect of us was a benign one. Many stores, such as Hilda's Style Shop, Sackett's Grocery, and the hardware store, extended credit to blacks, and the People's Bank of Crescent City never turned down qualified borrowers because of their race as far as any of us ever knew.

Our doctors and our dentist, all white, permitted blacks and whites to sit together in the same waiting room. Many other medical professionals in neighboring towns had segregated waiting rooms in those years.

Many older blacks and older whites developed the kind of intimacy peculiar to the generation that had lived as master and servant.

Still, the vast differences between our two worlds were manifested almost everywhere, especially at Lake Stella, where many children, black and white, spent their summers. We assumed that nature had drawn a line across the 308-acre lake, separating the white side from the black side. We swam and played on the "Babylon side"—named for the community that was home to the African-American graveyard—and whites used the "downtown side." It had white sand, which the town provided, on its shore. Our side was grassy and muddy and dotted with dead mussels.

Many of the whites had beautiful motorboats, and we envied the white children as they skimmed across the lake on colorful skis. None of our families could afford a motorboat, and none of us had waterskis. We enjoyed ourselves on the lake by creating games.

The greatest challenge, which most of us met with ease, was swimming from our side of Stella to Billy Goat Island. We had the most fun, though, playing a game called "gator." We would draw lots. Whoever drew the shortest marsh reed became the gator. The game's object was to outswim the gator. After the designated gator caught someone, a great struggle would ensue as the gator tried to pull the captive under water and hold him there. After freeing himself—or being released—the captive would become the new gator. Needless to say, we often came very close to drowning the weakest swimmers. But we had fun.

Even so, we felt the racial alienation. We could not, for example, eat at Thomas Drugstore's lunch counter or at Hap's Diner, which doubled as the Greyhound Bus Station. (In the early sixties, when a group of us tried to integrate the drugstore counter one afternoon, the owner threatened us with jail and telephoned our principal, Harry Burney, who dutifully informed our parents.)

At the town's movie theater, whites sat downstairs and blacks in the balcony. After the theater closed and became a bowling alley, blacks were no longer permitted inside.

Back then, busing for black children meant the opposite of what it means today. The cynical among us believed that the Almighty himself had created busing to keep "the coloreds" away from white children. Until the late 1950s, many students at all-black Middleton Junior High woke between 5:00 and 5:30 each morning and walked more than a mile to the bus that took us to Central Academy in Palatka. The direct route from Crescent City to the school, by way of U.S. Highway 17, was about 30 miles.

But we could not take the direct route. Too many kids lived back in the woods. The driver picked up the first students in the southern region called Long Station. Then she drove north to the other local black neighborhoods—Denver, Rossville, Whitesville, Babylon (where I lived), and Union Avenue. Leaving Crescent City, the 30 or more of us went southwest to Georgetown and Fruitland, then northwest to Welaka. From there, we drove northeast to Pomona Park and then due north on Highway 17 to Satsuma, San Mateo, and East Palatka. We would arrive at Central Academy between 8:15 and 8:30, barring mechanical trouble or a boat stopping us on the Dunns Creek drawbridge.

During the shortest days of winter, we left home in the dark and returned in the dark. But we did so happily because we thoroughly enjoyed school. For this reason, our bus rides were fun, with something new happening every day. Many of our lasting romances began on the bus. (Some who met on the bus are still married, some 40 years later.) We told one another our deepest secrets there.

In time we realized that, although school was fun and our bus rides were adventures, we were victims of Jim Crow's intentional cruelty. As our innocence died and as we absorbed the reality of living as Negro children in the segregated South, play became increasingly more important to us. We escaped the racial hostility of southern Putnam County through play. Because we were poor and could not buy ready-made toys and games, we had to invent and build.

A group of us performed our greatest building feat after watching several episodes of *Gunsmoke* on TV. We built our version of Dodge City. For several weeks, we collected scrap lumber, sheets of tin, and several pounds of nails; we chopped blackjack oaks and collected palmetto fronds. After about five weeks of sawing, hammering, and digging, we had built six mean structures, each with its own crudely painted sign: "Long Branch Saloon," "Doc's Office," "Marshal Dillon's Office and Jail," "Dodge House Hotel," "Livery Stable," and "Church."

We were happy. During the day, we played Gunsmoke and waded in brown brooks teeming with crawdads and tadpoles. At night, we built campfires and roasted hot dogs. Our folks let us sleep in Dodge as often as we wished. We never comprehended the incredible irony of our Dodge City experience: we were black children, locked in a black world, playing white characters and reenacting white situations, although blacks rarely appeared in the television show.

Bill at fifteen (back row, third from left) was vice president of his junior class. He attended the statewide Florida Student Government meeting at Bethune-Cookman College and appears here as part of the group of officers elected at the meeting.

As we grew older and the decade of the 1950s neared its end, we played fewer unstructured, escapist games among ourselves. Varsity football and basketball, pool, cards, talking trash, dittybopping, playing pinball at Chuck's Barbershop, and flirting with the girls became our new games.

At the same time, we had begun to hear of names such as the Reverend Martin Luther King, Rosa Parks, Elijah Muhammad, and Malcolm X. And, of course, we learned about the Montgomery bus boycott in school. Times were changing. African-Americans everywhere were beginning to speak out. The civil rights movement was in full force.

Gradually, I became keenly aware of the subtle dynamics in my encounters with whites. Increasingly, I noticed also that I was beginning to refer to whites as "crackers," even though I did not know what a cracker was. Many of my friends and teachers noticed that I was becoming aware of the gross unfairness in the black-white dichotomy and that I was becoming angrier.

My grandmother was a maid, and one of her sites was the Crescent City Women's Club. In addition to being a meeting place and a dining room, the facility served as the local public library, housing at least 2,000 books. When my grandmother took me with her to help clean the building one Saturday morning, I saw the books for the first time. The vast number of volumes and the smell of old leather and parchment were intoxicating. I was unfamiliar with most of the titles and authors. After that morning, I came with my grandmother every chance I got.

I spent more time reading than cleaning. At first, my grandmother would scold me for not working. Later, she encouraged me to read. Mrs. Anna Hubbard, the frail white lady who was often there, had a kind face and caring voice. Apparently noticing my interest in books, she began to suggest some for me to read—*Native Son, Of Mice and Men, The Sun Also Rises, Lord Jim, The Last of the Mohicans, Dracula,* and many more. Sometimes, Mrs. Hubbard would ask me about my reading. One morning, she sat down with me, and we discussed *Native Son.* During the three years that I knew her, we discussed many more books.

I remember being particularly embarrassed about discussing *Native Son* because the protagonist, Bigger Thomas, murders a white woman. Sensing my discomfort, Mrs. Hubbard asked encouraging questions and told me about plot, character, point of view, and other elements in fiction.

She also introduced me to writings about A. Philip Randolph, who was born in Crescent City in 1889. He was editor of the radical black journal *The Messenger* until 1925, when he founded the Brotherhood of Sleeping Car Porters.

Although Mrs. Hubbard and I did not become close friends, she sparked my interest in literature and writing. Her singular behavior relieved me of some of my growing hatred of white people. She convinced me that I was a good reader, that I had a gift for understanding the themes of books and the motivations of characters.

One afternoon, and I do not remember why, I told Mrs. Hubbard that I wished that she were one of my teachers. I will never forget her reply. "That's nice of you," she said, "but white people can't teach in your school." I told her that I understood. But I did not.

The race consciousness that kept the two of us apart made no sense to me. It was the same thing that had made the deputy in the courthouse do what he did. His actions made no sense. The white boy who broke my nose with his belt buckle—why had he done so? Why did blacks swim on one side of Lake Stella and whites on the other? Why were our football teams kept apart?

Why were black children bused so far? Why was I beginning to feel such profound contempt for white people? I did not understand. And I suspected that those responsible for the shape of our world at that time did not understand either.

Postlude — Crescent City

Today, this town of nearly 2,000 residents is still no utopia—for anyone. But it is a far better place than it was when I lived here as a child. Although the freezes of the 1980s killed the area's thousands of acres of citrus trees, the fern has taken up most of the slack.

The year after I graduated from all-black Middleton Junior-Senior High, Congress passed the Civil Rights Act of 1964, prohibiting discrimination in voting, employment, public facilities, and, of course, education. Unlike whites in many other small towns statewide, the overwhelming majority of whites here accepted the new legislation and straightaway built a new integrated junior-senior high school, turned the old white campus into an integrated middle school, and made the black campus an integrated elementary school.

Old Middleton is now Middleton-Burney Elementary, renamed to honor a black man, Harry Burney Jr., my principal, who died recently. And Crescent City Junior-Senior High School has a black principal, Joe Warren.

Incredibly, at least to me, Crescent City elected its first African-American city councilman, my social studies teacher, several years ago. Blacks now serve on civic boards and are welcome in all public establishments.

The other day, I visited the Women's Club, where once my grandmother and I were permitted inside because we cleaned it. Today black groups use the facility for social events. At the Crescent City Library, blacks and whites explore the world of books under the same roof.

For me, it is a significant personal triumph that many whites who know about my writing are proud of me. One old man, for example, who scorned me as a child, now brags that he is from the same town that Bill Maxwell is from. And John Reynolds, whose family owned Billy Goat Island, where my friends and I used to trespass, is now my friend and has invited me to his home. Such a relationship would have been unthinkable during the 1950s.

Although some of the vestiges of Jim Crow linger in Crescent City— huge gaps between black and white incomes, segregated housing—I am happy to see how much the town has changed, how the races are living together amicably and with great equality. My biggest regret is that my grandparents and other black people of their generation died before experiencing the new Crescent City. Their suffering, after all, made today's Crescent City possible.

Native Son

A Christmas bicycle illuminates the spirit of giving

December 25, 1994

> The gift, to be true, must be the flowing of the giver unto me,
> correspondent to my flowing unto him.
> **Ralph Waldo Emerson**

By now, most Americans have bought and received Christmas gifts. This annual ritual of mandatory giving and receiving has fascinated me since I was a young child.

Today, at age 49, I have vivid memories of some of my earliest gifts: cap pistols and colorful cowboy outfits; a hunting knife and a bolt-action .22-caliber rifle; a yellow tricycle; baseballs and gloves; footballs and basketballs; a bugle and a guitar; a Timex watch; a pedal-operated car that I drove onto a busy street, nearly getting run over by a real car; a wind-up train set; two red wagons.

Although I enjoyed these gifts, none meant very much to me at the time. They were routine, like those that other boys received. Another reason these gifts were not important then was that I had gotten them while my parents were living together, when we were a normal family, when we had extra money after the bills were paid. Even though we were poor, I had yet to comprehend the true meaning of poverty.

By my ninth birthday, however, my parents had separated. Because my mother, five siblings, and I had no money and lived in a two-bedroom apartment in a government housing project, I had begun to relish even the smallest gifts. For good or bad, I was learning to equate the value of gifts with the degree of sacrifice and wisdom of the giver and the appreciativeness of the receiver.

As the oldest child, I worried mostly about the cost of gift-giving in our family. Because my mother confided in me, I was fully aware of the paltry wages she earned as a maid on Ft. Lauderdale Beach. My siblings and I took nothing for granted, especially gifts.

When I was 11, my mother gave me a bicycle for Christmas. It was my first bike. I had set my heart on a slick one in the window of the downtown Western Auto and had shown it to my mother one morning in late October as we waited for the bus. I do not recall the bike's price, but it was a sum that made my mother shake her head. I had no real hopes of getting the bike.

But I was constantly encouraged when I would discover my mother secretly counting money. And my heart pounded with expectation after the bike was removed from the store window the week before Christmas. On Christmas Eve night, I lay awake listening to my mother plundering in the darkness, taking gifts out of hiding, putting them under the tree. My siblings were awake, too, whispering and giggling. As "the man of the house," I had to pretend to be asleep. At daylight, the other kids dashed into the living room and began ripping open gifts. I strolled in, fingers crossed, praying that the bike was there.

It was not.

Instead, a turquoise monstrosity that vaguely resembled an American Flyer stood near the stove. My heart sank. Aware of my disappointment, my mother said: "I couldn't afford the new bike. I had Mr. Dennis fix up one for you. He said it's just like new." Mr. Dennis was a piddler, scavenger, and handyman par excellence. With trembling hands, he could put together any contraption.

Initially, I hated the bike, a hulk of discarded parts and brush-streaked paint. The neighborhood boys laughed at it, calling it the "Mack truck." After about two weeks, though, when most of the new bikes were banged up or stolen, the laughing stopped. My turquoise monster was right at home. In fact, it was a godsend, with its three big baskets, one on the handlebar and one on each side of the rear fender. My mother did not own a car, so we rode the bus or walked everywhere. As the oldest child, I did a lot of the grocery shopping and running around for incidentals. When I shopped alone, I sometimes would have to walk to the store three times to collect all of the bags. With the bike, I could make one trip.

Why, of the many gifts I have received in my life, do I remember that bicycle so fondly? Because, for me, the experience related to it epitomized the spirit of gift-giving. Not only did my mother know how badly I wanted a bike, she also knew that, because of my duties as the oldest child, the bike would make life easier for me. She knew that it would give me some dignity. I would not have to walk everywhere or piggyback on another boy's bike. It gave me something in common with the boys whose families had more money.

In the spring, that bike did let me become "the man of the house." It gave me the opportunity to become a carrier for the *Fort Lauderdale News*. I was able to earn enough money to help my mother pay several household bills each week. That jerry-built bike gave me independence—a way to become self-reliant. My mother knew that, even as a child, I was driven by the desire to do for myself, and her gift was her way of acknowledging me. She has since told me so. To this day, my mother and I exchange gifts of mutual acknowledgement—if we are inclined to exchange gifts at all.

I am certain that I view gift-giving too seriously. Even so, I am convinced that Ralph Waldo Emerson captured its true meaning more than a century ago:

> Next to things of necessity, the rule for a gift . . . is that we might convey to some person that which properly belonged to his character, and was associated with him in thought. But our tokens of compliment and love are for the most part barbarous. Rings and other jewels are not gifts, but apologies for gifts.
>
> The only gift is a portion of thyself, Thou must bleed for me. Therefore the poet brings a poem; the shepherd, his lamb; the farmer, corn; the miner, a gem; the sailor, a coral and shells; the painter, his picture; the girl, a handkerchief of her own sewing. This is right and pleasing, for it restores society in so far to its primary basis, when a man's biography is conveyed in his gift . . . .

Is Emerson asking too much of us? Should we, especially during the Christmas season, think more seriously about our motives for giving?

Should we measure our feelings with greater care when we receive? If the day marking the birth of the Christian savior is important enough to honor, should the rituals related to this day signify more than a grand celebration of materialism?

With equal passion for all

NOVEMBER 12, 1995

In the wake of events such as the slaying of Israeli prime minister Yitzhak Rabin, the Oklahoma City bombing, and the furor over Nation of Islam leader Louis Farrakhan, I, like most other Americans, have been thinking about hatred.

As a black columnist who receives daily hate mail, I am acutely aware of this most destructive of human sentiments and my uneasy relationship to it.

Like most African-American children of my generation, I experienced hatred on a personal level as an ember that flared each time my presence intersected the lives of white people. I felt it, say, when I wanted to try on clothes in a downtown store, when I boarded a city bus, when I had business in a government office.

And, like my peers, I had no real sense of hatred as a system of thought, as a social, cultural, or philosophical construct that traps human beings in time, that makes groups and individuals blood enemies. Although I grew up reading the Bible and knowing that Jews were "different," for instance, I did not—and still do not—comprehend the world's profound hatred of them. My parents and grandparents were too unlettered, too unsophisticated, too busy making ends meet to teach me hatred as an abstraction.

I carried this ignorance with me to Wiley College, a small, historically black school in Marshall, Texas. There, in wonderful isolation, I became a voracious reader, fearing that if I did not have a book, journal, magazine, or newspaper open every second, I would miss out on something vital to the rest of my life.

Not until the second semester of my sophomore year did I learn that I was a freak on campus, one warily observed by many of the white faculty, by most of the black faculty, and, as far I knew, by all of the black students who knew me. I learned of my outsiderness one afternoon after overhearing one of my professors, a white Woodrow Wilson scholar from Rutgers University, tell a black colleague: "Our Mr. Maxwell hugs Anne Frank with one arm and Martin Heidegger with the other—all at the same time." Was this an insult or a compliment? Indeed, I had written a paper on *The Diary of a Young*

Girl. I was gripped by Frank's horrible experiences, especially the depictions of Nazis hunting Jews as if they were animals, of Jews having to huddle in smothering dens. But I was just as moved by this Jewish child's humor and insight, by her ability to remain an adolescent and fall in love under such circumstances.

At the same time, I had thrown myself into writing a paper on the development of existentialism, on Heidegger's discussions of "human existence" and "nonhuman presence." I was pulled into his complex prose, fascinated by the notion that, the more human beings become absorbed by "things," the less "authentic" their existence becomes. And I pondered then—and still do—Heidegger's expression: "Language is the house of Being."

I was considered an outsider because I did not discriminate among writers. I read and discussed all of them with equal passion and tolerance.

Even though I, like other students, had learned in lectures that Heidegger, a great German philosopher, was a Nazi who admired Adolf Hitler, I wanted to read him all the more. Unlike most other students on campus, I did not reject *Being and Time*, arguably Heidegger's most important work. Why should I have? It was not a tract of hatred. It did not discuss the man's private feelings. It laid the groundwork for his existentialist philosophy. To me, *Being and Time* was nothing more than the intellectual product of a brilliant mind. Furthermore, I wanted to know how such brilliance could accommodate hatred.

I went on to read Hitler's *Mein Kampf*, Friedrich Nietzsche's *Thus Spake Zarathustra*, Ezra Pound's *Cantos*, H. L. Mencken's commentaries, and the works of other well-known Caucasian haters. I also read black haters, such as Marcus Garvey, Richard Wright, James Baldwin, and Elijah Muhammad. I wanted to understand them all—black and white.

My interest in this subject was rekindled by William H. Honan's recent *New York Times* article detailing Heidegger's longtime affair with his student and fellow philosopher Hannah Arendt, a German-born Jew who, in the name of love, forgave Heidegger his anti-Semitism.

These new findings have ignited brush fires in academia. "Some of the greatest philosophers were despicable people," Arendt scholar Sandra Hinchman told the *Times*. "Rousseau abandoned his five children to a Catholic orphanage before writing *Emile*, his treatise on education. My fear is that if we concentrate on the lives of some philosophers, we may become prejudiced against their work."

Hinchman's is a tantalizing question: To what extent should we judge the works of influential thinkers by the vileness of their private acts?

Obviously, I do not have a definitive answer. I do suggest, however, that when we seek truth, we must try to keep the private acts of important thinkers separate from their work. And if we are trying to understand hatred, we must engage it intellectually. More often than not, hatred is irrational and emotional, and it cannot be countered with equal doses of irrationality and emotion.

Above all, we should not try to avoid hatred. It destroys us when we try to avoid it and those who espouse it. Avoiding it may give us the illusion of safety, and we may become smug in the process. But understanding hatred—reading about it, studying those who espouse it—remains the best way of defeating it.

Sunshine State's glitz melts the holiday spirit

December 22, 1996

Christmas in Florida is, like the state itself, a tropical bazaar. As a native Floridian, condemned to the perpetual heat, humidity, and greenery of Ft. Lauderdale, I always have had ambivalent feelings about Christmas in the Sunshine State.

Even as a young child, I knew that Christmas in Florida was a substitution, a contradiction, an overcompensation. I knew that Christmas was a time for Jack Frost; snow and snowmen; horse-drawn sleighs and bells; kids sledding down steep inclines. And I had witnessed scenes of carolers entombed in thick sweaters braving bone-chilling cold.

But, like other south Floridians, I baked on December 25. We went fishing, golfing, tanning, water-skiing, swimming. And believe it or not, many of us drank lemonade beneath sprawling banyans. Some of us even mowed the lawn.

And, of course, if venturing near a major roadway, past yards dotted with plastic pink flamingos, we worried about being run down by pale Canadians, Yankees, and Midwesterners. Christmas in Florida was and is the time of the tourist, when strangers have more relevance than relatives.

This old yuletide angst returned the other day when two colleagues invited me along to watch one of this area's plethora of annual boat parades. Instead of sleigh rides, Floridians deploy armadas of decorated watercrafts.

While living in Ft. Lauderdale, I never missed the boat parade, a bona fide Florida spectacle, some years attracting crowds as energetic as those at New York's Time Square celebration on New Year's Eve. Now, as then, most of the boats are wonders unto themselves, decorated with thousands of blinking lights in complex designs and topped off with live trees fastened to their guide towers.

The obscene, aerodynamic cigarette boats and their cargo are my favorite. Invariably, handsome young men, their deep tans the picture of wealth, guide these glossy, rumbling machines over the lightly chopping water. Hanging on to the men are beautiful, bikini-clad women, displaying perfect white teeth and waving to admiring crowds. Male spectators, many of them drunk on their duffs, especially love the flirtatious female boaters wearing those little red-and-white Santa caps.

As the evening grows darker, the colorful flotilla dips and twists like a too-long water creature coming apart.

This is Christmas in Florida.

So, too, are the mega-celebrations near Disney World, in the shadow of the now-familiar Earffel Tower, the municipal water tower decked out with Mickey Mouse ears. At the Magic Kingdom, Epcot, Universal Studios, Sea World, and other sites, carolers and spectators grasping candles throng the narrow walkways and plazas. Parades, complete with elaborate floats and human and animated celebrities, pass by with eye-popping regularity.

This is Christmas Florida style.

Here, commercial giants compete for who can do Christmas the biggest. Last year when I visited Mousedom, Sea World boasted that its 400-foot metal Sky Tower was central Florida's biggest Christmas tree. Not to be outdone, the folks over at Universal Studios had fake snow that looked very real on the park's lifelike New York Street set.

Disney-MGM Studios, never runners-up, sported a 70-foot tree with 2 million lights. And what is this monstrosity called? The wall of angels. And, still in the yuletide spirit, Disney-MGM flew in Buzz Lightyear, Woody, Bo Peep, and other characters from the hit movie *Toy Story*.

I try my best to avoid such gross commercialization because for me, Christmas is a time of remembrance, pure nostalgia, and sentimentality. Although many transplants fondly remember their first Christmas here, I cannot recall one that I truly enjoyed. I fondly remember my first white Christmas, however. It was in Chicago in 1952, at my uncle's home on the South Side. I was seven years old. Christmas has not been the same since.

Snow fell for two days, and I stood outside for hours, getting sicker than I had ever been. But I thoroughly enjoyed the experience of sailing down snow-packed slopes on trash can lids; flying off a snow-laden roof on an ironing board we had found in an alley; learning how to ice-skate on a real frozen lake.

And the snowballs. Instead of throwing chinaberries and oranges at my friends, I threw snowballs. My cousin and I even made a snowman in the front yard, trimming him with an old red coat, a brown stingy brim, and a Prince Edward cigar hanging punkishly from his mouth.

After I returned to Ft. Lauderdale, none of my friends believed that an entire lake could freeze over. And, for sure, no one could turn a trash can lid into a sled! But I had photographs and became something of a hero.

I long for that Chicago Christmas, when toys were simple, when the fellowship of family and friends was enough, when the atmosphere and weather were Christmas per se. Christmas in Florida has never been an intimate affair for me—but an event for serving the material needs of strangers. Here, cold temperatures are considered "bad weather."

Here, almost everyone is "from somewhere else," making Florida an escape, not just from bad weather but from bad lives, as well.

For most Florida residents, natives and transplants alike, Christmas is a state of mind. It has to be. Otherwise, few of us could tolerate its reality—its superficiality and commercialization.

Redeemed by Dali in half a day

DECEMBER 3, 1997

Ferris Bueller had his day off. On Monday, I had mine. Actually, I had a half day off.

En route to work, I drove, unaccountably, to the Salvador Dali Museum to see what time it opens: 9:30 A.M. During my nearly four years in St. Petersburg, I had not been inside the place. Because it is within walking distance of my house and because I pass it nearly every day, I had taken it for granted.

After our Editorial Board meeting, I left the *St. Petersburg Times* building. The day was perfect—the morning sun glistening in the bay, the boats in Bayboro Harbor gently rocking in the breeze, the sky an uninterrupted mellow blue.

Entering the museum, I immediately knew why I had come. Like Ferris Bueller, I needed a day off. I had to get away from the office, away from writing, away from my too serious self. I declined the guided tour, put away my reporter's notebook, and entered a world of, among other things, disturbing visions, eccentricity, "critical paranoia," irrational hallucinatory imagery.

The early works and those of the transitional period were interesting, but the surrealist works awakened all of my senses. I was particularly struck by *Eggs on a Plate without the Plate*. Dali claimed that it was inspired by an intrauterine memory. In other words, the vision came to him while he was in his mother's womb.

Lost in the richness of the colors—blue, orange, red, yellow—I ignored the periods of the works and began to appreciate them for their own sake.

Daddy Longlegs of the Evening—Hope! pulled me into Dali's psyche, and I identified with the artist's rejection of man's inhumanity to man, especially the human horrors of World War II. I could hear the unearthly sounds of war and the cries of pain and feel the anguish of the young artist, who had an aversion to organized mayhem, trying to understand himself.

Something in the room—perhaps a shadow or a voice or an odor—made me realize that I had traveled outside of myself and that I was no longer depressed, that Dali's very abhorrence of human cruelty had made me hopeful.

The sight of *Geopoliticus Child Watching the Birth of the New Man* enhanced this feeling, and the haunting eyes of *The Sick Child* made me think of the innocence and beauty of childhood, even though these paintings contain what I interpret as hints of nihilism left over from the long-gone Dada movement.

Perhaps the desolation of the landscape and the forlorn characters in the background influenced my thinking.

I marveled at *Broken Bridge and the Dream*. I did not try to understand this work. The imagery alone was satisfying: a damaged bridge is a stairway for angelic, fantastic creatures who float into the heavens. I wondered what awaits them beyond that dreamy horizon.

I learned later that, between 1948 and 1970, he produced 18 significant oil paintings that the museum's founder, A. Reynolds Morse, called masterworks, meaning that each painting measures at least five feet in one direction and intellectually preoccupied Dali for a year or longer. Partly because of their sheer size, Dali's masterworks are mesmerizing.

For more than an hour, I lost myself in the disturbing beauty of the masterworks—among them *Still Life—Fast Moving; Velazquez the Infanta Margarita with the Lights and Shadows of His Own Glory; The Discovery of America by Christopher Columbus; Ecumenical Council;* and *Hallucinogenic Toreador.* How, I wondered, did Dali manage to juxtapose the seemingly conflicting forces of destruction and healing, birth/death/rebirth, pain and suffering and love and redemption, and despair and hope to form an organic whole?

In *Galacidalacidesoxiribunucleicacid*, for example, the DNA molecule, the tragic flash flood in West Barcelona, Spain, in 1962 that killed 450 people, Arabs pointing guns at their neighbors, the Resurrection, and other surreal images are woven into a vision of hope for the human race.

Pulling myself away from this giant oil, I felt buoyant for the first time in weeks. I thought of Ferris Bueller, of how he and his two friends raised hell in downtown Chicago, of how one of the film's best moments occurred as the characters contemplated works at the Art Institute. Although Ferris Bueller, Sloane, and Cameron were escaping a world where adults took themselves and their affairs too seriously, the art scenes defined the truants as being worthy of respect.

Leaving Dali's masterworks, I was drawn into the Man Ray exhibit.

But that's a story for another day off.

Confessions of a bibliophile

JANUARY 11, 1998

During my recent travels to southern Virginia, I realized anew that, as surely as some people are addicted to drugs, I am hooked on books.

Indeed, I am a bibliophile, a lover of books. My bibliophilism has driven me to strange places, introduced me to interesting people, and forced me to commit acts that might call my sanity into question. I am also a bibliomaniac, one preoccupied with collecting books.

If I had enough money, I would become a bibliopole, a dealer of rare and curious books. Alas, my journalist's salary will not let me become a bibliopole. Just the other day, I considered buying an autographed copy of Truman Capote's *In Cold Blood*. I left this gem on the shelf because it would have set me back more than a month's rent.

Of course, I am a bookworm, a person devoted to reading and study. One of the world's best-known bookworms was author Katherine Mansfield. In 1922, while battling tuberculosis, she described her loneliness in terms of reading, expressing an ambivalence about the urge to read and her desire for human companionship: "Should I be happy with anyone at my side? No. I'd begin to talk, and it's far nicer not to talk."

No one should take reading for granted, for it is a complex process. Listen to Laura Furman and Elinore Standard, editors of the book *Bookworms*, describe book lovers and their obsession: "For the true bookworm it is sometimes hard to distinguish between what one has experienced and what one has read. We know that this is odd and even a little demented. . . . We are uneasy in a void with no book.

"Reading is a socially accepted form of hallucination. Through words we react to the ideas, memories and fantasies of people we'll never meet, whom we believe we know.

"Reading may be the last private act of our lives."

Reading, moreover, is powerful and inscrutable, so much so that dictators commit unspeakable crimes against writers (remember Russia's Aleksandr Solzhenitsyn, who was exiled for his books depicting life in the Soviet Union?); powerful enough to cause seemingly normal Americans to ban books from public schools and libraries.

In his book *Read for Life*, Joseph Gold cautions that reading is a subversive activity: "Reading has always been a political act, and the authorities have always known it, since writing was invented.

"Reading is dangerous to the status quo. To give reading power to the people is to undermine the power of reading authorities, to lose control of classrooms, to expose thoughts, feelings and attitudes to close examination, to challenge authority—in other words, to change the world.

"In short, a well-developed, fully responsive, free readership is the most powerful force for personal and social change."

My love of books also reconnects me with my past. In Exmore, on Virginia's eastern shore, the South Star Flea Market, a barnlike hulk that seemed vaguely familiar, caught my attention. There, among farm implements, cobwebs, and military gear, I found Cynthia Pearl Maus's 1947 book *The World's Great Madonnas*, one of the most beautiful books I have ever seen.

Thumbing through it, I became certain that I had been in this building before. More than 30 years ago, it had been a packinghouse, where, as a child farmworker, I had graded potatoes, where, during breaks, I had found quiet places in this drafty structure to read Richard Wright, Ring Lardner, and John Steinbeck. The current owner, Tom Carrick, confirmed that the building had been a packing facility.

Here in South Hill, I visited Our House, an antique store, and found a treasure trove of interesting old books, which included *The Ropemakers of Plymouth, Travels in the Old World, The Cyclopedia of Practical Quotations*. My best find was Noah Webster's *The Elementary Spelling Book*, written in 1886. My schoolmates and I had used this text—our copies were dog-eared discards from the white school—during the 1950s in Crescent City.

Jerrie Emory, the owner of Our House, saw my delight and told me that other books were beneath a table in back. "If you feel like crawling around and digging out the books, you're welcome to do it," she said.

For nearly an hour, I crawled on the floor, unstacked and restacked old volumes. Leaving Our House, I could barely wait to read Noel Sainsbury Jr.'s *Cracker Stanton*. This 1934 novel about a young Georgia cracker baseball player gave me a candid view of the enduring significance of class distinction among poor whites. *Cracker Stanton* has enriched my life.

Furman and Standard speak for me, a fellow bookworm, when they write: "Through reading, we intensify our capacity for pleasure, for sympathy, and for comprehension. What we read utterly changes our relation to the world. There is a thirst in all readers for stories that teach us about the world and ourselves."

Summer and the love of Stella

June 10, 1998

Each morning, I walk beside Lake Maggiore, relishing its beauty at sunrise. It is more beautiful than ever now that summer has arrived. Summer, I must acknowledge nostalgically, plays havoc with me, making me long to break free of this, well, this middle-aged body of a professional writer.

I want to be a barefoot boy again.

My happiest childhood memories are of Lake Stella in Crescent City, a fern-growing, bass-fishing town in northeast Florida. Stella held magic for my dozen or so buddies and me. It had that "special odor," as we called it. We could detect that odor after the late afternoon sun had warmed the grayish water and a gentle breeze blew toward Babylon, the unoffical name of our all-black settlement in the woods near the "Negro" graveyard. It was a mellow odor, laced with hints of decayed algae, cattail, and the black shells of mussels baking in sun.

Constance Howard, our homeroom teacher, said that we could not smell Lake Stella so far away. "It's all in your crazy little imaginations," she would say.

We did not listen to her. We knew that when that special odor came, summer—the most glorious time of the year—had arrived.

And school was out: No more "Connie," as we called Miss Howard. No more homework. No more cafeteria food. No more of those other strict teachers who made us behave despite ourselves. Summer was our time, when parents and grandparents gave us just enough freedom to get into just enough trouble to warrant an occasional smack beside the head or a day's grounding, the worst possible punishment because it meant being away from Stella.

Within easy walking distance of home, the lake was the center of our lives. Little more than 308 acres, it shimmered in the sun, and when a rare high wind blew, tiny waves stabbed at the grassy shoreline.

Most of us, all teenage boys, thought nothing of swimming nonstop from one side of Stella to the other. Our biggest problem was the game warden, a skinny, gnarled, old white cuss who actually cared for our safety. He would chase us out of the lake because of the alligators. Seeing them plunge into the water, we would wait before going in.

If gators were in the water, we stayed close to shore. After they returned to land—and we would count them—in we went. We took turns being sentinel, warning the others if a gator took to the water.

Over the years, we bought and borrowed several boats, sailing or motoring to every part of the lake. Our greatest adventure was an aborted all-night bivouac on one of the islands. One Saturday afternoon, 15 of us went there, making five trips in our tiny boat. We took hot dogs, marshmallows, and pork and beans.

We were having a great time—doing our Huck Finn thing—until about 9:00 P.M. Then, when mosquitoes began to reclaim their space with a vengeance, we realized that we were wearing cutoff pants and sleeveless tops. At first, we thought that a bigger fire would keep the bloodsuckers at bay. The plan might have worked had we not run out of usable wood.

"I can't take no more of this shit!" someone screamed. "Let's get outa here!"

The 15 of us dashed to the boat. Someone shouted that only three of us could go at a time. Everyone, of course, wanted to go first, which was impossible. We drew lots. Since I would be in the fifth crossing—each taking about 10 minutes one way, given the size of the engine—and because the mosquitoes were eating me alive, I decided to swim ashore and risk the gators.

Seconds after I dived into the black water, I heard several splashes. Certain that gators were after me, I closed my eyes. When I opened them, I saw more than half of my fellow campers swimming past me. We stroked toward shore, chastened by the pain of mosquito bites, exhilarated by the terror of being gobbled up by gators. All of us got to shore in one piece.

Today, when I look at St. Petersburg's Lake Maggiore, I wonder if my childhood buddies could resist the lure of this beautiful, dangerous body of water.

The young eyes of John Wise

September 20, 1998

I do not recall the year during the late 1950s when my uncle John Wise died, and I do not remember how old he was. When I was nine or ten, my grandmother said that he probably was in his late 80s.

My grandmother believed that he was born blind and never learned to read. As a young child, I became John Wise's windows to the world—his eyes. I read to him every day.

I was reminded of him a few weeks ago after I was asked to speak briefly at SpellDown '98, an annual fund-raiser for Read Pinellas, Inc. The program is usually held in September, National Literacy Month. In deciding on the theme of the talk, I, a former reading teacher and tutor, tried to recall the events that showed me that, in additional to being a source of personal enjoyment, the act of reading can be a service to others.

John Wise came to live with my grandparents, in Crescent City in 1940, five years before I was born. I used to watch my grandfather, a pastor, prepare his sermons by reading the Bible aloud so that John Wise could listen. In time, I took over and read the Scriptures to him. He preferred me to my grandfather because I made the Bible exciting.

I would read from a standard Bible but also would describe the paintings in an illustrated children's version that my grandmother had given to me as a birthday present. John Wise especially loved descriptions of the Garden of Eden, its beautiful rivers, the Tree of Life, "that damned snake," as he called the reptile that tempted Eve, the lovely Eve herself, and the rainbow painted against the Mesopotamian sky.

Of all of the books of the Bible, Exodus was the most fun to read. The dramatic images—the pharaoh, Moses among the bulrushes, the burning bush, the toiling Israelites, the plagues of frogs and lice and flies and hail, the death of Egypt's firstborn, the Passover, the parting of the Red Sea, manna from the sky, God's fearful presence upon Mount Sinai, the Ten Commandments—brought us back to Exodus time and again.

As I would read, John Wise's sightless gray eyes would roll in their sockets, and his head would rock from side to side. Both hands would rest on the cane in front of him. When he particularly liked a scene or passage, he would bang the cane on the floor, stomp, and laugh.

Although the Bible was our favorite text, we had a secret: Often when my grandparents were not at home, I would drag out my stash of 25-cent Signet paperbacks that I had found in a trash can outside a house where my grandmother was a maid. The first book I read to John Wise was Chandler

Brossard's *Who Walk in Darkness*, a 1954 novel about a group of young hipsters in New York's Greenwich Village. We loved the book's irreverence, the characters' jaded appetites for drugs and booze, the sex, their impulsive violence and profane voices.

Another favorite was Pearl Schiff's *Scollay Square*, a vivid novel of Boston's "pickup" street and a brief and violent tryst between a wealthy debutante and a salty sailor. John Wise particularly liked *The Hoods*, by Harry Gray. It was an intriguing account of gangster life, giving an inside view of a crime syndicate and of men who specialized in assault, robbery, drugs, and, of course, murder.

He also liked radio news but favored newspapers. I would read the local paper to him, but we thoroughly enjoyed the *Pittsburgh Courier* and *Grit*, two Negro weeklies that came in the mail. The *Courier* was especially enjoyable because it carried the predictions of "root workers" and other assorted Negro spiritualists, and it detailed the exploits of major leaguer Jackie Robinson.

Later, after I became the local delivery boy for the *Palatka Daily News*, I would read it to John Wise each night as he lay in bed. By the light of a kerosene lamp, I would read the sports pages first for news of the Brooklyn Dodgers.

Because of John Wise, reading became my conduit to complex ideas, distant places, and brilliant people. I served him, but he also served me by trusting me to see for him. I tried to imagine living in a world of darkness as he did, depending on another person to shape the contours of reality for me, to define the signposts that literally would guide my existence.

I was a mere child, but, already, I comprehended the power of reading. I knew that it was the beacon in a world of ignorance, that it deepened human understanding.

In 1958 or 1959, John Wise died while I was in Virginia with my father harvesting potatoes. My grandmother said that he asked for me during his final hours. He told her that I was a good reader for a child.

Finding a bit of heaven on a Harley

OCTOBER 28, 1998

I never pay attention to my birthday, but when it rolled around this year, a card arrived in the mail that transported me back to some of the best years of my life.

First, the card: On its front were the simple words "Happy Birthday." Inside, against a field of white, was the imprint of a kiss—fresh, ruby-red lipstick.

That was all. Just the outline of a distant kiss.

Who is this woman? The only clue was the St. Louis, Missouri, postmark. A similar card has come each year since 1978, when I left Chicago and returned to Florida for good. During my first year back, I was living in Key West when a card came from Chicago. Since then, cards have come from several other cities, including New Orleans; Madison, Wisconsin; Los Angeles; New York; Portland, Maine; Albuquerque, New Mexico; Tucson, Arizona—each a place I toured on my Harley.

My Harley was the reason that I left the Windy City and moved back to the Sunshine State: I wanted to be able to ride my Superglide every day of the year. What a great time—before I grudgingly accepted the enslavement of being an "adult male in society," before limiting myself to riding on weekends and vacations only.

My love of Harleys began in Ft. Lauderdale after I entered first grade, when my father would ride me everywhere on his baby-blue 1948 FL Panhead. I fell in love with the rhythmical ku-thunk, ku-thunk, ku-thunk of its engine. My father belonged to a touring club that consisted of African-American farmworkers who had made south Florida their permanent home. They would ride to cities statewide, stand around in large groups, talk trash, flirt with "the Ladies," drink Seagram's gin from the bottle, and admire one another's hogs.

I longed to have my own hog, not a giant, chromed dresser like that of my father and his buddies, however. I craved a sleek Knucklehead that could slice through the wind, that could send that Harley protest echoing for a mile.

My dream came true on my 15th birthday, when my father drove me to the home of a biker who was "hanging it up." There in his garage sat a cherry-red 1941 FL, the very "Knuck" that I wanted. From that day to now, I have never been far from a Harley, except for my stint in the military.

For me, as for everyone else in the hog brotherhood, riding a Harley is catharsis. Few things compare to the pleasure of feeling a V-twin thumping beneath you. As the massive pistons shove the bike forward, you feel the seamless vibrations. Your arms and legs become conduits of raw mechanical power. Your muscles tighten; your senses are energized.

I will never forget my first cross-country tour. Six other Harley owners and I left Daytona Beach in 1971 for Sturgis, South Dakota, and the Black

Hills Motorcycle Classic. It was a trip of equal parts courage, fear, exhilaration, and pain.

The open road was paradise. We streaked down winding highways, rarely under 70 miles per hour, as green fields, woodlands, valleys, mountains, rivers, and lakes rushed past us. Harley riders can rise into the air and look down upon themselves. I could see myself as an actor in a cosmic drama. I looked down the chrome forks, down to the glistening twirl of the wheel, down to the blur of black asphalt unwinding inches beneath the sole of my boots.

In turns, my companions and I would pull alongside one another, make eye contact, and, silently, speak a language that only Harley riders understand. It is a language of pride. After all, they own the most celebrated "sled" made. It is a language of awe. They—flesh, bone, and blood—are in control of an American myth, a wild iron horse.

The sense of speed is palpable; the torque, scary. They listen to the tailpipe as the wind intermittently thrusts that rumbling sound in front of them. They pass through it, then a momentary silence, then the ku-thunk. They can feel and smell the heat of the engine.

During ensuing years, I toured many other parts of the country, each trip always better than the last. Rain was never a reason to postpone a tour. Hell, we knew that we would run clear of the water somewhere down the road.

I had my best times when I rode with the Smokin' Wheels Motorcycle Club of Madison. We regularly partied from there to New Orleans and back—each of us with a beautiful woman luxuriating against the sissy bar. I can hear my girlfriends' laughter after all of these years and feel their arms wrapped around my waist as we roared along the nation's highways.

Which one, I wonder, still sends me a kiss on my birthday?

"Bloody Sunday" with the Reverend

JANUARY 17, 1999

The year was 1965, the time of my personal introduction to Martin Luther King and the Southern Christian Leadership Conference and my baptism into the civil rights movement. Dozens of nightstick-wielding state troopers, deployed by Alabama's Gov. George Wallace, stood at end of the Edmund Pettus Bridge on the outskirts of Selma. I was a 19-year-old junior attending Wiley College in Marshall, Texas. A group of my schoolmates and I had taken time out of school and had come to Selma to help initiate a voter registration campaign and, of course, to hear Dr. King speak at Brown's Chapel Methodist Church.

Fear, the stuff of black life in the South during those days, had always been my constant companion. But when the nearly 300 of us, led by King, Ralph Abernathy, and Andy Young, descended the hump of the bridge, I wanted to turn and run. The helmeted troopers, white men full of hatred and false courage, were determined to halt our march.

A fat trooper, standing behind a waist-high patch of grass, stared into my eyes. He understood my fear. Sensing his need to brutalize us, I was convinced that my life would end that day on the dusty easement of the Edmund Pettus.

Because I was near the end of the wave of protesters, I could not see King and the other leaders of the march. Looking into the faces of the other marchers, I saw fear and anticipation. I was surprised to see that about half of them were old people—women and men whose wrinkles and scars and slow gait chronicled the South's legacy of inhumanity. The presence of these elders made me hopeful and ashamed that I had waited so long to join the movement.

In front of me, a mass of bodies surged forward, heads bobbing rhythmically, and words to the song "We Shall Overcome" echoed in the warm air. Suddenly, a voice, amplified over a bullhorn, yelled, "Turn back and go home."

We moved forward.

"Disperse! Turn back!"

Frightened white journalists mustered the strength of mind to stay alongside us as we marched toward the courthouse, where we were to let the world know that black people in the South had a right to vote.

"Niggers!" another voice, somewhere beyond the first row of troopers, shouted.

"Turn back!" a trooper said.

We refused.

The marchers in front of me no longer moved as a single body. We became individuals, pushed by the realization that we would be attacked by white men who wanted to obliterate us.

The words "goddamn niggers" came from the crowd of white counter-demonstrators gathering behind the troopers.

Then, the screaming began.

Our women were the first to run as the troopers attacked, their nightsticks coming down like rain. For the first time in my life, I heard human bones crack. An old woman next to me fell to the pavement after a trooper backhanded her across the chest. Falling, she struggled to hold her green-and-orange gingham dress over her legs.

The trooper's next move shocked even me, a kid born and reared in a south Florida ghetto, who had seen violent incidents nearly every day. He kicked the woman in the stomach. As the crowd pulled me forward, I lost sight of her and never saw her again.

When tear gas canisters hit the bridge and a poisonous cloud rose into the air, the troopers, all wearing masks, rushed us and knocked many of us down. Not one of us fought back. March organizers had taught us that we would be whipped, injured, jailed, and perhaps even killed. The clubbing seemingly went on for an hour or longer as sheriff's deputies joined the troopers and encircled us.

The gas was overpowering, burning our lungs and eyes and nostrils. Most of us, at least those still standing, simply wanted to get out of the line of fire. By now, however, the cops had smelled blood—a lot of blood flowed that day known as "Bloody Sunday"—and were singling out younger males to chase and beat.

I was one of the unlucky ones.

A deputy struck me in the neck from behind with his nightstick, and, when I turned to face him, he jabbed me in the solar plexus with the weapon. My college roommate was beside me. He was hit in the face, and I saw blood stream down his cheek.

I could see King and Abernathy. Several deputies were dragging them toward a squad car. Young stood near an officer in charge, pointing at other officers beating three girls. Again, I was hit, this time on the forehead. Tasting my own blood, I raised my arms to ward off the blows. Women were screaming, and children were crying. But the cops continued to pound us.

That night at the church, I took full measure of what had transpired. We out-of-towners had far less to lose than the local black residents who participated in the demonstration. They stood to lose everything—their jobs, their churches, their homes. And, yet, they had the courage to stand with King on the side of justice.

Indeed, King deserves praise for making the civil rights movement a matter of conscience. But another remarkable side of the movement is rarely mentioned: that story is the bravery of the thousands of old people throughout the South who willingly faced the gas, the dogs, the truncheons, the guns. King knew how important these old folk were, for he routinely praised them in speech and in deed.

Martin Luther King has been dead since 1968, but I, along with others who had the honor of knowing him, remain touched by his courage and dedication to the cause of justice. He brought out the best in us. He taught us to overcome fear, to overcome hatred, and to turn the evil of the oppressor into a positive force in our lives.

Guess who's coming to dinner

February 7, 1999

My colleague Bonnie Blackburn, an editorial writer and columnist for the *Journal Gazette* of Ft. Wayne, Indiana, recently wrote a column about some of the famous people, living and dead, with whom she would like to have dinner. Bonnie's guest list was so interesting and the piece so well written that I am mimicking her. Following is my own short list of people with whom I would love to have food and drink.

Because I am as attracted to evil as I am to goodness, Adolf Hitler tops my roster. Yes, the führer himself. I would love to dine with Hitler. What, I would ask, drove him to such murderous hatred? I would look him in the eye as he tried to justify the unspeakable crimes at Auschwitz, Treblinka, and other death camps. In hindsight, would he treat Jews as fellow humans and spare them? Could he give me insight into the nature of human evil and help me understand today's human slaughter in places such as Africa and Kosovo?

Next, I would eat with Salvador Dali, one of my favorite 20th-century artists. After having read and reviewed Ian Gibson's recently published biography of Dali and watched a two-hour documentary of the Catalan surrealist, I am more intrigued by the man than ever.

I would not ask him about his art as much as I would ask about his incredible life—his sexual hang-ups, the paranoia, the chase after money, the egomania, the exhibitionism. At his death, he seemed to have come to some understanding of his excesses. Did he have any regrets? And, of course, I would ask him to tell me about Gala, his libidinous wife. Was she the enigma that she is reported to have been? Was she loving? Or was she just lustful?

May Sarton was the first professional writer I met as a college student, and I have always admired her poems and journals. Having her in my home for dinner would give me the opportunity to ask her about the aging process and writing. In one of the last journal entries before her death in 1995, she wrote: "I realize now that it will be good for me to talk about old age, find out where I should bear down more heavily on myself and where I should let things go." Specifically, I would inquire, did she bear down, and where did she let things go? Perhaps her answers could help me face old age gracefully.

Abraham Lincoln, the morose genius who freed my forebears from slavery, would be my next guest. I would like to know what he thinks of race relations in the nation today. Where did President Clinton's race initiative go wrong?—if it did go wrong. As a Republican, where does he stand on affirmative action? Are the vestiges of the "peculiar institution" sufficiently gone to permit us to declare—with honesty—that the playing field is level? What would he think of Ward Connerly, Clarence Thomas, and their white supporters who claim that race no longer matters? What advice would he give to John Hope Franklin, head of Clinton's race panel?

When Sylvia Plath arrives for dinner, I will tell her that *The Bell Jar* and her diary have been my constant companions since graduate school. "You had no right to kill yourself at age 30," I would tell her before serving the main course. "You left a void in many lives. Why?"

Then I would read to her one of my favorite passages from her journals: "I long to permeate the matter of this world: to become anchored to life by laundry and lilacs, daily bread and fried eggs, and a man, the dark-eyed stranger, who eats my food and my body and love and goes around the world all day and comes back to find solace with me at night." I would tell her that she died much too young, that I am mad at her, that her husband, British poet Ted Hughes, was not over her suicide when he died recently.

A meal with Ida Tarbell, one of my mentors, would be a special treat. She has been given many labels—feminist, statesman, social reformer, biographer, historian. To me, she will always be the *McClure's* magazine writer who, in 1902, broke the story detailing Standard Oil's monopoly. She became the nation's first "muckraking" journalist. The very thought of her made the corrupt and powerful run scared.

What, I would ask, does she think of today's "gotcha" journalism? What about the way we handled the Lewinsky-Clinton affair? How would she have approached this scandal? She was a pioneer in every sense of the term and, because of her writing, helped to make America a better place for ordinary citizens. Tarbell would be an inspiring dinner date.

I have always wanted to ask Giovanni Casanova how he did it, how he— magician, moralist, musician, philosopher, scholar, poet, and priest—became Europe's most notorious lover. After a few glasses of wine and a fine steak, perhaps Casanova would share the secrets of his charm, the forces that made women collapse in his embrace. Casanova understood human pleasure. He saw it not as a sin but as a natural, essential part of life.

I would ask him to share his wisdom, after dessert, of course. Enjoy these two gems:

Only human beings are capable of real pleasure, for endowed as they are with the faculty of reason, they anticipate it, seek it, fashion it, and reason about it after having enjoyed it.

The happiest of men is not always the most voluptuous but the one who knows how to choose the greatest voluptuous pleasures; and the greatest voluptuous pleasures, I repeat, can only be those which do not stir up the passions but increase peace of mind.

Who are the famous people on your guest list? Invite them for a meal and enjoy their companionship.

Bon appetit!

Finding happiness in the solo life

April 21, 1999

On Monday night, I ate supper at 12:49 A.M. As I ate, I began to write this column on my laptop while watching a movie on HBO. I made a pot of coffee about 1:15, poured a cup, and went outside. My senses were alive. The air was unseasonably cool, a few stars shone in the western sky, and the heavy odor of smoke from distant wildfires engulfed everything.

Back inside, I poured more coffee and wrote until 3:30. Tired, I lay on the couch and fell asleep. I awoke at 5:00 and went for a walk. Returning at 6:00, I microwaved the old coffee, read the *St. Petersburg Times* and the *New York Times*, listened to National Public Radio, showered, dressed, and arrived at work in time for my daily 9:30 editorial board meeting.

I did all of these things without disturbing anyone else. What I have described is a vignette from the life of one of America's 25 million adults who live alone. I did not know that we were so numerous until I read *Living Solo*, photographer Adrienne Salinger's beautiful book chronicling this "unique" way of life.

"Possibly," Salinger writes, "this is the first generation in which living alone is presumed to be a legitimate choice rather than a declaration of defeat; unprecedented numbers of people now choose to keep their own homes, to decorate them, and to entertain in them without overt societal pressure to adapt to specific notions of family living. . . . Until recently, living 'alone' was considered an aberration, a transient state within which individuals were identified by the culture as submissively awaiting mates in order to participate in society."

I have lived alone since 1988, when my marriage ended in divorce. During the first three months, I was lost—suspended somewhere without substantive form, incomplete without my longtime mate. As Salinger suggests, I was cut off from the "blissful union in which major purchases and life decisions [are] compromises of taste and desire."

Because my house was in the woods, more than 25 miles from Gainesville, I quickly adapted to living solo by reading and writing, walking the vast woodlands, growing vegetables and flowers, maintaining my three-acre lawn, caring for Fancy Pants, my Appaloosa, feeding the wild birds and learning to recognize them, and keeping my old Chevy pickup running.

At the end of the first year of being alone, I could not imagine living with someone else again, relinquishing the solitude that had forced me to feel comfortable with myself. Like Salinger, I am not talking about being "single," about giving up romantic and sexual relations. I am talking about celebrating my living space, about being alone in my book- and newspaper-strewn house whenever I wish—for as long as I wish.

Salinger, who has lived alone for years, captures the uncompromising essence of the solo life in both picture and word: "Without other people to help govern the events of daily living or judge the 'normalcy' of particular habits, a certain eccentricity is allowed to emerge. Eccentricity can be a good thing. It can make us unique, creative, unusual, mysterious, and sometimes idiosyncratic."

Who are these 25 million who live alone in the United States? "We have nothing in common," Salinger writes. "We have everything in common. We live in big cities and small towns. We eat over the sink and in bed—sometimes at a table. We find things where we left them. We always know where the good scissors are. We own the remote control. We are the people who sometimes celebrate holidays alone. . . . We are sometimes lonely. We are often successful and driven. We are sometimes poor and trapped. We have good friends. We have lovers. We are old. We are gay and straight. We are divorced, widowed, single, living on opposite coasts from our partners."

Indeed, for many individuals in a "couple," living alone suggests decadence and unnaturalness. I cannot count the times that people are shocked that I am not married. How often do acquaintances tell me to bring my wife when I come to dinner? When I say that I live alone, the tortured silence on the line confirms why I live solo. How often do people try to "set" me up (and I hate that)? How often am I called "weird" because I do things my way?

"It takes an enormous amount of courage to live alone," Salinger said. "You have no escape from looking at yourself."

More than most people, my favorite poet, May Sarton, who lived solo most of her life, understood the courage that Salinger speaks of: "The value of solitude—one of its values—is, of course, that there is nothing to cushion against attacks from within."

Others who live solo understand perfectly.

A human machine and a giant among men

JUNE 20, 1999

For the first time since I was a small child, I did not buy a Father's Day gift. My father died eight weeks ago.

He was one of the last of a group of black men who were "human machines," as they called themselves, and they had nicknames to match—Iron Man, Steelhead, Hammer, Tree, Dolomite, Dredge. My father was known as Big Man and Big Willie. He was 6 foot 6 and, in his prime, weighed 250 pounds.

Before farming, lumbering, and other harvesting fields mechanized, men like him literally did all of the heavy lifting.

They were the loaders. They were muscular and as hard as metal, not from workouts in the gym but from years of backbreaking toil in groves, fields, and woods. Not one was fat, each sporting broad shoulders, a massive chest, chiseled arms, and a slim waist.

To growers and crew chiefs, men like my father were the most important link in the process that took produce from the field to the table. These giants were so highly valued by some owners that they would give them vacations, loans, and pocket money. One of my father's bosses at Minute Maid co-signed for him to buy a new 1956 green-and-white Ford.

Theirs was a world of machismo, where physical strength meant everything. Intellect, of the academic kind, meant little, if anything, to them. I will never forget my father's words, for example, after I announced in 1963 that I was going to college: "What the hell are you going to college for? Get a man's job." He never openly forgave my "going off to college to be a damned sissy."

Even so, I have mostly fond memories of him, some of the fondest being those of him and other black men loading Florida citrus in the 1950s and early 1960s for McBride Fruit Company in Seville and Clark Fruit Company in Crescent City. Saturdays during the school term and weekdays during the summer, I accompanied my grandfather to the groves. My father was always one of our loaders.

McBride always used two to four trucks in each grove to transport the fruit to the packinghouse. Each truck had three loaders, one driver, one stacker on the truck bed, and a goat on the ground. My father was the quintessential goat—the strongest man in the crew who, each day, lifted hundreds of three-foot-long wooden field boxes onto the truck. Filled to capacity, each box weighed at least 300 pounds.

With gnats swarming around him, my father bent, grabbed the two end handles, straightened his back, and heaved at the same time. The boxes, swung at least five feet into the air, landed on the truck bed, where the stacker arranged them neatly in four six-foot-high rows to be secured with cables for transport.

Sweat poured from the men's bodies, but they worked until the load was complete. As a boy, I marveled at how the men's arms and chests strained under the weight, withstood the repetition, and endured the long hours. Everything was done with precision.

Competition among the crews was fierce. The men would bet big sums on which truck would be the first to load, reach the packinghouse, and return to the grove to repeat the cycle. If my father had a good stacker and driver, his truck, a wide-fender International, never lost a bet.

For their efforts, my father and his crew always received bonuses. Everybody wanted to vanquish Big Willie. Iron Man, a jet-black, bald-headed South Carolina Geechee, was the only other goat who regularly gave my father a serious challenge.

And these men played the way they worked: hard and rough. They armwrestled constantly, tussled, and boxed with bare knuckles. Amazingly, they rarely fought. Even when they punched one another savagely, they stopped at the first sign of blood. Apparently, they knew that their bodies were valuable property.

During the years that I followed my father up and down the East Coast to harvest crops, I admired his physical strength and wanted to emulate him. When I was in 11th grade, he became a crew chief for a potato farmer in Exmore, Virginia. I, along with four of my schoolmates, joined him there in the summer, and, to my surprise, he hired us as loaders. For two months, my buddies and I loaded thousands of bags of potatoes.

The other boys admired us, and the girls flirted. We could feel our muscles getting bigger and our backs growing stronger. We had become men—human machines like our fathers. Indeed, hard, outdoor physical labor was the litmus test for manhood in those days.

The week before my father died, I visited him in his hospital room in Ft. Pierce. A tube had been shoved down his nose and others pierced his arms. Having languished in this state for more than a month, he was no longer Big Man. Staring down at him, I recalled his glory days, when he could lift his own weight without blinking, how other awestruck men wondered how he could outmuscle them day after day.

When he whispered, "Don't let me die like this. I want to die like a man," I knew exactly what he meant. I spoke with his doctor.

Big Man died two days later—having held on to some of his dignity and manhood to the very end.

No illusions on next Africa trip

OCTOBER 17, 1999

During the mid-1970s, I went to Africa to fulfill a lifelong dream of re-connecting with the source of my beginnings. Never part of the politicized pan-African movement that captured the black imagination then, I went to Africa solely for personal enrichment. My 18-month itinerary took me to Cameroon, Eritrea, Ethiopia, Gabon, Ghana, Liberia, Niger, Nigeria, Senegal, Sierra Leone, and Zaire (today the Republic of Congo).

Did I reconnect with the source of my beginning? No. Did I feel the profound ancestral pull I had sought? No.

When I returned to the United States, I was a deeply disillusioned ex-pilgrim. Hardly anything about these African nations impressed me. In fact, I was appalled by much of what I witnessed—the violence and hunger, the disease and suffering, the graft and selfishness, the ignorance and vanity. After Marxist agents in Addis Ababa, Ethiopia, threatened to shoot my companions and me for being "CIA operatives," I left Africa and have not returned.

Next year, however, I plan to return to Ethiopia. This time, though, I will not pack naive illusions about the continent. Nor will I fool myself into believing that, for me to be a complete African-American with real sense of self, I must nurture an intellectual, a cultural, and an emotional affinity with the black peoples of Africa.

My planned return to Africa drew me to *Kinship: A Family's Journey in Africa and America*, Philippe Wamba's new book, which is a family and personal memoir about black America's love-hate relationship with Africa—a tortured romance that produced the self-immolating "blacker-than-thou" battles among black intellectuals and college students during the 1960s and 1970s.

Wamba understands all of it. His mother is an American black, his father Congolese. Born in Boston and a graduate of Harvard University, he spent many years with his family in Dar es Salaam, Tanzania. For him, and he makes his case compellingly, black people around the world have common interests, common goals, and a common destiny.

"I was born both African and African-American, but it took years for me to understand what that duality could mean," Wamba writes. "My blackness has been the bridge that has linked my two identities, the commonality that my split selves share. But it often seems a tenuous link. And not just for me. I have traveled the world, with my race as my constant companion and curse, and everywhere I have seen black people bewildered by a strange tension between feeling powerfully bound by what they share and hopelessly repelled by what they do not."

Indeed.

Each time I visit Israel, I am drawn to the Ethiopian Jews, and they are equally drawn to me. We stare at one another, sensing that somehow we are connected. Those who speak English ask if I am Ethiopian. Not directly, I tell them, but, on my mother's side of the family, I have Ethiopian ancestry. Nearly everything stops there, however, because, beyond DNA and skin color, we have few traits in common. I now realize that my fascination with the Ethiopians in Israel is primarily that—fascination.

Wamba probably would disagree, as would other prominent blacks such as W.E.B. Du Bois, Marcus Garvey, Malcolm X, Stokely Carmichael, and Jesse Jackson.

Like me, though, many other American blacks come away from Africa disappointed, some permanently alienated. In her 1981 book, *The Heart of a Woman*, poet and novelist Maya Angelou, for example, graphically describes her ill-fated marriage to a South African freedom fighter and her final disillusionment with many things African.

With the naiveté of an American black in the 1960s who is smitten by the ideal of Africa, Angelou summarizes her first impression of Vusumzi Make, her husband-to-be: "The man was blue-black and spectacular. His unquestionable dignity gave lie to the concept that black people were by nature inferior. His presence alone refuted the idea that our descendants had been naked subhumans living in trees three centuries before, when the whites raided them on the African continent. That elegance could not have been learned in three hundred years."

Later, she would see Make quite differently, realizing that his "Africanness" was nothing more than culturally defined male conceits and male domination. With insight, she began to see Africa as a place of oppression and pain.

More vehemently than any other black American writer, *Washington Post* journalist Keith Richburg argues that American blacks and Africans have nothing in common. In his 1997 book *Out of Africa: A Black Man Confronts Africa*, chronicling his eyewitness accounts of unspeakable horror, he demonstrates his contempt for the genocidal Rwandans, Somalis, Ugandans, Ethiopians, and others.

In a 1997 interview, Richburg responded to criticism from American blacks that his book reveals his hatred of Africa: "Well . . . actually . . . I don't hate Africa, and I don't hate Africans. What I end up saying is that I hate the corruption. I hate the brutality. I hate the inhumanity . . . I hate the kids who point guns in my face. I hate the big men who spirit away billions in the Swiss bank accounts. I hate the maddening propensity of Africans to kind of roll and wallow and endure this suffering without taking to the streets—and doing more to demand their own rights. I hate the people who toss firebombs in the offices of the opposition newspapers . . . I hate the way people can walk by the suffering." Richburg also says he rejoices that his ancestors escaped from Africa, coming to the American colonies in the holds of slave ships.

As I make plans to return the continent, I keep one eye on the foreign news headlines. As I write, I read this headline in the *Miami Herald:* "Ethnic hatred continues to divide Africa." The article describes how Rwandan Hutus and Tutsis are slaughtering one another.

Are these my people? Can I or any other honest black American ever reconnect with them? I wonder.

Was I afraid of the ghost? Just a little

OCTOBER 31, 1999

When I was growing up in rural Florida, Halloween was black children's favorite holiday. For many older black adults, however, it was a time of fear and trembling. In general, it was when the entire black community came together as a family, when we celebrated our good "luck."

We were careful not to mistake good luck for good "fortune" because, to us, fortune suggested a ton of money, big cars, travel to exotic locales, fine booze, luxurious pads, and romance. We knew precious few black folk who owned more than two decent slop jars, a No. 10 cast iron frying pan, a 'lectric washing machine, a gas stove, a Frigidaire, and a reliable car. Luck, on the other hand, meant that, as blacks in the antiblack South of the 1950s and early 1960s, we had managed to survive for another year without too many physical or psychological wounds.

We kids, boys and girls, thoroughly enjoyed Halloween. The main building of our all-black school campus in Crescent City, which doubled as the community center, became the place of an event that would have made All Hallows' Day progenitors Guy Fawkes and Muck Olla proud. Mrs. Iona Burney, our principal's wife, would organize an indoor carnival. Every organized event was held inside. My friends and I were in heaven.

We ducked our heads in tubs of water to grab apples between our teeth. Blindfolded, we tried to pin tails on poster-board donkeys. We threw darts at balloons. We square-danced. We played Simon Says. We had a spelling bee—the most creative phonetic spelling the winner. We had a kissing booth. We had a worst-dressed contest, an ugly-mask contest, a worst-singing-voice contest, and a dumbest-answer contest. I won the dumbest-answer contest three years in a row. Pete White won the kissing contest. The girls in the booth loved his big lips. They said Pete had sweet lips.

The Halloween bash would last from 7:00 P.M. to well past midnight. Most people never stayed out this late any other night of the year. Around 9:00, a few boys and I would sneak out of the building and go into the nearby neighborhood to pull a few practical jokes and pranks. Our favorite antic was tipping over the outhouse of an old hermit near campus. One time, he was in the loo when we toppled it. Feeling guilty, I never went to his place again after that Halloween.

We would sneak back into the school building just in time for the hayride on a real wagon pulled by two real mules. Our route took us through Babylon, the black neighborhood that was home to the cemetery. The wagon did not go through the graveyard because that would have been a sacrilege. We did, however, rumble and bump on the dirt road circling the site. We made the hour-long trip in silence, wondering if the stories of horror we had heard over the years were true.

What if Bone, the headless red mule, suddenly appeared in front of us? What if Bo Bo, the boar hog with that yellow cross on his back, plunged out of the shadows of the oaks and Spanish moss? Would these possessed animals kill us? The old folk said they would. Most of all, though, I wondered what would happen if the "hant in the feedsack frock" came out of the grave-yard. If this hant appeared, we knew we would die a horrible death.

One year, I realized that no older people came on the hayride. Everyone in the wagon, including the driver, was a teen or a preteen.

Why?

I did not learn the answer until years later, after researching the history of Bone, Bo Bo, and the hant in the feedsack frock: many of the older black people of my childhood were born before the turn of the century, had barely missed slavery, and were trapped in the superstitiousness that had arrived in the colonies in the holds of ships.

Many slave owners knew about African supernaturalism and invented ways to terrorize their chattel. In other words, a scared slave was a good slave. Many nonslave-owning whites in Florida who wanted to control blacks also adopted the campaign of fear. Indeed, a few blacks did see some-thing that looked like a mule without a head, and others saw what resembled a hog with a cross embossed in its back. Blacks did not know, however, that these apparitions were hoaxes staged by white people. As frightening tales do, these passed on to future generations.

Many older blacks in Crescent City, who spent their lives using one form of voodoo or another, really did believe in Bone and Bo Bo and welcomed a safe, indoor place on the last day of October where they and their loved ones could get out of harm's way. No headless red mule or evil hog in his right mind, after all, would come inside a well-lighted schoolhouse.

But the specter of Bone and Bo Bo did not strike fear like that of "the hant in the feedsack frock," a vengeful black witch who brought year-round grief to certain individuals, especially to adulterers of both sexes and those who were obnoxiously vain.

Recently, I was thrilled to discover Lorraine Johnson-Coleman's book *Just Plain Folks*, which explains the significance of the hant: "The hant is a woman who moves normally throughout the community during the day and then sheds her skin in the evening and terrorizes man and beast alike during the midnight hours. She slips through keyholes and under door cracks, and she sneaks into your room and 'rides you till you 'bout smother.' . . . The hant is really more mischievous than dangerous, but to keep her away there are some things you can do. You can keep a Bible underneath your pillow or a broom across your door."

My grandparents and their neighbors used a Bible and a broom. My friends and I did not believe any of the nonsense. But, just to be safe, we boys never left the Halloween fair without an amulet that would keep the hant in the feedsack frock at bay until next Halloween.

By the way, one of my childhood friends still has the goofer bag he bought nearly 40 years ago at a Halloween carnival. It contains the same grave dust and petrified frog's leg the local root worker put in it more than 40 years ago.

New York City, December 31, 1999: It was one magical night

JANUARY 16, 2000

If I live to become a grizzled centenarian with pâté de foie gras and merlot in my beard, I always will remember the stroke of midnight on January 1, 2000. I was here in Times Square—the fabled "Crossroads of the World"—with more than 2 million other Y2K revelers to see the crystal ball drop, to experience the countdown to what millions worldwide believed would be the annihilation of Planet Earth.

If the world were going to sing "Auld Lang Syne" for the final time, I wanted to be in NYC when the eternal silence fell.

When the U.S. Airways 737 approached New York Harbor and I saw the Statue of Liberty, my journalistic instincts instructed me to keep a journal of my experiences as the millennium clock ticked down. For me, Lady Liberty, one of the most majestic monuments anywhere, was a good omen. I felt like an immigrant seeing her for the first time.

Fittingly, the woman next to me—on her first trip to the United States—had flown from Mendoza, Argentina, for the celebration.

December 30, 11:50 A.M.: I arrive at my hotel, the La Samana at 25 West 24th Street, whose business card reads: "NYC's #1 Jacuzzi-Room Hotel: Art Deco Steam Room." The card also says, "Spoil Yourself!"

Actually, my room is twelve feet long by seven feet wide. The bed frame is some kind of plastic box, and the mattress is a three-inch-thick square of foam rubber. The cableless television is from a bygone era. The closet is the size of a full-sized refrigerator. I have a sink and a medicine cabinet–mirror. The ancient steam heater is no bigger than a carry-on suitcase, and pipes and sundry wires and lines crisscross the walls and ceiling.

The 10 or more guests on my floor share three bathrooms. One has a commode, another has a commode and sink, and the largest has a commode, a sink, and a shower.

1:21 P.M.: I walk to Times Square along Sixth Avenue. Already, thousands of people mill at 1 Times Square, ground zero of the ball drop. The Dick Clark stage has been erected. The temperature must be in the lower 30s.

3:06 P.M.: I walk along Broadway and pass dozens of portable toilets that seem out of place among the upscale shops and banks. A wedding is going on in front of Macy's. Hundreds of people stand in line to go inside the world's largest store. I go inside a restaurant to thaw and spend 30 minutes nursing a straight Jim Beam. Leaving the building, I have a nice buzz. The sidewalks are a mosaic of lovers walking arm in arm, locals doing their thing, and visitors trying to internalize forever the feel of midtown as the 21st century approaches.

4:51 P.M.: I buy Patricia Highsmith's novel *The Talented Mr. Ripley* at Barnes & Noble on Sixth Avenue. I walk to a restaurant near my hotel. Waiting for the main course, I nearly burn down the place when I flip the napkin covering my bread onto the candle on the table. Luckily, I extinguish the fire before too many other diners see it. The odor of burning cloth lingers.

6:15 P.M.: Back at the hotel, I shower, read the *New York Times*, the *Daily News*, and the *Post*. Then I watch ABC News. I pour a glass of Jim Beam and curl up in bed with Tom Ripley. In no time, I am a willing participant in his web of deceit and murder. I fall asleep before Tom kills Dickie Greenleaf.

December 31, 3:30 A.M.: Doors slam. Feet troop up and down the hall. Women and men laugh. Commodes flush. The shower runs. Minutes later, the unmistakable sounds of lovemaking echo all around. Now I am wide awake and return to Ripley.

6:30 A.M.: I walk to Times Square. The temperature is in the low 20s. I wear thermal underwear and snowmobile mittens. Incredibly, thousands of revelers—some in sleeping bags, others on cardboard pallets—sleep on the sidewalks. One young man is clad in a tuxedo. A couple snuggle beneath Old Glory. The wacky screech of noisemakers is already erupting. Midtown has come to life, and celebration has begun in earnest.

8:39 A.M.: Cops are everywhere, and I feel safe. I buy a cup of coffee and talk with a couple from Madrid, Spain. "I can't believe I'm actually here," the man said. "New York on New Year's Eve." A band plays on the Dick Clark stage, and, on a giant screen, dancers from an Asian country strut their stuff. Next to me, a man wearing a silly hat blows a noisemaker and pinches his girlfriend's fanny.

1:15 P.M.: At 47th Street and Broadway, giant balloon puppets float in a sea of confetti. People shout for joy. In the background, the Coca-Cola sign and Jumbotron TVs compete for attention. New Age music fills the air. A roar of voices goes up north of Broadway, causing dozens of cops to run in that direction. The subway rumbles beneath me.

3:30 P.M.: Two guys push a cardboard box in front of the McGraw Hill building on Sixth Avenue. A cop stops them and inspects the box. "Can't take any chances," the cop says. "Hey, we're Americans," one of the men says.

7:00 P.M.: As darkness falls and the neon twinkles, the crowd swells to more than 1.5 million. Cops are blocking off the streets with greater regularity. As each section is barricaded, I move farther south, not wanting to be trapped in the throng at midnight. I walk to Madison Square Garden, where the Knicks are playing and Billy Joel is singing. The night is taking on a sense of spirituality. The weather is a nice 38 degrees. I walk back toward Macy's and can see the ball clearly.

10:30 P.M.: The entire area is sealed. No one else can enter. Enough people—more than 2 million standing shoulder to shoulder. The energy builds. Suddenly, I feel that someone is staring at me. I move to a new spot, but the feeling persists. I turn to see a white woman about my age looking at me. She wants to speak to me. She assesses me. Approaching, she asks if I will sign her millennium book. She has the signatures of people from around the world. What a great idea. I sign the book, and we introduce ourselves. She is a high school guidance counselor from Chapel Hill, North Carolina. We are instant friends.

11:02 P.M.: She asks if I believe in angels. "I don't know," I say. She hands me a quarter-sized silver medallion of an angel. Now, I realize that I came to New York for this one experience. I give her my business card. She turns to a group of black girls behind us. She and they sing "Auld Lang Syne." I sing, too.

11:59 P.M.: Using my cellular telephone, I call friends back home. A young man in front of me proposes to his girlfriend. Minutes later, the revelers chant, "Ten, nine . . . three, two, one!"

Midnight: The noise is deafening. The girlfriend says, "Yes, I'll marry you" and locks lips with her man. The ball slides down the flagpole. Fireworks explode against the skyline. Blasts can be heard in New York Harbor. The year 2000 has come. The newly engaged couple pop an expensive bottle of champagne and hand out plastic glasses. I take one, of course, and drink. Two cops walk past and smile. Strangers kiss and hug strangers, shouting "Happy new year."

Walking back to my hotel along Fashion Avenue, I am swept up in the general euphoria. How could anyone have missed the best international party over the millennia? In my room, I pour a Jim Beam and read up to where Tom finally murders Dickie.

Again, the lovers on my floor wake me before daylight.

Public eye harsh when loved ones fall

FEBRUARY 23, 2000

As a person with a high-profile job and broad name recognition, I have walked in the shoes of St. Petersburg police chief Goliath Davis III, Tampa police chief Bennie Holder, Pinellas County sheriff Everett Rice, and others. Like them, I know only too well the embarrassment and shame of having a close relative on the wrong side of the law.

As we all know by now, for example, Davis's younger brother, 46-year-old Geoffrey Davis, is in the maximum security wing of the Pinellas County Jail and is unable to raise bail. His rap sheet is a doozy.

So is my son's.

My son has spent five of his 28 years on Earth behind bars for dealing drugs, robbery, assault, and violating parole. His last encounter with the law occurred while he lived with me in St. Petersburg three years ago. He had served two years in Putnam Correction Institution in East Palatka and was paroled to my home. I did everything in my power to get him on the right track: drove him each day to find a job, gave him pocket money, helped him get his driver's license, enrolled him in GED classes, and generally gave him a comfortable and safe environment in which to live.

To show his appreciation, he sold both of my expensive bicycles, my kayak, my antique double-barrel shotgun, my precious six-pack of Billy Beer (which I bought in Plains, Georgia), the color television in my home office, and one of my rare Mark Twain novels.

Why did he sell these items? For crack cocaine. Where did his propensity to use dope come from? I do not know. It certainly did not come from me or his mother. Illegal drugs were never in our home. My son was influenced on his own on the streets.

We did everything to keep him out of trouble. We did all of the counseling routines. We loved him. We bought him all of the things a normal American child receives. We read to him. We took him on fun vacations. I took him across the country on my Harley, and we camped in every state between Florida and California. It was a glorious, macho, man-to-man adventure, and I thought that we had developed a special bond that would endure and keep him out of trouble.

In addition to being his parents, we tried to be his buddies. We even took him to church regularly. Nothing worked. During his teen years, he started to act as if he had lost his mind. He broke into homes, stole cars, smoked pot. The list goes on. Needless to say, we spent thousands of dollars in attorney's fees, bail, and professional advice.

When he turned 21, however, I decided that enough was enough. NO MORE MONEY. No more sleepless nights. The time had come for him to grow up. The next time he was arrested, I let him stay in jail. He was convicted and sentenced to three years. Upon release, he promptly broke parole and went back to prison. He was released a year ago.

Since then, I have seen a remarkable change in him. He has studied culinary art and has landed a good chef's job in North Carolina. I believe that he has grown up.

My daughter (same genes), who turns 18 in May, is her brother's opposite. She has never been in trouble—even at school. She is studious, respectful of adults and her schoolmates, and the orchestra director at her school says she is one of the best cellists he has ever taught. She has performed both in the United States and abroad. She will attend college in the fall.

Why did these children turn out to be so different? I do not know. Do I take credit for my son? Yes and no. Do I take credit for my daughter? Yes and no. I have decided that when the time comes, children become self-actualizing people who do what they want. When I was 16, for example, I told my father that I was not going to be a farmworker and would not follow him through another season in which I would experience more hardship. I was going to college. And that was that.

Sure, Chief Davis, Chief Holder, and Sheriff Rice might be embarrassed, but they are in no way responsible for the troubles of their relatives. The problem is that the public, especially these men's detractors, love to hear that well-known people have scandal in their orbit. When my son was arrested in St. Petersburg, one of my critics who knew about the arrest stopped me in Publix, gloated, and told me that I was a hypocrite, that—because of my son's troubles—I had no right to tell blacks to take responsibility for their lives.

I spoke to my son last week and learned that he has earned the GED, has a great apartment, a three-year-old car, a new girlfriend, and a job that pays $20,000. Not bad for a young man who seemed hell-bent on self-destructing just a few years ago. He may make his old man proud yet.

The Noblest Profession

Don't undercut teachers' authority

November 16, 1994

The hypocrisy of many parents is undermining public education in the United States. Everywhere parents are complaining like never before that the public schools are doing a lousy job. Obviously, according to standardized tests and other indicators, many schools are failing to fulfill their academic responsibilities. Most parents, however, ignore their own vital role in the success or failure of the public schools. And one of the worst things that parents can do, which they do a lot these days, is to compromise the authority of the adults—the teachers, counselors, coaches, administrators, and others—in charge of the schools.

Nothing, in my estimation, is more harmful to adult authority than for irresponsible parents to side with their children in challenging rules intended for the good of the greatest number of students and to bring frivolous legal action against the schools. Such is the case at Hollidayburg Area Senior High in Pittsburgh, where a few parents are complaining that mandatory showers after gym classes violate their children's right to privacy. Bunk! Hollidayburg and other schools nationwide have had shower policies for decades, for darned good reason and without incident. Now, these modern-day, rights-obsessed parents and their peevish little darlings have been joined by the American Civil Liberties Union in challenging the school's authority. The superintendent, trying to balance the interests of everyone, modified the policy and had private shower stalls built. But the parents and their kids still want the shower policy itself killed.

In Florida, we have our share of kids and their parents challenging adult authority in the schools. Most of our cases involve distributing religious materials on campus, using unsavory and hurtful language, wearing apparel containing potentially offensive messages, and instances of sexual harassment. In too many cases, school officials, faced with the prospect of costly legal battles, back down, letting children win when they do not deserve to win. Religious pamphlets, for example, with headlines such as "Satanism bred in secular school system" and "Pro-choice women aid *Playboy* agenda" have no business in a public school setting—period. The parents of children wanting to distribute this junk should know better.

While these same parents are complaining that the schools are denying their children individual rights, they are griping, as hypocrites would, that the schools are not teaching their children well. How can the schools do their job when their authority to control the children has been weakened? A teacher who has no authority to discipline a boy for wearing a contraband T-shirt or a coach who has no authority to chastise a player for missing jump shots on the court, more often than not, will lack the authority to teach that child in the classroom.

Public schools, like the workplace and other environments requiring order, operate best when adults are firmly in charge. If you think I am being too harsh, take a look at the schools in your district, public and private, that boast of genuinely good academic records, and you will find strong adults in charge. You will find that most rules are nonnegotiable. You will find that kids do what they are told.

Today's new generation of spoiled, immature parents apparently needs to know that learning to follow rules is an integral part of their children's education and social development. They need to know also that their children's dislike of rules does not necessarily make the rules wrong. Most of all, these parents need to know that, when they help their children defeat adults, they undermine the system and jeopardize their children's education.

A firm hand for a troubled school

January 15, 1995

Sam Gaskins, an 11th grader at Dillard High in Ft. Lauderdale, followed a crowd toward the cafeteria, where many of the students ate breakfast before first period began at 7:45. Of course, hardly anyone would ever get to class on time. Breakfast was for hanging out before handing yourself over to the teachers and administrators for seven hours.

But something was different that morning last August. As the first wave of students approached the cafeteria, the words "All of you people need to get to class!" boomed along the breezeway, making Gaskins and everyone else stop. Gaskins turned. A few feet away stood the biggest, meanest-looking man he had ever seen.

He and his homies had met 6-foot-4, 310-pound John D. Kelly, Dillard's new principal. "I want everyone on this loge to get to first period—now," Kelly said. In the past, Gaskins would have moved, but slowly. On that morning, though, he broke from the crowd and hurried to class. As he walked, students milled in the halls even though classes had begun.

But no more. Today, nearly six months after Kelly's arrival, Dillard's hallways, loges, and yards are virtually free of students during class time. And Gaskins knows why. "Mr. Kelly makes you do what's right," he said. "He won't let the students be in the halls. You have to attend class, and we don't have as many people skipping the whole day. Dillard is different now."

Founded in 1907 in a one-room frame building, Dillard remained Ft. Lauderdale's black high school until it was desegregated by a federal court order in 1970. During the heyday of the civil rights movement, when many other black schools nationwide were shut down or transformed into middle or elementary schools, Ft. Lauderdale's black community, backed by the NAACP, won a court battle to retain the facility's high school designation.

But the school fell on hard times. After many veteran teachers were transferred to other schools, morale sank among the general staff and student body. As the economy faltered, neighborhoods around the campus disintegrated, and enrollment plummeted. As crime and drugs soared in the area, Dillard earned a reputation for being a place of violence and apathy, a place run by the students.

This reputation, fair or not, lingers in the minds of many Broward County residents. Kelly, who graduated from Dillard in 1962, has returned to change that image. "When you hear constant negatives about something you feel dear to, it bothers you," he said. "I was an assistant principal in Dade

County before I came here, and I heard about Dillard's discipline problems and inferior academics. I wanted to do something."

Last May, then-principal Benjamin J. Williams and a group of alumni asked Kelly, 50, to become an assistant principal. When Williams retired at the end of the 1993–94 term, Kelly replaced him. His return to his alma mater had followed a circuitous route.

After graduating from Dillard, he attended all-black Florida A&M University in Tallahassee on a football scholarship. From there, he played three years as a center for the Washington Redskins before injuries ended his career; he was the first black center in the National Football League. After leaving Washington in 1967, he returned to Dillard and coached football for one season before becoming offensive line coach and offensive coordinator at Southern University. Budget cuts cost him the job at Southern after several years. Then he took a job as a manager with New York Life Insurance. He was successful but unhappy. Missing the daily contact with children, he returned to the school system.

"I've come to one conclusion: God created me to deal with children," he said. "Dillard was part of God's master plan for me. So I jumped at the chance to come home and work with these kids."

Kelly's homecoming, though, has not been a honeymoon. From the outset, the huge number of students in the halls shocked him. "I mean, kids were walking and walking and walking and walking," he said. "There was no sense of urgency to get to class. I saw a lot of apathy. I saw kids who had given up. I can't accept that."

During his first meeting with the faculty, he outlined what he calls the rifle approach. "In the rifle approach, you've got to aim and hit what you're going to shoot at. You can't set your sights too high. First, I aimed at getting the kids in class. Then I aimed at discipline. These are simple things, but my most important goals right now. We must put our teachers back in control." He appointed a committee that developed tougher detention and tardy policies and stricter grading standards for regular students and for those in the magnet program. Magnet students, for instance, must maintain a 2.5 grade point average (out of 4) or return to their original schools.

Kelly does not believe in sending students home or expelling them. Instead, the staff uses in-school measures, including chores, such as cleaning the cafeteria's tables and floors, and mandatory study halls, to punish and motivate students. After these policies were established, copies of them were sent to all parents and guardians.

To enforce class attendance, Kelly, the six daytime assistant principals, coaches, and security staffers conducted sweeps of the campus each day, every period. During sweeps, teachers could not admit tardy students into the rooms. Now, the sweeps are strategically timed to ensure the element of surprise. Armed with a radio, Kelly prowls the campus each day, rousting students off the telephones, lecturing them, driving would-be lovers out of hiding, leading sullen star athletes to their classrooms. His determination to get students in class and keep them there is as practical as the man himself. "You can't learn if you aren't in class," he said.

Class attendance is the highest it has been in 40 years. But are the students learning their subjects? Not well enough to suit the new principal. He believes that discipline—appropriate behavior that makes learning possible—is still missing. Too many students continue to disrupt classes.

"Without discipline, nothing good can take place," he said. "I don't care how good the teacher is, if the teacher has to quit lecturing every five minutes to say 'stop' to an unruly student, she can't do her job. If you take five minutes from classroom instruction, you're now teaching a 55-minute period instead of a 60-minute period. If you have five or six periods a day, and you keep losing five minutes in each, in a year's time the student might miss six weeks of instruction. How can that student compete with a kid in suburbia where full 60-minute periods are taught?"

And what do Dillard's 2,800 students think of Kelly's radical changes? "In the beginning, we thought he was kind of mean and hard," Gaskins said. "But now that most of us have gotten used to Mr. Kelly, we are buckling down and studying. I think it's cool. I really like him, and most of the other students do, too." A few weeks ago, the student government held a school-wide program honoring Kelly.

Parents also support his tough policies. Like their children, though, most were skeptical at first, believing that Kelly was doing too much too fast. Some openly complained about the harsh punishment their children received, arguing that the new principal did not understand the 1990s generation of high schoolers. Today, however, few parents complain.

Dillard's teachers have the most praise for Kelly. "Mr. Kelly is innovative, he's willing to listen, and he brings discipline," said media center director Zonia Williams, who taught English from 1976 to 1988, before assuming her present job. "He's brought in a new administration and a new way of thinking. The tenseness on campus is gone. Although he is a big man, he is kind and gentle and approachable. He has big ideas."

Anderson Spince Jr., a Dillard graduate who has taught at his alma mater for the last 24 years, said: "For too long, teachers have had less power than the students. With the threat of lawsuits, HRS charges, and everything else, teachers were always on the borderline, always afraid to discipline the students the way they should be disciplined. It's like sitting on a time bomb trying to teach kids these days. Since Mr. Kelly came, teachers feel better about themselves and about the administration. The stress and pressure aren't like they used to be. Of course, we can still do a better job."

Indeed, all is not well at Dillard. Standardized test scores, for example, are still embarrassingly low, and the dropout rate, which has improved significantly, is still high. But Kelly has taken action. He asked teachers to drill and tutor seniors who were to take the exit exam in October. One result was encouraging: the students scored five points above the district average in communications, a first for the school. The previous year, Dillard had placed last.

But Kelly also worries about Dillard's magnet program, consisting of performing arts and high technology. "It's designed to pull white kids into a black community, but it has created a school within a school," Kelly said. "The black kids, 99 percent of them, who live in the area can't get in the magnet program. Of the approximately 700 students in the two magnets, very few are black. That breeds a lot of resentment between the races. I want to change that."

He wants to operate the entire school as a magnet, letting students' capabilities and willingness to work determine their academic status. "Everyone should really have a fair chance," he said. "Right now we have a system of haves and have-nots. I don't like it." He attributes the school's few cases of racial violence to the inequity the magnets create.

If he succeeds at Dillard, Kelly said, his race and gender will have a lot to do with that success. He also hired other black males, some of whom he has known since childhood, to bring meaning to the lives of Dillard's black male students.

"Let's tell the truth," he said. "The fact that I am a black male is super-important here in this environment. No matter how you look at it, socio-economically, the black male is the individual who is being lost. With me, they see one of their own. They see me working in their community, and they know I care about them. I can be tough on them because I am a good role model. I am one of them."

Sam Gaskins agreed that Kelly was correct in hiring strong black males. "Mr. Kelly graduated from Dillard, and he's returned to help us," he said. "That tells the rest of us—even the white students—that everything is possible. Mr. Kelly and some of the other black men on the staff came from these same neighborhoods and made it. That means we can make it, too, if we go to class and work hard."

A heartfelt tribute to teachers

May 5, 1996

Teachers, I believe, are the most responsible and important members
of society because their professional efforts affect the fate of the earth.
Helen Caldicott, author and peace activist

Of all of my teachers, Coach Bernard Irving had the most impact on my life.
Standing well over 6 feet and weighing about 230 pounds, he was our high
school's one-man athletic department. He coached everything—football,
basketball, softball, track, boxing, wrestling, soccer, and even fencing—and
played every sport expertly.

Because our school had the smallest student enrollment in our conference, we lost more often than we won. And here is where Coach Irving was
a formidable presence. Somehow, this gentle man could make a bunch of
losers feel like victors. One year, our football team lost every game. Even
worse, we did not score a single touchdown until the final minutes of the
final quarter of the final game. Coach did not berate us. Instead, he made
that one touchdown a reason to celebrate, to joke and laugh about the
season's misadventures, to hoist the player who had run the touchdown onto
our shoulders.

Coach, who also was a good chemistry and biology teacher, secured a
football scholarship for me to attend college. I would not have gone to
college if he had not helped me. To this day, I feel his presence. He taught
me and the other children at our all-black school to be tough: to accept
reality with as much good cheer as possible, to withstand adversity with
dignity, to forge ahead with purpose despite the obstacles.

Wherever you are, Coach Irving, I thank you for shaping my life, for
making me a survivor, for being the great professional you are. And because
Tuesday is National Teacher Day, this column is an unapologetic tribute to
America's other Bernard Irvings—our teachers.

Although they rarely receive thanks, teachers make positive differences
in the lives of children each day. The untold story is that, in addition to
teaching, most teachers invest in society by going beyond the call of duty, by
giving out of their pockets, by giving up their personal time, by nurturing
the children of strangers.

But rather than talk generally about the teaching profession, let us focus
on a teacher who, as Helen Caldicot said, affects the fate of the world. When
I asked several Pinellas County school officials to identify a teacher who
routinely serves beyond the call of duty, the name Deloris F. Bell consis-

tently came up. At age 54, Bell has worked for the Pinellas district for 30 years. For 18 years, she was an elementary teacher and now is a family involvement specialist for Title I, a federal effort that teaches basic skills to pupils in elementary schools with higher numbers of poor families.

After most other teachers have gone home for the day, Bell often is on the job, doing what she loves best: visiting the homes of children and their families. "It is important that families are involved in their children's education," she said. "I know that all parents want the best education for their children. When parents are involved in their children's education and communicate with the school and teachers, their children do better in school. We want to have a partnership between school and home to build a close relationship with the teacher, parent, and child."

And that partnership, which includes several intensive workshops, succeeds, in part, because of Bell's enthusiasm and commitment. In the computer training program, for instance, family members can borrow Macintosh computers and use them in their homes for up to three weeks after they complete a two-hour training. In the parenting workshop, Bell lectures and uses videos. "Families have an opportunity to share the joys, tears, and frustrations of parenting. This gives them a chance to talk with other parents and support each other," she said. "Some of the topics are building self-esteem, positive discipline, and rearing responsible children. We teach that communication between parent and child is crucial."

A top administrator said that Bell is one of the district's most valuable assets. "She will do anything to help the children," he said. "When we have kids having serious trouble because of low self-esteem, we try to put them in touch with Dee Bell. She works miracles almost every time. Even though she's busy in school, she's also very active in the community as a whole."

Several years ago, after learning of a neighborhood girl having problems at home, Bell went to the state Department of Health and Rehabilitative Services and won custody of the child, who lived with Bell for two years. For such efforts, Bell has earned the nickname "Mama Dee." Throughout the week and on weekends, children congregate at Bell's home. Many come for companionship, others for the fun, still others to find refuge from various forms of abuse. And at her own expense, she takes children to amusement parks such as Disney World and on educational field trips.

Deloris Bell, like Coach Bernard Irving, represents professionals who, too often, are discounted and made the scapegoat of society's failings. To the contrary, though, we owe our schoolteachers a huge debt of gratitude. Who, except a teacher, would respond as Bell did when asked to discuss the greatest rewards of her career? "I truly enjoy my job," she said. "I feel that my experience as a teacher has enriched my life and has given me the opportunity to grow and share my knowledge with others."

Such unselfishness deserves to be honored on Tuesday—National Teacher Day—and on every other day of the year.

Put the teachers first for a change

MARCH 14, 1998

When I was a child in Florida's public schools during the 1950s and 1960s, I admired my teachers. Along with being benign tormentors, my teachers were role models, neighbors, surrogate parents, friends. After becoming a college writing teacher in the early 1970s, I proudly encouraged many of my students to become schoolteachers. More than a few took my advice.

Today, however, I would be hard-pressed to advise a student to become a member of what used to be called "the noblest profession." Yes, teaching still carries many intrinsic rewards, such as the satisfaction of watching inquisitive minds grow intellectually or helping youngsters who lack self-esteem gain the courage to voice their opinions in class.

In far too many ways, though, teaching has become an ignoble profession, especially here in Florida, where public education per se is under siege on several fronts, where our GOP-controlled legislature and our new Republican governor, Jeb Bush, are treating teachers as if they were enemies of the people.

In addition to ramming through vouchers (using tax dollars for private school tuition), many Florida politicians are spewing punitive rhetoric that, among other things, casts teachers as slackers responsible for the sorry conditions in many school districts.

The governor, too, refuses to face the hard truth about what needs to be done to improve public education: Put teachers first. Every reliable study on the subject shows that teacher competence is the most important pedagogical factor in the classroom. Without good teaching, effective learning is virtually impossible for most students.

Bush and lawmakers should stop the sleight-of-hand approach to education immediately and pass legislation that sets teacher salaries high enough to attract the best and the brightest, salaries high enough to keep competent teachers in the classroom.

I am talking about salaries high enough to endow the profession with the dignity that it deserves. I am also talking about an attitude change, so that we treat teachers as professionals, as our children's allies—not as their enemies.

But nowhere does Bush earnestly address the issue of teacher salaries. When speaking most recently to the editorial board of the *St. Petersburg Times*, he claimed that he could improve teaching by increasing requirements for certification, rating colleges of education on their performance, and raising college admission standards for prospective teachers. These measures are part of a larger effort, not solutions unto themselves.

As for Lieutenant Governor Frank Brogan, having been in public education in Florida for nearly 22 years—as a fifth-grade teacher, middle school dean, assistant principal, principal, district superintendent, and state commissioner of education—he has become one more unprincipled politician who has turned his back on reality in the classroom. He recently wrote a guest column for the *Times* praising Bush's disingenuous plan for improving teacher education.

Unlike conservative politicians such as Bush and Brogan, who tell rich retirees and other right-wingers what they want to hear, administrators and professors—who direct the nation's colleges of education—struggle daily to attract, instruct, train, and, of course, retain the nation's public school teachers. They confront the problem with sincerity and candor. Last September, for example, I asked Roderick J. McDavis, dean of the University of Florida College of Education, to explain how—if he had the authority—he would attract excellent teachers who will not automatically abandon the classroom if another job comes along.

"From the standpoint of recruitment, we need to increase salaries. That's number one," McDavis said. "Today, when high school and middle school students look at careers, whether it's right or wrong, they look at how much money they can expect to earn. I think that's especially true with men. Young men tend not to look at education as a career path because they don't feel they'll be able to earn enough money to take care of a family. So we've got to find a way to increase beginning salaries for teachers and long-term career salaries."

The state also disregards teachers' need of money by not adequately funding an incentives program meant to bring teachers into academic areas where they are in critically short supply. Under the program, the state is supposed to either help pay off loans or reimburse tuition costs for new or veteran teachers who agree to take courses that prepare them for positions in "critical shortage areas" such as special education, science, and math.

For the second time in nine months, the state is scrambling to keep its end of the bargain. Hundreds of teachers, some having left other careers to work in the classroom, are awaiting money promised to them.

Why are we having this problem? Because elected officials apparently do not think that money for teachers is important enough to place them high on the list of legislative priorities.

The governor, because he is the state's chief executive officer, and the handful of right-thinking lawmakers in Tallahassee could fix the current problem by simply transferring funds. For the long term, however, they need to pass legislation that permanently guarantees adequate funding for the program. Our teachers deserve no less.

A rarely mentioned fact is that the overwhelming majority of public school teachers are caring, generous professionals who willingly compensate for the stinginess of their districts, as borne out in a survey by the National Education Association. In 1996, the NEA asked teachers how much of their own money they spent during the previous school year to meet the needs of their students.

Incredibly, 94 percent said that they had spent an average of $408 on everything from stickers to pencils to paper to pizza to shoes and clothing.

And what do elected officials and the rest of society give teachers for their generosity? Hostility from parents, unruly charges, mountains of paperwork, disrespect, unsupportive principals and superintendents, unnavigable bureaucracy, lousy legislation, low salaries.

As Florida rushes to improve public education by implementing vouchers, establishing charter schools, testing students every year from third through 10th grades, and raising standards for state-sponsored college scholarships, officials should listen to the University of Florida's McDavis. He wants to improve current teacher quality and recruit a new generation of public school teachers by making them—and their profession—feel valued.

"We've got to start saying more positive things about public education," McDavis said. "You've got to give a young person a reason to want to go into education. If all you read and hear about schools is negative, it's a turnoff. The perception these days is that our best and brightest do not go into teaching. Within our communities, we need to do more to honor teachers in a way that brings respect back to the profession. Teachers used to be highly respected. The level of respect has dropped off. People don't tend to go into a profession perceived to be disrespected."

Unfortunately, the measures and the rhetoric coming out of Tallahassee perpetuate disrespect. Because teachers have been demonized, their concerns are virtually ignored. Only enlightened, apolitical leadership can reverse this costly, destructive trend.

Teaching, the feminized ghetto

MARCH 24, 1999

In his new book *Jobs Rated Almanac*, author Les Krantz uses statistics from telephone surveys, the government, and trade groups to rank 250 occupations as super to the pits, according to six criteria: income, stress, physical demands, growth potential, job security, and work environment. If you happen to be one of the diminishing number of Americans who still idealize public school teaching, you should know that teaching ranks number 164, behind teacher's aide (111), janitor (154), and maid (157).

I am not surprised that teaching ranks so low. Indeed, the income is lousy; the stress level can threaten one's health; real growth potential is limited; unless one has a continuing contract, job security can be iffy; and, as we all know from recent shooting deaths and other attacks on campuses nationwide, the work environment can be dangerous.

"Much work in this profession, such as preparing lessons, grading papers and attending meetings, is done after the school day has ended," Krantz writes. "Teachers spend long periods of time on their feet. Working with rambunctious children can be fatiguing and stressful."

Krantz does not discuss what I believe to be the fundamental reason that teaching is such a lowly profession: It is a feminized ghetto—a field comprising mostly women who accept inconsideration as normal. In Pinellas County, for example, nearly 80 percent of the instructional staff is women. In the elementary grades, the percentage is even higher. Men do not teach at some American elementary schools.

In early America, before the government institutionalized the profession, nearly all teachers were men. After the government took charge of teaching, women became desirable because officials were hell-bent on paying teachers the smallest salaries possible. Most educated men would not accept such low pay for such difficult work.

Teaching became permanently feminized when the ideal teacher became the spouse of a successful man—a local businessman, an elected official, a pastor, and often a school administrator. Immediately, the woman's abysmal pay was treated as supplemental income to the husband's higher salary.

After writing a recent column arguing that teaching will become respectable only when teachers are paid much higher salaries, I received more than 30 letters from teachers throughout the country. Only one came from a man, a high school science teacher and football coach in upstate New York who agreed with me. I was disappointed by the number of women who disagreed.

In a letter that otherwise complimented my column, a longtime Pinellas teacher wrote: "My husband, who was in administration, used to say that it was not good for a teacher's salary to be too high because we didn't want 'just anyone' to be a teacher. There's something to be said for that line of thought, too."

Another woman wrote that her husband, who has a GED and is a sheriff's deputy, brags that he earns much more than she does. She ignores his braggadocio, she said, because she did not become a teacher for the money.

These two women and others like them affirm my thesis that as long as teaching is considered a woman's job—as mere supplemental income—the best and the brightest will continue to shun the profession. We hear tales about teachers who moonlight. Well, guess who the overwhelming majority of these moonlighters are: unmarried women, some single moms, struggling to make ends meet.

No one should be surprised that men who become teachers jump into administration—where the big bucks are—as soon as possible. Then they become the bureaucrats who see no need to fight for higher teacher salaries. Obviously, if more men were in the classroom, salaries would rise overnight. But men know better than to enter the field in the first place. Most of them simply will not become part of this invaluable, underpaid, widely disrespected profession.

Learning Curves

Universities should serve the nation

DECEMBER 18, 1994

As a former teacher at three state universities, I have always been dismayed that American taxpayers and donors make very few serious demands—outside of insisting on winning football and basketball teams—on these well-financed institutions. We should place great demands on our universities. These schools, in fact, should be leading the way in solving the nation's most pressing problems.

Some disciplines, such as those in the sciences, mathematics, agriculture, and medicine, naturally contribute to society's well-being. But other areas—especially some in the social sciences and the humanities—fail to serve the citizenry significantly.

How can the university best serve the citizenry? By helping government at all levels establish equitable, sensible public policies and by assisting in improving the quality of life in general. And given the nation's myriad cultural, economic, social, and political crises, the universities, home to our best and brightest minds, should be leading the way in finding real solutions, not providing ideologically expedient studies that serve powerful special interests and politicians. I was pleased, therefore, when Cornell University's newly appointed president, Hunter R. Rawlings, announced recently that one of his primary objectives would be "putting Cornell's great expertise to work in aiding New York State and the nation."

As a classics scholar, Princeton University graduate, and current president of the University of Iowa, Rawlings fully understands the larger role of higher education. "So many of our universities, like Cornell, have the highest academic quality, and our society has so many crippling problems," he told the *New York Times*. "I would like to convey some of that expertise in the service of the nation." Rawlings, a former Woodrow Wilson fellow, was referring to Wilson's 1896 speech, "Princeton in the Service of the Nation," when he said: "Wilson sounded the clarion call for universities to participate in the service of the nation."

Why are so many universities failing to work in the service of the nation? They fail for several reasons. Their presidents, deans, department heads, and research professors lack the necessary vision or fail to understand the essential mission of the university itself. These institutions are not ivory towers or Trappist villages. Nearly 100 years ago, Wilson described the appropriate role of the university: "It has never been natural, it has seldom been possible, in this country for learning to seek a place apart and hold aloof from affairs. It is only when society is old, long settled in its ways, confident in habit, and without self-questioning upon any vital point of conduct, that study can effect seclusion and despise the passing interest of the day.

"America has never yet had a season of leisured quiet in which students could seek a life apart without sharp rigours of conscience, or college instructors easily forget that they were training citizens as well as drilling pupils. . . . We can easily hold the service of mankind at arm's length while we read and make scholars of ourselves, but we shall be very uneasy. . . . College must use learning as a vehicle of spirit, interpreting literature as the voice of humanity—must enlighten, guide, and hearten."

Self-interest and greed motivate many scholars. Untold numbers of researchers quietly receive money and gifts to conduct studies for the sole purpose of validating actions that corporations such as agricultural chemical manufacturers, pharmaceutical companies, government agencies, and defense contractors want to take. Many presidents and scholars have literally sold their souls, relinquishing two of the university's most precious assets: objectivity and independence.

A recent example of such capitulation is the Stanford University president fired in part because he packed tens of millions of dollars of administrative overhead into research conducted for the U.S. Navy. Some of the expenditures included silk sheets and other frivolities. Add to the lure of money the political challenges of getting promotions and tenure, and a professorship at some prestigious university can become a pact with the devil.

Many universities fail to serve the national interest because professors fall victim to the specialization of knowledge. A lot of important research is too narrowly focused, too arcane to be of much use in the real world.

Poor writing—dense prose understood only among small groups of scholars—is another way that universities cheat the electorate and donors. The answers to some of the nation's most serious problems remain hidden in the pages of scholarly journals that few outside the university ever read. Inaccessible knowledge is dead knowledge.

Obviously, the public suffers when universities fail to deliver. The greatest harm is that think tanks, wealthy organizations staffed by modern-day Sophists and ideologues, eagerly fill the void left by the universities and help to establish the national agenda. Granted, many think tanks provide ideas and information that help make life easier. But too many—those deeply in the pockets of special interest groups, unscrupulous private companies, and unprincipled politicians with short-term, selfish goals—hurt public policy.

I am especially troubled by the influence of think tanks in today's cross-wired political climate. The handiwork of conservative think tanks can be seen everywhere. The Republican agenda for retooling welfare by investing in orphanages, for example, is fueled by the likes of the American Enterprise Institute's Charles Murray, coauthor of *The Bell Curve*. And, of course, the Democrats and President Clinton rely on think tanks such as the Brookings Institution and the Progressive Policy Institute.

The major problem is that hardly any think tanks are disinterested, making independent scholarship next to impossible. Essentially, legions of egg-heads compete on the Beltway for the biggest purses. I cannot imagine how the public interest is best served when policies are developed by mercenaries who say what they are paid to say. "Paid thinkers rarely marshal evidence and reach conclusions that generate ill-will with the payer," said Michael Warder, executive vice president of the Rockford Institute, a conservative think tank.

In short, today's national agenda amounts to what Warder calls the "relation of money and power to thought." The concept scares me. Think tanks are hardly new; they have been around for centuries. But contemporary tanks, employing the tools of cyberspace and traditional media, are more sophisticated than earlier ones, giving them power far beyond that held by the American electorate.

The university is the only other institution that can ease the think tanks' stranglehold on U.S. policymaking. But too many universities also are fettered by self-interest. Too many of them have abandoned Woodrow Wilson's vision. Until citizens demand that the universities become more assertive in helping to establish viable public policies, we will continue to follow the present fractious course, where solutions to our enduring problems are whatever the most powerful think tanks at a given time say they are.

Keep open the door to learning

MARCH 5, 1995

While erasing the chalkboard, I noticed the brooding eyes of a female student sitting in the back of the crowded classroom. I was there as an alumnus, a consultant at the annual Humanities Advisory Council Seminar at historically black Bethune-Cookman College. Later, the young woman shared with me the heartbreaking yet triumphant story of her life: "I'm 18 years old, and I didn't learn to read until I came here. I wanted to say something during the question-and-answer session, but I was kind of embarrassed."

Amazingly, she had spent 12 years in Florida's public schools without learning how to read. No one had diagnosed her dyslexia, an impairment of the ability to read, often the result of a brain injury or a genetic defect. Because she was always well behaved and well groomed, her teachers liked her and promoted her. Still, she was frustrated both in and out of school. "I tried and tried to read on my own, but I couldn't," she said. "I thought I was retarded or crazy or something. My parents didn't know what was wrong with me either."

Although her standardized test scores fell below average, she was determined to attend college. "Bethune-Cookman has an open-door policy, so they let me in," she said. "During my first month on campus, my teachers found out why I couldn't read. They worked with me every day. I am now a sophomore, and I can read well. It really feels good to understand what I'm looking at on a printed page. Now I can help other black children who have problems like mine. That's why I'm at Bethune-Cookman."

A major irony of this young lady's plight is that, even though she has the ability and the determination to help other African-Americans become productive citizens, very few schools, besides those that are private and historically black, would ever have given her a chance. Without institutions such as Bethune-Cookman, students such as this young woman would never come close to realizing the American dream.

Another irony is that now, as the nation adopts increasingly elitist views on who should and should not attend college and as federal student loan and Pell Grant funds face the Republican budget ax, this student and her peers attending historically black colleges face an uncertain future. The overwhelming majority of them receive federal loans or grants. Most come from poverty-level households, and untold numbers of parents have sacrificed everything—as they should—to send their children to college.

A professor shared with me more than 30 letters her students had written to their senators and representatives about the proposals to cut student financial aid and funding for historically black institutions. Each letter was a sincere appeal to keep the programs intact. Nearly every student at Bethune-Cookman and other such schools nationwide must work to support themselves, some even sending money home to help out. Many others are the first in their families to attend college. And for most, Bethune-Cookman is their only chance for success. Here are excerpts from some of their letters:

"I do not come from a rich family, and my college career depends on financial aid. Without financial aid, I would have to leave college, along with my sister, who is a freshman, and many of her classmates. I have no idea what I would do if I could not go to college."

"Being a young black woman, times are getting harder by the day. Not using race as an excuse—but more as a reality—it would be virtually impossible for me to continue my education in college without financial aid. My family can't support me."

"My family and the families of my schoolmates are not financially stable enough to help us much. We all work 5–8 hours each day off campus to pay our bills. We are struggling to stay in school. We aren't asking for a handout; we just need some help until we can get on our feet."

"If financial aid is cut, I won't be able to attend college because I also have a son to support. I made a mistake by getting pregnant, but I am getting my life back together here at Bethune-Cookman. I am striving to be the first one in my family to get a college degree. I want to be a role model for future generations. Please don't cut financial aid."

Like the young lady who has dyslexia, these are hardworking young people, the very ones for whom federal assistance was intended. Many are from the ghettos and housing projects of Tampa, Miami, Jacksonville, and other major urban areas in the state. Others are from migrant towns like Belle Glade, Ft. Pierce, and South Bay. They come from the neighborhoods that produce the human statistics in the crime reports that so frighten us.

But these young people are striving to be different. Historically black colleges are the last resort for many of them. Federal financial aid is essential for these students and their institutions. Together, they represent great investments, not liabilities to be toyed with in crass political games in Washington.

The success of these African-American students—like that of the young woman who labored to overcome the debilitating effects of dyslexia—is good for the nation. We should support them in every way. We should help them to thrive.

Pity the schools in these litigious times

October 6, 1996

Conservative pundits and sundry cynics smell blood. Their prey this time? Uptight public school bureaucrats who have let political correctness run amok, who do not know the difference between a young boy's innocent peck on the cheek of a female classmate and an act of bona fide sexual harassment. These critics fail to comprehend their sin: they are contributing to the devaluation of the nation's public school system.

The causes célèbres, or martyrs, are Johnathan Prevette, six, a first-grader at Southwest Elementary School in Lexington, North Carolina, and De'Andre Dearinge, seven, a second-grader at New York's Public School 104 in Far Rockaway. Both boys were suspended from school for "sexual harassment."

Johnathan's troubles started when he kissed a female classmate on the cheek. A teacher witnessed the act and reported it to the principal, who promptly suspended the boy for a day. Because he was absent from school, Johnathan missed an ice cream party honoring pupils with good attendance and was prevented from coloring and playing with his friends.

Several hundred miles to the north, De'Andre became persona non grata after stealing a kiss and ripping a button off a girl's skirt. Initially, he was given a five-day suspension. De'Andre said he kissed the girl because he likes her and wants to marry her. Okay, but why did he snatch the button? To pay tribute to his favorite fictional character, Corduroy, a teddy bear missing a button, he said.

Jackie Prevette, Johnathan's mother, complained that her son's punishment was too severe. After all, she saw his crime as nothing more than innocent smooching. Does the punishment—in either boy's case—fit the crime? Should either child be charged with sexual harassment? Yes, said Southwest Elementary's spokeswoman Jane Martin, referring to Johnathan. "A six-year-old kissing another six-year-old is inappropriate behavior. Unwelcome is unwelcome at any age."

Martin spoke these brave words days before the satellite trucks began to arrive from as far away as Canada, New Zealand, and Australia; before the likes of Rush Limbaugh, Oliver North, Kathie Lee Gifford, and, of course, the local mayor got into the act. After the school received a bomb threat, officials decided that they, indeed, would be "working on an age-appropriate revision" of the sexual harassment policy.

In Far Rockaway, matters were just as bad for school officials. After De'Andre's parents, the mayor, and the ubiquitous press came calling, officials threw out the suspension and started meeting to reconsider their sexual harassment guidelines.

All right, so the boys' parents got what they wanted. But what about the schools? What did they get? The nation's public schools do a thankless, Herculean job. They are, in fact, acting in loco parentis. That is, in place of the parent. Each weekday, for four to seven hours, school officials and teachers are responsible for every facet of their pupils' lives, including the children's right to be free from peer harassment.

Under Title IX of the federal Education Amendments of 1972, moreover, school districts are liable if they fail to act in instances of "peer sexual harassment," which is defined as "harassment that occurs during school activities or on school grounds by one student against another." Districts have latitude in interpreting the law, but they are required to have guidelines in place. In Johnathan's case, his parents, like other parents at the school, had signed a document stating that they had read the school's student handbook and had discussed the rules with their son.

The ugly truth is that public schools are held hostage by a litigious society that no longer supports the local schools. We come to school holding our children's rights in one hand and our attorney's business card in the other—all the while demanding that staff protect, nurture, and teach our little darlings. At the same time, though, we insist that our children enjoy every freedom and bask in self-esteem. In other words, we want it all.

School officials, far from being ogres, are victims who waste precious time seeking ways to stay out of court. On the one side of them stand the demands of the U.S. Education Department's Office of Civil Rights. On the other, parents and society wait in judgment, watching for a mistake.

As a former teacher, my biggest worry is that each time children are permitted to defeat teachers and administrators, each time a Jay Leno portrays teachers as fools, we further undermine the viability of public schools. We obliterate the necessary line between the child and adult authority. In effect, we force officials to overreact to protect themselves.

The wisest comments I have heard about this mess are those of Ellen Bravo, executive director of the 9 to 5 National Association of Working Women: "Clearly, local school officials overreacted in describing Johnathan Prevette's behavior as sexual harassment and punishing him for violating school rules. But the problem is the overreaction, not the rules. Can sexual harassment occur in elementary schools? It can, and it does. The degradation gets worse as kids get older—not innocent adolescent flirting and kidding around, but demeaning and abusive behavior."

Perhaps Bravo anticipated the case of Tianna Ugarte, now 14. When she was 11, a male classmate verbally and sexually harassed her. She and her parents complained to school officials and to the boy's parents. But no one acted. A few days ago, a jury told the Antioch School District near San Francisco to pay Tianna $500,000.

How will Antioch officials react the next time a student accuses a peer of sexual harassment? Officials elsewhere should stay tuned. They have excellent cause to ask if a kiss is just a kiss or if a kiss—in today's litigious climate—announces the beginning of big trouble around the bend.

When adults learn to read

April 13, 1997

Mattie M. Mathis, 52, a janitor and St. Petersburg resident, has a dream: to read well enough so that she can read to her grandchildren and help them with their homework.

A 45-year-old owner of a local tree service wants to learn how to read and spell to avoid embarrassment when trying to fill out a bill of sale in a client's presence and to be able to teach Sunday school.

Another St. Petersburg resident, 60, owner of a lawn service, is learning to read because, instead of having others complete his paperwork, he wants to write his own contracts, bid on jobs, and measure job sites. Most of all, he wants to write to his youngest daughter. He was unable to write to his other three children after they left home.

These residents, according to the U.S. Department of Education, are among the estimated 40 million American adults who "are—at best—able to perform tasks involving 'brief, uncomplicated text,'" given their poor reading skills. Incredibly, the United States has the highest illiteracy rate among all industrial nations, and untold numbers of citizens, especially blacks and other ethnic minorities, suffer a lifetime of limited options, unfulfilled potential, embarrassment, and fear.

Here in Florida, which has one of the nation's highest numbers of poor readers, one of five adults—1.7 million—cannot read adequately. Fortunately, adult students in this part of Florida who have severe reading problems can find empathetic volunteers at the Literacy Council of St. Petersburg. Each Monday and Wednesday evening, from 5:30 to 8:30, Virginia

Gildrie, 76, and 15 other tutors, who buy books and supplies out of pocket, meet at the Lakewood Community School to teach 18 to 20 adult students how to read.

Gildrie, supervising trainer of reading tutors, has volunteered with the council for 24 years. She assesses her mission modestly: it is to serve. "One of my most rewarding moments came," she said, "when a student told a tutor: 'I always buy Easter cards for my family, but for the first time, I was able to really pick the right cards because I could finally read them.'"

According to the most recent report of the National Adult Literacy Survey, Gildrie and her colleagues nationwide have good reason to be concerned about the personal and societal implications of inadequate reading:

- Four out of 10 job applicants tested in 1992 (the most recent year for which figures are available) for basic reading and/or math lacked the skills necessary for the job they sought.
- More than 50 percent of surveyed manufacturing companies indicate that more than half of their front-line workers have serious literacy problems.
- Nationwide, a correlation exists between reading difficulty and poverty, crime, unemployment, child abuse and substance abuse, teen pregnancy, homelessness, and high school dropout rates.

Experts say that these problems negatively affect quality of life and raise taxes for additional social services, prisons, remedial education, and police protection.

But politicians seem impervious to common sense and logic. Although less than 10 percent of the people who need help get it, decision makers in most parts of the nation slash adult education funds when budgets shrink. Moreover, public awareness and support of literacy efforts are fading. Most alarming, Gildrie said, is that while black adults have some of the most serious problems, literacy programs struggle to recruit African-American volunteers. The Pinellas organization, for example, recently enrolled its only black volunteer in eight years.

And how does Gildrie account for this shortage? "I think, considering the history of black people and how far they have come, that a person has to be very comfortable with what he is in his own skin before he can give of himself." More specifically, she explained, because they generally live in the same neighborhoods, attend the same churches, and shop in the same stores as their would-be tutors, blacks—believing that their secret will go public—shun those familiar with their reading problems. She added, "Blacks also feel that any black person who is able to read would look down on them because this person would say, 'I fought all of this stuff you're fighting, so what's the matter with you?' They don't think that other blacks would have the empathy. But that's changing."

The high number of young blacks under age 20 who refuse help is a serious crisis, said Sandy Thursby, a member of the Literacy Council's Board of Directors and an adult education coordinator for Pinellas County Schools. "They don't see the need yet," she said. "They start coming in during their mid-20s. That's when they start seeing the value of reading. They're either parents who suddenly become afraid, or they have job aspirations and realize that they need reading. Ordinarily, though, we seldom see young people."

A study by Laubach Literacy International paints a stark portrait of how the inability to read trapped adults: "It interfered with their work; it kept them from knowing exactly what their children were doing in school. It made them shy. It made them sad. And sometimes it made them feel like liars or impostors."

Learning to read can transform lives, Gildrie said. But thousands of new tutors—especially blacks—are needed immediately. If new tutors do not join the crusade, the problem will worsen.

Responsibility rests with the parents

MARCH 18, 1998

Since the woodshed has lost favor as a viable option for improving public education among children in Pinellas County, we need to move promptly to the next best option: active, realistic, excuse-free parental concern.

I am raising this issue because, in recent public meetings on school busing and related matters, hostile parents, most of them black, have blamed Superintendent Howard Hinesley for their children's poor academic performance and disruptive behavior. Most of these parents want Hinesley and School Board members to outline specific strategies for improving black student achievement, decreasing suspensions, and ensuring that more black students get into gifted classes. Currently, the perception is that too many black students are being dumped into classes for the troubled.

Obviously, as the trustees of the system, Hinesley, other administrators, and board members must be held accountable for much of what goes on in our schools. But parents who expect officials to be totally responsible for their children's learning need to have their heads examined.

Parents, not teachers, are the single most important influence on what, how, and when their children learn. Learning is an individual, private experience. In fact, it is a family value and a personal value in every sense—one that parents can most effectively instill. The inculcation of the love of learning occurs in the privacy of the home, around the dinner table, curled up in bed with a good book, on the laps of mothers and fathers and grandparents. A home devoid of this love is a wilderness, a wasteland. Indeed, teachers can inspire children to learn, but the appreciation of acquiring knowledge is a family matter.

My own life and the lives of many of my schoolmates are examples. As poor children attending inadequately equipped, all-black schools, we faced every conceivable disadvantage to learning. Yet we learned and were eager to do so. We learned because our parents—wanting us to "become somebody"—made us complete our homework before we did anything else, forced us to be home at "a decent hour," demanded that we respect adult authority, especially that of our teachers.

I do not recall anyone who was suspended. Expulsion was unimaginable. Our parents did their best to send a "good product" to school. My mother, for example, knew that teachers have an inherently tough job and do not need the added burden of peeling back deep layers of apathy, anger, unruliness, and other antisocial behavior. "Them teachers don't have time for your mess," she would tell us. "Don't make me have to waste time comin' to that school to see 'bout your behinds."

We knew what she meant. Today, I know only a handful of black parents in St. Petersburg who worry about the kind of "product" they are sending to school. I see far too many parents who are uninvolved in their children's school lives.

Most distressing is a scene I pass almost every day during my morning walk. Three or four boys, no older than 14, smoke pot while waiting for the school bus. These children are going to school stoned. What on earth can Hinesley do for them? Imagine the trouble the teachers face.

To help improve black student achievement—and to his credit—Hinesley has distributed to principals the names of underachieving students and has requested that officials establish ways to track the students and try to improve their progress.

And what is the response of black parents? Unfortunately, the blind defensiveness of Kim Saunders, a businesswoman and the mother of a kindergartener at Cross Bayou Elementary, is typical: "As a black American, I . . . feel insulted that the School Board feels like they have to have a special plan to help us learn."

Well, of course, a special plan is needed. Why? Because too many black homes lack a special plan, too many parents fail to discipline their children, and too many children have no sense of the long-term benefits of an education.

Meanwhile, Hinesley and other officials must hold their tongues. They are forced to devise quixotic academic improvement plans and pretend that they can perform miracles with children whose parents let them perpetually goof off. Nothing could be more unfair to these people and the many fine teachers who perform a thankless job.

One of these days, Hinesley may muster the intestinal fortitude to tell these parents to start taking responsibility for their children's rotten attitudes toward learning.

Listen up, parents: learning is free

April 1, 1998

Several weeks ago, I wrote that parents should be more responsible for their children's academic lives. The column was aimed mainly at black parents because of the high number of black children performing poorly and disrupting classes. Needless to say, and as I had anticipated, I received many angry letters and telephone calls from blacks who misunderstood me. Today's column is an attempt to expand on the notion of learning so as to clear up some of that misunderstanding.

All parents, especially black parents, should know this well-kept secret, one of the most important truths in the world: learning is free. I repeat: LEARNING IS FREE.

Education—the formal process of attending classes at an institution, completing assignments, and taking examinations to earn a diploma, degree, or certificate—costs money. But learning—the individual act of acquiring information, knowledge, and wisdom—is free. When prison inmates discover this truth, even their lives often improve. When I suggest that parents should do more at home to enable their children to benefit from the daily school experience, I am talking about inculcating a love of learning in their children.

To learn is to comprehend, to apprehend. It is to find a comfortable chair in the library, the best corner of your bed, a cool spot under a tree. It is to become excited—marveling over the beauty of a poem, accompanying Holden Caulfield as he confronts the world of adult "phonies," struggling to decipher an incomprehensible algebraic equation, discovering real connections between abolitionist newspapers and the Civil War, seeing why Americans celebrated John Glenn and Project Mercury.

In other words, no one else has to be there for a child to learn if the love of learning has been instilled.

During the rare times that I speak to black groups, I like to discuss the lives of our forebears, many of whom were slaves, who suffered the unforgivable sin of being prohibited by law from learning to read. I like to discuss how—without an official school or an official teacher—they learned to read and write and compute by stealing precious moments in hideaways. Tens of thousands of slaves and later generations of blacks liberated their bodies and minds through learning. Today, too many of us enslave our bodies and minds by refusing to learn.

Think, for example, of famous Floridians such as Josiah Walls. Born in Virginia in 1842, he fought for the Union, moved to Archer, and cut down trees for a living. He learned to read at night, thus launching his extraordinary career in politics.

As more blacks in Alachua County registered to vote, they saw the need to have their own representative. In 1867, Walls went to Tallahassee as a delegate to the state Republican Convention. The next year, he was elected to the Florida House of Representatives, and to the state senate the following year. Three years later, he was elected to the U.S. House, an office he held until 1876. In 1873, he bought the *New Era* newspaper in Gainesville, the first African-American-owned newspaper in Florida.

Mary McLeod Bethune, founder of Bethune-Cookman College in Daytona Beach, is equally inspiring. Born in 1875 on a five-acre farm that her father and mother, former slaves, sharecropped, she was one of 16 children. As a young child, she carried a book around and pretended to read.

"She wanted to go to school to learn how to read more than anything in the world," writes historian Maxine Jones. "But Mary's family was poor, and none of her older brothers and sisters attended school. She begged and begged until finally her mother agreed to let her go to the mission school. . . . This was the beginning of a life devoted to learning and to teaching others."

Presidents Coolidge, Hoover, and Roosevelt appointed her to important positions. Today, Bethune-Cookman, her greatest legacy, is one of the best black colleges in the nation, a place where thousands of African-Americans, including me, have been inspired to learn.

I could list hundreds of other blacks, many right here in St. Petersburg, who understand that learning is free, that it is for the taking. But I will not.

I will say, however, that more parents need to understand this simple truth and act on it.

Indeed, racism is a serious problem that disrupts the process of education, as I have defined it. But racism cannot stop black children who love to learn from learning. In fact, racism should be a great incentive to want to learn. Why? Because learning is the only sure way to free ourselves of racism's power to make us permanent victims.

Black colleges remain necessary

APRIL 8, 1998

Whenever I return to Bethune-Cookman College, my alma mater, I feel a sense of both pride and distress. A private, historically black institution, Bethune-Cookman is affiliated with the United Methodist Church and has 2,500 students, the overwhelming majority of them American blacks.

I am here in Daytona Beach to speak to the students majoring in journalism and public relations. My pride comes from knowing that the college—always struggling financially—has succeeded against huge odds in educating thousands of blacks who, like me, because of low standardized test scores and a lack of money, might never have attended college otherwise.

That said, I am distressed for at least two main reasons. First, I must again face the reality that the historically black institution is still needed in the United States. As the anti–affirmative action movement in admissions picks up steam nationwide, as merit becomes the most important measure for scholarships, and as Republican rhetoric grows more cynical and strident, increasing numbers of black students, who may have considered a mainline campus before, are finding the Bethune-Cookmans of the nation attractive.

Several students told me that, until last year, they had planned to attend a public university in Florida or elsewhere. But the nasty fallout from the successful anti–affirmative action campaigns in California and Texas and occasional reports of Florida's nascent effort make many students here believe that they are not wanted on traditional white campuses.

"I don't want to attend a campus where I'm going to be an outcast," said Michael Crooms, a freshman from Miami. "Here at B-CC, at least I know that the professors, students, and administrators want me to be here. I mean, it's like family. Sure, I would love to be in Gainesville. I think I would get a better education. But I don't know if I would feel comfortable there."

Another student, a sophomore from DeLand, said: "I don't think I would want to go anywhere else. I feel like a real person here. A lot of the brothers and sisters need to study more, but you can't study anyway when you've got a bunch of racists around like at the University of Central Florida. I wouldn't go to UCF, no matter how good the professors are."

The camaraderie that most of these students seek, however, leads to racial isolation, the second source of my distress. Such isolation can be protective, shielding students from the racism off campus. But isolation also can have the deleterious effect of perpetuating intellectual mediocrity and of fostering inadequate social skills, which impede success in a larger society. Too many students arrive with poor study habits and a lack of appreciation for learning. In fact, a large number still disdain "brains" and consider "being smart" as "acting white."

The concept of knowledge for the sake of knowledge has not caught on among most students. Many of them apply together, in small groups from the same cities in Dade and Broward, for example. They bring along their old habits and the antiintellectualism of the inner city. What many need, of course, is the challenge of different cultural experiences, interaction with other ethnicities, an infusion of new ideas, disparate ways of viewing the world and of seeing themselves.

Do not misunderstand me. While I see a need for historically black colleges and universities, I am aware that their very existence shows that America continues to turn its back on a large segment of taxpayers, that blacks and whites have immeasurable work ahead to narrow the racial divide. The black college, as much as I love returning to it, is not a sign of national health but a symptom of the cancer eating away at the nation's insides.

No, I do not suggest that blacks need to be in the company of whites to learn or to become fully socialized. I do suggest, though, that blacks must survive in an America where whites dominate in all important aspects. Further, self-selected isolation for culturally naive reasons is blind, and it will pay bitter dividends over time.

I would not object if my daughter attended my alma mater. But I would let her know that she would be delaying the useful experience of immersing herself in "real" America, a nation that, despite its instinct to discriminate along ethnic lines, is richly diverse.

Unfortunately, the nation's growing conservatism has made the black campus more important and appealing than ever.

Writing should not be a punishment

JANUARY 20, 1999

In his continuing zeal to embarrass President Clinton, U.S. Rep. Henry Hyde, on January 17, read a letter from a third-grade student in Chicago during his closing remarks at the Senate impeachment trial. The student, William Preston Summers, chastises the president for lying. Fair enough. Clinton should be chastised for lying, and he should be punished. But what punishment is appropriate?

William, eight, having been coached by his father and taught in an American public school, has the perfect punishment for the prez. Here are excerpts from his missive: "I have thought of a punishment for the President of the United States of America. The punishment should be that he should write a 100-word essay by hand. I have to write an essay when I lie. . . . I do not believe the President tells the truth any more right now. After he writes the essay and tells the truth, I will believe him again."

What was Hyde, a self-appointed keeper of the nation's morality, thinking when he shared a letter that describes writing as punishment? Hyde should be ashamed of himself. He has insulted every writing teacher in the United States who, each day, has to fight the perception that writing is drudgery.

A friend, a writing teacher at Eckerd College, told me about an incident involving her daughter, an elementary school student. When the child's class was preparing to play field hockey, she told the teacher that she did not want to play goalie because she "sucked" at that position. Her punishment? Write an essay discussing the inappropriateness of the word "suck." The mother went to the school and scolded the teacher for his crime.

In his book *Free to Write: A Journalist Teaches Young Writers*, Roy Peter Clark, a writing professor at the Poynter Institute for Media Studies, sees writing-as-punishment as a Skinnerian yoke: "Teachers try to modify the behavior of students by creating negative consequences for misbehavior. In one school, students who misbehave badly are given a choice between suspension or writing an essay (the death penalty or life imprisonment). The unintended side effect of this process is to create in the mind of the student a perpetual association between punishment and the act of writing, in the same way that the protagonist of *A Clockwork Orange* was conditioned to hate Beethoven."

"The tendency to equate writing with punishment is so deeply ingrained in our educational system that it has been reflected in popular culture," Clark writes. "During an episode of the television comedy *Different Strokes*, an otherwise enlightened teacher gives Arnold and his classmates a 100-word essay to write as punishment for misbehaving in the hallway."

If William Summers is typical of most U.S. public school pupils, then we are in big trouble. At eight, he already has been taught to hate writing. Reports claim that his father forced him to write the letter as punishment for having lied about not starting a fight.

William's father, 31-year-old Bobby, is in a prime position to ruin writing for future teachers and students. He is a graduate student in political science and a part-time college teacher. In a P.S. accompanying his son's letter to Hyde, Bobby wrote: "Dear Rep. Hyde, I made my son William either write you a letter or an essay as punishment for lying. Part of his defense for his lying was that the president lied. He's still having difficulty understanding why the president can lie and not be punished." If truth be told, I am willing to bet my paycheck that the elder Summers and Hyde are the ones having angst while trying to cope with Clinton's mendacity. William would much rather be at swim practice, where he was when he told the lie that landed him in trouble.

"When writing becomes punishment," Clark says, "all of the positive elements of learning—organization, discovery and communication—disappear. . . . In too many schools, writing is a recurring nightmare for students. . . . Their writing anxiety, their 'instinctive' hatred of writing, is not instinctive at all but learned."

Indeed, William has learned the hard way that writing is punishment. His parents told the *Chicago Tribune* that the Clinton letter to Hyde was the boy's third punishment essay on lying.

Hyde obviously believed that he was doing America a huge favor when he read the child's letter to the nation. Instead, he undercut the hard work of our thousands of writing teachers who must try to undo the damage done by the likes of Bobby Summers.

I want to see Summers and his hero, Hyde, punished. I do not want them to write essays. Who would read their sanctimonious tripe? I want them taken to the woodshed to have their rears whipped until they cannot sit.

Where adult-child relations make sense

May 2, 1999

A few weeks ago, I wrote about Piney Woods Country Life School, a 90-year-old, historically black, private boarding school 21 miles south of Jackson, Mississippi. It is one of four such institutions left in the nation.

In the wake of the massacre in Littleton, Colorado-where two students shot and killed 12 of their schoolmates, a teacher, and themselves—I felt the need to return to the inspiring story of Piney Woods and its 300 students. I am writing about the school again to purge myself of some of the pain and anger I feel because of the Columbine High School carnage. By reviewing my notebook, I wish to remind myself that many of our children can be innocent, playful, sweet, courteous, kind, and generous.

In March, I spent three days at Piney Woods attending classes and Sunday school with the students and staff, observing students working on the school's farm, visiting the boys' dormitory, eating in the cafeteria, strolling among the towering pines and the azaleas, interviewing students and personnel, traveling to Jackson to watch the chess team compete.

More than a month later, I am still impressed that all of the students, ages 12 to 18, look and act like children. Indeed, Piney Woods is a haven, a place where young people are protected from the encroachments of violence and other ills of contemporary America that abridge childhood. Here, for example, youngsters are not burdened by the need for "image," one of the major sources of the dysfunction and turmoil in many of the nation's public schools. On the simplest level, a strict dress code, in force on school days and during school trips from 7:00 A.M. until 5:30 P.M., eliminates many of the potential image problems. Furthermore, everyone is clean-cut and well-groomed. I did not see the hard, lifeless faces that I routinely encounter on the streets of St. Petersburg. I felt a sense of wholesomeness in the presence of each child.

The rowdiest moments on campus are the walks back to the dorms after meals, when the children, including the seniors, scream, romp, and engage in horseplay. One girl chased a boy and pulled his shirttail out of his pants—particularly amusing to me, a writer in what most people consider a cynical profession. Some of the administrators do not like such behavior. Others, however, welcome it because it epitomizes children being children.

Anger, resentment, and unhealthy rivalries are held in check. All negative excess is discouraged by students and staff alike. Kids openly correct one another's English. Everywhere I went on campus, they greeted me warmly and addressed me as "Mr. Maxwell" or "sir." Piney Woods is a place where adults are in control. Apparently, the kids want matters that way.

In the classes that I visited—math, Spanish, and English—the overwhelming majority of the students were polite, attentive, and eager to work. When someone did something wrong, the teachers stepped in immediately. When a boy interrupted the math lecture by continuing to talk too loudly, for example, the teacher said, "I told you to stop talking. You must not understand English. Don't say anything else." The room fell silent for the remainder of the lesson.

When a student fell asleep in English class, the teacher made him stand in a corner until he was fully awake. Good-naturedly, his classmates made fun of him until the teacher told them to shut up. This room, too, fell silent for the duration of the lesson.

In Sunday school, a boy in the seventh-grade class acted up. The teacher, a young black man, said: "If you want to be ignorant, take it outside. Right now, we're in God's house, and we're having Sunday school." The boy, mildly embarrassed, was a model student for the rest of the service.

Even when they are away from campus among students from other counties, Piney Woods boys are respectful and obedient. I drove with members of the chess team to Jackson, where they participated in a tournament at Hinds Community College. During a break between games, the boys came outside with dozens of students from other schools. Several Piney Woods boys and others started to walk through a bed of flowers. Michael Cox, the Piney Woods adviser, yelled for his players to get out of the flowers; they obeyed without complaining. Other children took their time, even kicking some of the plants.

I was even more impressed with the boys after we went back inside for the matches. I sat near the door away from the players. One Piney Woods boy approached me and said that he was going to the bathroom and would return shortly. I was puzzled as to why he spoke to me. A few minutes later, another Piney Woods boy did the same. Back on campus, I asked one why he had told me where he was going. His answer? Because I was an adult accompanying his teacher, he thought that I deserved the respect of an official chaperone.

These incidents may seem inconsequential to most readers. To me, however, each is a lesson about one of the precious things we have lost as a nation: common sense in adult-child relations in the school setting. No good has come of our smug permissiveness, as the staff, students, and parents at Piney Woods know only too well.

I would love to see the nation's failing public schools export the best of Piney Woods.

"Failing" school finds many successes

December 15, 1999

Last Friday afternoon, the Liberty City Charter School—Florida's first charter campus—held its fourth annual Christmas program. All 205 pupils in kindergarten through fifth grade were there, and all 11 teachers were there.

Amazingly, at this time of day, more than a dozen parents were there, too. They had taken off work to be with their children. The significance of this fact alone accounts for much of the school's early success. During the program, each class either performed a skit, recited a poem, danced, or sang. The kids had fun, and the mothers and fathers watched adoringly and applauded.

Four years ago, before Jeb Bush, then head of the nonprofit Foundation for Florida's Future, and T. Willard Fair, president of the Miami Urban League, founded the school, such a scene would have been impossible to imagine in this, the poorest area in Miami, where the public schools are some of the nation's most dysfunctional.

Despite its recent failing grade of D on the state's new tests that evaluate public schools, Liberty City Charter is thriving. Although disappointed that her students failed and believing that the tests cannot accurately measure intangibles such as parental involvement and campus safety, principal Katrina Wilson-Davis supports the grading system.

"Our being rated a failing school has been a shot in the arm in a lot of ways," she said. "It's something like taking an immunization shot. At first it makes you sick, but it makes you well. It helped us to focus on our children more. It told us what we can do for our children and make them better than they currently are. Being rated a failing school is not an easy thing to swallow—not by any means. But still, I will venture to say that in the long run, it's going to be good for our children."

Wilson-Davis is optimistic because, as a charter school—an independent public institution free of many of the Department of Education's restrictions—Liberty City is not trapped in the one-size-fits-all philosophy governing traditional campuses. She has the autonomy to establish a curriculum and other services that best serve her all-black student body, selected by lottery from various income levels. A major portion of each school day, for example, is dedicated to character building and citizenship, subjects absent from nearby public schools.

But Wilson-Davis and her faculty face some major obstacles in teaching the children of this community that is separated both physically and economically from Miami's bustling downtown by Interstate 95. "We basically have an uneducated population," she said. "By uneducated, I mean un-knowledgeable. The adults aren't fully educated on the things they can do to help their children. A lot of parents trust the school to do their job and, in some instances, don't take an active role in making sure their children are ready when they come to school.

"A lot of parents complain that the homework is too difficult or that they can't help their children with the homework. Our parents are great if they're told what to do. They need to know, though, that their children need to be prepped much earlier. Kids are now starting kindergarten knowing the al-phabet, knowing how to read, and how to write. Some children are already computer literate. Our kids are coming to the table without having these experiences. In too many cases, the preschool preparation has not been done, so we're working against the grain. We must teach some of our par-ents that education is a value. So the continuum from what the school is doing and what is being reinforced in the home is not there a lot of the time."

Another problem, Wilson-Davis said, is that many pupils watch TV and videos into the early morning. They come to school tired and unproductive, disrupting the equilibrium of their classes. She said she spends many hours explaining to parents the importance of sending their children to bed early and to getting them to school on time—and feeling positive about them-selves.

Plainspoken and charismatic, Wilson-Davis envisions a bright future for Liberty City Charter. She plans to build a new facility with classrooms equipped with the latest technology. "Mainly, though, I expect to have a student body that is strong academically," she said. "I expect parents to be heavily involved, trained, and acclimated to the demands of this school and their children. I expect to have a top-notch school. Our goal is to become a beacon of hope for children coming through here. We want to provide them with an essential education, to lay the foundation for them to be able to do anything they choose to."

Living While Black

In a black straitjacket

JANUARY 12, 1997

As a 51-year-old black professional endowed with at least average intelligence and skills, I am sick and tired of being the guinea pig for social scientists, the exotic primitive for linguists, the "special student" for educationists, the cause célèbre for black ideologues, and the elixir for healing the consciences of assorted white liberals.

I, like other Americans, want to be permitted to be a normal human being. For me, along with hundreds of thousands of other blacks, the heaviest burden of wearing black skin is being forced to live with the world's expectation that I, a lifelong adherent of solipsism, must think like other people of color, that I must be the spiritual double of, say, some wino in Little Rock whom I will never meet.

By contrast, does anyone seriously expect all whites to think alike? Of course not. Why, then, do we foolishly expect all blacks—some 37 million of us, born to diverse backgrounds and blessed or cursed with distinct propensities—to be of one mind? Is the legacy of slavery so powerful that it alone has become the common thread that forever joins us at the social, cultural, and intellectual hip?

To be black and to deviate from the philosophical norm is to be labeled abnormal, a freak. What do I mean when I say that I want to be permitted to be a normal human being? I mean that, like the average white person, I want to be able to say, think, and do as I please without facing special judgment. In other words, I want to be free to be my own person. And being my own person means regularly traveling roads not traveled by other black people.

Let me demonstrate with a simple example. I became fed up with forced conformity several years ago after I told a black acquaintance that I liked the Tracy Chapman song "Talkin' 'bout a Revolution."

"That confused broad sings like a dizzy white chick," he said.

"And how does a dizzy white chick sound?" I asked, expecting too much.

"Like she ain't got no SOUL," he said, mocking me.

"That pretty much sums it up," I said.

He will condemn me for sure after reading this column and learning that I enjoy some of Natalie Merchant's music and that Toni Braxton's interminable, sound-alike croonings grate on my nerves.

But conformity in music is benign when compared with conformity in other areas. I am thinking generally about politics and specifically about the tortured public life of Supreme Court Justice Clarence Thomas. He recently turned down yet another speaking engagement with a black audience because some leaders of a local branch of the National Association for the Advancement of Colored People threatened to protest. Why? Because, they argued, Thomas "is not a good role model for black youngsters."

And what is Thomas's transgression, his deviancy? The man dares to be a conservative, for heaven's sake—a condition that, in reality, is just as normal as being a fuzzy-headed liberal. But because he is black, Thomas is diagnosed as being abnormal. Would we call Barbara Bush, Ronald Reagan, and Elizabeth Dole abnormal simply because they are conservative? No, because conservatism is within the realm of normalcy for whites.

For the record, I also have contempt for Thomas, not because of his conservatism but because he became the worst kind of hypocrite by badmouthing affirmative action. The truth is that no other black has benefited more from affirmative action than Thomas, who, at the time of his nomination, was an inexperienced functionary unqualified for the nation's highest court.

As black society grows more Afrocentric, the demand to conform increases and casts a wider net. Journalism is a field that should remain free of such influences. But it has not. Many black journalists, in fact, are ideological zealots who are leading the conformist movement and are the first to call their renegade colleagues abnormal, Uncle Toms, and other names. These writers are black first and journalists second—a conflict that compromises their ability to write the truth on most subjects involving their own. For these writers, areas that portray blacks negatively are off limits. They simply do not write these stories, depriving readers of valuable information. But I, along with many others, see myself as a journalist first and black second.

"Bill, you aren't normal," a black colleague in Ft. Lauderdale told me a few weeks ago when I said that I was preparing a piece critical of black leadership in St. Petersburg. "Why do you want to come down on the brothers and sisters so hard?"

My comments about "professionalism" and "journalistic integrity" fell on his deaf ears. Conformity is everything to him. He would not write negatively of other blacks, so as not to give cover to conservatives and racists.

The real horror of black America's unthinking need to conform is that few of us have developed honest, wholesome relationships with other blacks. In general, we relate to one another on the fringes, in the shadows, in whispered code. Too often, to avoid ugly truths, we lie to one another. Real relationships cannot exist in such a smothering climate, where taboos outnumber freedoms, where normalcy—thinking for oneself—is a liability and a cause for ostracism.

Unfortunately, matters will get worse before they get better. The main reason is that increasing numbers of blacks in the nation's urban centers believe, with compelling evidence on their side, that racism is on the rise. As a result, black groups that fought among themselves just a few years ago are now establishing alliances that place conformity at an even higher, more dubious premium.

A refreshing insensitivity

MARCH 23, 1997

As I stood at the checkout counter of a convenience store in South Hill, Virginia, trying to locate a bookstore, the old white man behind me said, "You ain't from 'round heah."

I explained that I was a vacationing journalist from St. Petersburg, a book collector, and an incurable explorer. "We don't git many colored newspaper people 'round heah," he said, grabbing the bib of his work-worn overalls. "What's a colored fella like you doing in South Hill?" His tone was a combination of curiosity and amusement.

"Colored"? When had I last heard that word or seen it in print? Back in St. Petersburg, we refer to ourselves as either black, African, African-American, or people of color. Suddenly, I realized that I was going to have a great seven-day vacation, among simple folk in a rural region where life is stripped of smothering pretense. Here was a place where honest talk is as natural as a sunrise, where eye contact is 20–20.

"I'm just trying to relax and find a few good stories," I said.

"Well, we got lots of good stories 'round heah."

Indeed, after we walked outside, the man told me about several "good colored families" in South Hill and in the neighboring towns of La Crosse, Brodnax, Union Level, and Ebony. When I told him that I also wanted to meet some "good white families," he said, "They probably won't talk to you. They ain't used to talking to coloreds."

That word again.

I did not press the issue because his unrehearsed candor, emitted between chomps on a plug of Virginia chaw, was persuasive.

In Chase City, a few miles down the road from South Hill, I witnessed marvelous, real-world political incorrectness. The assistant manager of a grocery store, an overweight white woman with a beet-red proboscis, stormed out of a produce cooler, saying, "Men are all alike. They can't do any darn thing for themselves!"

Everyone, including the men, in the closest checkout lane laughed. Attempting to show off among strangers, I said, "That sounds like sexism to me."

The woman who had made the remark looked me straight in the eye and said, "It is sexism." She ended any hopes of clever conversation that I, a big-city writer, had entertained.

Now I became the object of derision. All eyes seemed to be asking if I, an outsider, was from an alien planet. Amused by my own blunder, I paid for my orange juice and bananas and walked into the parking lot. Standing beside my car for a few minutes, I watched dozens of local residents come and go.

Men opened doors for women and tipped their sweat-stained baseball caps; a few older black men greeted white women but kept a "respectful" distance; rifles and shotguns hung from the rear windshields of many pick-ups; white men, young and old, spat tobacco juice on the asphalt.

At Head's, a black-owned barbershop in Chase City, I was honored to be part of a spirited debate about the worsening plight of young black males. For the first time in many years, I saw black men—unfettered by political ideology and the need for popularity—strongly disagreeing without calling one another Uncle Toms, radicals, fools, and other epithets. I actually saw them take opposite positions on the issue of self-reliance, all without resorting to knife play and fisticuffs.

Piedmont Mall in Danville, Virginia, gave me yet another surprise: smokers were everywhere, puffing away inside the complex itself. Spotting a security guard, I knew that he would snuff out the cursed weed. To my utter consternation, he, too, was spewing cigarette smoke like a hyperactive Humphrey Bogart.

"What's going on? How can people smoke inside?" I asked a bookstore clerk.

"This is Virginia—Tobacco Country," she said incredulously. "Where're you from anyway?"

An hour away in South Boston, I went into a local eatery and saw a scene worthy of an unreformed Epicurean. Grossly overweight men and women, unworried about their waistlines, attacked some of the thickest, juiciest steaks I had seen in years. Greasy home fries, magnificently browned bis-cuits and cornbread, collard greens, okra and tomatoes, and macaroni and cheese laced the huge platters in front of the guests.

Because of my diet, this spectacle, replete with wondrous aromas, was overpowering. I bought a cup of coffee and left as quickly as I could. Why am I on a diet? I asked myself. Why am I not washing down a plate of fried chicken with a few drams of Jim Beam?

On the morning that I prepared to leave southern Virginia, I had an anxiety attack. I had to return to St. Petersburg—to civilization—to a self-conscious workplace where the slightest cultural, racial, ethnic, or gender indiscretion could jeopardize a career. I had to return to a city that is afraid to speak its mind; where candor is a liability; where we wear our sensitivities on our sleeves; where we are scaring ourselves to death with paranoia and pessimism and ignorance and denial.

And if this is the price of "civilization," I would rather be vacationing.

Sick of white liberals' "understanding"

OCTOBER 22, 1997

I cannot speak for my brethren, but I am one black man who is tired of the insufferable "understanding" of white liberals—the group claiming to comprehend the black man's condition. Such "understanding" is as harmful to our well-being as our own bad behavior. Moreover, their well-intentioned but naive assessments of our problems and their empathy have aided in producing generations of social engineering that has rendered many blacks intellectually and ethically impotent and unemployable.

White liberals should demand of blacks the same positive values and high standards that they demand of themselves and other select groups. Like other people, blacks need honesty, thrift, self-reliance, cleanliness, studiousness, sobriety, punctuality, calmness, and, of course, cold introspection to prosper.

My wariness of white liberals has returned as St. Petersburg residents, especially whites, struggle with the significance of last year's riots, which wrenched the city out of its complacency about race relations. Sadly, this kind of communal soul-searching produces high levels of guilt and sentimentality, both of which encourage many liberals to make the felonious appear heroic; the law-abiding, villainous.

Many "understanding" white liberals have, for example, joined blacks in excusing the behavior of TyRon Lewis, the 18-year-old black motorist who, after disobeying direct police orders, was shot to death last October 24, sparking the worst race riots in the city's history.

These same liberals are vilifying Officer James Knight, who, perhaps fearing for his life, shot Lewis. I am not suggesting that Lewis should have died. I suspect, though, that many whites condemning Knight would be much less "understanding" of Lewis if he had been a white man. A white motorist, after all, should have known better than to challenge a cop whose adrenaline was flowing, whose pistol was drawn and pointing at his chest. Alas, Lewis, a black male, knew no better.

This is paternalism at its most contemptible. It also pervades public education, where many "understanding" white teachers force white students to work hard but let black students—viewed as victims of a culture of poverty—do little or no work.

Several years ago, I visited my son's school after he and a white kid had fought in class. When I arrived, my son was in the back row of the classroom, his head on his desk. "Why wasn't Dustin taking notes like the other students?" I later asked the teacher, a white woman in her mid-30s.

She merely shrugged, her expression suggesting an "understanding" that turned my stomach. I reminded her that she was professionally obligated to push my son as hard as she did her white students. I told the principal the same thing. He, too, was despicably patronizing.

I also am sick of white liberals who, while living in their gated cul-de-sacs and rarely setting foot in the black ghetto, claim to "understand" the dynamics of crime among blacks. These same whites value the rights of black thugs more than those of frightened, law-abiding property owners. These same whites tie the hands of police officers working the most dangerous streets in the ghetto. Some of these same whites even claim to "understand" why black males gun down one another.

White liberals also "understand" pregnancy among black girls—those "poor dears" who are ignorant of contraception and so starved for love that they fly into the the arms of older black men. These lechers impregnate more than half of their young conquests.

For sure, white liberals "understand" the sociology that contributes to widespread drug and alcohol abuse among blacks. They "understand" black males who lack the gumption to polish their shoes and join the unemployment line like everyone else. How often have I heard some white, born and reared in a suburb, idealize poor blacks and excuse their self-destructive behavior?

As a practitioner in the workplace, I am especially troubled when white liberals blindly accept black mediocrity. How often have I seen "understanding" whites protect unqualified blacks whose poor performance often taints the fine work of truly qualified blacks?

Few things are more insulting than being a member of a group that is "understood" to the point of being routinely forgiven our misdeeds.

All that said, I wonder sometimes if I am not being too harsh on white liberals. Perhaps they are good people who simply do not know what the hell they are doing.

Misunderstood on "understanding"

October 29, 1997

During an interview shortly before his death in 1994, historian and social critic Christopher Lasch, whose parents were influential progressives, was asked why he apparently had turned against liberalism.

"My father is puzzled by my attacks on liberalism," Lasch said. "'Why are you so hard on liberals, and why do they seem to take the brunt of your attack?' Having been raised as a liberal, I appreciate what is valuable in the liberal tradition, which seemed to me at one time to offer the best hope of a decent kind of politics, and for that very reason liberalism strikes me as more worthy of engagement and criticism than other traditions.

"If I seem to spend a lot of time attacking liberalism and the left, that should be taken more as a mark of respect than one of dismissal. You don't bother to argue against positions that aren't worth arguing with."

Lasch's comments sum up my purpose in writing a recent column with the headline "Sick of white liberals' 'understanding.'" Because the column brought an outpouring of anger, disbelief, and even pain, I am writing a follow-up. Mind you, this is not a mea culpa but an explanation.

I, too, was reared in a liberal environment, where to use the word "conservative" was to risk a whack to the keister. My family, friends, and teachers never questioned the tenets of liberalism. As a result, in 1963, I went away to college already a blind disciple of Camelot and the New Frontier. Like Lasch, I believed—and still believe—that liberalism offered the "best hope of a decent kind of politics." I believe also that liberal ideals still offer the best chance for large numbers of blacks to achieve the American Dream.

I know that I, along with other ethnic minorities, owe a huge debt to liberals. Without affirmative action, for example, I could not have attended the University of Chicago. Without affirmative action, I could not have taught at Northern Illinois University or at the University of Illinois at Chicago. And I am certain that the desire for more ethnic diversity on the editorial board played a role in my being hired by the liberal *St. Petersburg Times*.

I know, too, that the G.I. Bill, Pell Grants, Social Security, Medicare, and Medicaid are invaluable liberal contributions. And here in Florida, most of our best social programs, such as Healthy Start, came from progressive governors. The column in question in no way discounts the significance of these programs or mocks the viability of liberal ideals. It does, however, challenge white liberals' naive belief that they "understand" black folk. Perhaps much of the confusion over the thesis of the column came from my failure to define how I used the term "understand."

Webster's New World Dictionary offers two definitions pertinent to our discussion. One states that to "understand" is "to know thoroughly; grasp or perceive clearly and fully the nature, character, functioning" of the object. The other states that to "understand" is "to have a sympathetic rapport with" the object. My point is that white liberals can never "know thoroughly" or "grasp or perceive clearly and fully" the plight of blacks. At best, they can have "sympathetic rapport with" the black condition.

Such rapport, because it is based on emotion and intuition rather than on conscious reasoning, is superficial. And, of course, it is dangerous because it leads white liberals to rationalize the self-destructive deeds and misdeeds of blacks. It makes white liberals see blacks as victims who need handouts and pats on the head. Unwittingly, such "understanding" also makes white liberals feel superior to blacks, which invariably leads to condescension. Moreover, I agree with Lasch's observation that many American liberals tend to "regard themselves as a civilized minority, an enlightened elite in a society dominated by rednecks and other 'anti-intellectuals.'" They also see themselves as the "therapeutic caretakers of a country that is . . . deeply sick"— with African-Americans as regular patients.

I will accept the advice of a letter writer and distinguish between "liberals who have compassion and think" and "the pseudo-liberals who only have compassion." I am wary of the latter, those who merely have "sympathetic rapport," who do not employ conscious reasoning when reacting to black people and their problems.

Again, I challenge liberals because I appreciate what is valuable in the liberal tradition. But given the failure of so many areas of that tradition— especially the paternalistic treatment of blacks—liberals need to examine their philosophy. And while they are at it, they should cultivate the capacity to handle criticism.

Come look within the outsider

November 16, 1997

Like many other Americans, both black and white, my life often is mired in the putrefaction of race.

How I wish that I could find a way to let whites everywhere enter my consciousness, to experience what I experience as one who must cope with depersonalizing assaults on my sense of being a human being. But I cannot provide a way for them to enter. Even if I could, they would not see what I see. Or feel what I feel. Vicarious experience is never enough when race is involved.

As a black man, my place in America is like that of the protagonist in Ralph Ellison's classic novel, *Invisible Man*. It is a "warm hole in the ground," a place of hibernation, where I too discovered the paradoxical condition of invisibility, where, as the protagonist says, "I am neither dead nor in a state of suspended animation."

The English language lacks the words to help black people adequately describe our burdensome awareness. How do we explain that invisibility provides us a unique freedom while being an entrapment at the same time? Or that, in another way, invisibility is a state of isolation, an outsiderness that a white person will not experience as a lifetime condition? And while whites condemn irresponsibility among blacks, they fail to understand that invisibility absolves people of responsibility. I am not whining, by the way. I am informing whites of a core truth they would rather ignore.

Try to imagine having to perpetually search for personal meaning because of your skin color, a circumstance over which you have no control; because of being out of sync with the world around you. Listen to Ellison's hero: "Invisibility . . . gives one a slightly different sense of time, you're never quite on the beat. Sometimes you're ahead and sometimes behind. Instead of the swift and imperceptible flowing of time, you are aware of its nodes, those points where time stands still or from which it leaps ahead."

At another time, he says: "All of my life I had been looking for something, and everywhere I turned someone tried to tell me what it was. I accepted their answers, too, though they were often in contradiction and even self-contradictory. I was naive. I was looking for myself and asking everyone except myself questions which I, and only I, could answer.

"It took me a long time and much painful boomeranging of my expectations to achieve a realization everyone else appears to have been born with: That I am nobody but myself. But first I had to discover that I am an Invisible man!"

Can a white person ever understand the experience Ellison describes and the multitude of horrors related to it? Few white people have earnestly tried to understand. Oh, many whites talk about black problems and read about them and write news stories and columns and books and make movies about them.

But few, if any, have gone to the extraordinary lengths of, say, author John Howard Griffin. In 1959, he left his wife and two children in Mansfield, Texas, for six weeks to have his skin darkened with the drug oxsoralen and travel through the South passing as a black man. The result was his 1960 best-selling book, *Black Like Me*, which became a blockbuster movie. In the preface, Griffin outlines his struggle to come to grips with this nation's living legacy of racism and its centuries of grievous wrong against a people. "Some whites will say this is not really it," Griffin writes, explaining the purpose of his metamorphosis. "They will say this is the white man's experience in the South, not the Negro's.

"But this is picayunish, and we no longer have time for that. We no longer have time to atomize principles and beg the question. We fill too many gutters while we argue unimportant points and confuse issues.

"The Negro. The South. These are details. The real story is the universal one of men who destroy the souls and bodies of other men (and in the process destroy themselves) for reasons neither really understands. It is the story of the persecuted, the defrauded, the feared and detested. It could have been a Jew in Germany, a Mexican in a number of states, or a member of any 'inferior' group. Only the details would have differed. The story is the same."

In the first chapter, he writes: "How else except by becoming a Negro could a white man hope to learn the truth? Though we lived side by side throughout the South, communication between the two races had simply ceased to exist.

"Neither really knew what went on with those of the other race. The Southern Negro will not tell the white man the truth. He long ago learned that if he speaks a truth unpleasing to the white, the white will make life miserable for him."

Obviously, I would not expect the average white person to do what Griffin did to learn what being black means. But I would invite all whites who care about our race dilemma to stop being so scornful of the black perspective, a perspective derived from the ugly reality of being treated less than human each day of your life.

But given the sophistry surrounding the current affirmative action debate, along with other issues of racial equity, in Congress and elsewhere, I am not hopeful of the future. Moreover, I hear too many seemingly bright white people uttering the language of deep denial when race is at issue. I see bright white people treating race as if it were a unicorn—a creature that never existed. Heck, if race never existed and does not matter today, then affirmative action is unnecessary and bad.

Again, who in his right mind would ask a white person to emulate Griffin? I would not. But I do suggest that all whites, especially opinion leaders and lawmakers, read *Black Like Me*. I see the book as a sincere effort to find real answers to a problem white America itself created but, apparently, refuses to repair.

In 1976, Griffin, still haunted by the hatred and soul-scorching slights he encountered while passing for black, explained what he had learned: "I was living in a land where there were so many myths and racial stereotypes, it sinks into the blood. And I would never have gotten them out of my blood unless I lived them."

Supper with a serving of racism

February 4, 1998

As I write, I feel dirty from the stench of racism—acquired on Monday night at Phillippi Creek Village Oyster Bar at 5353 South Tamiami Trail in Sarasota.

A former colleague from my college teaching days, a Jewish woman, and I went there to discuss a highly successful national mathematics program that she directs. She was in town for a two-day conference. I wanted to talk with her because I intend to write about the program and arrange a meeting with the editorial board of the *St. Petersburg Times.*

Upon entering the restaurant, I saw no black people. Suddenly, the place fell silent as a sea of white faces stared at us. Our waitress reluctantly seated us.

She asked if we wanted drinks. I said that we would have a bottle of merlot. The house brand is Corbett Canyon, one I had never had.

"May I taste it first?" I asked.

"No," the waitress said, in a hostile tone that surprised me.

"Miss, I'm not going to pay 12 or 14 dollars for a bottle of wine that I can't sample. May I taste the merlot?"

"No," she said, indicating that she would return for our food orders.

My companion, who travels the nation and regularly dines out, was outraged. "I don't believe this," she said. "I'll bet that if I ask to taste it, she'll let me. She won't refuse a white woman."

She waved the waitress to our table. "I want to taste your merlot. If you sell it by the glass, I can certainly taste it." The waitress promptly left, returned with an opened bottle, poured a finger, and set the glass in front of my companion.

"My friend ordered the wine, and he's the one who wants to taste it," my colleague said, handing the glass to me.

Feeling the sickening weight of outsiderness, I wanted to leave. I remained calm, however, tasted the merlot, which was quite good, and ordered a bottle. From here, matters deteriorated. As she took our orders for stone crab, the waitress could not conceal her contempt for me and, of course, the white woman brazen enough to be with me.

While we waited, our waitress chatted with other waitresses and bus help. Several passed our table, staring. Soon, the manager prowled the floor, surreptitiously glancing at us. Our waitress and a bus worker openly laughed at us after she had brought our food. After a while, the bus worker came over and reached for my plate before I was finished. I let him take it away rather than cause a ruckus.

My companion could barely control her anger. I struggled to conceal my shame. Whenever I am the victim of a racist act, I feel more ashamed than angry. We watched as our waitress let white customers automatically sample their wines. I made sure that the waitress saw me observing her, which had no positive impact on her. She grinned while giving her white customers the superior service the place is known for.

"I don't believe this," my colleague shouted. "This is racism."

"I don't believe it, either," I said, wanting the staff to know that I, too, was offended. The white couple behind us, angry at my companion and me, walked out before ordering. The man hurled a racial epithet over his shoulder.

We paid the bill, and my colleague insisted on seeing the manager, which I said would be a waste of time because he would turn us—the victims—into instigators. He did exactly that, feigning incredulity and voicing faith in his staff's professionalism.

I knew the technique well: demonize the nigger, get him to become loud or violent, then call the cops, who will gladly drag the black troublemaker off to jail. Avoiding further abuse, I walked out into the rain and waited for my colleague. If the restaurant's policy is to keep out blacks, the staff succeeded with me. I will never return to Phillippi nor recommend it to others.

After saying good night to my friend, I drove back to St. Petersburg, hurt and ashamed. My sense of self had been assaulted by strangers who know nothing of my life, my modest successes, my love for America and hope for a society free of racism.

When the Sunshine Skyway Bridge came into view, I realized that I, an ex-marine and world traveler, was crying. Back inside the safety of my home, I showered for the second time in four hours, trying to wash away the foul experience, to restore my sense of self. I studied my black skin in the mirror, trying to see what the waitress had seen, trying to understand racism and the acts of deliberate cruelty that it produces.

From a wrong, many rights

FEBRUARY 8, 1998

I must publicly acknowledge that I am overwhelmed by the outpouring of letters, telephone calls, and e-mail messages I am receiving in response to my recent column describing a racist encounter that a white female colleague and I had at a Sarasota restaurant. The sheer volume of correspondence aside, I am awed by the caring expressed by the readers—most of whom are white.

In the column, I wrote of how I, along with my companion, was humiliated by the restaurant's serving staff. I tried to capture the personal nature of the racist act: how the victim carries a deep, private hurt and a sense of hopelessness hidden from public view; how an assault on the sense of self can devastate even a worldly-wise black male.

At last count, three days after the column was published, I have received more than 300 messages. One reason for writing this follow-up, therefore, is to tell my readers that I do not have the time to return all of their calls and reply to their letters and e-mails. I want everyone who contacted me to accept this column as my heartfelt thanks for his or her concern.

But my real purpose is to say that much of my faith in the goodness of most white people has been renewed. And I do not think that I am being naive.

A black friend cautioned that what I am witnessing is the "gushing of white guilt," belated acknowledgment of generations of inhuman treatment of African-Americans.

Perhaps. But I do not care if what I am getting is an expression of guilt. The fact remains that these readers, unlike many pundits and conservative politicians, understand that race is an enduring problem in America, that untold numbers of black individuals—inured to poor treatment—suffer in silence. The first step toward racial understanding is acknowledging that racism exists in the first place and that it matters. My readers are doing just that.

A cynical colleague said that my celebrity as a columnist, not the incident per se, has caused the outpouring of responses. I will not argue this point, either. I will say, however, that if most white people are to respond appropriately to acts of racism, they must identify with the victim in a personal way.

In my case, people feel that they know me because I have shared parts of my life with them in other columns and speak at many social functions. The column in question gives white readers a vicarious experience real enough to touch them where they are most human and honest—and most vulnerable.

I am appreciative and I feel fortunate to know that so many strangers care about me. I am one person with modest celebrity who has been able to elicit widespread empathy for me as an individual. I think, however, that few of the readers who took the time and spent the money to contact me will look at race in the same way again. I suspect that they have changed fundamentally, that I have been an avenue by which they can empathize with other black people describing similar encounters.

One letter writer expresses my point better than I can: "You made the awful incident into a shattering reminder of just what we put black males through, what patience they have shown, and how slow we whites ought to be in lecturing black men on their excuse of victimhood. With whites like those in the restaurant, who can blame them? You are victims, still and constantly."

Students talk about racism with candor

November 21, 1999

I must acknowledge that on most days I am pessimistic about the state of race relations in America. So when Joan Warrick, an English teacher at Indianapolis's North Central High School, asked novelist Beverly Coyle, who is white, and me to discuss with students our experiences growing up in Jim Crow Florida during the 1950s, I agreed to the engagement with trepidation. (Beverly and I had written essays about our childhood experiences for the 1999 summer issue of *Forum*, a magazine of the Florida Humanities Council. To our surprise, various organizations had begun to invite us to do readings from the essays.) I assumed that North Central High's students, like most adults I know, would be in deep denial on race and race relations.

I was dead wrong.

For an hour, Beverly and I described how, because of racist attitudes and various forms of legalized segregation in Florida, we led parallel lives. Born a few months apart, living within a few miles of each other, and traveling the same roadways, our lives—one white and one black—did not intersect and could not have intersected in any meaningful way.

At the end of our talk, we invited the students to comment and ask questions. For more than 30 minutes, Beverly and I, jaded veterans of America's race culture, listened to the most candid discussion on race relations we had yet encountered. Most remarkably, the students did not, as adults do, substitute affirmative action for race. They talked about race without recrimination, and they did so openly and eagerly.

Surveying the approximately 200 faces in the audience of sophomores, juniors, and seniors, I saw real America: most black students sat together in small groups, and most white students did the same. I was drawn, however, to the handful of white and black kids sitting together. Because I could not take notes, I will try to paraphrase what some of the students said.

An African-American senior in the front row said that until recently, she had no white friends. Her parents and grandparents had taught her to distrust whites. Even now, she warms up to white people reluctantly, she said.

A white male, sitting next to a black male, said that Indianapolis is rife with racism. He said that he sees evidence of it every day, almost everywhere. He reminded his schoolmates and teachers that Indiana, including neighborhoods in and around Indianapolis, still has a large population of Ku Klux Klansmen. He also said he had no doubt that blacks are victims of discrimination in almost every way.

I was surprised, but heartened, when a white girl discussed her mother's latent racism. One day, while she and her mother were stopped in their car at a busy intersection, two black males walked to the corner, and her mother automatically locked the car doors. The girl said she was appalled by her mother's behavior, the snap judgment that the boys would rob them.

Another white male talked about restaurants that hire blacks to work in their kitchens but refuse to let them work on the serving lines and in the dining rooms.

Over and over, the students described their experiences with racism. But what impressed me most were the students' lack of defensiveness and their refusal to blame the victim. Again, this was a new and surprising experience for me.

After the session, a white girl came to me and expressed her disappointment with the way adults handle issues of race. "Most of them don't tell the truth about racial stuff," she said. "My parents say they aren't racist. But they are. They and their friends do stuff that I see as racist. Then they say blacks caused all the problems. Maybe blacks do cause some of the problems, but somebody else had to start all this stuff in the first place. I don't believe what grown-ups say about race. I see things with my own eyes."

Warrick, who teaches senior composition, Western literature for seniors, and sophomore composition, has spent her entire 24-year career at North Central, which has 3,100 students. Of that number, 33 percent are black. Realistic about her students and race relations in and around Indianapolis, her reason for bringing Beverly and me to campus was simple: "I want North Central's students to have an awareness that people have different kinds of experiences, that people come to their attitudes, their ideas about life, through their experiences."

She believes that North Central, like the rest of America, has racial problems and that they must be addressed honestly. As such, many of her assignments deal directly with racial issues. For example, students must read Prescott King's essay on the Montgomery bus boycott, and they watch the movie *The Long Walk Home* in class. Along with the essay and the movie, they must interview a parent or a grandparent or someone else who was alive before or during the civil rights movement. The interviewee is asked about race relations and their perceptions and personal experiences at the time.

"It's a wonderful assignment because what happens is I always have kids who had grandparents who grew up in South," Warrick said. "They always learn something that was never discussed before. It's so funny. The child interviews a parent or grandparent and comes back with these huge eyes saying, 'My gosh. You won't believe what happened to my dad when he was traveling or what happened to my grandparents who were in Kentucky.' It's a real eye-opening experience for kids. It's one thing to hear that segregation occurred, but it's another when, man, it's your own family. I think it makes kids aware and really brings it home to them that this kind of thing happens."

A white student who did not get a chance to ask her question during the session, escorted me to my car. "We really thank you all for speaking to us," she said. "Everybody wanted to talk about race. It was cool."

Warrick's efforts are worth emulating in every public school in the nation because school is the ideal place to start excising the cancer of racism. "I look at North Central and I look at how large it is, and I see all the different ethnic groups," she said. "North Central is a microcosm of society. It makes me happy that our kids are aware of the problems and that they are anxious to talk about them. These kids seem willing to do something about these problems. Their honesty is pretty wonderful. It's the thing that makes me keep teaching after 24 years. It's that hope, and it's the fact that kids are not jaded like adults. They still have optimism about race and the world. It's wonderful. My job is to help keep them hopeful."

America remains mired in racism

February 16, 2000

During the more than 15 years I have written a column, I have responded in print to a letter writer only three times. The unspoken rule is to let the reader have the last word.

Occasionally, however, I must respond. A Tampa reader took me to task for being inconsistent. He loves for me to tell blacks to take responsibility, but he hates for me to remind whites that white racism still exists. Actually, the two things are not connected in any way. My critic is simply illogical.

"Perhaps," he wrote, "Maxwell should read William Raspberry's February 1 column on Alan Keyes, 'When conservatives look beyond race.' Many whites have gotten beyond race and class while black liberals have not."

NOW HEAR THIS: not a single living soul—black, white, red, brown, or yellow—in the United States has gotten beyond race and class. White conservatives darn sure have not gotten beyond it. Trust me when I say that one person who has not gotten beyond race is the one who insists that he has.

The naked truth is that the United States is defined by race. I do not know where my Tampa critic lives, but I will bet that his world is not slopping over with folks of darker hues. If he is retired, I will bet that his former workplace was not jam-packed with my ebony brethren in important positions.

Look around.

St. Petersburg, where I live and work, is one of the most segregated cities in the nation. Tampa is just as segregated as St. Petersburg. One of the things I like about the mayor of St. Petersburg is that he does not deny the enduring taint of race. During my years at the *Times*, the mayor has openly discussed race with the editorial board. And he tries to solve some of the problems. And before the mayor set out to solve problems of race, he first acknowledged that racism exists.

Look around.

Much of the strife in the St. Petersburg Police Department involves race. The black chief and many of his white officers will never get along because the department has a long history of racial antagonism.

Pinellas voters have never elected a black person to their School Board (Governor Reubin Askew appointed an African-American to the board years ago, but he was defeated when he came up for election). Why? Race. Until the late Governor Lawton Chiles appointed Calvin Harris to the county commission, a black person had never served. Why? Whites— mostly Republicans—would not vote for a black.

Now, let me share a secret about white conservatives and Alan Keyes, the black Republican who battles windmills in each presidential campaign: Keyes gives cover to whites who have spent their lives discriminating against black people. Keyes gives them a way to relieve themselves of guilt, by saying, "See, I have gotten beyond race because I support Alan Keyes." If truth be told, thoughtful white people do not waste their time with Keyes, whose presidential campaign will not go anywhere—not now, not ever.

Making matters even more convenient for his white fans is that Keyes made his name by condemning his own people to the point of obsession, by pretending that race no longer matters. Keyes says exactly what the nutty right wants to hear about blacks and race. Keyes gives these people a snug hiding place. He is their mouthpiece.

Keyes also gives whites a way to misuse Martin Luther King's words that called for a time when blacks could be judged "not by the color of their skin but by the content of their character." Only the most pernicious hypocrite would use King's words to argue that race and class are dead in America. King was speaking of a nation that was mired in racism, where blacks were judged only by the color of their skin.

Well, guess what? America is still mired in racism. Blacks are still judged by the color of their skin. Our public schools are more segregated now than they have been in years. Racism still keeps blacks and whites in segregated neighborhoods. Banks still turn down qualified loan applicants because they are black. Real estate agents still steer blacks away from white neighborhoods.

King, whom I knew personally, would be appalled that his words have been appropriated in such a way. He was a realist and, were he alive, would dare anyone to claim that race and class are no longer problems, that his children and grandchildren are now judged solely by the content of their character.

Enough of the nonsense already.

The dangers of a love affair with New York City

March 29, 2000

As a lover of New York City, I go there every chance I get. I will be there this weekend taking Robert McKee's famous screenwriting course that will be held at the Fashion Institute of Technology.

Although I am excited about being in the Big Apple for four days, I am worried about my personal safety for the first time ever. I have always taken to the streets of New York like a child taking to the sights and sounds of the circus. New York is pure excitement—the ultimate love affair. Today, however, the prospect of going to the city scares me because of the attitudes of the New York Police Department, the city's taxi drivers, and far too many residents. I worry because I am a dark-skinned black male, a target that attracts trigger-happy boys in blue and the wrath of cabbies.

During the past 13 months, NYPD's finest have killed four unarmed black men on the street. The latest victim, Patrick Dorismond, was standing on Eighth Avenue, near the theater district, hailing a taxi when an undercover cop, seeking to buy drugs, approached him. Moments later, Dorismond was lying in his own blood—dead.

As usual, Mayor Rudolph Giuliani demonized the victim and defended the cop—even before knowing all the facts of the case. Apparently, the NYPD has its marching orders: get black males by any means necessary. That scares me. What would I do if a noncop-looking person approached me trying to buy drugs? What would I say? Would my actions be my last? -

Black men on New York streets can feel the personal danger. When I was there alone for the millennium celebrations, I was careful to avoid any contact with cops or situations that would demand their presence. I stayed on busy thoroughfares, among crowds, and, except for my cheap hotel, inside upscale businesses. In Central Park, I steered clear of lone white women and made every effort not to surprise them.

In short, I tried to avoid any behavior that could have been misinterpreted as threatening. And what is threatening? Anything a white person, especially a business owner, deems so. Whenever I hailed a taxi, I did so in busy, well-lighted places. I remembered actor Danny Glover's now-famous media blitz about his trouble getting a cab. Had he not been a movie star, he easily could have wound up dead on a Manhattan sidewalk.

Another trick I use to call a cab is to be in the company of a white person. Drivers usually do not pass me by when I am with a white person, especially a male. Or, offering a good tip, I have an attendant at my hotel call one for me.

I feel safest in Harlem. There, I encounter fewer whites who may feel threatened. Whites in Harlem want to be there. They want to eat at Sylvia's, see the Apollo Theater, attend service at the Abyssinian Baptist Church and listen to the choir, tour the Schomberg Center for black culture, and generally enjoy the unique ambience. These are whites who have come to terms with Harlem and its denizens. They tend to be more cosmopolitan and harbor fewer fears of African-Americans.

Fear creates unnecessary ethnic friction, which engenders incidents that bring in the police. Last summer, when I came to New York to cover the Million Youth March, I had to walk from Grand Central Station to 125th Street in Harlem because I could not find a cabbie to drive me there.

A few years ago, I would walk into any neighborhood. Today, I am smarter. I know that I can get into big trouble simply by crossing a street, from one deeply ethnic neighborhood to another. Here is how one travel guide describes the city: "New York is the world's most ethnically diverse city, with different nations in different territories. The cityscape changes and so do the faces, customs, and languages. It's around the world from barrio to Chinatown to shtetl."

Frankly, I will not go alone into some of these "territories." The mere sight of me in, say, the Bensonhurst section of Brooklyn would be bad for my health. I most certainly would not venture alone into Crown Heights. I would, however, walk the streets of Spanish Harlem anytime. The vibes are positive there.

As a dark-skinned black male in New York, I know that I must battle the old forces: the perception—and perhaps the reality—that we are overrepresented in street-level crime, that we are violent. As such, I choose to navigate the city by minimizing even the slightest confrontations that may bring me face to face with the NYPD. I choose to take responsibility for my human environment, learning the lay of the land, knowing my place.

Anyway, I fly to Gotham City on Thursday and hope to return on Monday.

Where Have All the Children Gone?

Alicia's anchor

OCTOBER 27, 1996

The journalist's instinct of taking a final look at everything in the area at the end of an interview caused me to notice seven-year-old Alicia Downing.

I was in a sugarcane-growing town in western Palm Beach County to write about an honor student at the local community college, a story that interested me because the student is the first member of her family, four generations of migrant farmworkers, to attend college. Having pocketed my notebook, stashed my tape recorder, slung my camera over my shoulder, and walked out the door of the apartment, I noticed the tiny figure at the end of the dingy breezeway.

There, at a picnic table, sat a girl. She was gripping a book, reading as if her very existence depended on finding just the right answer to a mysterious question.

"That's my niece, Alicia," said Tonya Harvey, the student I had come to interview. "Alicia reads all the time. Sometimes she reads to me, and I read to her."

I automatically walked toward the child, snapped her picture, and turned on my recorder.

"What's the name of the book you're reading?" I asked.

"*Pocahontas*," Alicia said. "She's an Indian girl; she lived a long time ago; she saved Captain John Smith's life and became a princess and went to England. She's real pretty and has long, long hair. I like her. She's my favorite. I want to go to England, too."

For more than an hour, Alicia and I sat in the cool afternoon shade and talked. A second-grader at Pioneer Park Elementary School in Belle Glade, she enjoys reading more than anything else.

Why reading?

"It makes me happy," she said, pointing to a picture of Pocahontas and her father, Chief Powhatan.

Even before she answered, I knew that the two of us were soul mates in many ways. As a child, I, too, had lived in Belle Glade. My family had been migrants and had cut sugarcane and picked vegetables here every season. I, too, had read most of the time.

Alicia lives with her grandmother because her mother, a farmworker with an uncertain salary, cannot adequately care for her precocious daughter. At the apartment complex where Alicia lives, drugs, violence, and other problems have made life precarious for young children and teenagers alike. She does not venture far from the front door without either her grandmother or Tonya in tow.

And like thousands of other youngsters in farmworking families nationwide, Alicia finds refuge in books. Reading connects her with the rest of the world—letting her share experiences common to people everywhere, taking her to distant lands that she may never actually visit, introducing her to ideas and information that will help her shape her views.

In her immediate environment, reading helps Alicia cope with the tragedies, personal and otherwise, in a town that recently was called the "AIDS capital of the world," where farmworkers have little hope, where children too often internalize and emulate the worst of adult behavior.

Alicia, who plays with Barbie dolls, knows girls who are mothers. She also has known children who have died violently. She knows people who have contracted acquired immune deficiency syndrome, and she knows of teenagers and adults who have died of the disease.

At school, fortunately, the innocence of Alicia gets a measure of protection, and she enjoys some control over her fate, as she and her classmates get to choose many of the books they read. When talking about the joys of reading, Alicia uses words that flow like those of a character in a stream-of-consciousness drama: "I pick lots of books and read and read until I get tired, and when I read, I dream about going to the places I read about, and I dream about meeting some of the people and animals, too. In *Danny and the Dinosaur*, the little boy goes to lots of baseball games, and I like to go to baseball games. My cousin takes me sometimes.

"I read another book called *Chicken to Egg*, and I learned that a chicken has to stay in the egg 21 days, and I read about snakes, and I'm scared of snakes, but I like to read about them. I'm going to read some more books about snakes, and when I grow up and get a job, I'm going to buy lots of books and let kids read them, and I want to write books for kids to read."

Reading is Alicia's anchor.

It gives her peace of mind and helps ease the pain of being separated from her parents. Each afternoon after school, she submerges herself in the colorful pages of books—a safe place where her imagination soars, where she can create ideal parents and friends. This is an orderly place where she is protected from harm, where she experiences certainty.

The act of reading, writes Alberto Manguel in his new book, *A History of Reading*, is "an intimate, physical relationship in which all of the senses have a part." Obviously, Manguel was not thinking specifically of Alicia, but he perfectly describes her relationship with her books and with life around her.

Instead of leaving Belle Glade feeling my usual sense of hopelessness, I left thrilled to have discovered another soul mate. And to my list of special people to whom I give books, I shall add the name of Alicia Downing.

Bringing dignity to the lives of children

June 29, 1997

Tanika Thornton, a 21-year-old single mother, is infected with HIV, the human immunodeficiency virus, which causes AIDS. Most days, she is too weak to care for her rambunctious one-year-old daughter and three-year-old son for more than a few hours and must take a break from them.

Fortunately for Thornton and many other parents in this mostly black area of north Tampa, the Great Day Respite House, which opened two years ago, is a few blocks away. Great Day, an affiliate of the not-for-profit Family Enrichment Center, cares for 35 children, infants to six-year-olds, whose families have in some way been affected by AIDS.

Although games and field trips are part of its activities, Great Day is more than a baby-sitter, program supervisor Rhenita Reeder said. Depending on their needs, the children receive free academic, social, and motor skills training. Thornton's son, for example, has been in the program since June 1996 and has learned his alphabet, colors, and numbers.

"If I didn't have this place, I don't know what I would do," Thornton said.

Part of the mission of Great Day is to prepare the children and their relatives for the loss of a parent. If she dies while they are young, Thornton wants her children to have a permanent, loving home. Reeder understands the plight of women such as Thornton. The AIDS epidemic is leaving many children orphaned in Tampa. In fact, according to the Centers for Disease Control, AIDS is now the leading cause of death among black women aged 25–44, including those in Tampa.

And nearly 80,000 children nationwide have been orphaned because their mothers died of AIDS. Authorities predict that by the year 2000 that figure will reach 125,000. In Tampa, the Family Enrichment Center is assisting such children through its foster care and adoption programs. Founded in 1992 by the College Hill Church of God in Christ, the center runs the only black-owned adoption agency in the southeastern United States, one of only six in the country. The center now has its own charter and no longer is affiliated with the church.

With an annual budget of only $275,000—most of that sum coming from the Ryan White Title I Provision Act, Hillsborough County, the City of Tampa, and the Florida Department of Children and Families—the center has become one of the most effective social organizations in the state.

During each of its two years of existence, executive director Olga Williams said, the center has placed more "special-needs" children into adoption than any other private agency in Tampa Bay, exploding the myth that blacks do not adopt. Special-needs children are eight or older, are often siblings, may have been identified as having a developmental disability, or have been registered in the state's adoption exchange for at least six months. They are the most difficult to place because many clients want young children.

Williams explained that the center's uniqueness accounts for much of its success. "We're in the heart of the black community, and you can walk in," she said. "That makes us unique. Our families are connected somehow to the church or to other relatives. We grow by word of mouth. We're unique also because the faces in our office don't change as often as they do in the larger agencies.

"We never want to have more than 50 or 60 adoptive homes under our care at one time so that we can stay familiar and accessible. We're user-friendly, a place where people can feel comfortable, where they can get services from people who look like them. We understand our clients' histories, and we listen. We understand their language. Another strength of the center is that several members of our Board of Directors have adopted children. They empathize with the community people."

Furthermore, Williams said, the center uses common sense to streamline the process for becoming a foster parent and for adopting. For example, the center has legally reduced the mandated parenting classes from 10 weeks to four by requiring clients to meet more often during a shorter period of time.

And although the organization is black-owned and -operated, Williams said that she would place a black child in a white family. "We put the child in the best home for the child," she said. "The center matches families to children, not children to families."

Despite its extraordinary success, however, the center struggles to survive. Two major problems are that local black people do not, or cannot, donate money, and no corporate angel has stepped forward. A more urgent problem is that Florida lawmakers seem not to take black children's groups and support systems seriously. For example, during the last legislative session, State Sen. Jim Hargrett, who represents the district to which the center belongs, pushed a proposal to fund the organization. The proposal failed. One reason is that it came up for review midway through the session, a time when most dollars for such efforts had already been appropriated. Hargrett has said that he will reintroduce the proposal.

Williams, along with her staff, remains optimistic. She wants a new building, additional key employees, and a $1 million budget to bring dignity into the lives of children needing stable homes. Parents such as Tanika Thornton also hold to these dreams because for them, the Family Enrichment Center is a place of hope.

Innocence found

OCTOBER 5, 1997

I have a special place, a place where I read, write, and observe a group of boys fish and play on the shore of an inlet in south St. Petersburg. Sometimes only two boys show up, other times as many as seven. The youngest is probably 9, the oldest perhaps 13.

I spoke to three of them for the first time the other day as I was about to take the maiden voyage in my new kayak. As I pushed the sleek yellow craft into the water, the youngest boy said, "Mister, that's a nice canoe."

"It's a kayak," I said.

"A what?"

"Kayak."

But I digress.

This place is special because the boys are special. They are black. They are innocent—a quality I do not take for granted, given the powerful lure of street life in the economically depressed neighborhood where they live.

And what do these children do along this shore? They pretty much do what my friends and I did 40 years ago, before television and other electronic gadgetry changed the way black boys play, when being a boy meant flying kites, shooting marbles, casting yo-yos, capturing lightning bugs, pushing car tires, playing cowboys and Indians.

These boys, like my friends and I did, invent, create, experiment, learn. They are not getting into trouble, and they apparently are thinking the thoughts that kids their ages should be thinking. Sure, they are rough-edged, and they compete—vying to see who can skip a rock on the water the farthest, who can catch the biggest sheepshead, who can stay submerged in the brackish water the longest. But their play in general lacks the serious meanness I so often see among many other black boys whom I encounter in my travels.

The mere fact that they choose to play in nature—in an area that is a gateway to the Gulf of Mexico and a window to the breathtaking Sunshine Skyway Bridge—tells me that they have a sense of beauty inside them. They, like my friends and I did, feel the pull of open spaces, where naturalness has a soothing effect, where lasting friendships based on mutual respect can be established, where openly caring for others is not laughable.

I watch them closely each time I come here. I have seen the oldest show the youngest how to make a rock jump three or four times off the surface of the water. The one who wears the Chicago Bulls jacket taught the one they call "Li'l Red" the difference between a snapper and a mullet. Everyone gathers around when the tallest kid opens his slick tackle box. One afternoon, he took out something called a "wet fly" and something else called a "nymph."

I have been coming to this spot at least once a week for more than a year, beginning just after the riots that left several poor people homeless, many businesses burned, and a handful of people injured. I came the first time to get away from the newsroom and the incessant talk about the fires and the shootings. The boys also started coming here at that time. I felt that they, too, wanted to get away from the violence and the mean rhetoric around them.

The heavyset one always arrives first, sits alone on the seawall. He often brings a bag of peanuts or bread and feeds the gulls. More than a dozen of them flutter overhead, diving and screaming, as the boy tosses food into the air. From the look in his eyes, I guess that he marvels at the birds' freedom and their easy acceptance of the freebies. Sometimes he talks to them, inviting the less aggressive ones to eat from his hand. He is always careful to finish this ritual before his pals arrive. This, I tell myself, is a special moment he reserves for himself.

I identify with this kid. He, like I was at his age, seems to be dreaming of things he dares not tell anyone else about. Why? Because some things are so innocent, like feeding gulls, that secrecy is the only way to protect their dignity and magic.

I distinctly feel also that the other boys in the group, who come here with fishing rods and night crawlers, will not tell their tougher peers where they spend their time after school. After all, who would care? What could be of interest along a mangrove-lined shoreline that carries the perpetual odor of low tide muck? How can that be cool?

Again, their innocence makes this place special for me. And on this day, dark clouds gather in the east over Tampa Bay. I want to launch the kayak, but I know that rain will fall within 15 minutes. Plus I see lightning in the distance over the mainland.

As I pull the kayak out of the water, the youngest boy comes over. I ask him to help me carry it back to my Blazer. He agrees.

"Grab the stern," I say.

"Where's that?"

"Back there."

"Yo, what's this thing called again?"

"A kayak. K-a-y-a-k. Kayak."

He asks if I will take him out sometime.

"You got it," I say, realizing that I will need to speak to his parents first.

Child's play: a thing of the past?

November 15, 1998

Nearly 100 years ago, Swedish author and reformer Ellen Key wrote *The Century of the Child*. The book argued that the 20th century would liberate children from the demeaning shackles of the past, creating a world where, for example, they would be free to play rather than work in fields and factories, and enjoy good health instead of dying prematurely from infectious diseases. In many ways, Key's prediction has played out in the United States: modern medicine has all but eliminated childhood diseases; counseling has replaced the strap; universal education has replaced labor as the norm.

Beginning in the 1970s, however, many U.S. scholars and authors began to notice that the nation's attitude toward child rearing—even childhood itself—was changing for the worse. One of the first alarms came in a 1983 book, *Children without Childhood*, in which Marie Winn argued that childhood was slowly vanishing. Neil Postman confirmed Winn's findings in his 1994 book, *The Disappearance of Childhood*.

Now, as 2000 nears, a University of Michigan Institute for Social Research study indicates that childhood, as we know it, may be even more threatened than Winn and Postman believed and may prove that *The Century of the Child* had a false thesis. According to the study, as summarized in the *New York Times*, American children 13 years old and younger, as compared to those 16 years ago, spend more time studying and doing household chores than playing, watching TV, and just being kids.

The biggest source of the problem, said Sandra Hofferth, a University of Michigan sociologist, is that busy parents are transferring the squeeze on their time, along with the troubles caused by it, to their children. "Children's lives have become increasingly structured," Hofferth told the *New York Times*. "Kids are feeling the time crunch, just like their parents are. They are spending more time in school and preschool. As a result, something has to give at home. What gives is unstructured play—tag, hide-and-seek, board games—all the things that children do."

Experts see pitfalls in the trend of replacing unstructured activities with structured ones. Instead of naturally organizing their own games of stickball, marbles, foot races, pickup basketball, and playing with dolls, children are being forced to accompany their parents on errands or participate in organized sports such as soccer. And if they are not under the direct control of an adult, most children are studying.

Some of the report's specific findings of today's children ages 3 to 11 are startling:

- On average, they spent six hours a day in preschool or school in 1997 compared to four hours in 1981, when a similar study was conducted.
- In 1997, they spent an average of six hours a week doing household chores. In 1981, that figure was two and a half hours a week.
- In 1997 there had been a 50 percent overall increase in the number of hours girls and boys spent in organized sports, compared to 1981. The study also showed a 30-minute decrease each day in time spent in unstructured play and outdoor activities.
- Another surprising finding indicated a sharp drop in the number of hours children spent watching TV, which some experts consider a form of free play. In 1981, they spent 15 hours and 12 minutes a week in front of the tube; in 1997, 12 hours and 5 minutes.

In addition to having their free time squeezed at home, children are seeing play eliminated from the public school as well. Nationwide, recess—when children romp, invent their own rules, solve problems, and associate with peers without adult intervention—is becoming a thing of the past. In Florida, the move is on to keep children in school longer and test them more often, thus further curtailing playtime.

Each new encroachment on play shortens the length of childhood, jeopardizing children's well-being, wrote noted psychiatrist Bruno Bettelheim shortly before his death in 1990: "A hundred years ago the span of childhood was more than 10 or 11 years; now the years from about 5 or 6 to 13 years constitute childhood—at best some eight years.

"So while childhood has not disappeared, it has been cut nearly in half and, what is worse, even those few years are encumbered by adult concerns. Today's children are too often cheated out of their childhood because too many parents (and the media) worry them with adult problems."

The Michigan researchers see no immediate letup in the diminution of childhood in America as the number of dual-earner families increases and as schools push to eliminate play in return for academic achievement. Structure, of course, is essential. But at what price in relation to the long term health of the nation's children?

Bettelheim, who studied child development for more than 70 years, aptly captured the essence of play and why we should recommit ourselves to protecting it: "Besides being a means of coping with past and present concerns, play is the child's most useful tool for preparing himself for the future and its tasks. . . . Through his play, the child expresses what he would be hard-pressed to put into words."

A rich experience in a poor country

April 25, 1999

Whoever stereotyped Gen-Xers as being apathetic, laconic, lazy, and unfocused has not met Eckerd College students Christie Biggs, Daphne MacFarlan, Maria Manteiga, Patricia Manteiga, Tammy Olivier, and Taryn Sabia. For the last two Januarys, while many others of their generation went about their business on campus, these six were placing themselves in harm's way to help 26 orphans near Port-au-Prince, Haiti.

Eckerd, a private liberal arts college, has fall and spring semesters, with January as a winter term sandwiched between. Instead of taking courses on campus, these young women decided to use the winter term to establish an independent study program in a foreign country.

Haiti was easily accessible. The parents of Maria and Patricia Manteiga, who let the students live with them in Port-au-Prince during the project, belong to the U.S. Foreign Service and have been stationed in Haiti for the last two years. Wanting to work in a social service setting, the students contacted a colleague of the adult Monteigas who told them about La Fraternité de Notre Dame Orphanage, operated by an order of nuns based in New York and France.

"We wanted to help people who really need our help, to take care of children, and to demonstrate that, as little as it is, there is something everybody can do for a small part of the population," Maria said.

By any measure, this "small part" is invaluable to the Haitian children and to the Eckerd students. When they first came to the orphanage in 1998, the Americans fell in love with the Haitian children, ages 1 through 15. But they had to adjust to daily existence in the poorest nation in the Western Hemisphere.

The nuns, who came to Haiti years ago, had little intention of establishing a large-scale orphanage. But after the island's poverty destroyed families, leaving children abandoned on the streets or curled up in the beds of pickup trucks, they established the facility. One severely malnourished boy, Joseph, was found tied to the back of a donkey, where he had cried for several hours before a passerby notified the nuns.

In the dry months, a dusty riverbed separates the girls' side of the orphanage from the boys' side, a 45-minute walk in the hot Haitian sun between them.

On a typical day, the students begin the morning on the girls' side of the orphanage. There they spend about an hour playing with the children, singing, and teaching English. Then they walk to the boys' side. There they help construct new buildings that, when completed, will allow the girls and boys to share the same campus for the first time. In the afternoon, they return to the girls' side, to play with the children and teach them. The gentleness and innocence of the children have endeared them to the Eckerd students. Simple games, such as musical chairs, keep the children happy and away from the dangerous streets of Port-au-Prince.

"The high point of the trip is just working with the children," Daphne said. "For me, going back this year was extra special because the kids recognized my face and could call my name. They just came up to us and started singing. It feels good to come back and see how the children and the orphanage are growing."

The very presence of the Eckerd students has been central to the orphanage's success. "The local Haitian community didn't know that this orphanage existed when we first got there," Daphne said. "Here we were, six light-haired, blue-eyed American girls running around Haiti. We stuck out, and people were asking, 'Well, what are they doing? Why are they here?' We had so much fun spreading the word in Haiti and back here on campus and in our hometowns. I went to my church last summer and raised over a thousand dollars for the orphanage." Indeed, several embassies in Port-au-Prince are donating money and personnel and have installed water pumps for the orphanage.

The students' work does carry some risk. Although they live in the gated home of career diplomat Felipe Manteiga, the students' safety is threatened by the government's instability. Parliament has been dissolved, and new elections are not scheduled until 2001. Violent political protests regularly occur, forcing the students to stay inside for several days at a time.

They recall the day when they were strolling a few blocks from downtown and heard a huge crowd. The embassy radio, which they are required to carry whenever they are out, crackled as a security officer told them that more than 1,000 protesters were headed their way. Two minutes later, the crowd had grown to more than 2,000, then to more than 3,000.

"The security officer told us to get in our car, leave the area, and go home," Maria said. "The political turmoil put a lot of stress on us."

"Many Haitians dislike Americans," Daphne said. "They know what diplomatic cars are. They know your license plate, what kind of vehicle you travel in, the route you take to the office. We're easily tracked."

Despite the dangers, the students worked with the orphans as often as possible, absorbing the new culture. They were most impressed by the children's love of learning. Patricia Manteiga recalls a boy who once wailed without pause all morning. At noon, a nun explained that he had made a lower score on a test than that of a younger boy.

"When I quizzed him on the test material, he knew everything and made no mistakes," Patricia said. "He was so frustrated that someone else would do better than him. He wouldn't eat lunch. The nun explained that education is such an amazing thing to them that if they had a holiday and didn't have classes, they would ask the sisters why they were punishing them like this. What had they done to be grounded? They realize that they are lucky because the illiteracy rate in Haiti is incredible."

The students say that their lives will never be the same after working with the orphans. Before going to Haiti, Maria, for example, had pretty much decided to complete a premed major. "The orphanage helped to make up my mind," she said. "I now know that I want to work with children and make them happy, to be able to teach them on a daily basis. This is definitely a life-changing experience, as cliché as it sounds. I'm definitely thinking about joining the Peace Corps when I get out of college so that I can continue to work with children."

Daphne, a marine sciences major, said: "It's the same for me. There's got to be a way of incorporating my major into something more people-oriented. The trip put everything in perspective. Everything that we take for granted—from clean drinking water, to hot showers, to clean laundry, to having water to brush our teeth—is stuff that these children don't have on a regular basis. The little things. They teach you not to take what you have for granted—ever."

From Haiti to America in servitude

OCTOBER 27, 1999

People who do not live in south Florida or pay attention to local media probably have not heard of Charlyne—the name the *Miami Herald* gave to a 16-year-old Haitian girl in a small town between Ft. Lauderdale and Miami.

Charlyne belongs to a brutalized group of children who get less attention in the United States and elsewhere than do black slaves in the African nation of Sudan. The United Nations also has slighted these children. And the Florida Department of Children and Families is just now waking up to its responsibility to protect them.

This problem has been ignored because Haitians, especially female children, do not evoke deep sympathy and popular humanitarianism like people in other parts of the world.

But Charlyne's story is compelling. Like thousands of other children in Haiti and the United States, she is a "restavec"—the Creole term for the turn-of-the-century institution of involuntary child servitude in Haiti. More than a decade ago, monied Haitian immigrants nationwide secretly imported the restavec system to the United States. South Florida has the highest number of restavecs in America.

Three weeks ago, the system came to light after authorities discovered another enslaved 12-year-old girl, this time in the home of a Pembroke Pines couple. According to Haitian-American human rights activists, the girl was forced to perform around- the-clock household chores without pay. In return, she received room and board.

Children take these jobs, both in Haiti and in the United States, because their parents are told that their children will be blessed with a better life, including savings for college and other paths out of poverty. But the children rarely receive anything resembling the promises. Instead, besides being forced into hard labor, many are physically and emotionally abused. The Pembroke Pines girl, for example, was sexually abused, Leonie Hermantin, an executive with the Haitian American Foundation, told the *Herald*. "The family clearly brought her from Haiti to be placed in servitude," she said.

Hermantin's comment understates the problem. Her colleague, Jocelyn McCall, head of the National Coalition for Haitian Rights in New York, said: "Anything goes as far as ill treatment. The rape of young girls is far more common than usually acknowledged in Haiti or Haitian immigrant communities."

Top brass at the Department of Children and Families have dropped the ball with these children but have promised to do better. The problem, of course, is that a restavec, like the black slave of old, is an invaluable piece of property, and, in most cases, everyone, including African-American big shots, will remain silent.

According to the last reliable report, more than 240,000 restavecs were in Haiti in 1990. Because Haiti is and has been the poorest nation in the Western Hemisphere for decades, people have grasped for any possible relief. Many parents, unable to make ends meet, believe the only way to ensure good lives for their children, especially their girls, is to ship them to the United States as restavecs.

"The restavec is probably the ugliest instance of a whole lot of ugly things that are the result of desperation, poverty and marginalization, not having any recourse," Miami Roman Catholic bishop Thomas Wenski told the *Herald*.

The underlying sin is that Haitian government officials in Miami will not discuss the problem. I tried three times to speak, for example, with Consul General Jean-Gabriel Augustin but was rebuffed. His refusal to speak underscores the horror of the restavec system—as manifested in the treatment of Charlyne. When the child was five, her mother, then living in Port-au-Prince, contracted her daughter to a family. The mother then emigrated to the United States, leaving Charlyne behind.

At 5:00 A.M. each day, Charlyne told the *Herald*, she fetched water from a stream, cooked meals, and washed clothes. If she displeased her masters, she was beaten with a leather whip. Eventually, she emigrated to south Florida to live with the mother who abandoned her in Port-au-Prince.

And how is Charlyne faring?

Herald writers April Witt and Jacqueline Charles described the child's condition: "The lash marks on her legs and back have healed. But she's withdrawn, has few friends, and hasn't bonded with the mother who left her behind to seek a better life in Florida. Charlyne speaks little, but expresses her rage at abandonment, at times slashing her mother's clothing and furniture with knives and scissors."

Student rises above adversity, follows her dream of a bright future

FEBRUARY 27, 2000

Shenique Gilbert is a 17-year-old senior at Hallandale High School, a sprawling urban campus between Ft. Lauderdale and Miami.

The mean streets of this south Florida city—the violence, the lack of economic opportunities, the low expectations—have destroyed many lives and prevented countless professional careers from taking root. Most people agree that only the smart, the hardworking, and the very lucky can successfully escape this environment.

Count Shenique among the smart and hardworking.

One of six children reared by a single mom, she has won a $10,000 Horatio Alger Association scholarship. The scholarships are given to 105 students nationwide who have overcome adversity and who have reached specific goals.

Alger, who died in 1899, wrote 100 best-selling books for boys. The stories, such as *Ragged Dick, Luck and Pluck,* and *Tattered Tom,* were about poor newsboys and other menial laborers whose honesty and industry pushed them beyond adversity and gained them economic success.

Indeed, adversity has been one of Shenique's constant companions. Her father spent 10 years in prison, and her older sister dropped out of high school. Her mother, Eddie Mae Ware, is a devout Christian who has supported her children—alone—as a house cleaner. Drugs have been in Shenique's face all of her life, and world-hardened brothers and sisters at first tried to lure her away from her dream of attending college and becoming a high school history teacher.

But she has chosen to follow her dream.

Shenique is president of Hallandale's student government, a star in five sports, and a scholar in the top 10 percent of her class. In the fall, she will attend Florida A&M University in Tallahassee.

Shenique is not perfect—but try to find someone who has anything negative to say about her. Deidre Mobley, lead instructor for the school's Institute of Business and Entrepreneurship, said Shenique has more "drive" than any other student she has ever taught. The program is tough, teaching students how to write résumés, how to dress, and how to venture into business with confidence and assertiveness. Each student is carefully selected.

"Shenique is out of this world," Mobley said. "You don't see this kind of motivation in most people her age. She will succeed because of her positive attitude toward education. She looks toward the future. When I first met her two years ago, she was quiet and shy.

"But she had a spark in her eyes, and she paid attention in class. She has changed a lot. Now she is outspoken. She has leadership both in class and out of class. I am very proud of her. This is a tough two-year program."

Shenique said she does not care if she is called a goody-goody. "I am doing well because of God, my mother, and my family," she said. "All of my teachers, coaches, and our principal help me. My classmates are real supportive. My mother, though, is my role model. She works hard and takes care of us. She motivates me, and the rest of my family motivate me. They are depending on me to succeed.

"I will be the first one in my family to attend college. I'm a good basketball player, and I hope to get a basketball scholarship, too. I want to succeed for me and for them. After I finish college, I want to come back here and teach history and own a business."

In May, when Horatio Alger scholarship winners travel to Washington, D.C., Shenique will be there. She and her peers will spend a week visiting the Smithsonian Institution, touring the capital, and listening to some of the nation's political leaders, including Supreme Court Justice Clarence Thomas, who will deliver a special motivational speech.

Meanwhile, she will continue to study, run the student government, play sports, help her mother clean their home, and keep her three siblings still living at home out of trouble.

Paradise Lost

The native's true love

July 5, 1998

In these past one hundred years, man has reshaped and relandscaped the
peninsula, leveling forests, draining its marshes. The process continues at
such a rapid rate that many residents of more than a decade barely recognize
the areas around their homes.

Mark Derr, *Some Kind of Paradise: A Chronicle of Man and the Land in Florida*

Born in Ft. Lauderdale in 1945, when the eastern edge of the Everglades was a few minutes from my back door, I am one native with a bad attitude. Hold that thought for now.

We native Floridians and other residents are preparing to elect our 42nd governor. Will he be Democratic Lt. Gov. Buddy MacKay, Democratic State Rep. Keith Arnold, or lone Republican Jeb Bush? All of the smart money is on JEB! Indeed, if elected, he might make an excellent governor—even though, at age 45, he has never been elected to anything.

But politics is not my current concern. I am worried about how we are losing forever that abstract idea of the Sunshine State that only we natives comprehend. I am talking about a special love, one that does not take its strength from profit, expediency, or comfort. For us, Florida is not the Great Escape, as it is for the thousands of tourists and transplants who flock here. It is our home, an indefinable part of our identity.

I recently was reminded of the importance of this affection as I traveled the state to interview the gubernatorial candidates. I met Bush, a real estate developer, in his office in Kendall, a sprawling suburb south of Miami. We had a pleasant visit, and I left with a better understanding of many of his positions and with more respect for him as an individual.

But as we spoke, something kept bothering me. His words? His tone? His "vision thing"? What was it?

The answer came a week later in Winter Haven while I was interviewing Democrat Rick Dantzler, who since has become MacKay's running mate. Dantzler, born and reared in Polk County, has one of the biggest rattle-snakes—mounted, of course—that I have ever seen. The office walls are a gallery of paintings and photographs, a monument to Florida's great outdoors.

Like Bush, Dantzler, a lawyer, talked politics. But he talked just as eagerly about his love of Florida. I quickly learned that he had fished nearly every body of water and hunted in every woodland in the central part of the state. If asked to identify the species of fish in a particular lake, he could. He celebrates the Sunshine State and its rich natural resources for their own sake.

Now, my misgivings about Bush began to translate: he is a native Texan, an interloper who does not share the native's unique love of Florida.

Arnold, too, is a native Floridian, whose family has always farmed in the southwest region. From his office in the renovated courthouse on Main Street in Ft. Myers, Arnold looks down on a scene straight out of Mayberry. This is Old Florida. As he spoke of the land, the wide-open spaces that farmers covet, I sensed a regret, a longing for the unspoiled shorelines of his childhood, when sea oats, sand dunes, and blue herons outnumbered snow-birds and the imported flora choking the coast. Like me, he keeps a wary eye on the talking mouse that is gobbling up Orange, Lake, and Seminole Counties.

MacKay, favored to beat Arnold, is a true-blue Florida cracker. The state is his life, and he knows every part of it. And like his boss, Gov. Lawton Chiles, MacKay, whose roots are in rural Marion County, understands that the urban centers of Dade, Broward, Palm Beach, Duval, Hillsborough, and Pinellas are not the state of Florida by themselves. He understands the special needs of the Panhandle and the forest and sandhill and cattle regions that make up most of the peninsula.

He knows that beyond the glitter of a towering skyline, real souls sweat and toil in ordinary jobs that support much of the economy. He has touched the muck of Lake Apopka and the Okeechobee basin surrounding Belle Glade, South Bay, and Clewiston. He understands, as does environmentalist Mark Derr, that the "tale of Florida's development is often sordid, marked by the greed of people intent on taking whatever the land offered and leaving nothing in return."

I would be dishonest if I did not acknowledge that since he lost to Chiles four years ago, Bush, a native Texan who moved here as an adult, has been educating himself about the state that he wants to govern. He has visited many schools, some in small towns. Even as I applaud him, though, I worry about his acceptance of huge sums of money from oil interests outside the state. How will these contributions affect his environmental policies, especially negotiations for oil drilling rights off our coast?

At the outset, I said that I am a Floridian with a bad attitude. What I mean is this: I, along with tens of thousands of other natives, resent how our state has been pillaged, our beachheads privatized, our forests and farms bulldozed. I hate the condos, the strip malls, the traffic. I also resent the smugness of people such as *Orlando Sentinel* columnist Myriam Marquez, a Miami-reared Cuban who sees politicians with cracker roots as hayseeds. In a recent column, while questioning the wisdom of MacKay's selection of Dantzler as his running mate, Marquez disparaged this native duo: "Two white, Southern fellas would have made for a winning ticket in 1960, even into 1980. But heading into the 21st century, Florida has a much more diverse and cosmopolitan society than it did when Chiles first walked the state in his hee-haw shirt, looking like Jed Clampett of *Beverly Hillbillies* fame."

Marquez has plenty of company, including transplants who do not know a damned thing about the "real Florida" and interlopers who escape to this paradise to grab what they can. They do not want to understand this beautiful place that many of us call home.

Spoil paradise, and pay

JUNE 22, 1997

In her 1984 best-selling book, *The March of Folly*, historian Barbara W. Tuchman discussed a problem that imperils human existence. It is one with which Florida politicians at all levels and urban planners should become familiar, lest we lose the quality of life we have come to expect in paradise.

"A phenomenon noticeable throughout history regardless of place or period is the pursuit by governments of policies contrary to their own interests," Tuchman wrote. "Mankind, it seems, makes a poorer performance of government than of almost any other human activity.

"In this sphere, wisdom, which may be defined as the exercise of judgment acting on experience, common sense and available information, is less operative and more frustrated than it should be. Why do holders of high office so often act contrary to the way reason points and enlightened self-interest suggests? Why does intelligent mental process seem so often not to function?"

Granted, Tuchman was speaking of military war, but her message is germane to this discussion because many Floridians also are waging a war, one against the environment. In the Sunshine State, gangs of fools have backfilled our swamps, bulldozed our trees, butchered our mangroves, gouged our shorelines, and paved over our grasslands, all in the name of development—a policy inimical to our long-term interests.

The results of this greed-driven madness can be seen everywhere. But south Florida is a living museum to our environmental folly, as demonstrated by the haphazard, unrestrained development in Broward County that has swallowed up nearly all of the Everglades south of Interstate 75 and west to U.S. 27.

Mammoth residential enclaves with names such as Weston, Chapel Trail, and Silver Lakes mushroom out of what used to be the unspoiled domain of alligators, deer, waterfowl, insects, fish, Indians, crackers, and familiar "colored" fishermen. The sounds of wild creatures have been replaced by the voices of children on playgrounds. And the natural activities of natives eking out livelihoods have been replaced by the unnatural roar of lawn mowers and, of course, by the drone of cranes, backhoes, and hammers.

Yes, life is "good" in these gated subdivisions. But how much longer will the shine last? On the social level, from the sprawling Kendall development in Dade County to densely populated Weston near Ft. Lauderdale, many public schools (some newly built) have too many students. In southwest Broward alone, where construction is most intense, about a dozen schools are overcrowded. According to the *Miami Herald*, students "study in cafeterias and offices that serve as classrooms, or in portables on land once reserved for ball fields."

While school overcrowding is an irritant, the real problem is water—either too little of it or too much of it. This situation is life-threatening and is the direct result of cronyism, cowardice, fear, stupidity.

South Florida Water Management District officials say that by the year 2010 water supplies will be at an all-time low, frequent shortages will be routine, and restrictions on watering lawns and washing cars will be tighter than ever.

On the other side, however, an overabundance of water will be a major problem as more and more pavement and rooftops prevent rainfall from flowing into the Everglades and other natural sites and seeping into the aquifer. This excess water will collect in yards, in parking lots, in posh bedrooms. Following major storms, flooding is a certainty.

"[South Florida] got piecemealed to death by development after development," Nathaniel Reed, noted conservationist and a former Water Management Board member, told the *Herald*. "They just kept on coming, and nobody ever looked at the area as a whole. These developments may be pleasant places to live, but we have a huge dilemma, and it's still ahead of us."

How did we get into this mess?

When thousands of development applications poured into the Broward Planning Council offices during the mid-1980s, only State Sen. Howard Forman (D–Pembroke Pines), then a county commissioner, had the courage to publicly oppose the land-use changes that gave builders the green light to destroy the environment. "The facts were there, but even the staff did not say a thing," Forman told the *Herald*. "They were too afraid of losing their jobs."

This was a time when vast agricultural tracts, especially sour pastures, were considered eyesores and liabilities and were sold to developers for a pittance. This land is gone forever, buried beneath miles and miles of sewer lines, roadways, and assorted kitsch.

And now the Water Management District, fully aware of the looming crisis, struggles to establish a 66,000-acre buffer between suburbia and the Everglades. People need to be protected from flooding, and the Everglades need to be protected from the pollution that comes with human habitation.

Experts predict that "build-out" will occur in southwest Broward by the year 2020, when the population will have tripled. Will residents have enough water to drink? Many of the experts do not think so.

Enlightened self-interest must become part of the south Florida landscape, because desperate efforts such as man-made wetlands will not solve our problems. Attitudes toward Florida must change. Residents, most of them from somewhere else, must learn that we cannot continue to rape the state.

We must protect paradise or lose it.

The monster isn't always the monster

OCTOBER 8, 1997

This column is about the meaning of the death of the longest alligator recorded anywhere. The gator's death reminds me of a 1963 John McPhee essay about travel and nature. In the essay, the author speculates about the existence of the Loch Ness Monster.

Concealing the theme, McPhee weaves personal narrative and informative reporting to demonstrate that the real monster is the creature hunting the Loch Ness Monster: humankind. He describes the monstrous behavior of people like those in the narrative who have come to Scotland to see the monster. Combined with current action are flashbacks that show how carnival owners imprison a young black bear in a cage and drive him crazy, and how a man kills a harmless, nonpoisonous snake with a shovel just because it is a snake.

McPhee suggests, of course, that a similar fate awaits the lake's mythic creature, a sentiment voiced by one of the officials living near the loch: "With enough time, we could shoot the beast with a crossbow and a line, and get a bit of skin." Observing an image of the monster embroidered on the man's necktie, McPhee says: "As I studied it there, framed on [the man's] chest, the thought occurred to me that there was something inconvenient about the monster's actual appearance. In every sense except possibly the sense that involves cruelty, the creature in Loch Ness is indeed a monster. . . . Its general appearance is repulsive, in the instant and radical sense in which reptiles are repulsive to many human beings."

Now, back to central Florida waters and our 14-foot, 800-pound gator—a monster in every sense of the term. In a four-hour struggle, it was killed in Lake Monroe near Sanford. Its spinal cord was severed by hunters Barry

Lardner, 34, and Mike Taylor, 37, shown in a photograph lying beside the dead, magnificent beast.

Why did they kill this animal, which, by many estimates, was more than 60 years old? Sure, the most direct reason is that area residents were afraid and that it felt at home in a boat basin. The greater reason, however, is that, as with our images of the Loch Ness Monster, our perceptions of gators force us to confront many of our primal fears. Most of us, for example, fear and loathe reptiles, especially big ones. We imagine the savagery of the gator as it kills and eats its prey. In some of our worst nightmares, we see ourselves being devoured by a reptile emerging suddenly from deep, dark waters.

Some of my faith in humankind returned after several readers wrote to the *Times* expressing anger because we featured a front-page photo of the Lake Monroe gator and its killers and because wildlife officials did not spare the animal's life.

Eva DeHart of Palm Harbor lamented: "What was [his] crime? That he grew too long?"

Seminole resident Moira Dean asked: "How about some compassion? It could have been transported somewhere safe to live out its life."

John V. Calhoun of Palm Harbor commented that he was reminded of "old photographs from the turn of the century depicting 'great white hunters' in Africa kneeling over their trophy lions and elephants."

This gator story and the letters about it remind me of an incident a few years ago on State Road A1A near Callahan involving another reptile. The van driving toward me suddenly did a U-turn, went off the road, then went back and forth on the embankment, turned around, and went back and forth again.

The cause? The driver had risked his life and mine to kill a defenseless rattlesnake in the wild. I saw the snake's thick body, its colorful, shiny skin writhing in the grass. Why did the driver feel compelled to kill? For the same reason, a combination of the tangible and the symbolic, that Lardner and Taylor killed the Lake Monroe gator: dominion over all things wild, a repulsion of reptiles, and an irrational fear of the unknown.

By the way, the gator meat has become restaurant fare, the hide a trophy. And the real monster? McPhee's answer would be unequivocal.

One way or another, the woods will burn

June 24, 1998

In 1994, I owned and lived in a house on 3.5 acres deep in the woods outside Bronson, a small town near Gainesville. My street, North Tulane Drive, was a two-mile-long lime rock rut slicing through sand hills covered with several varieties of moss-draped oak and slash pine, deep-green fern, palmetto, Florida rosemary, and hundreds of wildflower species.

Today, I am returning to check on the five-acre pasture I still own, to see how vulnerable it is if the wildfires in nearby Alachua and Bradford Counties move southward. When I lived here, the area's beauty would have delighted the most jaded member of the Audubon Society, I am sure. But then, as now, this subdivision was a volunteer department's worst nightmare waiting to happen.

My nearest neighbor, rhythm-and-blues legend Bo Diddley, lived about a mile away, and we often talked about the wonder of having these woods all to ourselves. Even as we patted ourselves on the back for living in the "middle of nowhere," as we called it, we knew that we were one lightning strike, one cigarette butt, or one spark from a barbecue grill away from an inferno. All around our homes, decades' worth of dead leaves, sticks, shrubs, grasses, pine needles, and branches blanketed the ground beneath the trees and bushes. Scrub oak, some stands so thick that they were impassable, stretched for a mile. Bo and I and our distant neighbors were living in a fuel tank waiting to ignite.

Occasionally, and to our relief, small fires would break out, burning some of the deadly fuel. Each spring, I would gather my water hoses and nozzles, for safety's sake, and burn my lawn and the perimeter of underbrush. That was 1984.

Three years later, Bo and I were surrounded by dozens of mobile homes, some more than 20 years old. Our new neighbors were afraid of fires—as they should have been. But their fears unwittingly placed all of us in grave danger. Each time a small fire started, they would immediately call the fire department, which would call the forestry department, which would snuff out the flames long before they burned off much fuel.

As more and more people moved in, the place became more dangerous. Gone were the low-intensity blazes that had been common to the area in earlier times, when burnable material did not accumulate to dangerous levels. When small fires did occur, north central Florida residents rarely had to worry about the kind of conflagration that has consumed 60,000 acres in the state so far this year.

And matters will get worse before they get better, says Steve Linderman with Tall Timbers Research Station near Tallahassee, an organization well-known for fire ecology research. Controlled burns, intentionally set fires, are necessary, he says. But the influx of new residents has forced fire officials to cut back on such burns. "We're definitely faced with a challenge," he said. "We have to keep letting them know that we have a need to burn."

Another big problem is that thousands of acres are owned by timber companies, such as Georgia-Pacific and Rayonier. Wanting to protect their trees at all costs, they no longer burn but have turned to herbicides. Trees are their bottom line. Rayonier alone owns 30,000 acres in Union, Bradford, and Alachua Counties. It lost 2,000 acres to fire last week, and it does not want to lose any more, a spokesman says.

Forestry officials constantly preach that, like it or not, Florida's woods should and will burn. "You can't have wildfires if you have a prescribed fire," biologist Jim Stevenson says. "There's no better insurance." However, each new house built in areas that were once woods makes fire officials wary of controlled burns. Against their better judgment, and worried about liability entanglements, they are giving in to the concerns of residents. Thus more fuel is allowed to pile up on the forest floor. But as they douse every flame and complain about controlled burns, residents had better prepare for more wildfires.

Looking at my old house, I am amazed at the tons of dry material so close to it. The new owners covet their privacy and are willing to let the underbrush multiply and the petrified thatch mushroom. The only open space within a mile of them is my pasture.

Driving away, I count my blessings that I no longer live in an area that has been taken over by people who do not understand the relationship between fire and the land.

This time, the river and its fans win

August 5, 1998

The Timucua Indians called it Welaka, or "River of Lakes." We moderns call it the St. Johns River. To have lived near the St. Johns and played in it is to love it. During the 1950s and early 1960s, my friends and I spent much of our childhood canoeing, kayaking, and fishing the St. Johns, some of its many tributaries, and several of the lakes into which it dumps.

As a native Floridian, I am thrilled that Congress has designated the St.

Johns an American Heritage River. Only 13 other rivers nationwide have been so designated, the St. Johns being the only one in the Sunshine State.

The announcement brought back many memories, reminding me of the St. Johns's primitive beauty. In Crescent City, where I spent many happy years as a boy, Lake Crescent was one of my playgrounds. A huge body of water by any standard, it is connected to the St. Johns by a tributary that winds through central Putnam County.

A few miles west of Crescent City lies the small town of Welaka. Here we found the real thing, the St. Johns River itself, its blackish water reflecting the trees on its banks, bream and bass leaping in the sunlight. At the main dock, my friends and I would launch our canoes and kayaks and paddle north—"up the river," as we called it. We learned from old-timers that the St. Johns is one of the few rivers in the country that flow north.

On a few stretches, the banks were as magnificent as they had been when John James Audubon described them in his 1834 *Ornithological Biography*. "Myriads of Cormorants covered the face of the waters, and over it Fish-Crows innumerable were already arriving from their distant roosts," he wrote. "Now, amid the tall pines of the forest, the sun's rays began to force their way, and as the dense mists dissolved in the atmosphere, the bright luminary at length shone forth."

Harriet Beecher Stowe, who owned a farm on the river, also immortalized beauty of the St. Johns in her writing. Another notable, botanist William Bartram, thought that Welaka Springs was one of the most beautiful places on earth.

The St. Johns's heritage designation is a personal and a political coup for Jacksonville mayor John Delaney, a certified river rat who white-water rafts, hikes, and camps along the 310-mile-long river, the northern portion of which snakes through the heart of his city. Republican Delaney had to battle heavy hitters in his own party, such as Cliff Stearns, Tillie Fowler, and Dave Weldon, who tried to kill the proposal in Washington.

Their reasoning? The heritage designation would ban development on the river's banks. State Rep. George Albright of Ocala and other Republicans in the pockets of developers threatened lawsuits and made fools of themselves during meetings. Ostensibly defending "property rights," they called Environmental Protection Agency officials "communists," arguing that EPA chief Carol Browner wanted to hand the river over to the United Nations. *Florida Times-Union* columnist Ron Littlepage aptly summed up the tawdry truth: "Let's be honest here. This isn't about property rights. It's about development rights, the health of the river be damned."

The American Heritage River designation is more than symbolism. It means that the St. Johns will be eligible for federal preservation and cleanup funding. A "navigator," a full-time federal employee, will work closely with towns along the river's banks and assist officials applying for appropriate federal grants.

Delaney's victory is one for all Floridians who care about the environment, but it is especially significant to residents along the river because its health will improve immediately. Already, the Jacksonville municipal government has allocated $260 million to clean up the heavily polluted basin. And "Operation River Rat," a sting operation, has nabbed nearly three dozen people for dumping toxins into the St. Johns.

For lovers of the river, Steve Mihalovits, a Jacksonville Beach information systems specialist, has set up an excellent Web site on the St. Johns at http://www.stjohnsriver.org. I consulted the site for this column and found it valuable. Mihalovits truly grasps the river's meaning. "The St. Johns River," he said, "is as important to North Florida as the Everglades are to South Florida."

True. But my concern is this: Will our next governor—Jeb Bush or Buddy MacKay—support people like Delaney and Mihalovits and environmentalists who know the difference between property rights and development rights, when our irreplaceable environmental treasures are at stake?

Lake Apopka, taxpayers' money pit

December 13, 1998

Florida taxpayers have been fleeced. The fleecing, both environmental and financial, is contributing to the misery of a select group of workers.

We have been swindled by our own state government, by the governor, by the legislature, by the St. Johns River Water Management District. We have been ripped off by the farmers who, for more than 50 years and until June 30, grew vegetables on the black muck that used to be the bottom of Lake Apopka—Florida's second-largest lake before officials poisoned it, dredged it, diked it, and drained it.

At one time, images of Lake Apopka graced postcards, and the lake was advertised nationally. It was one of the most vital fisheries in the nation, serving 29 fish camps on its shores and producing lucrative incomes for the owners of hotels, motels, restaurants, and other businesses catering to thousands of sport fishermen who came here every year.

The lake's slow death began at the turn of the century, when authorities dug a navigation canal that altered natural outflow and disrupted water level patterns. But the real end of a healthy Lake Apopka came in the early 1940s—after state officials allowed farmers to remove nearly 20,000 acres of marsh on the northern rim of the lake by diking it to grow vegetables.

Keep in mind, too, that the lake bottom is public property, but the farmers were allowed to treat it as private property and amass fortunes from it. Today, because of decades of farm-related nutrients and pesticides and industrial and municipal sewage discharges, Lake Apopka has been shrunk to a shallow, pea-green soup that supports gizzard shad and other hard-to-kill trash species unfit for a respectable dinner table.

During the 1960s, environmentalists initiated a movement to stop the pollution and restore the lake, located in west Orange and east Lake Counties, to its pre-1940s condition. The first stages of the proposed solution have been dramatic, bringing about the financial fleecing of Florida. In a series of legal but shameful deals, the St. Johns River Water Management District used Florida tax dollars to buy out the 14 large muck farms on the lake's northern shore at a cost of $91 million, plus an appraised value of $29 million in equipment acquired during the buyout.

Here, the saga takes on the appearance of a deal put together by mob bosses. A 1996 state law classified the equipment as surplus and determined that it should be auctioned to assist the more than 2,200 farmworkers—many of them longtime homeowners and most of them American citizens—who lost their jobs after the farms closed.

The law earmarked up to 20 percent—or a projected $6 million—of the money raised for retraining farmworkers. The rest of the money was slated to go to the regions most impacted by the shutdown. The same law, however, gave the management district permission to retain any equipment deemed necessary to restore Lake Apopka. Taking advantage of this loophole, water district officials kept $2.6 million's worth of heavy equipment, including a fleet of pickups that, they claim, is needed to restore the marsh and clean the lake.

Besides the fact that the management district kept so much equipment, only a small part of the tax dollars spent has been recouped because the very men whom the state bought out—the former owners—were first in line to buy back their equipment at bargain prices. Here is an example of this public rip-off: the Water Management District paid Zellwin Farms $33.5 million for its operation based, in part, on the $14.2-million appraised value of the equipment. Specifically, the district paid Zellwin $1.4 million for its state-of-the-art vegetable precooler. On the first day of the auction, Zellwin general manager Glenn Rodgers bought back the precooler for $35,000. Another farmer sold the state processing machinery for $500,000. He bought back the same stuff for $50,000. These farmers, along with others, will simply ship the equipment out of state, where they have other farms. In the case of Zellwin, the precooler is going to its vegetable processing facility in Lake Park, Georgia, near Valdosta.

Public outcry in Apopka, whose economy stands to lose $110 million annually as a result of the shutdown, has been swift and fierce because the auction lost millions. One official said the water district is earning pennies on the dollar. Generally, farm equipment is auctioned for about 30 percent of its value.

Most upset are advocates for the farmworkers, such as Jeannie Economos of the Farmworker Association of Florida, based in Apopka. "I'm disgusted," she said. "At this rate, what's going to be left for retraining workers? By the time farmworkers get this 20 percent, how much will be left, what are they going to use it for, and who is going to be left to use it?"

Farmworker Association leaders said that, although county retraining efforts include a small stipend, child care, and gas reimbursement, many workers have trouble using such benefits. Because they are so poor and must feed their families, they must find work each day and, therefore, cannot "waste time," as one worker described it, in classrooms or shops learning new subjects and trades. Economos said that many workers have taken low-paying jobs in daily labor pools. Others—rising before dawn and returning near midnight—travel long distances to pick citrus in other counties. Still others have left the area altogether. Most are also having serious housing problems because they no longer qualify for farm-related subsidized housing.

What happens to the millions of dollars in equipment that did not sell during the weeklong auction? It will be sold "dirt cheap" or "virtually given away," an Apopka official said. Florida taxpayers, especially farmworkers, are the clear losers in a buyout scheme that made the already rich much richer.

The fleecing of the Sunshine State continues.

Before all the cypress are turned to mulch

February 28, 1999

Last year alone, I drove at least 30,000 miles statewide, from the once-bustling village of Flamingo in the Everglades to the tiny burg of Walnut Hill in the western Panhandle. The environmental devastation I witnessed—deforestation, unnecessary forest fires, dredging, backfilling, excavating, paving, and the spreading of herbicides—makes me want to chase the perpetrators into the sea or, at the very least, force them into Alabama and Georgia.

As the Florida legislature prepares to go into annual session, natives like me want our new governor, Jeb Bush, a wealthy developer from Texas, to know that our peninsula is a special place and that the wholesale raping of our pristine treasures—some of the most magnificent flora and fauna anywhere in the world—has to end.

In case no one except natives has noticed, our paradise has become a victim of its own allure, as tens of thousands of people a year make Florida their permanent home and as millions of others visit our beaches, amusement parks, and other entertainment venues. "The tale of Florida's development is often sordid, marked by the greed of people intent on taking whatever the land offered and leaving nothing in return," writes Mark Derr in his book *Some Kind of Paradise: A Chronicle of Man and the Land in Florida.*

Few contemporary trends illustrate Derr's observation more than the coast-to-coast destruction of our cypress trees. Although these trees symbolize Florida almost as much as alligators and oranges, their disappearance, unlike that of mangrove trees, has gone virtually unreported. As a result, no important citizen protest has emerged to send a warning to elected officials.

Exactly how important are cypress trees to the long-term health of Florida, the state with the most beautiful name? Second only to pines in sheer numbers, cypress occupy 1.6 million wetland acres and are essential for water purification and flood control, and as habitat for wildlife.

Some cypress stands, especially those in the swamps, ponds, and backwaters in the southern region, are being wiped out to make room for housing developments and new municipalities, such as Abacoa, a *Truman Show*-type city being constructed near the Loxahatchee River in Palm Beach County. When completed, Abacoa will consume 2,055 acres.

Statewide, however, most cypress stands are being cut for mulch. That is right: our cypress trees are being reduced to mulch for flower beds. For many homeowners, in fact, cypress mulch is a horticultural must. According to a report by the University of Florida School of Forest Resources and Conservation, most of the old growth—including the mammoth trees hundreds of years old—was harvested before the 1950s and was used to manufacture furniture, shingles, paneling, beehives, and water tanks.

Today, however, 85 percent of the trees are bagged as mulch. In assessing the extent of the devastation, a federal study shows that cypress harvesting increased from about 19 million cubic feet in 1980 to 42 million cubic feet in 1995, an amount that would fill a 90-story bin the size of UF's Florida Field.

As if the uncontrolled harvesting is not bad enough, we are not regenerating trees fast enough to make up for the losses. "It warrants an alert," said Judy Hancock, who belongs to the Florida chapter of the Sierra Club. "There's just major devastation going on. You can see it just rolling down the road."

What are local and state officials doing to halt the destruction? Hardly anything. State forestry bigwigs and timber moguls are commissioning studies to determine the impact of increased harvesting on wetland stands and to discover ways to regenerate trees. Officials, wary of angering homeowners, hope that the new studies will bring voluntary rules for harvesting.

The hard truth is that voluntary guidelines will not work in an industry that has a trendy, lucrative product such as cypress mulch. Mandatory guidelines are needed. And we need to use the best science available to determine—once and for all—how fast cypress stands regenerate and under what conditions. What level of stress, for example, does heavy harvesting place on the general ecology?

We do not have reliable answers because officials let the mulch industry virtually regulate itself. Meanwhile, the Sunshine State is losing trees that beautify our roadsides, nurture our wildlife, and help keep our groundwater potable.

We are fools to let this continue. "There are as many reasons for moving to Florida as there are people," Derr writes, "and the problem becomes less one of controlling the influx than of assuring that the state's prime resources are cared for and respected. . . . That can come about only if those officials and voters shaping the state's destiny approach their responsibilities with a feel for the land and water that transcends desire for quick profit. Once used up and despoiled, it is paradise no more."

Environmental cures are worse than the disease

August 8, 1999

When flora and fauna are involved, Floridians, especially elected officials and other sundry bureaucrats, are some of the dumbest people in the Union—perhaps the world.

We, the human menagerie who have chosen paradise as our home, love to import exotic stuff. However, almost every time we bring home a botanical or zoological stranger and sink it into our tropical soil, cage it, imprison it in an aquarium, or float it in our waterways, we regret our actions.

Each year, though, we welcome dozens of noxious outsiders that cost us millions of dollars in equally exotic efforts to control them. Most of these invaders are nature's own. Others are man-made, like the new phantasm called *Fusarium oxysorum*, a "mycoherbicide" that is being developed by the Montana company Ag/Bio Con.

And just what is a mycoherbicide? It is a fungus that kills plants. In this case, it is a real "weed" killer, manufactured to destroy marijuana plants in the Sunshine State. That is right. Governor Jeb Bush's handpicked zealot of a drug czar, Jim McDonough—himself a New York transplant—is so determined to rid Florida of pot that he wants to release into our fragile environment a soil-borne fungus that we know diddly-squat about.

McDonough is embracing the word of Ag/Bio Con that *Fusarium oxysorum* "does not affect animals, humans, or any other crops," and he is hoping that experiments at the University of Florida will prove that the fungus is safe.

Fortunately, David Struhs, secretary of Florida's Department of Environmental Protection, and his scientists are not being swept along by Ag/Bio Con's claims. If they err, they apparently are choosing to do so on the side of putting the environment first. Struhs expressed his alarm in a letter to McDonough: "It is difficult, if not impossible, to control the spread of *Fusarium* species. The inability to guarantee that the organism will not mutate and attack other plant species is of most concern. Mutation of the organism would not only threaten Florida's natural environment, but would also put at risk our economically vital agricultural industry. . . . Without considerably more information to address these concerns . . . I strongly recommend that Florida not proceed further with this proposal."

Too late.

Emboldened by the support of antidrug crusaders such as U.S. Rep. Bill McCollum (R–Longwood), who calls the fungus the "silver bullet," Tim Moore, director of the Florida Department of Law Enforcement, and Betty Sembler, the influential wife of one of the GOP's best fund-raisers, McDonough is plowing ahead with his fungus scheme.

Native Floridians and transplants who love the state's natural wonders should actively oppose McDonough's blind tinkering with nature. After all, his mission is not so much about eradicating marijuana as it is about right-wing Republican politics.

Lest we forget, we have a long history of creating environmental Frankensteins that could have been avoided had we proceeded with "good" science and common sense. In trying to establish dominion over the environment and rid nature of phenomena that inconvenience humans, we repeatedly concoct cures far worse than the disease.

One of the most boneheaded feats of environmental engineering was the planting of Australian melaleuca to drain the Everglades. Decades later, the thirsty trees have more than done their job—draining the River of Grass beyond recovery and drying up thousands of acres of other south Florida wetlands. We have no way of accurately measuring, in dollars or human effort, what we squander on efforts to strangle the melaleuca menace.

Do not discount the invasive prowess of kudzu, the supercharged Chinese vine that grows like Jack's bean stalk along Florida roadways. Our prescient leaders, cocksure that it posed no threat to the environment, imported kudzu in the 1920s to control erosion. Well, guess what? This exotic pest grows a foot per day under the right conditions.

For shade and windbreaks, our bureaucratic wunderkinds brought in Australian pines. These nonnative giants seeded rapidly and often bunched in the hundreds on single lots, tearing up sewers and buckling sidewalks and foundations.

Developers and ordinary citizens have been just as misguided. A nice little lady brought the prolific water hyacinth from the World's Fair in New Orleans and plopped it into a pond in Putnam County. Today, the weed rules many waterways. As we try to drown it with pesticides, we wind up killing valuable aquatic life.

Here on the Suncoast where I live and work, residents often travel abroad and return with nonnative plants. A famous example is Flora Wylie, who brought the seed of an *Ochorisia eliptica* tree from Italy in her shoe. The seed passed to a local nurseryman, who propagated it into what has become a favorite tree throughout the state at Christmastime. No matter how much people love the *Ochorisia eliptica*, this Italian interloper, which crowds out native varieties, does not belong in Florida.

Another misadventure, which began innocently enough, gave Florida yet another exotic. In 1989, Alan Bunch, in the town of Seffner, traveled to Hawaii and went bananas over the *Plumeria rubra*, popularly called frangipani. Back home, he could not forget the fragrant blossoms of the tree. Well, Bunch went to work, growing the plant and selling it to all comers.

When will this lunacy stop?

The state has a so-called Upland Invasive Plant Program, but I do not see much evidence that it is effective. Palm Beach County is the only region that seems to be serious about ridding its environs of exotics. Officials there have updated their 1992 code to require residents in all unincorporated areas to eradicate certain nonnatives on their property by 2006. Here are the plants and trees that must be removed in Palm Beach: air potato vine, Australian pine, Brazilian pepper, schefflera, kudzu, earleaf acacia, carrotwood, melaleuca, and the small-leaved climbing fern.

Because Florida is a keystone state, one that disproportionately attracts new permanent residents each year, officials at all levels should follow the example of Palm Beach County and adopt environmental policies that protect our two most important economic assets: tourism and agriculture. And what does each industry depends on for its viability?

The environment.

Hopes should not run high, however, that most officials will come to their senses any time soon. Why should they be expected to when one of the state's most powerful men—the drug czar—wants to introduce a pot-killing fungus into an environment that already struggles against too many nonnative life forms?

Environment, economy clash in south Florida

August 15, 1999

Environmentalists and developers nationwide are watching events in south Florida, where politicians and their supporters have petitioned Attorney General Janet Reno to expedite plans to turn old Homestead Air Force Base into a modern jetport, with up to 650 flights a day.

Pro-jetport people say, "Let the 747s fly." Environmentalists say, "No way. We already have Miami International up the road." Although the ultimate answer will yield results directly salient to South Dade County residents, it may affect similar disputes between business and environmental interests nationwide.

The issue: Homestead Air Force Base, closed after Hurricane Andrew destroyed it, once pumped $480 million into South Dade's economy each year. Within days of its closure in 1992, the Bush administration and then-presidential candidate Bill Clinton pledged to immediately transform the base into a commercial complex generating thousands of jobs.

Local officials and businesses established a redevelopment committee and wrote a plan to turn the base into a commercial jetport that would employ as many as 14,000. First, though, an environmental-impact study had to be conducted. The air force produced the first study in a nine-month blitz instead of the usual several years that such studies take. The entire plan was derailed in 1994, however, after the County Commission, in a no-bid process, granted exclusive building rights to Homestead Air Force Base Development, Inc.

Environmentalists and their allies cried foul and demanded a new study, one that seriously assessed the proposed airport's potential to further degrade the Everglades, Biscayne Bay, and other natural treasures. The air force and the Federal Aviation Administration asked for a second study in 1997. Officials say a draft of the study will be released at year's end and will be finalized in March.

Here the saga takes an unusual turn, one that could change how redevelopment wars are fought countrywide. A group calling itself the Equal Justice Coalition—including, among others, the mayors of Homestead and Florida City, two bank presidents, the executive director of the Dade County Farm Bureau, and the president of R-C-H Haitian Community Radio—have hired a high-powered Washington lobby and have filed a "Petition for Extraordinary Relief" with the attorney general.

In a press release that quotes its own petition, the coalition writes that the "petition seeks an end to 'unjustifiable, continuous imposition of irreparable harm' to the health and welfare of the poor and minority residents of the communities surrounding Homestead Air Force Base as a result of unconscionable delay in the redevelopment of the base. The petition urges [Reno] to intervene and enjoin what the coalition believes are clear violations of federal civil rights, environmental, and environmental justice laws by the Department of Defense, the Department of the Interior, the President's Council on Environmental Quality, and the environmental groups that have acted under their cover."

Homestead mayor Steve Shiver said the petition—perhaps even further legal action—is necessary because a commercial airport would revive South Dade's economy overnight. Although the rest of the nation and Florida are benefiting from a booming economy, South Dade remains one of the poorest sectors in the country, with more than a third of the population of Florida City and Homestead living below the poverty level and unemployment near 15 percent in Florida City alone, he said. If Shiver is right, local unemployment is twice as great as that of the rest of the county.

As to Homestead being the location of a new jetport, Shiver said: "This is the only site in the county that is feasible. Late last week, Mayor Alex Penelas's office reiterated his strong support for a reliever airport, and his conclusion that Homestead is the only place where it can be done. We are asking the attorney general to free us from this bureaucratic stranglehold, fueled by the callous indifference of powerful environmentalists, so that our community can be free to enjoy the full rights and privileges which come with being Americans."

Environmentalists dismiss most of the pro-development's jetport argument as being pure bunk. First, many business owners and officials say that another airport is unnecessary. But the heart of the environmental position is the preservation and rejuvenation of Everglades National Park, Biscayne National Park, and southern Biscayne Bay—all threatened natural resources. Homestead is less than two miles from Biscayne National Park and about seven miles from the Everglades. A major concern is that the $7.8-billion restoration plan in the works for the Everglades will collide with a multibillion-dollar jetport in the park's backyard.

"There are no existing laws, in fact, capable of protecting the parks once this airport is permitted by the FAA," said Alan Farago, chairman of the Sierra Club Miami Group. "So we've been fighting on both the issue of direct impact, which is noise, disturbance, and impacts on wildlife, and indirect impact, which has to do with the conversion of the last farmland in south Florida into a virtual industrial park.

"Were that to happen as an indirect impact, we can confidently predict that the flow of water to southern Biscayne Bay and into the national park would be irretrievably damaged, and the park and its resources would be lost. No commercial airport is next to a national park in any other part of the nation, and the environmental groups don't want to see a precedent set in South Dade." From the beginning, environmentalists argue, local politicians, along with business people, have been hell-bent on building an airport—and nothing else.

For most environmentalists, however, the issue is having or not having an airport per se. They know that South Dade has not recovered from Andrew, that the closure of Homestead devastated the economy, that new jobs are needed. Their major concern is bringing in a sustainable, nonpolluting project. Ideally, they want to use the parks' natural amenities to attract appropriate commercial development.

Farago is not hopeful, though. "We have one of the most rabidly antienvironmental corners of the nation down here," he said. "It has really been a battle at every single turn. We wind up confronting the same issues, the same cast of characters. And this [environmental justice petition] is just another manipulative ploy that is very sad."

Unfortunately, the battle for Homestead is so adversarial that an outside entity must step in. Meanwhile, as the two sides trade salvos, South Dade remains one of the most economically troubled parts of the the nation.

Cattails endanger the River of Grass

February 9, 2000

> There are no other Everglades in the world. They are, they have
> always been, one of the unique regions of the Earth, remote, never
> wholly known. Nothing anywhere else is like them.
> **Marjory Stoneman Douglas**

The Everglades, as Marjory Stoneman Douglas wrote and spoke of them, are dying much faster than the general public and most politicians think.

Cattails, tall marsh plants with reedlike leaves, are the culprit. According to figures in the *Miami Herald,* cattails have devoured 61,053 acres of the Everglades, or 14.5 percent of the area state researchers have mapped in the swamp. Cattails have become superplants in the River of Grass because they feed on phosphorus, a nutrient that farmers use to produce crops and that homeowners and businesses use for green lawns.

Environmentalists and researchers are asking some scary questions: Has the continued trade-off of supercrops and manicured turf over the environment doomed the Everglades? Can we save them? How can we stop pumping phosphorus into the region?

At ground zero, in the national park itself, cattails are smothering sawgrass and other flora that normally thrive and nurture animal life. Unfortunately, Florida International University ecologist Joel Trexler told the *Herald,* reversing decades of damage may be next to impossible. Even the smallest traces of phosphorus can accelerate the growth of cattails, seriously mutating soil and plants.

"In the Everglades, it's easy to get too much of a good thing," Trexler said.

When cattails proliferate, they form a thick cover on the water that keeps out sunlight and robs the water of oxygen that aquatic plants and animals require. The result? Too much bacteria and "everything crashes," Trexler said.

In a paper on the impact of phosphorus and cattails in the Everglades, Trexler said phosphorus that is not captured by cattails saturates the soil. The soil stores the nutrient and releases it during dry times after lightning-induced fires burn muck, producing yet more cattail stands.

"Over time, it is almost certain that any area of the Everglades will experience a 'natural' disturbance (such as a drought and fire) that will clear out [sawgrass and other vegetation] and permit a race by plants for dominance,"

Trexler said in the *Herald*. "Cattails will out-compete the typical low-phosphorus plants if the soil has accumulated enough phosphorus prior to the disturbance."

Officials with the South Florida Water Management District told the *Herald* that, since the 1970s, phosphorus buildups have tripled in some parts of the Everglades. The good news is that the sugarcane industry, one of the region's worst polluters, reduced its total phosphorus discharges by 49 percent last year alone. By all measures, this is a remarkable achievement. Other polluters—cattle producers near Lake Okeechobee and housing developments—need to follow Big Sugar's lead and triple efforts to clean up their acts.

The last chapter of Douglas's book *The Everglades: River of Grass* is titled "The Eleventh Hour." Indeed, the clock is ticking down for one of America's unique natural treasures. The campaign to rescue the Everglades from cattails and other threats will demand shared investments of time, hard work, creativity, sacrifice, and money.

Our Own Worst Enemy

Sapped by intellectual incest

FEBRUARY 5, 1995

After becoming the president and chief operating officer of the National Urban League last July, Hugh P. Price gave a speech that angered many leaders and rank-and-file members of mainline civil rights organizations such as the National Association for the Advancement of Colored People and the Southern Christian Leadership Conference.

Price, 52, became anathema because he focused on self-reliance and publicly de-emphasized white racism as the most significant cause of poverty among urban blacks. While acknowledging racism's undeniable reality and its well-documented pervasiveness in areas such as black employment, lending, and housing, Price cautioned: "We must not let ourselves . . . fall into the paranoid trap of thinking that racism accounts for all that plagues us. The global realignment of work and wealth is, if anything, the bigger culprit.

"For all our suffering, we cannot become so fixated on our problems that we ignore our commonality of interests with others. If we're ever to deal with [black problems] on a scale remotely equal to their size, we must coalesce with people of other complexions who feel the same pain, even if it isn't as acute."

By expressing these ideas, Price stepped outside the ideological grid that the civil rights establishment follows in lockstep. Armed with the experience of having been vice president of the Rockefeller Foundation, he rejects the intellectual incest—grounded in victim-consciousness—that has sapped the vitality of the nation's major civil rights groups. Intellectual incest is the political, although not necessarily the personal, act of selecting the fellowship and advice of only those who share your Weltanschauung.

Let me differentiate between personal and political selectivity. A man might personally believe that black people must assume responsibility for their own well-being. The same man might, in fact, be a model of self-reliance. But to remain an acceptable member of the political family, he chooses not to publicly advocate the unpopular notion of black responsibility.

Intellectual incest is one of the main reasons that the National Association for the Advancement of Colored People, for example, is near collapse. Since its inception in 1910, when W.E.B. Du Bois merged the Niagara movement with that of a group of whites, many of them Jews, the NAACP has been the country's most powerful civil rights organization to exploit white racism and violence.

As a result, the group has developed a culture of blame and victimhood. Its 64 trustees and its regular members feed from the same trough, sleep in the same bed, as it were, have the same vision of America, and believe in the same anemic solutions to black problems.

The truth is that the NAACP, like most other civil rights groups, has not had a significant infusion of positive, new ideas in many years. Its intellectual gene pool is weakening by the day. It needs fresh, vital blood. Even though Benjamin Chavis, fired last summer as director, at first seemed to have some new ideas, he proved to be another in a long line of race-baiting demagogues who hurt civil rights efforts.

And, as much as I admire Myrlie Evers-Williams, the 64-year-old widow of slain NAACP field director Medgar Evers, I do not believe that she can cure the chronic ills of the organization if she becomes its new executive director. Too much of the old culture's blood runs through her veins.

The NAACP aside, most other areas of African-American culture also suffer from intellectual incest, a condition that is exacerbated by today's preoccupation with Africa. Yes, word is out that black thought is not monolithic. But people who challenge tradition—those whose pragmatism can literally save future generations—are ostracized.

To truly appreciate this fact, take a look at the Black History Month speakers' lineups for most cities. You probably will not find these names: Glenn Loury, a conservative political economist at Boston University who lectures about the "enemy without" (racism) and the "enemy within" (dysfunctional behavior responsible for dependency and poverty); Thomas Sowell, a Senior Fellow at the Hoover Institution, who blasts the need for preferential programs; Shelby Steele, author of the book *The Content of Our*

Character, who wants blacks to shed their victim persona; Robert Woodson, founder of the National Center for Neighborhood Enterprise, who advocates "interior activism" (self-help).

In *Challenging the Civil Rights Establishment: Profiles of a New Black Vanguard*, Joseph G. Conti and Brad Stetson explicate the philosophies that set Loury, Sowell, Steele, and Woodson apart from influential civil rights leaders. Although these social critics represent a wide spectrum of opinion, they agree in several important ways:

- They reject the notion that racial loyalty requires ideological homogeneity.
- They argue that a self-destructive silence has been imposed upon an inner-city culture of poverty by black activists who believe that publicly discussing black problems plays into the hands of racists.
- They insist that racism alone does not account for black poverty and other social ills that African-Americans experience.
- They condemn civil rights leaders for relying on the political capital of white guilt.

Members of the "new black vanguard" are despised in traditional African-American circles. I, too, often disagree with them, and I believe that Sowell is too mean-spirited. But their bold ideas are exactly the new blood that the establishment needs to save itself from the slow, certain death of intellectual incest.

Members of the old guard must face the ultimate truth: Their solutions have failed. The time has come to try new ones.

When old haunts turn into an urban nightmare

July 30, 1995

Whenever I return here to the Fort Lauderdale neighborhood where I was born and spent much of my childhood, I feel like I have landed on an alien planet in a faraway galaxy.

I do not recognize the buildings. The corner stores where we bought Sugar Babies and jawbone breakers, the cafés where we ate delicious greens, chitlins, and sweet potato pies, the clubhouse where we dreamed of being rich—all are dilapidated or abandoned or torn down now.

Nor do I recognize the landscape. The parks where we played touch football and the once-manicured backyards where we shot marbles are now strewn with debris. Even the vacant lots have no grass, wildflowers, or fruit trees.

And the laughter of children has disappeared; so have the old men who "shot the breeze," played checkers, picked their guitars, blew their harmonicas, and sang the blues under the city-block-wide banyans.

Worst of all—and here is the central point of this writing—I no longer have much in common with the people, especially the young ones. Their words and their behavior dismay me. Their values are altogether unlike those I learned as a child.

On my most recent trip here, for example, I was first in a line of seven shoppers in the grocery store near my mother's apartment. A young male, dressed in his generation's signature butt-dragging pants and high-tops, barged in front of me and placed a can of Pepsi on the counter.

Surprised, I looked around at the other customers. All of them, older than I, stared either straight ahead or at the ceiling or at the floor. Their faces wore the blankness of perpetual fear. The cashier, a polite Haitian woman, looked away from me in embarrassment and reached for the boy's money. I could not believe she would wait on him first. Nor could I believe that he, perhaps a 13-year-old, would break in front of a group of adults.

Apparently mistaking my surprise for fear, he said: "Whuzup, ol' nigga? Whuzup? Whuzup?"

Now I was angry. The courtesy that I am accustomed to—the respect that individuals give to others in public places—was suddenly turned on its head. Pushed beyond tolerance and risking arrest, I grabbed the boy and flung him headfirst onto a row of watermelons near the exit. He was too shocked to move immediately. I paid for his Pepsi and handed it to him where he lay.

"Learn to get in line like everybody else," I said.

The other customers cheered. But I wondered who would stand up for them the next time a young tough discounts them or is about to crack their skulls or blow them away for their Social Security money.

Nearly everywhere I went, lawlessness, disrespect, intentional cruelty, and self-destruction prevailed. This, I thought, is a world of chaos, an urban black hole. Most cops, even those born and reared here, have stopped pretending to give a damn.

According to street wisdom, the "real deal," or unwritten policy, is containment: Let those people do what they want—sell their drugs, beat their women, abuse their children, steal from one another, kill one another. Just keep them on their side of the tracks.

I see evidence of such benign neglect all over. One morning, as I sat in my car at Northwest 14th Avenue and First Street—across from the Police Department—five males, none older than 14, were selling crack and pot. How could such illegal activity go down fewer than 100 yards from police headquarters? Because it occurred on the other side of Broward Boulevard—on the black side, where the only free people are the criminals who terrorize the innocent. Where innocence is a liability.

Some blocks away, as I drove to a gas station, four teenage girls blocked my path. Cars were parked on the other side of the street, creating a narrow lane for oncoming traffic. The girls sat on the curb, their legs extending into my side of the street. Had I driven around them, I would have struck the cars on the other side. Had I driven ahead, I would have run over their legs. I stopped. The girls were laughing. Two of them stood, did a vulgar dance, and sat again.

I put my car in reverse and took another route.

Sure, I could have asked them to move; they would have refused. I could have argued with them. But I might have gotten shot or cut. Or I could have driven over them and gone to jail. Instead, I drove away, knowing that in this neighborhood, the girls' rules are law—a law that does not favor the polite, the law-abiding, the normal.

That night, my mother told me that she is afraid to go beyond her apartment complex. "The teenagers are dangerous," she said. "They'll kill you just for looking at them the wrong way."

A few hours later, I heard two gunshots. They were nearby. I was about to go to bed when sirens screamed and police and emergency vehicle lights flashed through my mother's bedroom window. I stayed inside. Bone-jarring rap music kept me awake most of the night. My mother complained, too, but warned me: "Don't say nothing to these fools 'round here. They'll shoot you over that damned rap mess. The police can't do nothing. Nobody can."

I learned the next morning what had occurred the night before: a teenage boy had shot and killed another over a foul call in a basketball game played two days earlier. When I walked to my car that afternoon to drive back to St. Petersburg, I saw some of the dead boy's dried blood on the hot asphalt behind the dumpster.

I do not belong here, I thought, driving along filthy Sistrunk Boulevard, the street that had been central to my life as a child. It had been a clean, prosperous street, where I had wandered without a care, where a generous old man had sold the "sweetest homemade ice cream in the world." These were the words scrawled on the wooden sign beside his hand churn.

He even kept his money in an open King Edward cigar box next to cones and silver scoops.

The true color of bloodsuckers

November 5, 1995

Recently, I went into a popular fish market in the oldest black section of Ft. Lauderdale. I had expected to see the familiar, smiling old black couple behind the counter fileting and frying fish.

The new owners are not black. They are Korean. And on that day, they were not smiling, their expressions shifting from glum, to quizzical, to exasperated, to scared. Their customers, however, were the same as always—poor, mostly black. The prices were a lot higher than I remembered, so high, in fact, that I became righteously outraged and refused to buy anything.

But before denouncing these merchants as "bloodsuckers," as Nation of Islam minister Louis Farrakhan refers to them, my rational side reminded me of an ugly truth about the bloodsucker, the so-called greedy, unprincipled outsider who takes money from the black community without giving back anything: immigrants struggle financially and risk their safety and their very lives to provide essential services to poor, often crime-ridden, black communities. These people—Korean, Vietnamese, Arab, Hispanic, and Jamaican—fill a void that too many American blacks refuse to fill.

What happened to this fish market is typical of what happens in black communities almost everywhere. When it went up for sale, no blacks with viable means and business savvy came forward. The Korean family, looking for a good investment, stepped in.

If these people had not bought the shop, it would have rotted, and the city would have boarded it up, as it does other long-abandoned properties in the area. The residents, many of whom do not own cars, would have had to travel several miles by taxi or bus to find a comparable business. Even with its high prices, the market, which stocks dozens of other foods, cooking supplies, and household products, is a lifeline in a community where so many immigrants now stand behind the counters.

And, yes, these Koreans, who work 18-hour days, leave my old neighborhood each night, taking their money with them to another part of the city. Are they bloodsuckers? If they are, then we, black people, are willing hosts.

Why do we not have more black proprietors? Here are some hard truths that most of us refuse to confront:

Both as a group and as individuals, too many of us lack the family solidarity required to start and operate a business. Immigrant businesses, in general, are run by relatives willing to work long hours for little or no pay. These extended families may live together for years in cramped quarters, saving their money and spending among themselves and others of their kind. They trust and rely on one another for everything. They delay personal gratification. After they save a few thousand dollars, their first stop is not the Mercedes dealer or the travel agency to book a voyage to the Bahamas or Cozumel.

Too many blacks lack the personal responsibility and self-discipline required to succeed in business, as Farrakhan has said for many years. Success comes from personal sacrifice, from the cultivation of positive habits, from self-respect, from not having to rely on alcohol or narcotics to function.

Individually and collectively, blacks, unlike immigrants, place their hopes in politics, not in commerce. Unfortunately, black culture does not respect commerce and is suspicious of people who succeed financially.

A *Washington Post* poll conducted during the Million Man March to measure what marchers identified as the single most important reason for their participation showed how little we care for commerce. Twenty-nine percent came to support the black family; 25 percent to show support for black men taking more responsibility for their families and communities; 25 percent to demonstrate black unity. And a mere 7 percent said that they came to demonstrate African-American economic strength—the one area that truly is our salvation.

While Hispanics and Asians have been establishing banks and international trade firms, for example, to build fortunes for themselves personally and for their people, too many outstanding blacks have been running for political office, a profession that benefits the officeholder more than it does constituents. Nationally, compared to blacks, fewer Hispanics and Asians are in the legislatures of the states and the U.S. government. But compared to blacks, these groups have amassed more wealth and enjoy a better quality of life.

Alas, we have digressed too far from our discussion of bloodsuckers. Immigrants do, of course, take black people's money in exchange for goods and services. And, yes, they do not live in the communities where their businesses are. And, yes, they do not give to charities in the communities or offer college scholarships or volunteer in area crime-watch programs.

But these immigrants are no worse than blacks who own businesses in black communities and also do not give back. These immigrants are no worse than black preachers and their trustees who collect hundreds of thousands of dollars each year from low-income parishioners while giving back very little.

Who, then, are the real bloodsuckers?

No bloodsucker is more injurious than the black bloodsucker who vamps on his brethren, who, as Farrakhan describes bloodsuckers in general, attaches himself to human flesh "to suck the value of its life without returning anything."

The worst slum lords in most black communities nationwide, for instance, are prominent black people—many of them elected officials, civic leaders, doctors, judges, and pastors. What do they do with their money? How much do they give back?

Minister Farrakhan correctly identifies the bloodsucker as an enemy of black communities. But he attacks the bloodsucker of the wrong color. And, by the way, Jews stopped operating businesses in black communities a generation ago.

We need to lighten up

APRIL 21, 1996

When I told an acquaintance, a woman in her late 40s, that I collect *Amos 'n Andy* videos and cassette tapes, she was outraged.

"How can a black man mess with that racist crap?" she asked.

"Because it's funny," I said.

"You're sick!"

I had expected such a reaction. Because black people have been abused from the moment they were dragged onto America's shores, my acquaintance, trapped in an ethos of real victimization, is emotionally and psychologically justified in her sentiment. After all, vicious humor was used to deny black people a soul, which is one reason that most of us now reject humor that puts us down in any way.

Although she may be forgiven on emotional and psychological grounds, she has no intellectual justification for reacting as she did. In fact, her behavior is the product of contemporary ethnic correctness. Blacks, like Jews, Hispanics, and other marginalized groups, traditionally have used humor to their advantage. "From a marginal position one sees things more clearly and therefore more comically!" writes historian A. Roy Eckardt in a 1992 article on Jewish humor.

Not until the 1960s, during the height of the civil rights movement, did the likes of *Amos 'n Andy* become taboo. Most blacks rejected the show because its creators were white, which should not have mattered. During this time, too, blacks as a group began to lose the benign side of their humor, their spirited self-mockery and self-deprecation. We also began to lose our awareness of humor's life-giving power.

Sure, today we may laugh at sitcoms, such as *Martin* and *Living Single*, and the stand-up smut on cable. But the public banter and infectious joking that sustained us during centuries of inhumane treatment are waning, especially in the middle class and other polite circles, where smugness is the mask of choice. Genuine joking has been replaced by gangsta rap, snaps, and other antisocial genres.

What a shame. During my childhood, I heard great jokes all the time and everywhere—in the barbershops among the old men, in school yards among the boys, and in the kitchens among some of the older women. I recall the catharsis, the fellowship, the fun of it all.

We even laughed at lynching. Listen to this joke: A Philadelphia-born teenager went to visit his kin in a small Alabama town. After arriving, he didn't see any other black people. He turned to a redneck and asked, "Where do all the colored folks hang out in this town?" The redneck pointed to a live oak in front of the courthouse and said, "See that limb?"

The very act of telling such a joke made lynching less frightening, thus empowering us.

Blacks correctly suspected that they received unequal justice before the law, which made the courtroom a source of ironic humor. Here is a gag that my grandfather loved: "It is the opinion of the court," intoned the Mississippi judge, "that this innocent Negro is guilty as charged!"

Illiteracy, because of prohibitions against educating blacks, also served as a rich source of humor. I often heard this one: Little Henry came home from school and said to his father, "Say, dad, I need help with my 'rithmetic. The teacher says we got to find the least common denominator."

"My Gawd, ain't they found that thing yet?" the father shouted. "Hell, they was looking for it when I was a boy."

Africa, our ancestral home, provided unlimited hilarity: A white missionary trekked into a remote part of Africa and met the chief of a cannibal tribe, "Do your people know anything about religion?" he asked. "Well, we got a little taste of it when the last missionary was here," the cannibal said.

Humor was the slave's talisman. Folklorist W. D. Weatherford explains humor's efficacy: "No master could be thoroughly comfortable around a sullen slave; and, conversely, a master, unless he was utterly humorless, could not overwork or brutally treat a jolly fellow, one who could make him laugh."

For society's pariahs, humor supplies a rhetorical effigy, having the power to destabilize the enemy's control. I grasped this truth several years ago while reading Steve Lipman's book, *Laughter in Hell: The Use of Humor during the Holocaust.* How, I wondered, could Jews find humor in the worst evil ever perpetrated by humankind? Dutch Jew Rachella Velt Meekcoms, who staged vaudeville shows with other teenage inmates in Auschwitz, comments in her diary: "In spite of all our agony and pain we never lost our ability to laugh at ourselves and our miserable situation. We had to make jokes to survive and save ourselves from deep depression."

Earlier generations of blacks, like Jews, told jokes to save themselves. Today, we blacks still need to save ourselves from hostile forces, both external and internal. We need to lighten up, to stop taking ourselves so seriously, to stop turning many innocent comments about race into insults. And for goodness' sake, get out and tell a few good jokes.

Skin color, for example, is a major concern in black life, so here is a joke fit for the most discriminating repertoire: Dwayne was indignant to learn that his main squeeze had refused to marry him because of his black, black complexion. To complicate matters, she had nicknamed him "Captain Midnight."

"She got no business callin' me Midnight," he protested. "That gal is pretty close to 11:30 herself."

No promise of delivery

JULY 21, 1996

After 14 of his drivers were robbed and one was shot to death in a high-crime neighborhood, the manager of a Miami taxi company warned his cabbies against picking up suspicious fares in the area. When the new manager of a Chicago pizzeria learned that several of the company's delivery people had been robbed in a high-crime district during the last two years, she declared the area off-limits after sundown.

These are not isolated cases. Many similar ones occur nationwide each year, according to a recent study of workplace violence by the National Institute for Occupational Safety and Health. The report states that, statistically, workers who deal directly with the public by exchanging money and delivering goods and services face the greatest risk of being killed. Twenty workers are murdered and 18,000 are assaulted each week, with cabdrivers dying most frequently. In 1994, 84 cabbies perished at the hands of assailants. Pizza deliverers also face a high number of threats.

Despite these dangers, many cities—by using appeals to civil rights and by threatening to levy huge fines or snatch occupational licenses—often try to intimidate and shame companies into sending their workers into all neighborhoods. Recently, for example, the San Francisco Board of Supervisors passed the first law in the nation that prohibits businesses from refusing to deliver in certain communities that otherwise would be part of a regular route. Although the law is virtually unenforceable, it sets a troubling precedent for retailing and other service industries.

The San Francisco law, according to the *New York Times*, is the brainchild of 72-year-old Willie Kennedy, a black member of the Board of Supervisors. She proposed the measure after her grandson, William Fobbs, could not get a nearby Domino's Pizza to deliver to his home in Hunter's Point, a mostly black district with a reputation for being crime territory. Kennedy also lives there.

But Hunter's Point no longer deserves much of its bad reputation. Many of the drug dealers and other hoodlums are gone, and attractive new homes have replaced much of the run-down public housing. Civil rights advocates believe that Domino's redlined the area solely on the basis of class and race. "When people advertise that they deliver, they should deliver everywhere," Kennedy said. "They judge all of us by the worst of us."

What the San Francisco Board of Supervisors sees as blatant discrimination, the California Restaurant Association and Domino's Pizza see as a logical way to protect innocent workers.

Should a pizzeria be forced to deliver in a high-crime area? Invariably, the question leads to a skewed discussion of race. Most delivery personnel—the victims—are young white males. And most high-crime areas that are off-limits are black. As ugly as racial discrimination is, no boss should knowingly send workers into a neighborhood where other workers have been attacked.

Racism is bad, but reckless laws can be deadly. Knowing this fact, Fobbs, manager of a private security company that patrols federal housing developments, and David Wilcox, owner of the Domino's that refused to deliver to Fobbs's home, together inspected every street in Hunter's Point. Afterward, Wilcox said that he would deliver to selected streets in the district. Other streets, though, still would be off-limits. Fobbs agreed, admitting that even he would avoid some parts of his own neighborhood because they are too dangerous.

A policy like that of San Francisco is written by politicians who believe that the delivery of goods and services is a right. This is a laudable, democratic concept. But the delivery of goods and services in the private sector is a privilege, not a right.

Dan McCarthy, manager of the Yellow Cab Company in Gainesville, Florida, operated on this principle last year when he incurred the wrath of city commissioners. One night, two young black males tried to rob a Yellow Cab driver. McCarthy, who is white, said that the driver, who is black, had nearly been robbed because he had violated a company policy forbidding him to pick up young black males who did not give a specific address.

Even though he apologized to the black community and promised to abide by ordinances that require any cab company with available vehicles to pick up a fare, McCarthy had used common sense in formulating the company policy. As manager, he had a duty to protect the drivers. After all, law enforcement officials reported at the time that all of the six cab robberies and scores of attempted robberies on record during the two years prior to the McCarthy flap were committed by young black males.

Apparently, San Francisco and Gainesville officials want to be fair. But they and other lawmakers err when they try to send highly visible delivery workers and cabbies—who carry cash—into crime zones without providing additional city-sponsored protections. If city leaders do not provide such protections, they should be held liable if workers are harmed as a result of misguided ordinances.

After collecting their wits, members of the San Francisco Board of Supervisors amended the law to let businesses refuse to deliver if the firms demonstrate "a reasonable good-faith belief" that a delivery poses "an unreasonable risk of harm."

And the Gainesville City Commission seems to have come to its senses by amending its ordinances. Now taxi drivers can refuse to pick up fares if the drivers believe that their safety is in imminent danger.

These are wise changes because—taking race into account—they balance the customers' desire for services and the workers' right to be protected.

Put the scapegoats out to pasture

OCTOBER 13, 1996

If the Central Intelligence Agency was involved in selling narcotics in mostly black South Central Los Angeles during the 1980s to finance the Nicaraguan Contras, as the *San Jose Mercury News* alleges, those responsible should be imprisoned. And even if the allegations prove false, California

Rep. Maxine Waters and others should be commended for persuading the CIA and the Justice Department to investigate, because the truth must be ascertained.

All that said, however, this and most other black conspiracy theories should be called what they are: self-destructive traps that are bound in history and perpetuated through scapegoats. For blacks, the ultimate historical scapegoat is slavery, along with its institutionalized legacies.

I must point out from the start, though, that groups other than blacks nurture scapegoats. Miami Cubans burn Fidel Castro in effigy each day; Asian-American citizens remember the U.S. internment camps; white southerners, especially low-income rural males, instinctively reenact the Civil War; American Indians dwell on the specter of pioneer savagery.

All groups either succeed or suffer according to how effectively they periodically expel their scapegoats, while taking control of events on terra firma. Although many Miami Cubans are obsessed with having been victimized by Castro, today they dominate most areas of life in Dade County. After being treated like prisoners of war, Asian-Americans now excel in every facet of American society. Small pockets of white southerners let "damn Yankees" influence them, but most are unaffected by this attitude. While many American Indian groups act as remnants of manifest destiny, many others have used enterprises such as bingo and casinos to improve their lives.

And blacks? Far too many of us live squarely in the past, rallying around scapegoats on which to unload our real and imagined problems. Ron Daniels, executive director of the Center for Constitutional Rights in New York, expresses a time-worn view: "Repairing the divide between white America and black America must begin with reparations for slavery. This country has never accepted moral responsibility for either its role in slavery or the devastating effects of slavery on African-Americans. At the heart of the crises afflicting black America today is not welfare, drugs, or single mothers but the failure of America to consciously heal the wounds of slavery." Columbia University law professor Patricia Williams, who is black, agrees. "The individual unifying cultural memory of black people is the helplessness of living under slavery or in its shadow."

Such an absorption with grievance prevents rational thought, making us susceptible to the most outrageous conspiracy theorist or demagogue. In the book *I Heard It Through the Grapevine: Rumor in African-American Culture*, University of California African-American studies professor Patricia Turner writes that some conspiracies are real—like the Tuskegee syphilis experiment, in which scientists withheld treatment from 400 black men.

But, she maintains, paranoia has caused many blacks to believe, for instance, that national fried chicken outlets are Ku Klux Klan fronts and season the chicken with an illegal spice that sterilizes black men.

And when the likes of former Nation of Islam spokesman Khallid Abdul Muhammad and other provocateurs come along, we slobber all over them, easily believing that government and industry are destroying the black community with, among other things, crack and AIDS.

Paranoid rumors can be beneficial, Turner argues, if they are used to mobilize resistance against economic exploitation and government indifference to black concerns. Moreover, such rumors can be even more beneficial if we examine their implications and ask why we are so easily subjected to them. In other words, we should start using paranoid rumors as a springboard for introspection.

Of all of the places in the United States, why did the CIA—if the rumor proves true—dump crack cocaine into South Central Los Angeles? Were agents looking for a certain profile? Well, of course. You do not need to be a genius to know that dozens of black drug dealers will—and do—kill to sell dope to young black children in South Central L.A.

No, I am not blaming the victim. But I am saying that the victim does not have to sell crack to his own people just because CIA agents make the drug available. Pure greed and a lack of values motivate dope dealers. And black people do not have to buy the CIA's dope.

Instead of crafting a complex conspiracy theory that leads us away from the truth and instead of nurturing a scapegoat that saps our creative energy, we should be looking inside ourselves, asking hard, uncomfortable questions: Why, for example, are we such easy prey for every vice that comes along? Why do demagogues, devils, crooks, and fools single us out? Exactly what kind of values do we possess that makes us so attractive?

We need to give honest answers to these and other questions each time we flail at a scapegoat or try to expunge an imagined demon. For the sake of argument, let us say that CIA operatives did bring crack into South Central L.A. in the 1980s. What must we do now? Create more workshops? More congressional investigations? More highly paid speakers with new civil rights careers?

No, we need to come to our senses about the meaning of living in the past and the inevitability of the future. We need to acknowledge the huge role that we play in our own plight, get a grip, and then move on. Large numbers of blacks are doing just that. The rest of us need to start listening to them.

Stop protecting "Brother" and teach him to grow up

July 6, 1997

The music, poetry, chants, drumming, and speeches delivered during the final memorial to the late Betty Shabazz and the gathering of the rich and famous in the pews were impressive. But funereal formality and communal pathos aside, the ceremony perpetuated one of the most serious problems plaguing black society: excusing or ignoring the felonious behavior of black males.

Shabazz, 61-year old widow of slain Black Muslim leader Malcolm X, died on June 23, after suffering third-degree burns over 80 percent of her body in a fire in her Yonkers apartment. Police suspect that Malcolm Shabazz, her rebellious grandson, intentionally set the blaze on June 1. He confessed as much to his mother.

Glaringly missing from the events surrounding the fire and the death of Betty Shabazz is any serious discussion by African-Americans of young Malcolm and the larger meaning of this horrible crime. The serious discussion has been left to authorities, who want to charge the boy with murder, or manslaughter at the least.

Poet Maya Angelou alluded to 12-year-old Malcolm during the memorial, calling for black America to see him not as a perpetrator but as a victim who needs protecting and nurturing. "God created him," Angelou said, with the gravity that has become her signature.

Although her words were appropriate for the occasion, bringing the crowd to their feet in applause, the message was, as one wag said, "so female." He could have gone much further: for the betterment of black life in America, Angelou's message was, and is, wrong. Instead of so readily forgiving them, black people—especially women—must start forcing our males to grow up, to learn the meaning of responsibility itself, to accept responsibility for their actions.

Novelist James Baldwin wrote about this female-produced dynamic in his book *The Evidence of Things Not Seen*: "There is . . . a disease peculiar to the black community called 'sorriness.' It is a disease that attacks black males. It is transmitted by Mama, whose instinct—and it is not hard to see why—is to protect the black male from the devastation that threatens him the moment he declares himself a man.

"All of our mothers, and all of our women, live with this small, doom-laden bell in the skull, silent, waiting, or resounding. . . . Mama lays this burden on Sister, from whom she expects (or indicates she expects) far more than she expects from Brother; but one of the results of this all too comprehensible dynamic is that Brother may never grow up."

In fairness, I should point out that a strain of sorriness exists among all groups, especially among those that are matriarchal or those in which extended family relationships protect the male, while demanding much of the female. Many rural southern white families resemble black families in this regard and sometimes rear males considered "sorry."

After Malcolm X was gunned down by fellow Muslims in 1965, Shabazz never remarried, and she reared her six daughters alone. Her demanding parenting style is legendary, and she sent all of the girls to excellent schools. Although she later had legal problems, Qubilah Shabazz, the second-oldest daughter and young Malcolm's mother, graduated from the U.N. School in Manhattan and attended Princeton. The other daughters include a professional singer, a lecturer, a city administrator, and a playwright.

But young Malcolm, or "Brother," as Baldwin would have called him, was sheltered, pampered, and prevented from maturing. Shabazz, like untold numbers of black grandmothers, went to great lengths to keep her mentally troubled grandson out of jail and, ironically, away from mental health professionals, who probably could have helped him. Before she died, Shabazz had brought the boy from Texas to live with her, to protect him from the bad influences of the world. Her other daughters also took turns protecting the boy.

And even now, after Shabazz has been buried, the daughters and other African-American women, such as Coretta Scott King, the widow of Martin Luther King Jr., Myrlie Evers-Williams, the widow of Medgar Evers, and actress Ruby Dee, want to protect Malcolm from the press, the judiciary, and the penal system. They are not, however, seriously speaking of ensuring that the boy learns to take responsibility for this crime if he committed it. Taking responsibility is one of the first steps in becoming a mature adult. Again, this crucial rite of passage has mostly been reserved for girls.

If recent trends hold, life in black society will get worse before it gets better. Why? Because too many of today's mothers rearing boys are themselves mere children. Who, then, will teach the boys? Who will inculcate in them the right values? Who will demand that they grow up to be real men?

The obvious answer, of course, is that we should look to black men. Makes perfect sense, if all black men were college-educated and middle- or upper-class fathers, who felt duty-bound to provide for their families and help rear their sons. But in the nation's bleak urban centers, where so many older males have not grown up, expecting them to rear their sons is unrealistic. We should still hold them accountable, but we might also look to successful black men with the financial resources to intervene and teach their less fortunate brethren to help their women rear their sons.

The "doom-laden bell in the skull" of the women that Baldwin writes about must be silenced. For all of their maternal strength, women such as the courageous Betty Shabazz need equally strong black men beside them if "Brother" is to grow up, if he is to become a real man and assume his responsibilities.

Service with a sneer

August 2, 1998

Anita Taylor, a divorced mother of three, is a proud African-American. But she, along with dozens of other blacks interviewed for this column, hates to shop or otherwise do business in St. Petersburg's black community. She simply cannot tolerate the widespread rudeness and general lack of professionalism.

Typically, after getting off work at 6:30 P.M., Taylor stops at either the Winn-Dixie grocery store on Dr. M. L. King (Ninth) Street South or the Food Lion on 34th Street South in St. Petersburg near her home. Even as she pulls into the parking lot of the stores, she braces for a humiliating experience.

"I go into Winn-Dixie and spend my hard-earned money, and these people—I mean black people—do not even greet me or anybody else, fellow black people," Taylor said. "They never say, 'Thank you, have a nice day' or whatever. Sometimes they don't even tell you what your total is. You have to rely on the computer or the cash register to know what you're paying. Or you're standing in line, and you've got to listen to the cashier and the bagger waste time talking about what they did the night before. They don't pay attention to their customers."

Taylor and others complain also that black workers at Publix near Coquina Key treat customers rudely. Taylor said that on several occasions, she—the lone customer—has waited for as long as 10 minutes at the bakery counter while the clerk talked on the telephone with friends. A black manager at the store acknowledges that many of his black workers, especially the teenagers, are insensitive to customers.

A technician for Biomedical Housecalls in Tampa, Taylor, 38, was born in Dothan, Alabama, and reared in St. Petersburg. She recently bought a modest house on Coquina Key, a racially integrated island south of downtown St. Petersburg.

On evenings that she does not cook, the family grabs something from a fast-food restaurant. Service is no better and often worse at these places if they are in the black community, she said. She and her children have been mistreated, for example, by black workers at the McDonald's, the KFC, and the Wendy's in or near the area where riots destroyed several businesses nearly two years ago.

One of her worst experiences occurred earlier this year when she and one of her daughters went to the Wendy's on 34th Street South. They took their place in line at 7:50. When the line had barely moved after 25 minutes, she and other customers began to complain. Taylor noticed that only three employees and a manager were operating the place. She suggested to a server, a black male, that someone should have calmed emotions by explaining to customers that the store was short-staffed, perhaps even offering a free soft drink for their patience.

"He told me that if I didn't want to stand in line I should leave," she said. "I told him that he had the wrong attitude, that we were his customers. I admit that I was angry by now. I asked to speak to the manager, who was black. She walked away, telling me she was busy. The guy waiting on me went so far as to say, 'If you don't want to wait in line, you can take your ass home and cook.'"

Denny Lynch, vice president of communications for Wendy's International, acknowledged that the store on 34th Street South, which does a high volume of business, "gets some complaints but not enough to make them stand out. Excellent customer service is a daily priority and a challenge. We train our employees to treat our customers special. What the employee said to Miss Taylor does not represent the way our employees are trained. We make mistakes, but we correct them as quickly as possible. One mistake is one too many."

Black workers were also remarkably rude at the Pizza Hut on 34th Street South, which ended up closing. A spokesman for the company said that the store will reopen in a few weeks—minus table service. All food will be carryout. Taylor is not surprised.

In these and similar incidents, Taylor believes that she sees the source of what ails St. Petersburg's black community and those elsewhere: a profound self-loathing that has caused African-Americans to act harshly toward those who look like themselves. It also causes black customers to willingly and silently accept nasty behavior from other blacks. "We must get out of the mind-set that bad service from our own people is okay," Taylor said. "It's not okay. I'm so concerned about it that when I receive good service from a black person, especially a young person, I compliment them.

"I went to Publix near Coquina Key last Sunday, and a young male cashier said, 'Hi, how are you today?' When he was done waiting on me, he said, 'Thank you. Have a nice day.' I told him that I was proud of him. But what he did was not exceptional. That's just how it should be. That's your job. I did not tell him that, though."

St. Petersburg's black community has all of the symptoms of an abused spouse, Taylor said: In other words, blacks have been cruel toward one another for so long that we have internalized the belief that such cruelty among ourselves is normal. When we accept this treatment, we in turn treat other blacks likewise, she said.

Besides rude behavior, black residents encounter many other manifestations of this internalized abusiveness. Taylor said that most businesses in the riot zone are not well kept. Many mom-and-pop restaurants, for example, have dirty floors, shabby furniture, and walls needing fresh paint. Landscaping is virtually nonexistent, and the sidewalks are filthy. Chain restaurants are no better.

"You couldn't get away with this stuff on the north side," she said. "White people won't tolerate it. But because we're black, we allow these things to happen to us on this side of town. If people can get away with it, they'll keep doing it to you."

The abusiveness and its acceptance also show up at the gas pump. Every station on M. L. King Street South—the very heart of the south side—requires prepayment. "That means that I've been labeled a thief even before I steal," Taylor said. "I went off one morning at the Chevron station because I don't appreciate that. I told the owner that he had no reason to believe that I'm a thief. He said, 'I understand what you're saying, but put yourself in my shoes—where you lose $30 to $40 a day because these people drive off without paying.' I am still insulted. I feel abused. These other blacks think that prepaying is normal. I do not."

Taylor is insulted also because all of the fast-food restaurants close their dining areas early, at least two hours before the area businesses shut down for the night. "You can't sit down and eat a meal after 9:00 because you're in a black area," she said. "We let them do that. If McDonald's wants to close their lobby at 9:00, then how about we just not go there?"

Even more insulting are the thick Plexiglas windows separating customers and staff inside the restaurants, Taylor said. "It's not normal," she said. "We're being caged off like animals because of where we live. In the same way, Walgreen's put up a fence around their store, and Badcock has those metal roll-up doors that make the place look like a fortress. I'm insulted."

Another double standard, which most blacks on the south side see as normal, concerns the Walgreen stores on Dr. M. L. King Street South and on Central Avenue, where mostly blacks shop. Both stores require a deposit to get film developed. The ones serving mostly white areas do not require a deposit. Needless to say, Taylor is livid. "One day, I asked the manager in Central Plaza why I had to pay a deposit," she said. "Do you know what he said? 'Because it's predominantly black, but if you went to 49th Street North, you wouldn't have to leave a deposit.'"

And just try, she said, to find an automatic teller machine near the riot zone. The one near Bayfront Medical Center shuts down at 9:00 P.M.

What about pizza delivery in the black community? Because of real violence or perceptions of it, few companies will risk sending drivers there. "Can you really blame them?" Taylor said. "Nothing is normal about this."

Nor is anything normal about law enforcement's apparent acceptance of drinking alcohol on south-side streets, Taylor said. "I don't want my children seeing grown men walking up and down the sidewalks drinking liquor," she said. "Why do we accept this kind of behavior? I hate it."

As the mayor and others dream up exotic schemes to improve life on the south side, they had better include bona fide seminars on courtesy and professionalism, Taylor said. Until blacks stop abusing one another and stop accepting such behavior as normal, we will never overcome the abused neighborhood syndrome. We will continue to receive inferior goods and services.

A foolish suspicion of learning

July 7, 1999

A recent *New York Times* article about the concern among educators that the academic achievement of middle-class and upper-class black students perpetually falls below that of their white counterparts prompts me to revisit a volatile issue in American education and African-American culture: black people's suspicion and dislike of fellow blacks who achieve in school by virtue of their brains, especially those who speak "proper" English and write well.

The article quotes several overachieving black youngsters describing the taunting they endure from black schoolmates. An Illinois girl who is taking advanced placement and accelerated classes said of her experiences: "People were like, 'Oh, you're an Oreo.' Getting good grades was always connected with white people. So they're like, 'Are you going to be white and achieve?'"

Another Illinois student, whose parents are from Panama and Belize, describes the stigma of speaking perfect English: "You learn to switch it off. When you're on the streets, you speak Ebonics. When you're at home, you speak Creole. When you're in school, you speak proper English. But when you talk too proper, your peers will call you white and say you're a cracker."

Accusing others of "acting white" is one of the most self-destructive problems in black society. It has been worsening in many urban centers since the 1980s with the rise of hip-hop, a rap subculture that celebrates negritude—genuine pride in the positive aspects of black life and tradition. Too often, though, hip-hop celebrates pseudo-negritude—misguided pride in the negative or self-destructive parts of our culture.

Because of pseudo-negritude, too many black teenagers embrace unwholesome sacred cows, emulate unsavory personalities, adopt self-defeating behavior, and rationalize selected forms of criminal and antisocial behavior. Worst of all, pseudo-negritude generates a cult of silence that prevents us from honestly and openly discussing serious problems, such as our contempt for intellectual and well-spoken sisters and brothers. Black children and adults alike know firsthand that the "acting white" admonition paralyzes thousands of our children each year. Yet I rarely hear anyone, including leaders of important organizations, publicly confronting this problem.

As a result of our silence, black children must hide behind a veil of mediocrity or stupidity to please their peers. Having and using a brain should not be a liability. Making excellent grades should not bring ostracism. But it does.

How did our thinking become so convoluted? Like many other deep-seated cultural problems in black society, our dislike of intellect and articulate speech comes directly out of slavery and the racism and other forces it has spawned through the generations. From the moment the slave population grew into the thousands, owners used handpicked slaves to help organize other slaves. Most often, these privileged few were the most articulate and intelligent. In time, they became a class apart, many becoming highly cultured and learned. They often lived in or near the master's home, met the rich and powerful, ate good food, and traveled throughout the colonies and abroad with their masters. Many had more material possessions than their fellows.

During Reconstruction and later, this class of blacks, smart, articulate, and financially better off, became leaders of their communities; whites depended on them to keep other blacks in line. They became the "spokesmen for the black community," the voices whom whites used to conduct business on the other side of the tracks.

And, in too many cases, many of these very blacks became snitches, the eyes and ears of the white power structure. Because they possessed more and lived better, they naturally incurred the envy, suspicion, and wrath of the less fortunate. History holds many tales of articulate blacks profiting by helping to repress others.

All of the traits that typified the white man, especially intelligence and proper speech, became the very traits that blacks who "acted white" manifested. They became symbols of racial disloyalty, shorthand for blacks with "white" minds, everything that the descendants of slaves despise. A list of contemptuous terms grew out of this dynamic: Uncle Tom, Aunt Thomasina, Aunt Sally, handkerchief head, Oreo, hincty, sellout, yard jockey, house nigger.

Unfortunately, as the *New York Times* article indicates, race and its vestiges continue to influence our perceptions of ourselves—especially our perceptions of academic performance.

How about a little neighborly respect?

JULY 21, 1999

By now, most Tampa Bay area residents know about the "KKK" graffiti painted on the garage door of Melissa Metcalfe and Frank Jackalone, who live in St. Petersburg at 6734 30th Street South in Pinellas Point. Metcalfe and Jackalone are white.

They suspect that their neighbors across the street, Harold and Betty Jones, are at least indirectly responsible for the graffiti. Betty Jones is the mother of Los Angeles Dodgers outfielder Gary Sheffield and the sister of Cleveland Indians pitcher Dwight Gooden. Metcalfe and Jackalone say they have reason to suspect the Joneses, who are black. Metcalfe and Jackalone, along with several of their neighbors, have filed noise complaints against the Joneses and believe the graffiti is retaliation.

During the last two years alone, police have received 25 complaints about late-night and early-morning noise coming from the Joneses' $243,400 house. One complaint came in at 5:53 A.M. Metcalfe and Jackalone say they have personally asked the Joneses to turn down the volume, only to be insulted or threatened. The bottom line is that Metcalfe and Jackalone are having trouble sleeping in their own home, and they believe that the Police Department is insensitive to their pleas.

"KKK" graffiti suggests, of course, that Metcalfe and Jackalone are racists. I have met the couple and am familiar with their years of civil rights work in Florida and Georgia.

"We moved here because we wanted to live on a racially mixed block," Metcalfe said. "We felt that it was really important to show that kind of confidence. When we moved in, the riots had just happened. When we bought the house, we also bought the black T-shirts that read 'St. Petersburg Together.'"

What I have described above is one side of this nasty drama. Here, now, is the other side, the one that most of us are too afraid to discuss openly: all too often, black people bring trouble—especially loud music—to previously tranquil neighborhoods, which is what has happened on 30th Street South.

I know many people—some of them black, including several coworkers at the *St. Petersburg Times*—who must endure their noisy black neighbors. I, too, have had noisy black neighbors. Most recently, a man on a street behind the house I rent would play loud music after midnight. Two of my white neighbors asked for my advice. Knowing that the police would act anemically, I went to the man's house the next morning and told him that his gangsta rap was keeping his neighbors awake.

His response? "Get the fuck out of my yard," he said. I left, but not before telling him—in equally profane terms—that we were not going to tolerate his noise. I told him that his kind of black makes life unnecessarily tough for other blacks, that people like him cause "For Sale" signs to mushroom after we move into an area. I also told him that he is a redliner's dream. His kind, I said, causes realtors to demand disproportionately high down payments from African-Americans, that he and his ilk cause property values to plunge.

Over the years, I have heard blacks claim that loud music is part of our culture. Nonsense. Loud music at inappropriate times, in inappropriate places, is uncivil and has nothing to do with black culture. Such behavior belongs to blacks who disrespect both themselves and others.

Unlike the Joneses, however, many other blacks have lived peacefully with whites in Pinellas Point for many years. They, too, play music and have parties. But they do so appropriately, respecting the rights of their neighbors—white and black. Neighborly respect is not a white thing or a black thing. It is the right thing. Metcalfe and Jackalone, whose home I visited, are just asking for a little respect and a little sleep. Nothing more.

"This noise problem is not an issue about race," Jackalone said. "Look at Chunky Sunday. Black people are victimizing black homeowners in the Barlett Park area. Black people are complaining about black people. It's about noise and urinating in people's yards. That's not about race. For us, when we cannot sleep and must go to work the next day, when we cannot function because of someone else's noise, that's the problem. When we go ask our neighbors to turn down the volume and they threaten us, that's what the problem is. It's not about race."

Unfortunately, Jackalone is only half right. This scenario is not about race per se. But it becomes a matter of race when negative stereotypes—such as that of blacks being noisy—are acted out. These stereotypes, then, are the source of slogans such as "There goes the neighborhood" when black people move in. Now, we are talking about race and perceptions of race.

Black people hurt themselves by vandalizing, neglecting their communities

March 5, 2000

Throughout the nation, self-destructiveness continues to trap many black communities in poverty and crime. This self-destructiveness is expressed in many ways, but three of the most telling manifestations of it are vandalism, theft, and the refusal to donate money to black causes. Monetary costs aside, the long-term damage of these phenomena can be measured by the degradation heaped upon adults, the fear instilled in outsiders—especially potential investors—and the sense of hopelessness adopted by far too many children.

Here in St. Petersburg, where I live and work, vandals and thieves struck with a vengeance the other night, derailing, at least temporarily, a self-help entrepreneurial project that would help hundreds of residents if it could get off the ground.

The old Yellow Cab Company building, located in a blighted area, had been vacant for several years when Rodney Bennett and others reopened it as a nonprofit business and training center. Although the organization, called New Beginnings, is struggling to find money, it manages to provide jobs for young people and offers inexpensive vehicle services. Bennett, who volunteers his time, also wants to offer service and training in computer repair, and he wants to start a community radio station.

But some area thugs gave Bennett and others in the group a dose of reality by breaking every large window facing the side street, pulling light fixtures from their sockets, vandalizing and overturning desks, ripping the alarm system from the wall, and ripping doors off their hinges. The thugs went outside and damaged several recreation vehicles and buses that were being restored, and they stole thousands of dollars in furniture and appliances.

Needless to say, these acts are a morale killer. And the irony is obvious. "Some of the kids who did this are probably some of the kids we'd be trying to help," Bennett told the *Times*. "Some of these kids have too much time on their hands. . . . I can't say bad kids did bad things. Unfortunately . . . they've hurt a serious community effort. This kind of thing really set us back."

Perhaps these are not "bad kids." But they certainly did a bad thing, an act indicative of a do-nothing attitude that blocks progress in many black communities nationwide. New Beginnings could be a valuable incubator for many offshoot businesses if it were supported by black residents, especially those who have money. Instead, black residents are doing what they too often do—nothing.

Following riots in 1996 that left many businesses destroyed or damaged, a flurry of activity occurred at the local, state, and national level to assist the area. Since then, however, the old behaviors and attitudes have returned. Not enough middle-class blacks, who are beyond living from check to check, are pitching in to help take care of their own. Even though many of these people were born and reared in St. Petersburg, they lack a sense of owning and nurturing their old turf.

Self-help organizations such as New Beginnings are forced to go outside the black community to get support, financial and otherwise. And, more often than not, they must go to white people. This is not the way matters should be. Blacks should be the biggest benefactors in black communities. Black children should see adults writing checks, so that giving—instead of vandalizing and stealing—will become a natural part of their lives.

A newly established private school in St. Petersburg's black community is illustrative of black stinginess. Academy Prep was founded more than two years ago by a white couple and a black couple. Because I am a mentor at the school, I know a lot about it. One thing I know is that the overwhelming majority of the school's donors are white people. One of the best things that could happen at the school is for the black students to see many more black names on the roster of donors. Think of the wonderful lesson the kids would learn.

Meanwhile, the New Beginnings, the Academy Preps, and other organizations in the nation's black communities must go begging to outsiders. The lack of giving by blacks is especially shameful because many have the money, the time, the knowledge, and the expertise to improve the places where they live.

Blacks could make streets safer simply by helping police

APRIL 30, 2000

Police and witnesses say that on April 24, 16-year-old Antoine Jones shot seven youths at the National Zoo in Washington, D.C. As of this writing, the 11-year-old boy who was shot in the head remains in critical condition, kept alive on life support so his organs can be donated. According to unofficial reports by observers on the scene, the shooter and his victims, the oldest 16, are black.

On one level, the incident shows that random violence can strike anywhere, even in the exclusive Woodley Park residential neighborhood in northwest Washington, which is home to the 111-year-old zoo. On another level—one with ramifications that should concern African-Americans everywhere—the incident shows that when black people assist the police, black-on-black crimes can be solved and the cycle of violence among black people can be broken for good.

By now, most Americans are aware of the irony surrounding the tragedy: the shootings occurred on a day celebrating the African-American family. Since the turn of the century, Washington's African-Americans have convened at the zoo on the Monday after Easter to enjoy picnics, hunt eggs and roll them down the park's landscaped slopes, display original arts and crafts, watch African dancers, listen to music, and, of course, observe the zoo's many animals.

This event should have been the last place at which black-on-black violence erupted. It was the first time such violence had occurred. Irony, frustration, and shame laced the comments of Washington's black leaders.

"It is a rare event that happens at a national site like the National Zoo," Washington's Mayor Anthony A. Williams, who is black, told the *New York Times*. "But quite frankly, it isn't rare, it's all too frequent, in our neighborhoods."

Again, the mayor, in the *Washington Post:* "I think this is particularly a tragedy because it happened on a day of celebrating the African-American family. . . . It's a particular tragedy because all of us are tired of talking about this, and we're tired of talking about something that happens all too often."

Metropolitan Police Department chief Charles H. Ramsey, who is black, said during a press conference: "Parents and other adults need to take a new look at the way in which violence is promoted as entertainment, through music, videos, and television. All too often, we as adults seem to instill in our young people the notion that violence solves problems—when, in fact, violence only leads to more violence. So we really need a wide-ranging approach to this problem."

The "wide-ranging approach" the chief refers to includes courses that teach young people to manage anger and to resolve conflicts without resorting to violence, various communitywide efforts, and quality parental involvement. As a law enforcement officer, Ramsey also wants more black inner-city residents nationwide to follow the lead of the black Washingtonians who identified Jones as the gunman.

From the beginning of modern law enforcement in the United States, many blacks—seeing law enforcement as one of their oppressors—generally have refused to cooperate with the police, even refusing to identify armed robbers and murderers. Each year, police departments nationwide complain that thousands of crimes go unsolved because of the black wall of silence.

In the zoo shootings, however, matters were different, Ramsey said. Thanks to forthright witnesses, the suspect was arrested exactly 24 hours after the attacks. "We were very fortunate that so many witnesses stepped forward with information about the incident and the person responsible," he said. "Detectives were able to identify the individual, his last known address, as well as places where he was known to frequent. . . . We need that same kind of cooperation in all of our cases. . . . Unfortunately, it is unusual for this large a group of witnesses to step forward. This just highlights the need for people to get involved in helping us solve crimes in our communities."

Many black people around the country need to learn, as some in D.C. apparently have, that identifying suspects is a citizen's duty and that leaving criminals on the streets perpetuates crime in black communities. Listen to an African-American mother living in a black community where residents do not cooperate with police: "I no longer let my kids go out and play. And I rarely take walks in my Northwest neighborhood anymore."

Clearly, black people are responsible for their communities. A white reporter speaking at the police chief's press conference may have sounded cynical and inappropriate to many black listeners, but the subtext of the reporter's comments went to the heart of the nation's black-on-black crime crisis: "What do you think it will take to get an influential member of the African-American community to stand up and say, 'Enough. Let's get our communities under control'? I'm talking about someone like Michael Jordan, Magic Johnson, Jesse Jackson. . . . Jesse Jackson was very vocal about making sure the young black men involved in a high school fight weren't suspended. Why doesn't anyone spend equal effort trying to stop the carnage? I think the white community is powerless to help. It has to come from within."

I also ask: when will our most prominent national, state, and local leaders declare "Enough"?

On the Outside

Haunted by faces of homelessness

October 1, 1994

Turning onto Miami's Southeast First Street, I saw a man begging a woman for money. His clothes were filthy, his beard matted and nappy, the hair on his head a tangle of ancient dreadlocks. He had a dirty burlap bag slung over his shoulder. He was skinny and had the glare of a person not in control of his senses. As he walked, his brogans seemed to hydroplane on the rain-soaked pavement.

I'd forgotten about him as I pulled into the parking lot near the Occidental Plaza Hotel, where I would stay for three nights. Once settled in my 10th-floor room, I stared out the window facing glimmering International Place. I looked down at the street and was surprised to see the same beggar. He turned right, went past the James L. Knight Center parking garage, and disappeared into the throng of shoppers.

As I was about to turn away from the window, I spotted piles of cardboard, vegetable crates, old sheets, and carpet remnants under the Metromover platform. I couldn't believe that heaps of trash were so close to the Occidental, the Hyatt at River Walk, and fewer than 200 feet from the front door of Bijan's on the River restaurant. With room rates at $120 a night, I was ready to become angry until I saw a pile of trash moving. Then another moved. A stack of carpet remnants moved. Crates moved. Several sheets moved.

All of that trash was alive. Slowly, arms, heads, and legs appeared. These were people. This was a homeless squatter camp.

Sure, I'd been around the homeless all of my life. But this seemed different. Perhaps the elegance of my room and the fact that my boss was footing the bill made this encounter different. No matter. I felt guilty. Sick to my stomach. Then, as if to remind me of my good fortune, the beggar reappeared, walked to a pile of cardboard, and crawled inside. As heavy rain began to fall, I took a shower and watched CNN. After about an hour, the rain stopped, and again I looked out the window. The homeless camp was flooded, but the piles of trash were still there.

A few people emerged to survey the damage. I wasn't ready for what happened next: a young woman and a small child crawled from the stack of cardboard the beggar had gone into. Both were emaciated and dirty. I wanted to cry. Then the beggar came out and stood beside the woman and the child. All three were soaked. Off they went, toward Brickell Avenue, the child grasping the man's hand. That night as I was returning from dinner, I saw them begging in front of the Holiday Inn restaurant. I gave the man five dollars. Then I looked into the little girl's beautiful ebony face and handed her five dollars.

What else could I do? I had to buy some peace of mind. That night, I kept getting out of bed, staring down at that stack of cardboard, wondering about the child. Is she wet, hungry, scared? Will she have a future? What kind of future? Three days later, I drove home, knowing that I would never see the little girl again. The five dollars I'd given to the child hadn't eased my pain. I wanted to return for her. I didn't, of course.

Our growing inhumanity

April 23, 1995

DISPATCHER: "911. Is this an emergency?"

BRUCE SILVERMAN: "Yes, it's an emergency. I need an ambulance. I have a two-year-old daughter that's passed out on me."

DISPATCHER: "Okay. Where do you need the ambulance?"

BRUCE SILVERMAN: "I'm in front of the emergency exit in Coral Springs Hospital."

DISPATCHER: "You're right in front of the emergency exit?"

BRUCE SILVERMAN: "Yes, that's exactly where I am. And they won't do a goddamn thing in this place."

Silverman is the 30-year-old auto body shop manager who, on February 12, rushed his daughter, Alexandra, to the emergency room of the Coral

Springs Medical Center. The child was suffering from vomiting, dehydration, and diarrhea.

The 911 dispatcher dialed the emergency room.

DISPATCHER: "There's a guy that says he's right outside your emergency exit. And he needs an ambulance. He said his two-year-old daughter is dehydrated."

EMERGENCY ROOM WORKER: "This is a guy who wants to be seen quicker. We're busy. So he figured if he called 911, he'd be seen quicker."

DISPATCHER: "Well, he's saying that he needs an ambulance right away. Is somebody going to go out there or not?"

EMERGENCY ROOM WORKER: "There's nothing we can do."

On the advice of the 911 dispatcher, a Coral Springs police officer drove to the hospital. A few hours later, Alexandra was admitted and placed on antibiotics and an IV.

Before sunrise, however, doctors had declared her brain-dead. Three days later, after life-support systems were removed, the little girl with the sweet face, the big brown eyes, and the warm smile was dead. Now lawyers, strangers, and the relentless wheels of an uncaring bureaucracy are soiling the memory of Alexandra's short life.

This scenario, along with Silverman's words—"They won't do a goddamn thing in this place"—has replayed itself in my mind many times since I first heard it recently on a nightly newscast. Alexandra's treatment, along with that of dozens of other examples elsewhere, underscores the vast reach of this country's growing inhumanity.

But nothing captures the cruelty at the heart of Alexandra's death more poignantly than the clinical words of Jason Moore, the hospital administrator: "While we can sympathize with the Silvermans' grief and express our heartfelt condolences, we are still of the opinion that our hospital treated their child appropriately and did nothing to cause the unfortunate death of their daughter."

Alexandra was not treated appropriately. This innocent child, a month away from her third birthday, did not have to die.

I am not questioning the motives of the Almighty, as Brother Juniper does in Thornton Wilder's novel *The Bridge of San Luis Rey*. Brother Juniper is a Franciscan friar who wonders whether the collapse of a bridge in Peru in 1714 that kills five travelers was an accident or a deliberate plan of God. Each time I hear of a tragic death, I am reminded of his query.

In Alexandra's case, I am convinced her death has nothing to do with providence. It is the indirect result of what America has become, the result of our growing callousness toward the well-being—and the very lives—of others. Busy schedules, heavy workloads, and financial strains aside, we have become a nation of insensitive, arrogant pseudo-individualists who would tell the frightened father of a sick child: "There's nothing we can do."

As conservatism takes root and spreads, our insensitivity and arrogance deepen. By its very nature, contemporary conservatism is cold and punitive. In the name of saving a buck, for example, we deny health insurance and care to whole classes of people. To save a buck, we take shortcuts in providing health care, risking the lives of patients. To save a buck, we throw people out of work. To save a buck, we pollute the environment and destroy our wetlands. To save a buck, we shut down day-care centers. To save a buck, we refuse to buy textbooks for our children.

Only a very thin line separates today's retooled social Darwinism from social barbarism. If you listen to the muscular rhetoric of the 1990s, you can hear its meanness, its class and race consciousness, its creeping misanthropy. No amount of subterfuge, of pretending to care about the state of the Union, can hide our growing contempt for those different from ourselves.

The behavior at Coral Springs Medical Center is par for the course in today's climate. If you click on the news, you can hear U.S. House members comparing single mothers on welfare to alligators and lower primates. Shall we mention talk radio? Harshness is everywhere; it has become normal—even chic. It pervades every corner of our lives.

The ugly spirit displayed on the 911 tape is common in our dealings with one another. If we do not regain some semblance of our old compassion, more young children like Alexandra Silverman will be turned away and denied the milk of human kindness. And we will hear more Bruce Silvermans saying of the institutions in which we place our trust, even our lives: "They won't do a goddamn thing in this place."

A sweatshop here, a godsend elsewhere

August 4, 1996

All of the hand-wringing over Kathie Lee Gifford's and Michael Jordan's affiliations with products made in foreign sweatshops takes me back to my travels in Central Africa during the 1970s. The controversy also reminds me of how ignorant most Americans are of other cultures.

Everywhere, I mostly saw poverty and misery, especially in the harbor town of Dixcove on Ghana's Gold Coast. As a member of a group of American college teachers studying Ghana's oral tradition, I lived at the edge of a river in an airy bungalow. Sea mists and the moisture of fetid marshes and lagoons shrouded the bamboo huts and tin shanties. Trash littered the dirt streets, fly-infested piles of goat and chicken manure lay everywhere, and streams of raw sewage crisscrossed some alleys. Big flies attacked everything that moved.

Pot-bellied tykes roamed the streets in search of food and whatever else they could beg or steal. As American blacks, we were prime targets. A nine-year-old boy, who had a runny sore on the back of his neck, followed me everywhere, and I grudgingly adopted him during my two months there. I gave him money, junk food, a University of Chicago sweatshirt, and a Chicago Cubs baseball cap.

After he took me to a smelly hut to meet his family, my heart went out to him. His 12-year-old sister supported the family as a prostitute. Three of his siblings had died during birth, and his parents suffered from onchocerciasis, or river blindness. I later learned that the father also had leprosy.

I have not gone back to the area, but a former colleague who traveled there earlier this year tells me that few things have changed: river blindness, malaria, gastroenteritis, and pneumonia still afflict hundreds; life expectancy remains about 52.2 years for the men, 55.8 for the women; infant mortality is still high.

And just as significantly, few children attend school, making illiteracy extremely high. Because of their illiteracy and lack of technical training, many Dixcove residents are virtually unemployable by American standards. In U.S. currency, the average worker earns about $1,800 a year.

Dixcove residents are typical of millions of others in Third World nations. They need plenty of steady, unskilled jobs. If we Americans could set aside our concept of the superiority of Western cultural values, we would realize that people like these would welcome a chance to sew fabric for Wal-Mart's Kathie Lee Gifford line or stitch leather for Nike's Air Jordans and soccer balls.

I am not advocating the establishment of sweatshops in Third World nations. Nor am I excusing Gifford and Jordan for lending their good names to businesses that reportedly abuse children. I contend, though, that most things are relative, that too many Americans are ignorant of employment and labor standards in other nations, that we are too quick to demonize what we do not comprehend.

A recent *New York Times* article about sweatshops in Honduras points out, for example, that what Americans view as exploitation, Hondurans, whose per capita income is $600 a year, see as a godsend. With unemployment at 40 percent, Hondurans, including children as young as 14, eagerly work long hours for Global Fashion, the company that makes the Gifford line.

In Honduras, 14-year-olds can legally work up to six hours a day if their parents and the Labor Ministry approve. Rarely does anyone disapprove. Many of the sweatshops provide medical care and subsidized lunches for employees. If Global Fashion did not hire these children, they would be on the streets begging—or worse. Few of them attend school after the sixth grade, and their families depend on their wages to make ends meet.

As to the other side of the globe, child-labor activists in the United States point out that the monthly wage of the average Nike worker in Indonesia is about $117, or 53 cents an hour. This amount is about the price of a pair of Air Jordans. If those figures are appalling, consider these: Indonesia's minimum wage is $56 a month, or 25 cents an hour for a 55-hour workweek, much less than what Nike pays. What appears to be mere pennies to Americans—53 cents an hour compared to 25 cents an hour—to an Indonesian family can mean the difference between eating or starving, between sleeping on a mattress or wallowing on the ground.

Would these Third World families be better off if Wal-Mart and Nike shut down their plants? I do not think so. And neither do most of the workers. From my American perspective, I certainly believe that Gifford is on the right track in trying to improve sweatshop manufacturing both abroad and here at home. Wages should be raised, and working conditions and benefits should be upgraded. But before we condemn working conditions in faraway lands, we should try to understand the realities of these economies.

Listen, for instance, to Evangelina Argueta, a labor organizer in San Pedro Sula, Honduras, speaking to Americans wanting to remove children in her community from their apparel factory jobs. "This country is not the United States," she told the *New York Times*. "Very few Honduran mothers can afford the luxury of feeding their children until they are 18 years old without putting them to work." When these children are kicked out of the garment factories, Argueta said, many are forced to settle for more abusive work for less pay. But most buy phony identification and re enter the apparel industry through the back door.

To most Americans, this arrangement is tantamount to abuse. To Honduran children and their families, however, it is survival.

Fanning the flames of homophobia

October 14, 1998

Matthew Shepard, 21, is dead. Hate—of a special American kind—killed him.

Still on a ventilator, he died early Monday. His parents were at his bedside. Matthew, a University of Wyoming student, was savagely beaten last week, apparently because he was gay.

He was not just gay. This courageous student lived his gayness in the sunlight—just like the rest of us live our lives, openly and freely.

According to the police, Russell Henderson, 21, and Aaron McKinney, 22, lured Matthew out of a local bar and into a pickup by pretending that they were gay. Then, police say, the duo kidnapped Matthew, whipped him with a .357 Magnum, tied him to a wooden fence, and burned him over part of his body.

He remained there for about 18 hours in near-freezing weather until a bicyclist, thinking at first that he had seen a scarecrow, discovered the victim. In addition to the other wounds, Matthew's skull was crushed. Police officials say that Matthew, of small stature, begged for his life. But his attackers, driven by hate, pounded him into unconsciousness.

The hate that killed this young man—an ever-growing homophobia in the United States—is the same brand that is being spread by some of the country's most powerful elected officials, including Republicans Trent Lott and Dick Armey. These men, who should be inculcating wisdom on the airwaves, are teaching citizens to hate by calling homosexuality an "evil." Apparently, Lott and Armey do not know that hate is the real evil.

Worse, however, is the role of organized religion in this campaign of inhumanity. Each Sunday, too many ministers are using their pulpits to wage an unholy war against gay people. Early last Sunday, for example, I listened to a televangelist inveigh against "homosexuals" for more than 15 minutes. This preacher and others like him are partly responsible for the climate that created the killing of gay people. Instead of being places of understanding, civility, and love, many churches are incubators of intolerance. In August, if you recall, the world's Anglican bishops, meeting in Canterbury, England, voted 526–70 to adopt a resolution condemning homosexuality as being "incompatible with Scripture" and advised against ordaining gays and lesbians. No good will come of this move. It is a ticket to hate.

The Christian Coalition, with close ties to the national Republican Party organization, may have done more than any other group to condemn gay people to violence—and murder. In an attempt to distance itself from Matthew's murder, the Christian Coalition's national office released a statement on Monday calling for "zero tolerance for such crimes."

In the Tampa Bay area, the Indian Rocks First Baptist Church has been distributing material, published by David Caton's Florida Family Association, attacking a School Board member who approves of a gay support group on campus. I have read the fliers and can report that they are intended to create the kind of climate that killed Matthew Shepard. Many gay students in the area have said that they feel threatened.

Why is a church—with the word "Christian" in its name—engaged in such a hateful, ungodly campaign?

And I am sad to write that most black churches are no better than the Indian Rocks First Baptists of the nation. Gay-bashing long has been the black church's middle name. And many black gays have been brutalized and murdered because our churches, black culture's most important institution, have condemned gay people to lives of hell on earth.

I do not put much stock in comments like those of the Christian Coalition that follow tragedies. Why not issue statements of tolerance each day? Why not make tolerance official policy?

That is what Unitarian Universalists nationwide do. I attended services at the Unitarian Universalist Church in St. Petersburg last Sunday, where the Reverend Dee Graham is the pastor, and was inspired when a girl lit a candle for Matthew Shepard. Little did we know that Matthew would die a few hours later.

For me, the Unitarian Church in St. Petersburg is an oasis in a world of hate. Listen to part of its "Vision" statement—a statement that embraces Matthew Shepard: "We cherish and celebrate our diversity. Let us love and inspire one another to change the world."

Deporting a parent

November 29, 1998

Latisha Espinosa, daughter of farmworkers, is a high school senior who has spent much of the last two years patiently raising twin brothers on her own. Her father, a Mexican-born man who has toiled the fields of the United States much of his adult life to provide for his children, made a mistake in 1993. He tried to sell some marijuana, and he was sent to prison for it.

Now, the U.S. government wants to make Luis Espinosa pay twice. Not content with the 15 months he has served in prison or the 29 years he has lived and labored in this country, the Immigration and Naturalization Service is determined to deport him. More to the point, the INS will strand four children with no mother or father.

"My dad paid for his crime," Latisha said. "They're now punishing us."

Can such punishment possibly make sense?

Espinosa, 47, is a painful example of what ails our immigration system, of how the political momentum to close the nation's borders has produced unintended consequences. In his case, the 1996 Illegal Immigration Reform and Immigrant Responsibility Act has gone too far. It has taken a family of children who are surviving against enormous odds and is throwing them the cruelest curve of all. It is taking away their father—their only reliable provider.

Espinosa, a farmworker from Ruskin, Florida, sits in the Federal Detention Center in Oakdale, Louisiana, awaiting deportation to Mexico in a few weeks. His two girls, Jessica, 19, and Latisha, 18, his 10-year-old twin sons, Luis Jr. and Mario, and a 2-month-old granddaughter live alone in a Ruskin labor camp. The children's mother, who left their father in 1993, lives in another part of the state. How Espinosa wound up in a Louisiana lockup is a simple enough tale, but the forces driving his case—the reasons for his deportation—are ironic and eerily harsh for the American Way.

Born Luis Espinosa-Hernandez in 1952 to a poor agricultural family in rural San Francisco del Rincón, Mexico, Espinosa never attended school. Wanting to find a better life, he crossed the border into the United States in 1969 and became a farmworker. In 1983, he married Anna Maria, who was born in the United States. He returned to Mexico for three weeks in 1986 to qualify for immigrant status in America based on his wife's citizenship.

In 1993, his troubles began. He traveled to Mississippi to look for work. Anna Maria had already deserted him, so he left the children in Ruskin with his wife's father. After the crop in Mississippi failed, Espinosa became desperate to earn money to send to the children. A friend persuaded him to drive marijuana from Texas to Florida. He was arrested en route to Florida in Rankin County, Mississippi, for possession of more than 1 ounce of marijuana but less than 1 kilogram, an amount not considered an aggravated felony by the INS.

He was arraigned, given a court date, and released on bail. He returned to Florida, settled back into life as a farmworker, and never went to court. In 1997, he returned to Mississippi to work and was arrested as a fugitive. The judge gave him a two-year sentence. He was released after one year for good behavior. The problem was that he was handed over to INS and brought to Oakdale.

While Espinosa has been in prison for the last 15 months, his children have had to fend for themselves in a two-bedroom mobile home that does not have air conditioning. To look inside the lives of these children is to witness a crisis that the U.S. government never should have created and probably did not intend. Even after their father was convicted, the children, all born in Florida, believed that he would return home soon. But as the days stretched into months, the children resigned themselves to living alone and together as a family.

Latisha, or Letty, was nearly 17 when their father was locked up. Now a senior at East Bay High School in Gibsonton, Letty assumed full responsibility for her siblings. Jessica, a year older, dropped out of school. She recently had a baby.

A studious child, Letty was at first angry that she had so many adult responsibilities. "Why me, I kept thinking," she said, her stoical eyes surveying the small room where her brothers and their friend sit on the worn couch. "But I refused to let my family get split up. I decided to take care of the boys, my sister, and her baby."

Letty and the twins qualify for free breakfast and lunch at school. Other than that, they receive no government largesse. Their grandfather, a crew leader for farmworkers, gives the children $60 a week. Their mother was ordered by the court to pay $400 a month in child support. A farmworker who follows the East Coast migrant stream, she sends what she can, when she can. Often, she has nothing to send.

Letty and her siblings feel no bitterness toward their mother. "Our mom calls," she said. "Sometimes she comes to visit. She doesn't have much time because she is a farmworker. She works very hard to send us money."

Having learned to manage expenses, Letty, with her grandfather's financial and moral support, consistently pulls together the cash to pay the $87.50-a-week rent and the telephone and electric bills. She struggles to keep enough money for food. And when the boys need clothes, she finds ways to dress them. "I am the boys' mom, dad, sister, cook, and nurse," she said.

She gets up each morning at 5:00, gets dressed, wakes the twins, and walks them to the bus stop. She catches the school bus at 6:20. The boys are already back in the camp when she arrives home at about 3:15. She oversees their homework, cleans the mobile home, and prepares dinner if Jessica has not done so. Whenever the boys are ill, Letty nurses them. She cuts their hair every three weeks and referees disputes when they get into trouble in the camp or fight with each other.

Letty, who is slated to graduate this spring and who wants to be a computer analyst, has no social life. She does not date or attend school sporting events or dances. "I'm mostly here all of the time, just taking care of the kids," she said. "I just go to school, come back home, and shop. I don't have a car. My grandfather has to drive me."

The twins seem to understand Letty's sacrifices and try not to give her too much trouble. Because they are poor, the boys watch a lot of television and invent games and toys. They spend many hours in a nearby wood that they call "the clubhouse." There, they and a friend play cowboys and Indians and engage in other roughhousing.

Even when life goes smoothly, however, Letty knows in the back of her mind that she and her family are victims of a cruel waiting game. When their father is deported after December 7, she believes the Florida Department of Children and Families will try to take the twins. "Splitting us up is the worst thing that can happen," she said. "I want to go to college, but, because I just turned 18, I may quit school, get a job, and take care of the kids. I don't want us split up. The kids are better off with me."

Letty's calm exterior belies a bitter wisdom that comes to the children of immigrants caught in the legal nightmare of inflexible immigration policies. "Our dad committed one stupid mistake," she said. "We don't know what we're going to do after they deport him. If my dad was here, everything could be fine like before. I could get a part-time job and help him out and still go to school. That's what we had planned.

"They're taking our dad away from us, and we're not able to live our normal lives ... My dad is a good person. There was no work. He was taking care of four kids on his own. He didn't want to drag us all up north—to Georgia, Tennessee, and Michigan—so he tried to make some fast money for the first time in his life. He used to work three jobs to support us. He would do any kind of work. He would work anywhere. Now he's being taken from us. What are we going to do?"

Espinosa's pro bono attorney, Alicia Triche of the Catholic Legal Immigration Network in Oakdale, Louisiana, said that her client's punishment far outweighs his crime, that he is a victim of a law that is too restrictive.

When convicted in 1997 for possession of marijuana and of jumping bail, Espinosa was ruled deportable. Triche filed for a hardship waiver, which, prior to 1996, would have protected her client from deportation because he had resided in the country for seven years. The revised 1996 immigration act, however, retroactively made any legal immigrant with a drug conviction subject to immediate deportation—no matter how long ago the conviction occurred. Before 1996, Triche said, an immigrant ruled deportable could ask the judge to waive that provision because of the "equities," the positives, the person had built while in the United States.

The case law still allows the judge to decide if the immigrant is basically a good person, to determine the number of relatives in the United States, how long the person has been in the country, the family life, the work history, and then the nature of the crime and whether he or she is contrite.

"The judge decides if you're good enough to stay in America," Triche said. "And our judge did decide that Mr. Espinosa was good enough to stay. He said, yes, this crime is egregious, but it is outweighed by the way Mr. Espinosa has taken care of his children, by the way that he has worked hard in the United States. Unfortunately, the judge also said that Mr. Espinosa's waiver requires that he had to have lived in this country seven years after being legally admitted."

Therein lies his problem. Even though Espinosa had been in America since 1969, he was not legally permitted until receiving his green card in 1986. Here, Triche said, is where the law, as interpreted by the judge in the case, is too narrow. When does permission begin? But more important, when does it stop? In Espinosa's case, the judge said his permission stopped when he was arrested—not when he was convicted. The result is that Espinosa missed the seven-year-residency requirement by only a few months.

"This portion of the law is open to interpretation, and I want to appeal it," Triche said. "But Mr. Espinosa has been in jail for over a year now and insists that he wants to be released at any cost—even if it means deportation. We have a good chance of winning on appeal, but he doesn't care to wait the one to three years it takes to do an appeal before the Board of Immigration Appeals. He's anxious to go back to Mexico so that he can start sending money to the children. He's desperate to start supporting them."

Barring complications, Espinosa should be back on Mexican soil before the end of December. He will leave America without having seen his new granddaughter.

"There's no common sense in this," Letty said. "If we're split up, I'll quit school if I have to and follow the boys. I have to help them out. The boys don't say much. They don't really understand what's going on. I try telling them, but they're too young to understand."

In a key immigration case of nearly two decades ago, federal immigration judge Irving R. Kaufman wrote: "Deportation is not, of course, a penal sanction. But in severity it surpasses all but the most draconian criminal penalties."

The Espinosa children may soon find out just how draconian the INS can be.

Ordered out of house and home

MARCH 21, 1999

Imagine this scenario: You are a legal, hardworking, 40-year-old farmworker from Guatemala. You and your wife, a 38-year-old Guatemalan, have been in the United States for more than eight years. You both have limited knowledge of English. The two of you saved enough of your combined $16,000 annual income to buy a lot and a dilapidated mobile home. More than 15 years old, it needs repairs that you cannot afford. Your daughter, 13, and your son, 10, both speakers of English, attend a local public school. They are good students and never get into trouble.

On this day, you and your wife leave home at 5:00 A.M., as you do each weekday this time of year, and catch a van to the strawberry fields, where you pick all day, returning home at about 5:15 P.M. Curiously, the kids are not inside watching television. They are outside sitting on the makeshift bench beneath the only tree in the yard.

As you approach, the girl points to the green sticker that a county code enforcement investigator has pasted near the door: "NOTICE: This Building Is Declared Unfit for Human Habitation and Ordered VACATED. It Is Unlawful for Any Reason to Enter This Building."

You and your wife panic. You have never been in trouble with the law and will not start now by going inside the trailer. The sticker says that you had better not. Your wife sobs and hugs the children. You and your family abandon the trailer and go to the home of friends across town.

Your world has fallen apart.

This scenario is not imaginary. It is reality for 25 farmworker families in Wimauma, Florida, a tiny agricultural town in southern Hillsborough County that recently were greeted by "vacate" stickers like the one described above. Don Shea, the county's operations manager for community improvement, said that the condemnations are part of a countywide effort responding to complaints about deplorable housing conditions.

Shea, who directs the office of code enforcement, said he was especially concerned about properties with multiple mobile homes on them, where unsanitary conditions and safety violations decrease "quality of life." Some people in the neighborhood in question live in dangerous sheds. Shea is careful to note that this area of Wimauma is not the only section of the county being targeted.

For government officials such as Shea, condemning property—ordering residents to either fix up their property or move out—is merely a part of their job, said Rocio Rocha-Smith, unofficial spokesperson for Wimauma's farmworkers. But for her and the six other members of her extended family, Shea's efforts are life-changing. The family returned home one afternoon last week to discover a "vacate" sticker pasted on their trailer.

Rocha-Smith, 27, a graduate student in public administration at the University of South Florida and a program supervisor with Mental Health Care, Inc. of Ruskin, is not a troublemaker. She is, in fact, vice president of the Wimauma Civic Association, the very organization responsible for trying to beautify the town.

For Rocha-Smith, a native of Brownsville, Texas, the story behind the condemnations is a human tragedy caused by bureaucratic insensitivity.

"Basically, I have a conflict of interest," she said. "I believe we should beautify. I know that the city has a valid point and a formal process that people must go through. But what happens to those people who you just put out of a house, those who can't afford to fix up their place or move? I want to know about plan B and C. What happens to you when your home is gone?"

Rocha-Smith said that she is angry because the man responsible for pasting the stickers on the homes, Jim Ellington, chief inspector for Hillsborough code enforcement, expressed a callous attitude toward the residents' plight. Ellington, in a telephone interview, deflected questions to his superiors.

"He told me that it's 'just an inconvenience. Everybody can start over. Everybody can buy a home as long as you own the land,'" Rocha-Smith said. "I couldn't believe he said that. It's true for some people but not for most. My family is fortunate because, although our home has been condemned, we own the land and can start over. But it will be hard for us, too. If it's hard for us, think of how it is for people who don't have anything. Jim Ellington offended us by calling this just an inconvenience. It's our homes—our lives. It is not just an inconvenience."

Whenever the government throws the lives of the poor, especially farmworkers, into disarray, children suffer the most, as is the case in Wimauma. A teacher with the migrant education program said that 10 percent of the farmworker children at one middle school alone are missing class to acompany and translate for their parents as they seek new housing. Other children are staying out of school to help their parents pack and move. How many children are affected, no one seems to know. In visiting just 7 of the 25 condemned trailers, Rocha-Smith said that she counted 30 children.

For many of the residents, especially those who do not speak English, getting assistance is a nightmare. Even the warning letter the county mailed to the residents is misleading. In addition to announcing the condemnations, it lists nonprofit organizations that the residents should contact for help. The problem? None of the organizations can help these people.

Evan Jorn works with Beth-El Farmworker Ministry in Wimauma, and he is chairman of the South County Coalition for Community Concerns. He said that the nine organizations listed, including Catholic Charities, did not know why they were included. When he called code enforcement, officials could not give him a straight answer, he said.

Jorn is particularly upset because the "vacate" sticker, which says that the property is unfit for human habitation, does not tell residents that they have at least 30 days to move or make repairs. "Many people were too afraid to enter their homes and went elsewhere," he said. "They are law-abiding pickers and were too afraid to cross the line because the sticker said 'Do not enter.' I called Mr. Shea, and he said that if residents had been home when his inspectors arrived, his people would have explained to the residents that they had some time. But if they are not home, all they see is the sign. That is causing a lot of people a lot of sleepless nights."

Shea said that legal residents can apply for assistance through his office. Qualified renters, for example, can apply for federal rent subsidies, and owners can apply for other aid. He said that only a small number of residents have contacted his office. Some residents refuse to telephone his office because they think they are not qualified, while others simply do not want to participate in government programs, he said.

Rocha-Smith offers yet another explanation: "These people work 40 hours a week. Some used to get government subsidies but are now trying to build their lives and homes without government help. Now the government is demolishing their homes and telling them to get government help. You're putting people back into the cycle of dependency that they worked their way out of. All of us work full-time, and some of us go to school part-time. We don't want to be in the cycle."

The county has every right to bring properties up to code, but officials should temper policies with fairness and understanding, especially when dealing with those who have nothing and are being thrown out of their homes, Rocha-Smith said. "The problem is that people don't know the history behind other people. They don't know what's going on in the lives of farmworkers, the tragedies and hardship. For example, my brother died last year, and we had to basically give all the money we had to the funeral. Do officials know that? Do they care?

"Do they know that my parents' house burned down and that they couldn't rebuild completely? No. Unless you're in the family or care to find out what's going on, you won't know. If officials knew the history of these farmworkers, they wouldn't call uprooting them from their homes an 'inconvenience.'"

A setting for the absurd

April 4, 1999

Ever wonder why the setting of Carl Hiaasen's novels is south Florida? And what about Elmore Leonard? Ever thought of why he often places characters in this sun-baked arena?

One major reason is that the so-called Gold Coast—a conglomeration of too many out-of-state retirees, every ethnic group under the sun vying for the same karma, too much conspicuous consumption and poverty side by side, too many controlled substances, runaway land development, too many crooked and crazy politicians, too many students, and too few schools—is one of the zaniest regions in the world.

Where else, for example, would you find the following agricultural scam so blatantly carried out?

Dr. Harold Dubner of Boca Raton, who owns hundreds of acres of land in western Miramar near Ft. Lauderdale, keeps 30 cows to save thousands of dollars in property taxes. Okay, so what is wrong with keeping 30 bovines to save money? Nothing exactly, until you look at the details. The cows are kept on two gravel "pastures," as they are called, off busy Miramar Parkway within a stone's throw of Interstate 75. The nearest green grass is on well-manicured berms and lawns out of the cows' reach.

Wait, there is more. Those gravel "pastures" are actually two lots—in a highly developed subdivision—facing the bustling parkway at Southwest 148th Avenue and Flamingo Road. The emaciated animals have nowhere to graze, standing 24 hours a day on rocks. Hay and grain are trucked in, and the cows drink from holes and ditches. Local residents said that they have never seen such skinny cattle.

"If they are on rock or concrete all day, that's bad for their feet," says Dr.

Frank Bernard, of the University of Florida's College of Veterinary Medicine in Gainesville. "They need to be able to graze properly so they get nutrition. They need shade so they don't get heat stress." Here is what Dubner gets for mistreating his suburban cattle: In 1998, his property at 148th Avenue was valued at $114,840 for taxes. The tab would have jumped to $812,280 without the agricultural tax break. The Flamingo Road lot was assessed at $7,350 for taxes. Without the tax break, it would have been valued at $257,320. Meanwhile, the 30 cows keep getting thinner.

Only in south Florida.

Just up the road from Miramar, in western Boynton Beach, is probably one the worst examples of selfishness anywhere. For several years, the Palm Beach County School Board has known that a new middle school had to be built. The problem, of course, was finding a suitable site. By every measure, a parcel on Woolbright Road was ideal, and the board voted for it. Trouble is, the site is near an upscale retirement community.

When a brigade of elders organized and trotted into a meeting with signed petitions, board members, being the politically expedient creatures that they are, realized that middle school kids do not reelect them. Old folks do—in blocs. Given the old-timers' reaction, you would think that the county was putting a landfill or a shooting range or brothel or a topless doughnut shop in the area. You might even think that a black family was moving in.

What did the board do? It reversed its vote and is now looking for a new place for the badly needed school. Meanwhile, thanks to these well-heeled oldsters, many of the youngsters who live in the Woolbright Road area will continue to be bused 40 minutes each way to school.

Hold on, there is more to this south Florida tragicomedy.

The major excuse that the retirement gang used to block the school reflects an incredible mix of chutzpah and goofiness. Here is how *Sun-Sentinel* columnist John Grogan describes it: "In a letter to Superintendent Joan Kowal, Mitchell A. Radin, an opposition ringleader, said children might end up injured or worse, given the driving abilities of seniors. 'Our eyes and reflexes are not acute,' he wrote. Boy, there's an admission I'd like to see carved in stone. Isn't it convenient? The same folks who ferociously fight any attempt to impose safety tests on older drivers are trotting out their infirmities when it suits them."

Alas, south Florida.

A few miles south of Boynton Beach, city commissioners in Lauderdale-by-the-Sea proved that they also have have been out in the sun too long and have far too much time on their hands. They unanimously passed a law that prohibits residents from interrupting a council meeting or making "personal, impertinent or slanderous remarks" or becoming "boisterous."

The mayor, Oliver Parker, swore that the ordinance was not intended to curb free speech or public debate. "We're not going to be using this to bust people's chops," the enlightened leader promised. Taxpayers who run afoul of this law, however, can be fined $500. By the way, other south Florida towns, such as Margate and Pompano Beach, that also are populated by a bunch of Yankees and midwesterners, have similar draconian ordinances.

Is it any wonder that Hiaasen and Leonard love to place their amoral, psychologically challenged characters in zany south Florida? For all of its wealth and leisure, the region is pure theater of the absurd.

The Fruit of Their Labor

Harsh memories of migrant work

DECEMBER 10, 1997

As I watch migrant farmworkers in Immokalee, Florida, battle tomato growers for higher wages, I recall 1954 and 1955, when my father and I picked in these same fields. We, too, struggled to buy food. We scrimped to keep gas in our beat-up Ford and send money back home to my mother and siblings. I was nine years old in 1954.

My father and I lived with about 80 other pickers, all black, in a migrant camp about six miles south of town. Conditions in this camp, along with others we lived in from Belle Glade, Florida, to Long Island, New York, were brutish and nasty. Disorder and apathy prevailed.

Our living quarters were a tin-roofed, wooden, windowless bullpen where 10 to 15 men and boys slept on pallets. Because our crew chief was a devout preacher, whose wife and daughters accompanied him, married couples, families with children, and single women slept in shacks across the compound from the men. The females had three fly-infested, two-holed outhouses; the males, two one-holers. Mosquitoes attacked us inside these stinking buildings, which is why so many of us urinated and defecated elsewhere. Real toilet paper was coveted like gold. Most of us used newspaper that we softened by rubbing it between our hands. Sometimes we used Spanish moss.

The crew chief's dwelling and the shacks of the families had electricity and running water. The rest of us pumped water by hand from a well. Good hygiene was next to impossible. And a moment of individual privacy or romance was rare. We males ate our meals, prepared by the crew chief's wife, on makeshift tables. Families with children cooked their own meals. Single men paid $12.50 per week for lunch and dinner. A bottled soft drink or a jar of Kool-Aid was extra.

For many of us, especially males who were physically weak or who had hot tempers, life was violent and often short. Few men were shot back then. The knife was the weapon of choice. Our sense of manhood, even for young boys like me, framed our relationships. We cultivated it like the crops we planted, tended, and harvested.

My saddest memories are of men who had been badly knifed in the stomach. I still see them: bent over, groaning, holding their intestines in their hands, blood streaming through their fingers. Most fights erupted during games of craps or cards. Cheating or bragging too much could get you killed.

Hard work—stooping and sweating all day—was at the center of our lives. We belonged to the crew chief and the grower. We rode from field to field on the beds of trucks and in old school buses that broke down more often than they operated properly.

My father and the other men who sent money back home complained about the low wages. For the men without women in their lives, money was used for physical pleasure. They spent most of their time in the camp's juke joint looking for sex. Venereal disease was rampant.

Although a preacher, the crew chief recruited few souls among the pickers. Most of them wanted no part of God because the majority of their encounters affirmed God's rejection of them. Rarely did I hear a prayer.

Life outside the camp was more demoralizing than life inside. We were despised by most local residents, white and black. "Colored Only" and "White Only" signs controlled our movement. Whites were openly contemptuous. And local blacks, except for the dandies who preyed on our women, treated us worse than the whites. We despised the whites and resented the blacks.

The feeling of being the outsider weighed on all of us, especially the children. We did not fit in our schools: our clothes were different, our food was "weird," many of us did not read or speak well. Our parents could not vote or belong to organizations. We were strangers.

Immokalee has not changed much since those days. Sure, American blacks have been replaced by Guatemalans, Haitians, and Mexicans, but the conditions are much the same. On December 3, for example, more than 1,000 workers, roughly half of all Immokalee tomato pickers, refused to work in protest of low wages. They are asking growers to raise the piece rate from an average of 40 cents per bucket to 60 cents, which would be their first raise in 20 years.

Gargiulo, Inc., Collier County's largest grower, agreed to pay 45 cents now and 50 cents next November. The other growers have refused to budge. Meanwhile the pickers are sliding deeper into poverty. For me, these are times of déjà vu down on the farm.

"We wouldn't let this happen to dogs"

MARCH 25, 1998

The building is small, windowless, filthy on the outside, squat. Until a few weeks ago, two men, called ticket takers, stood in the doorway and sold condoms for $20 apiece. Inside, the johns had intercourse with the women waiting in dirty, unventilated stalls.

Today, they stand empty, the building boarded up, not a john in sight.

Federal marshals shut down this brothel, along with those in four other Florida cities, after learning that 10 women and 3 girls, all Mexican, were victims in a prostitution ring for migrant farmworkers.

This is how the scheme works: Eight male members of the Cadena family crime ring of Veracruz, Mexico, seek women in Mexico and other Latin American regions and promise them jobs as tomato pickers and house cleaners in the United States. After the women are smuggled into this country, however, they are enslaved and forced to work as prostitutes. The $20 they earn per john goes to their captors. The women can win their freedom only after selling their bodies enough times to pay a so-called transportation fee of $3,000, federal officials said.

Three of the Cadenas, being held in the Palm Beach County jail on federal slavery and prostitution charges, are in the custody of the U.S. Marshal's Service. Officials in Mexico, Texas, and Florida are still trying to find four other members of the crime ring who are wanted on the same charges.

In several ways, the women have been victimized. First, of course, they were tricked and forced into sexual slavery. On top of that, they are pariahs among their own people and are despised in the neighborhoods where the brothels are located. And to make matters worse, they have been in jail since the brothel was shut down.

Last Friday, they appeared before U.S. Magistrate Judge Frank J. Lynch. He informed them that they would be released today on $25,000 bail apiece. Clad in green two-piece uniforms and white socks to protect their ankles from their leg irons, the women seemed oddly out of place as they occupied two rows of the courtroom gallery.

Nothing about them suggested that they are prostitutes, willing or unwilling. The youngest ones giggled and softly spoke in Spanish. The older ones sat silently. They seemed frightened, disoriented, and humiliated as they listened on headphones to translations of the proceedings.

Lou DeBoca, a U.S. Justice Department attorney specializing in indentured-servitude cases, said that the women's futures look bright for the first time since they have been in America. In an elaborate process, U.S. marshals will bring the women to the Mexican consulate after they are freed, then fly them to the Bahamas and back. This flight is necessary so that they will touch foreign soil. Otherwise, they cannot be legally admitted into the United States.

After being released today, the women will be given jobs in companies near a Miami safe house and will be permitted to come and go as they please as long as they remain in south Florida. "We're going to find them good, legitimate jobs, the kind most of them were promised when they were taken to our country," DeBoca said. His biggest concern at this point is ensuring that the women will not flee to Mexico before their captors are brought to trial. "We've got a pretty good safety net in place," he said.

Outside the courtroom, a translator said that federal authorities have been slow to go after criminals operating prostitution rings in migrant communities: "It's like these people don't really matter. It seems like the only thing they're good for is picking our fruits and vegetables. Who cares about them? These kinds of things shouldn't happen to human beings. We wouldn't let this happen to dogs. How can we let men force women to sell their bodies for $20? It makes me sick."

Federal authorities say that they have no real way of determining how many women are being held hostage in migrant communities but fear that the numbers will grow because more money is needed to hire more agents and to establish networks among local officials in U.S. cities and their counterparts south of the border.

Hector Cruz, an advocate for farmworkers, said that women such as these are easy prey because they face severe economic hardship in their countries and are desperate to help support their families. "People like the Cadenas can easily take advantage of these women," he said. "They simply want honest work, but they get sold as sex slaves in America."

40 cents a bucket plus free abuse

April 7, 1999

Isolation and intimidation are the main tools that the owners of Six L's Farms use to control the more than 400 workers in the company's East Naples labor camp, say spokesmen for the Coalition of Immokalee Workers, a nonprofit labor advocacy organization based in Immokalee. The barracks-style camp is in the Everglades, five miles south of Alligator Alley and seven miles east of Naples. For the overwhelming majority who do not own vehicles, the nearest store is an hour's walk along a dusty road.

Before the coalition began showing up a few months ago, the camp did not have a telephone. Pickers were cut off from the outside world. Anyone who did not own a vehicle and who needed to make a call had to trek to a store on U.S. 41. Today, because of media coverage and pressure from the coalition, Six L's owners, the Lipman brothers, have installed four pay telephones.

In addition to blocking workers from communicating by telephone, Six L's prevented them from having visitors at the camp. This practice went on for years, until the coalition complained to company officials and the press.

Each time pickers invited coalition representatives to the camp, the supervisors ordered the advocates off the property. When they agreed to leave, the supervisors would call the police anyway. The advocates would then go to the nearest convenience store and speak with pickers in the parking lot. Recently, a supervisor accompanied by police officers followed the advocates to the store. An officer asked coalition members for identification. After they complied, the cop handed the information to the Six L's supervisor.

A few days ago, coalition workers and a legal adviser returned to the camp at the invitation of pickers. Again, a supervisor ordered them off the property and called the police. "The supervisor told us to get out," said Lucas Benitez, a coalition spokesman. "'This is my camp, and these are my people,' he said, and called the police. I told him that these are not your people. The camp may be yours, but these are not your people. People aren't the property of anyone." This time, though, officers asked the pickers if they had invited the coalition. In one voice, the group shouted "yes." The officers left, telling the supervisor that the coalition had broken no laws. Florida law states, in fact, that farmworkers—living in housing owned by growers—must be treated as tenants with the right to have visitors in their rooms.

Six L's has a long history of calling the police on workers who complain about abuse. "It's an attempt to intimidate the workers," said Greg Asbed, a coalition spokesman. "It's a system of isolation that keeps workers divided and unorganized. As a result, Six L's workers were the last to know that pickers in other companies got raises in the piece rate."

Only now, after the coalition's persistent efforts, have Six L's pickers been given a raise, from 35 to 40 cents per bucket—the industry's lowest rate. This is the company's first rate increase since 1979. Six L's was the last company of the "Big Four" tomato producers in southwest Florida to raise pay last year. The Gargiulo company, for example, raised its rate from 40 to 50 cents per bucket following strikes in Immokalee and after talks with the coalition. After Governor Jeb Bush intervened, Pacific Land Company and Nobles Farms, Inc., followed Gargiulo and gave 5-cent raises, from 40 to 45 cents.

Despite its raise, Six L's refuses to follow other growers by using a variable per-bucket rate in successive picks in the same fields. Because tomatoes are less plentiful each time the same field is picked, Nobles, for example, pays 45 cents on the first pick, 50 on the second, and 55 on the third. Six L's pays a flat rate of 40 cents for all picks. Owners argue that they must pay the low rate because they provide free housing—four people to a 40-square-foot room that has no air conditioning.

Yes, Six L's provides housing, but the trade-off of lower wages for so-called free rent is a net loss for the workers, Asbed said. "The amount lost at the lower piece rate compared to workers picking for Pacific or Nobles is far more than the amount saved by living rent-free at the camp," he said. "Gargiulo also provides housing at reduced rates yet manages to pay the highest piece rate of all of the large area companies."

Even as the coalition attempts to persuade the owners of Six L's to sit down and talk with the pickers, the intimidation and other abuses continue. "Here at Six L's," Asbed said, "you're little more than a tool put into a shed overnight to be taken out in the morning to be put back to work again."

Displaced farmworkers deserve help

August 11, 1999

Esteban Almeda is an American citizen. For nearly 20 years, he was a farm laborer for A. Duda and Sons. He and his family lived in a mobile home on company property on the edge of Lake Apopka. His children were born and reared in the area and attended Lake County schools. Teachers say they were well-adjusted, good students who had plenty of friends. A few weeks ago, the Almedas were forced to move to Mission, Texas, to stay with relatives in a run-down, crowded house.

What has happened to the Almedas is a human rights tragedy. They, along with several hundred other farmworkers like them, are the undeserving victims of an insensitive bureaucracy that takes no interest in their plight.

On June 30, 1998, the St. Johns River Water Management District and the U.S. Department of Agriculture's Natural Resources Conservation Service shut down the muck farms on Lake Apopka's shores. This action was taken to clean up the once-pristine lake that has become a pea-green broth as a result of more than 50 years of farming.

After the farms closed, nearly 400 farmworker families, mostly Hispanic, who lived in labor camps in the impacted area, were forced to move. Under provisions of the Uniform Relocation Assistance and Real Property Acquisition Act of 1970, the workers, many of whom owned their homes, were supposed to receive cash to find new housing. Those forced to relocate had 18 months to apply for assistance. "When the government displaces people, they have to make sure they don't suffer in the interim," said Greg Schell, managing attorney for the Migrant Farmworker Justice Project.

Nearly 14 months later, however, no workers have received a dime.

Why? USDA officials claim the Water Management District waited for months to tell them workers were being displaced. After learning about the displacements, the USDA initially argued that the workers did not qualify for federal money. Schell and his office struggled for weeks to convince the officials otherwise.

But the real crime is that—as the 18-month deadline nears—the USDA still has no system for accepting applications from the farmworkers. "Unfortunately, the process of locating and entering into an agreement with a contractor to begin the process of determining relocation benefits under the URA has been progressing much slower than the department anticipated," wrote David Harris, USDA associate general counsel, in a recent letter to Schell.

"If this had been middle-class white folk, the funding would have been in place before the work," Schell said. "These folks are unfamiliar with the system and reluctant to complain."

Of course, Schell is right. Months before the farms closed, officials had arranged to pay the 14 farmers on the lake's northern shore a whopping $91 million for the land, plus an appraised value of $29 million in equipment acquired during the buy-out.

Advocates for the farmworkers, who are trying to help the workers get money to relocate, are working against the clock in more than one way. Each passing week, workers such as the Almedas are scattering throughout the country, making tracking them more difficult. When, and if, the USDA develops an application process, many workers qualified to receive relocation money will be long gone and may not know that they had money coming to them.

In addition to federal officials, including Agriculture Secretary Dan Glickman, Schell has written to U.S. Senators Bob Graham and Connie Mack and to U.S. Rep. Bill McCollum. Without committing themselves, Mack and McCollum responded with brief letters. Graham, who rarely does anything to help farmworkers, has not responded.

Such foot-dragging is unacceptable. More than a year before the farms were shut down, representatives of the Farmworker Association of Apopka pleaded with the water agency and local government officials to begin looking into relocation benefits for the soon-to-be-unemployed field hands.

Schell said the USDA's Harris claimed the agency probably will start accepting worker applications within a month. "This is the first hopeful thing I've heard," he said. "But we'll just have to wait and see. Time is running out on these farmworkers."

Meanwhile, Esteban Almeda would like to use the money owed him to return to the Apopka area, where he can find a suitable home for his family, where his children can attend school with friends. The relocation project may owe his family as much as $10,000—no small sum for poor people who lost everything to government displacement and bureaucratic insensitivity.

Paradise Found

Florida's best-kept secret

JULY 9, 1995

> I come here to find myself. It is so easy to get lost in the world.
> **John Burroughs**

At least once a month, I drive here to beautiful Lake Mountain Sanctuary, known today as Bok Tower Gardens. It is in Polk County, 85 miles east of St. Petersburg.

Like writer John Burroughs, I come here to find myself, to ease the sting of the insults I receive in letters and telephone calls, to quiet the din of politics ringing in my ears, to temper the guilt of constantly falling short of my personal and professional goals.

Each time I visit Bok, I am renewed and emboldened to accept the next stint in the world outside—a world where the respect you receive is determined mostly by the capriciousness of birth and wealth. At Bok Tower Gardens, the rules are sane. "Here," reads a plaque, "all living things are respected, all people are welcomed."

I felt a change even as I pulled into the parking lot. I felt refreshed, deep down inside. At the café and gift shop, pleasant volunteers served me, answered my questions, and started me on an enriching experience.

From the visitor center, an authentic "cracker" house, I walked only a few paces before the mixed fragrances and bright colors of native plants, and the songs of thousands of birds, enticed me into this 130-acre paradise. No matter which path I choose, I will walk beneath a canopy of live oaks draped with Spanish moss. If a gentle breeze blows, the moss sways, forming lazy semicircles in the light streaming through openings in the foliage above.

On this day, I chose the North Walk, on which I passed a giant crinum with its lilylike flowers. Looking toward a patch of lantana at the base of a palm, I saw a butterfly flittering from petal to petal. I stood there, intrigued that this tiny creature could fill me with such wonder. I wanted to touch its beauty, to experience its freedom.

A mockingbird sang overhead, and two red-bellied woodpeckers dipped toward a petrified pine framed against the sky. A rabbit hopped within a few feet of me. A squirrel begged for food. A spider's web, glistening silver and green, hung across two ferns. A hummingbird, like a friendly ghost, darted in and out of the shadows and alighted on a blooming *Abelmoschus*.

The winding path was trimmed on each side with thousands of camellias and azaleas. As I paused to admire a flowering *Mussaenda* and a row of coleus, my eyes were pulled to the darkest clump of leaves of a bay tree. The two big eyes there belonged to a great horned owl. I wondered if anyone else knew that it was there.

Feeling my secret was safe, I followed a trail that opened onto a bigger one. Leaves crunched beneath my feet, and the sounds echoed for a moment. From here, I could see the reflection pool where two swans maneuvered effortlessly around a big lilypad. As they moved in the direction of the pink bell tower, I looked to the sky.

Music filled the air. I felt as if I were outside of my body. I was at peace. The adults around me spoke in hushed tones. Even the youngest children apprehended that something special was taking place. They, too, were quiet.

The carillon was as melodious as ever. An older couple stood near the bench where I sat in the shade. The man's eyes were closed; the woman stared at the goldfish in the pool. She embraced him. The two of them rocked back and forth, letting the music have its way. Watching them, I recalled a comment attributed to Edward W. Bok, the sanctuary's founder: "Not only must the carillon be in tune, the hearers must be in tune with the carillon."

From there, I walked to the Window by the Pond, my favorite place. No other spot, except the tower, represents Bok Tower Gardens more than this window in the small wooden nature observatory. It faces the pond, letting visitors view birds and water creatures undisturbed. A sign says it all: "Be patient here. This is nature's show and it does not necessarily match our schedules." On this day, after about a 30-minute wait, I saw alligators, egrets, herons, kingfishers, blackbirds, thrushes, gallinules, wood ducks, blue-gray gnatcatchers.

By no accident, Bok Tower Gardens, Florida's best-kept secret, is on the top of Iron Mountain, the highest point on the peninsula. From Lake Pierce Vista, guests can look down upon land that was part of the ocean floor half a million years ago. The fossils of prehistoric creatures—dinosaurs, mastodons, tigers, camels, and lions—are buried beneath centuries of sawtooth palmetto, wild grasses, prickly pear cacti, and scrub oak.

I was looking at humanity's past. I felt small yet significant at the same time. I felt alive. A breeze swept over me, wafting heat and the odor of magnolia. A dragonfly danced before me, pulling me out of my reverie. Turning to depart, I experienced anew the real secret of Bok Tower Gardens: its quietude, a spiritual presence that induces a feeling of contentment.

Again at the reflection pool, I stared at my image, this time silhouetted by the late afternoon sun. A swan passed, sending symmetrical ripples across the dark water. The infinite expanse of the sky shone in the pool, endowing everything with beauty. I was part of it all.

Florida bound: the wild life

JANUARY 5, 1997

Here in Flamingo, less than two hours southwest of Miami, history and nature intersect, creating a panorama of subtle environmental wonders that will give the average tourist and native alike an unexpected sense of the Sunshine State.

Forget about sandy beaches and elegant hotels. Forget about mouse ears and monorails. And Flamingo, like the rest of Everglades National Park, does not hit the visitor with the spectacular scenery and towering vistas of some of the nation's western parks.

But Flamingo is just as special and pristine in a way that inspires awe. It is a step back in time. In 1893, when the ragtag band of sugarcane growers, moonshiners, smugglers, and plume hunters at the rim of Cape Sable established a post office, federal officials ordered them to give their mosquito-infested village a name.

The most cynical residents believed that "End of the World" was perfect. After all, most of them had run away from troubled pasts, and their fishing settlement, accessible only by boat, was at the southernmost tip of the Florida mainland. But finally, observing the flocks of magnificent wading birds that gathered, the settlers became less philosophical and appropriately dubbed their outpost Flamingo.

The village never became a boomtown and was unknown to most of the outside world. In 1947, however, the U.S. Department of the Interior recognized the importance of Flamingo's estuary system to the region's marine fishery and wildlife and made the town part of the Everglades National Park.

All visitors drive into the park, and the trip to Flamingo, 38 miles from the park entrance, is a delight. The first stop should be the park's Visitor Center, which offers information, exhibits, an 18-minute video about the park, and a bookstore and gift shop. This is the place to pick up reading material—books, brochures, and maps—that will help make your stay pleasurable.

On the drive to Flamingo, points of interest dot both sides of the highway. Do not wait for the River of Grass, which is mostly flat, to overwhelm you. It will not. Rather, you should stop at as many of these designated points as you can. Each site has a short trail and a display explaining the flora and fauna for that area. Gumbo Limbo Trail, for instance, is a 1.5-mile trip through a subtropical paradise, a hardwood hammock of gumbo-limbo, strangler fig, live oak, sumac, and red maple.

Pa-hay-okee Trail Boardwalk and Tower are required viewing. The boardwalk takes the visitor to an observation platform overlooking the "true" Everglades, vistas of sawgrass prairie the Indians called "pa-hay-okee," or grassy waters.

Today, Flamingo is not a town per se but a well-maintained oasis for visitors in what are otherwise 1.5 million acres comprising one of the most inhospitable ecosystems on earth. The Flamingo region remains much as it was before the turn of the century—and it has some of the best canoeing and hiking trails in the southern United States. All self-guided trails can be reached from the park's only highway, and many of these trails are clearly marked throughout.

At Coastal Prairie, for example, the hiker steps back into time, along an old road once used by black cotton-pickers and fishermen. Shady button-woods line the trail but regularly give way to open expanses of coastal plants. Eco Pond, entirely freshwater, is a favorite of various wading birds, song-birds, alligators, and other animals. The best times to come here are at sunrise and sunset. Bring plenty of film and binoculars and stake out a quiet spot on the wooden ramp.

Rugged canoeists should try Hells Bay, nine winding miles of sheltered mangrove creeks, ponds, and small bays. This trail got its name, according to old-timers, because it is "hell to get into and hell to get out of." Park Service officials, apparently believing the old coots, have marked the trail with 160 numbered poles.

Noble Hammock is another challenge. A two-mile loop, the trail is a maze of shady, mangroved-lined creeks and small ponds. Sharp corners and narrow passageways make this trail tough even for experienced canoeists to navigate.

Do not hesitate to walk, to get close to the environment. The miles of lush greenery and animal life on the road to Flamingo will take on a special meaning—an intimate experience that will last a lifetime. To visitors who have the time and want to explore and enjoy the real beauty of this part of the Everglades, I suggest that they set up base in Flamingo and stay a few nights or a week. For those wanting the amenities of home, the Flamingo Lodge Marina and Outpost Resort provides the perfect vantage point. Facilities include a modern motel and cabins and a restaurant with a great view of Florida Bay. Breakfast, lunch, and dinner are served. Drinks and light fare are available in the first-floor lounge.

For the hardier visitor who loves sleeping under the stars, the Park Service provides an excellent campground at Flamingo with nearly 100 tent sites and more than 200 sites for motor homes. Ample grills, picnic tables, bathrooms, and showers are available. At the marina store, visitors can buy groceries, gasoline, propane, camping and marine supplies, gifts and souvenirs, and, of course, that essential: insect repellent.

The waters of Florida Bay continue to attract sport fishermen from around the world, and the Flamingo marina offers a wealth of supplies and services. Visitors can rent boats with outboard motors and a variety of fishing tackle. Generally, the fishing is excellent. During my most recent visit,

I saw happy tourists showing off snapper, redfish, and sea trout. Many visitors prefer charter fishing boats, which depart from the marina each day.

Because much of the region is remote and accessible only by water, I highly recommend a day or more on one of the marina's houseboats, either a 37-foot-long Gibson or a 40-foot pontoon. Each boat will sleep six to eight and comes with propane, pots and pans, dishes, linens, navigational charts, and safety equipment.

Renters do not have to be boating experts; skilled, patient staff offer a complete orientation. A houseboat, moreover, provides great photo opportunities and chances to get intimate glimpses of some of the park's most exotic birds and other wildlife. The marina also rents bicycles and canoes.

Those who prefer organized sightseeing can take advantage of daily staff-operated cruises into Florida Bay and the mangrove estuary. A tram tour offers a good introduction, and Park Service personnel conduct daily workshops and demonstrations during the winter season.

After arriving at Flamingo, the end of the road, you can relax and enjoy a drink and good meal. Then, before turning in for the evening, prepare yourself for sunset over Florida Bay—one of the most spectacular sites in North America.

Now, a warning: beware of mosquitoes! Stuart McIver, in his book *True Tales of the Everglades*, writes of the old days: "One of the settlers' worst enemies were mosquitoes. Stories abound that they had been known to kill cows and mules left out for the night." At any rate, if you follow these dos and don'ts, provided by the National Park Service, you should enjoy your visit to Flamingo:

DON'T roll down your windows when stopping along roadsides to observe wildlife.

DO avoid grassy areas. Walk only on paved areas.

DON'T wear colognes or perfumes.

DO apply mosquito repellent before getting out of a vehicle.

DO wear long pants, long sleeves, and closed shoes.

DON'T leave doors open longer than necessary.

DO avoid areas under trees and in the shade of buildings.

A little wilderness close to home

November 3, 1999

Wilderness is always on my mind.

I am a Florida native, a dwindling breed, who remembers our peninsula when it was more pristine than developed, more sand dune than pavement, more earthy green and brown than kitschy pastels, more shoreline than seawall.

As a St. Petersburg resident, I escape the city as often as possible to recapture at least a handful of Old Florida. Jumping into my Blazer and leaving the area for the weekend is not always an option. During the last four years, I have learned how to enjoy Old Florida within a 30-mile radius of my home.

My secret? A yellow kayak.

When I need to stay in town, I haul my kayak to Fort De Soto Park and put in at Mullet Key Bayou along Anderson Boulevard near the fort. For visitors who have never been on the side of Anderson away from the beach, a world of beauty awaits in the backcountry, as it were.

Last Sunday, I paddled from this site to the family picnic area and then to the southernmost islet near Sister Key, all the while witnessing the perpetual dance of seaweeds on both sides of the kayak as I skimmed across the flats. Hundreds of insects and spiders sinuated themselves through the brine.

Near the shore, I enjoyed a sense of being in the wilderness. A strong breeze hailed from the Gulf of Mexico, making the going challenging in open areas. I saw several pink flamingos, two with white necks, feeding in and around the fingerlike roots of mangroves. Several varieties of hawks surveyed the shallows. Snowy egrets, spoonbills, and ibises waded in the flats, where seaweeds had collected on top of the water. Cormorants dried themselves on posts and tree limbs, and brown pelicans hovered nearby in hopes of getting a free lunch.

Everywhere, mullet leaped into the air, sometimes startling me. As I rounded the bend near the picnic area and entered deep water, several dolphins broke the surface of the blue expanse and disappeared just as quickly. Here I stopped to rest, waiting to see if my companions would show themselves again. About 30 seconds later, the dolphins, like children in a giant pool, circled my kayak and suddenly went out of sight. I did not see them again until I entered Bunce's Pass and approached the open waters of the islet where I took out.

Here the shore is snowy white, and I took off my sneakers to enjoy the soft sand. Overhead, laughing gulls circled and glided in the wind drafts. To the east, I saw a dark shadow creeping across the sand. As I approached, the shadow moved faster, its shape changing with each second. On closer inspection, I realized that the shadow was an army of ghost crabs. When a gull descended, every crab disappeared inside tiny holes in the sand. After I backed away and the gulls retreated into the distance, these clawed apparitions came out and cautiously marched toward the water's edge. Each movement of my feet would make them stop.

I walked around the entire islet and went for a swim in the cold water, where I saw starfish, brittle stars, sea cucumbers, and sea urchins. Back on land, I discovered the petrified shell of a horseshoe crab at the base of a tree. Called a "living fossil," the horseshoe crab is not a crab at all but one of the last of an ancient species closely akin to scorpions and spiders.

As the breeze swept the area, a stand of sea oats bent from left to right beneath a bank of pure-white clouds that seemed to touch the distant sea. I could not believe that I was only a few miles from downtown St. Petersburg, where many residents are oblivious to this wilderness paradise.

On my return trip through Bunce's Pass, I crossed to the other side of Mullet Key Bayou and skirted the shore of St. Christopher Key. Farther on, I approached an oyster bar, where two raccoons feasted undisturbed. Again I sensed that I was in a wild place that people had somehow missed and had not ruined with their luxury homes and effluents. In the distance, giant mangroves sheltered a small rookery.

Viewing the setting sun, I let the kayak drift for about 10 minutes before it hit a mudflat and made me realize that I had a long way to paddle back to land. As I paddled, I could not keep my eyes off the enormous orange ball falling into the Gulf of Mexico. A blue heron flew overhead, and gentle breakers licked at the sides of the kayak as my Blazer came into view.

My next kayak excursion will be a day on the Little Manatee River a few miles to the south. After that, I may try to paddle the Braden River, then the winding estuaries of the Ding Darling National Wildlife Refuge.

Race Matters

We should celebrate our cross-racial friendships

JANUARY 22, 1995

American novelists Bebe Moore Campbell and Joyce Carol Oates met recently at the request of the *New York Times Magazine* to discuss gender and race. Campbell is black, and Oates is white.

Campbell, whose latest novel, *Brothers and Sisters*, is a riveting account of the friendship between a white woman and a black woman, identified a simple way to greatly improve race relations in the United States: "One of the things that really strikes me about America, and it's kind of the under-reported story, is that in spite of all of the racial trauma we go through, there are black and white people who like each other very much, even love each other. And I'm not even talking about romantic love. I'm talking about males liking each other and respecting each other, and women. We don't really talk about those friendships and how to make more of them."

What a great notion—talking about our cross-racial friendships and making more of them—especially today, when race consciousness is more widespread than ever, when racism seems to be growing deeper than ever, and when the race card is being used more effectively than ever by politicians, attorneys, and other groups that gain from such conflict.

But do we need to discuss our cross-racial friendships? Should we bring attention to them?

I believe that we should. We talk a lot about role models and their value in teaching children right from wrong, showing them the heights to which they can soar, demonstrating the rewards of leading decent, law-abiding lives. Why, then, should we not use our friendships in the same way? Think of the good that we, black and white adults, could do if we were honest about our friendships, if we discussed these relationships with our children and encouraged them to emulate us.

I cherish the memory of my first white friend, whom I met in 1963 when we were both freshmen at a college in Texas. I believe that our friendship holds lessons for others. She was the young wife of my language professor and one of two white students attending this historically black school. Because I had been reared in the South and had had no intimate contact with whites, especially women, I was initially uncomfortable that she followed me everywhere. We became friends because we had a lot in common, particularly our love of books. Some of the happiest times in my life came when her husband drove us to bookstores in Dallas twice a month. We would spend the entire day there, exploring rows and rows of books, daydreaming about the brooding best-sellers we would write. I would spend every cent I had.

She and her husband taught me to play bridge and chess, two games I had only heard of before college. But the lasting lessons they taught me emerged over time, as our relationship seasoned. He was at least 40 years older than his wife. His kindly face, with a thick mustache and bushy eyebrows, was framed by an Albert Einstein head of hair.

I loved to watch and listen to him lecture, his hands trembling slightly, the ill-fitting tweed jacket smothering his long, skinny arms, the thick Hungarian accent, full of caution, searching for just one pair of sympathetic ears among a sea of black faces. Recognizing his distress, I always made a point of raising my hand and reciting in class. "Please keep responding in class," she would say. "It makes him feel like he's doing his job."

Slowly, the couple's amazing past unfolded as I inquired about the many strangers who frequently came to their home in the evenings. The professor had been a leading member of the anti-Communist movement when the revolution broke out in Budapest in 1956. A bounty was placed on his head. When the Communists installed former Premier Imre Nagy to lead the new government, the professor fled to New York, bringing along the frightened teenage girl he had met one night in a field near the Austrian border.

Using connections in New York, he obtained a work visa and eventually came to the Texas college. During the three years that I knew the couple in Texas, their home was a clearinghouse for other Hungarian immigrants trying to start new lives in the United States. Their telephone rang constantly, hot food was always on the stove, and cots were everywhere. Their guests were so deferential and would disappear as quietly as they came. They always left behind the most interesting books, magazines, and newspapers.

The husband died in 1986. The wife, now in her 50s, is an English professor and a poet. She still writes to me and telephones regularly. I adore and admire her. Besides teaching me that a man and woman can have a genuine platonic friendship, she taught me that I am defined by my skin color only if I choose to be so defined.

She taught me this lesson by treating me as a human, as another world traveler. She made me, a boy from a backward southern town, feel good about myself. Our endless discussions of literature, philosophy, and history made me believe in my own intelligence. I learned to like myself. I learned that we should not choose our friends according to race. Friends should happen. They should be the natural outgrowth of common interests. Friends are soul mates.

Because of her influence, I have many white friends today. I celebrate these friendships because they are special. Unfortunately, many blacks will condemn me for admitting that I have white friends. Some will applaud. I do not know what whites will say.

Do I care? Yes, I do. I care because by not celebrating our cross-racial friendships, we cheat our children of the opportunity to create a peaceful society. They should know that white and black people can be friends.

Black culture is part of the whole

June 11, 1995

Take this pop quiz. In two or three sentences, explain the intellectual significance of at least 10 of the following accomplished African-Americans: Amiri Baraka, Charles Waddell Chestnutt, Meta Warrick Fuller, Zora Neale Hurston, Aaron Douglas, Palmer Hayden, Alice Walker, Ishmael Reed,

Nikki Giovanni, William H. Johnson, Toni Morrison, John Edgar Wideman, Augusta Savage, Lorraine Hansberry, Phillis Wheatley.

Did you pass? If you are white and attend or attended an American college or university, you probably have heard of no more than six of these novelists, poets, painters, playwrights, and sculptors. Most of your black peers, by the way, would not score much better. If, however, we give the same quiz to our European counterparts, many would score higher.

Why? The answer is familiar but one that needs repeating: Racism is so widespread and institutionalized in this nation that black intellectuals and artists are virtually unknown, even to many of the learned. America does not value black culture enough to accept its creators and their artifacts as integral to the nation's intellectual life. In fact, many conservative intellectuals and their political supporters have condemned multicultural attempts to recognize and teach more black culture.

The opposite is true and has been occurring for decades in many European nations. This fact was the focus of a recent Associated Press article about the Collegium for African American Research that met in Puerto De La Cruz, Canary Islands. As its name suggests, the collegium is a group of European scholars committed to studying black life and its relationship to American culture. Many of these academics first experienced black culture as children after World War II through the jazz recordings on U.S. Armed Forces Radio. Josef Jarab, rector of Palackeho University in Olomouc, Czech Republic, told the AP that when he was young, black jazz let him "fly to freedom." As an adult, he played a major role in making courses in black literature and music part of his university's curriculum.

"There is an enormous amount of skepticism among European students about what America represents in the world," Maria Diedrich, a professor of American studies at the University of Münster in Germany, told the AP. "But at the same time there is a fascination with the country, and much of this has to do with African-American culture."

Although black studies have been a staple of many American university curricula since the 1960s, these programs—because of institutionalized indifference toward black culture—are not as effective as those in Europe. And here is why. Conferees at the collegium produced evidence showing that many American campuses teach this curriculum as black studies courses per se, often physically isolated from other parts of the campus life. An American professor, for example, will spend weeks fleshing out meaning in August Wilson's play *Fences*. But the professor will not show how *Fences* contributes to the whole of society. Most respected anthologies of American literature contain black selections, but even they are taught as black literature, not as American literature. On many of our campuses, black culture is a ghetto in the ivory tower. As a result, few white students leave our campuses with the knowledge to discuss competently the major work of a single black intellectual.

European professors, according to those attending the Canary Islands conference, integrate black life into American or English studies programs. They do not teach black subjects in isolation. Another difference between the two systems is that most black studies lecturers in the United States are black, while most in Europe are white. This fact alone makes the two systems seem like night and day—like different views of the world. The obvious advantage in having more whites teach black courses is that the courses more easily blend into the curriculum and are more acceptable to a wider audience.

American universities' treatment of black culture shortchanges everyone, and it especially keeps young whites ignorant of the many contributions their black compatriots make to the various academic disciplines. Such ignorance produces distorted views of blacks and discourages the urge to learn more about them.

Ironically, many black students leave traditionally white colleges and universities with a broader liberal arts education than their white peers. In my own case, my black classmates and I, as English majors, not only read every Dead White European Male author tossed our way, but also read and discussed every black writer we could get our hands on. Today I believe that most of us, compared to our white classmates who did not read blacks, have a broader understanding of American culture. A few of those white classmates have said as much.

Despite the dire warnings of neoconservatives and their apologists that the left is trying to kill off classical knowledge, I believe that, for the good of the nation, U.S. colleges and universities should adopt the European approach to teaching black life: treat it as a natural, inseparable part of America's intellectual esprit.

"Superblack," honorary white

September 24, 1995

Most commentators, because of either ignorance or political correctness, are disregarding the less benign reasons for Gen. Colin Powell's wide appeal among white people as a serious presidential candidate. The comments of *Washington Post* editorial writer E. J. Dionne Jr. are typical: "Powell's appeal is that he is a compelling human being who has lived an admirable life, overcome obstacles and demonstrated leadership. He exudes strength—or, as they prefer in presidential politics, 'character.'"

Dionne is right. But millions of other blacks are compelling human beings who live admirably, overcome obstacles, demonstrate leadership, and exude strength and "character." Yet white folk do not ask them to live rent-free at 1600 Pennsylvania Avenue.

Dionne, along with others, simply has presented the safe, generic side of Colinmania, the side that does not distinguish Powell from other Beltway operatives. The other side, the underside, shows that much of Powell's allure is cloaked in the complex race psychology, the collective guilt, the double standards, the desire for atonement, and the hypocrisy that define black-white relations.

Powell is, in fact, one of that rare breed of black men who has become an honorary white person. And one of the most powerful sources of Powell's acceptance is his fair skin. This truth will disturb many readers because it taps into an ugly strand of the American character most of us would rather ignore. Cox Newspapers columnist Howard Kleinberg expressed it best: "Racist white America always has had an easier time accepting a light-skinned black than a dark-skinned one."

Whites who believe that they like Powell the man should ponder Kleinberg's words, and they should consider yet another source of their adulation: Powell is the offspring of poor Jamaican immigrants who came to America of their own volition, who succeeded in the mythic tradition of Ellis Island. Would these same whites adore Powell if he were an equally successful, American-bred, dark-skinned homeboy from the Mississippi Delta, whose parents had been on welfare?

Another reason that many white people like the idea of a Powell candidacy is that it would give them a ready-made chance to prove that they are not racists. Although Powell supports affirmative action, many right-wing whites will support him. Sadly, his presence gives these hypocrites and their strident, phony arguments against affirmative action an undeserved reprieve.

In a literal sense, he gives all reluctant bigots something palpably black that they can support, a specific name on a ballot. Symbolically, however, Powell is one of those Ralph Ellison ectoplasms to whom hypocritical whites refer when they say, "Why, some of my best friends are black."

Ultimately, Powell's "sensible centrism" notwithstanding, he appeals to white America because he is the quintessential "superblack," the ideal my grandparents and other older blacks wanted their grandchildren to become: "If you want to make it, you have to be better than white people. You have to be the best."

If any black person is to enjoy broad white appeal, he cannot be, say, a Ronald Reagan, a Jimmy Carter, a George Bush, a Dan Quayle, a Phil Gramm, a Bob Dole, a Patrick Buchanan, a Bill Clinton. In other words, a successful black cannot be average or merely competent. He must be larger than life—a Moses come down from Mount Sinai, a Horatio Alger wowing Wall Street. He must be a Colin Luther Powell, the nation's youngest chairman of the Joint Chiefs of Staff and the first black to hold that position.

Powell already is etched in white people's fantasies of what a "good" black can and should be. He is, as *Chicago Tribune* columnist Clarence Page writes, a flesh-and-blood affirmation "that the American dream and its fabled meritocracy still work, that all of us, regardless of race, creed or even gender, can get our just rewards by playing by the rules."

Page is right, of course. But because Powell is a superblack, his uniqueness prevents him from being a black Everyman. If he becomes president, whites can respect him while simultaneously despising the rest of the black race. And, unfortunately, this former four-star general flies too high above radar to be an accessible role model for most troubled young black males who could benefit from his example.

Nonetheless, Colinmania is authentic. Few men of any stripe in U.S. military history have been promoted as quickly as Powell. And few things endeared him to whites more than the moments when he held the world rapt as he pointed his baton at the map during the televised Persian Gulf war briefings and explained, in vintage GI minimalism, the nation's mission: "Our strategy in going after this [Saddam Hussein's] army is very simple. First we are going to cut it off, and then we are going to kill it." This was the stuff of legend. The setting was a perfect stage for hero making. It was complete with the high adventure of lightning-fast aircraft, mega-guns, massive tanks, and Americans stalking the evil enemy—all commanded by a superblack.

If he does not open too many veins during the next several months, Powell will remain an enigmatic figure, as most superheroes are. As the nation's first superblack, his personal capital will rise and his mystique will grow, teasing the imaginations and consciences of white Americans seeking atonement.

Image of Betty reflects our ethnic health

MARCH 24, 1996

Have you heard the one about Betty Crocker? She backed into an oven and burned her buns. Just joking, folks.

All right, let's get serious about Betty Crocker, an icon of the American kitchen. Have you seen her new look? That's right. On the occasion of her 75th anniversary, America's most-beloved baker has been recoiffured, tanned, face-lifted, nipped, tucked, liposuctioned, and sartorized, as it were.

Today, instead of being "a paragon of white Middle America: a cheery homemaker with blue eyes, creamy skin and June Cleaver features," as the *Wall Street Journal* calls her, Betty has been digitally "morphed" into the nation's latest multicultural pinup. General Mills, Betty's owner, re-created her using the best features of 75 real women—from ages "18 to 118," from many ethnicities—who mailed in photographs of themselves.

Perhaps Betty's new look is intended to measure the state of womanliness in the republic. I don't know. One thing I do know, however, is that Betty's image (along with that of Aunt Jemima, which I'll say a few words about later) is not only a bellwether of the woman's place, or perceived place, in America but also a reflection of our collective ethnic health. By studying Betty's changing physical traits, we can ascertain which persona females assumed at any given time in recent U.S. history and, subsequently, understand American society at large.

The first Betty, ladled out in 1921 to answer customers' questions about baking, isn't represented in a portrait. She is a mere signature that, for a time, becomes as familiar as that of John Hancock. Betty is depicted in a portrait for the first time in the 1930s, as a somber, "motherly" figure who accurately reflects the strong, nurturing women of the Great Depression era.

In 1955—as the economy merrily sails along, as suburbia becomes the new Eden with the "housewife" as the new Eve, as President Eisenhower signs into law the $1-an-hour minimum wage, as television comes into its own, offering facts, fantasy, and fun—Betty is given her first smile, befitting an era of prosperity.

Ten years later, Betty changes again, reflecting the angst among the populace. Some highlights: the United States takes the offensive in Vietnam, causing Alice Hertz, a 72-year-old war protester, to sit down on a Detroit street and set herself on fire; an assassin's bullets kill Malcolm X; Watts burns, baby. And how does Betty respond? Appropriately, she casts off her smile, ditches her white collar, and dons a pearl choker.

In 1972, Gloria Steinem creates *Ms.* magazine, heralding a new age of freedom and entrepreneurship for women. And Betty? She wears business clothes for the first time. This makeover, her owners claim, symbolizes " the American woman's newly significant role outside the home."

In 1986, the Supreme Court endorses affirmative action as a remedy for past discrimination against minorities and, of course, women. Betty—recognizing the ruling's significance to her sisters in real life—sports a bow tie. Betty's new power-attire, General Mills says, shows her as a "professional" who is "as comfortable in the board room as she was in the dining room."

And now, on her platinum anniversary, the only things left of the original Betty are her red outfit and vaunted ability to bake unblemished buns. Barry Wegener, a General Mills spokesman, says the company wants Betty to reflect the nation's diverse consumer population: "The ultimate goal is to have this picture represent all the women in America."

The artist who painted Betty's new image says, "I've portrayed a woman who is exceptionally knowledgeable, yet imminently approachable and genuinely caring."

Perhaps. Perhaps not. Either way, the whole effort is noble, which brings us to Betty's African-American counterpart, Aunt Jemima, who made her debut in 1889 as a fat, jolly, black, black woman wearing a kerchief wrapped around her head, a loose-fitting feed sack dress, and holding a wooden rolling pin at the ready.

But Auntie J. too, has seen a few makeovers that directly reflect the nation's evolving, albeit ambivalent, relationship with blacks. She has gone from being a slave cook—a laughable creature lacking a Christian soul—to a modern housewife with a bright smile, intelligent features, walnut-tinted skin, and "good hair."

When I place the new Betty Crocker alongside Aunt Jemima, I sense that they could be next-door neighbors who could prepare a multiethnic meal together that might include spareribs, tamales, pasta, chow mein, braunschweiger, apple pie, and herring in cream sauce.

Yes, I already hear the denunciations of General Mills for bowing to political correctness, for transforming Betty Crocker—an identifiable WASP—into Everywoman. I hear, too, the shrill voices calling me a damned liberal or worse. So be it, for I know that I would feel comfortable sitting any day at the table of both Betty Crocker and Aunt Jemima for a meal.

Alas, though, I must confess that I draw the line when the fates of certain cultural icons are threatened. Take, say, the case of Ace Hardware. Remember its jingle, "Ace is the place with the helpful hardware man"? Well, Ace now advertises itself as "the place with the helpful hardware folk."

Egad! What, pray tell, are "hardware folk?"

And while we're on the subject, what are they planning for Uncle Ben? Haven't seen much of him lately. Has the Big Guy, along with his rice, been converted? And into what? Will he reappear sometime soon as a trash-talking dude with chiseled pecs?

To lift a community: a death, a riot, and responsibility

NOVEMBER 3, 1996

In his 1994 article "Newspapers' Quest for Racial Candor," former *Milwaukee Journal* editor Sig Gissler wrote: "Race—it is America's rawest nerve and most enduring dilemma. From birth to death, race is with us, defining, dividing, distorting."

As our rawest nerve, race is a subject most Americans try to avoid. Now, though, in the wake of the recent riot, St. Petersburg residents know that long ago race turned this city into two camps. Here is where blacks, some of them armed with guns, battled police and burned and looted businesses their relatives and neighbors depended on.

But because race is encrypted in our every word and thought about the riot, we are engaged in a skewed debate laced with personal attacks, lies, and dangerous fallacies. The result is that we cannot honestly search for the root causes of and solutions to our enduring problems.

Some background to the crisis: As has happened elsewhere, white cops chase a speeding car driven by a black male in a low-income, mostly black area. After the stop, one of the cops shoots and kills the driver. In this case, which occurred on the afternoon of October 24, police say that the officer fired because the car "lurched" forward. Witnesses say, however, that the car "inched" forward.

My purpose is not to sort out what happened at that intersection. Instead, it is to examine some of the issues that spokespersons on all sides of the tragedy do not talk about—such as a "culture of poverty" or a "culture of welfare."

As word spread that a white cop had shot a black teen, a mob gathered, pelting police with rocks and bottles. More police arrived. One officer was shot in the shoulder, and a few journalists were injured. At nightfall, the burning and looting began. Officials imposed a state of emergency. Twenty arrests were made. National Guard troops were encamped.

Even before the flash point had cooled, black activists were saying that racism had killed 18-year-old TyRon Mark Lewis. Time may prove them right. But many activists went off track, claiming that police brutality is what ails St. Petersburg's black neighborhoods. They are wrong. The problems are systemic.

Still, a veteran black city commissioner added to the volatile mix by saying that white officers come to the black community with "their minds cocked and their guns cocked." Many blacks of this mind-set justify destroying property in their own communities and assaulting white motorists. White liberals also weighed in, arguing that the residual effects of slavery, centuries of racism, poverty, joblessness, bad housing, misery, low self-esteem, and the Republican-led 104th Congress caused the conditions that ignited the violence.

Most rational leaders on all sides agree that unemployment and low earnings have destabilized the riot zone more than anything else, prompting one writer to label the incident a "poverty riot." The 1990 census found that more than 96 percent of area residents are black, while citywide the number is 20 percent black. Median income for the city is $23,577 annually but $14,000 for this sector. Citywide, 14 percent of residents are below the poverty level, while the figure stands at 37 percent here. Twenty-three percent of households are on welfare, while citywide the number is 6 percent. And 10 percent of residents 16 and older are jobless.; for the entire city, the number is 5 percent.

These statistics show the stark disparities between this area and the rest of the city. And, for my purpose, they form the basis for discussing a culture of poverty, which cannot be separated from race, as a possible source of many intractable problems in the riot zone.

In his latest book, *When Work Disappears: The New World of the New Urban Poor,* based on research conducted in Chicago, Harvard professor William Julius Wilson argues that long-term economic decay breeds "cultural traits and behaviors" that trap inner-city residents in misery. A close adviser to President Bill Clinton on social issues, Wilson writes that low wages, the perpetual failure to get and hold steady work, the flight of positive role models from the neighborhoods, and the lack of viable community networking have eroded moral standards. As these conditions persist, the sense of powerlessness widens and deepens. The result is that irrational, self-destructive behavior and lifestyles and negative attitudes become the norm. In time, these pathologies assume a life of their own.

The greatest tragedy is the perception of the family. In a recent *New York Times Magazine* article, Wilson made this point by comparing inner-city blacks and other groups, especially Mexicans, who come to the United States with a solid commitment to the traditional family unit, who view men as the main wage earner. Although Mexicans may accept the extramarital affairs of men, single pregnant women are "a source of opprobrium, anguish or great concern." Parents of the pregnant woman and those of her lover pressure the couple to marry.

"The family norms and behavior in inner-city black neighborhoods stand in sharp contrast," Wilson writes. "The relationships between inner-city black men and women, whether in a marital or non-marital situation, are often fractious and antagonistic. Inner-city black women routinely say that black men are hopeless as either husbands or fathers and that more of their time is spent on the streets than at home.

"The [black] men in the inner city generally feel that it is much better for all parties to remain in a non-marital relationship until the relationship dissolves rather than to get married and then have to get a divorce."

In *When Work Disappears*, Wilson maintains that a culture of poverty has been most destructive in employment. Work "constitutes a framework for daily behavior and patterns of interaction because it imposes disciplines and regularities," he writes. "The fact that blacks reside in neighborhoods and are engaged in social networks and households that are less conducive to employment than those of other ethnic and racial groups in the inner city clearly has a negative effect on their search for work. In the eyes of employers . . . these differences render inner-city blacks less desirable as workers, and therefore many are reluctant to hire them."

Currently, St. Petersburg officials are asking the federal government for $28 million for an antipoverty effort. The bulk of it will be wasted, however, if plans ignore the culture of poverty, especially the harmful effects of poor employability skills. Tough conditions, including specific outcomes, should be placed on groups and agencies wanting to participate.

Officials also should consider some of Wilson's proposed solutions to the inequalities threatening inner cities. As a first step, the mayor and others should establish public-private partnerships that have real, not token, long-term goals to fight poverty. City and school authorities should create policies that require youngsters to perform at high levels before they can receive diplomas. And black students should be taught to encourage one another to meet these high standards. "Students who meet high standards are not only prepared for work but they are also ready for technical training and other kinds of post-secondary education," Wilson writes.

The $28 million certainly should include plans to improve child care in the area so that parents, many of them single moms, can afford to work and buy health insurance at the same time. Private and public institutions could jointly begin to solve this serious problem.

Far too many parents in the riot zone have poor parenting skills. Leaders should establish programs to deal with this problem. The mayor and the commission would be smart to look next door and seek the wisdom of people such as Johnnie Mack, a 70-year-old neighborhood leader, who understands the culture of poverty. "All I can say for the neighborhood is that parents, they need to get up and teach their children to have respect for the law and respect for themselves," she told the *St. Petersburg Times*. "You got to respect yourself before you can respect someone else."

In the United States, "history is against you"

AUGUST 17, 1997

We Americans, like people elsewhere in the world, often need the dispassionate eyes of outsiders to help us understand our problems, especially the controversial ones that lay bare our deepest emotions. The editors of the *New York Times Magazine* obviously had this notion in mind as they planned the June 8 issue. Correspondents from 18 countries were invited to share their views of the United States. For me, the most important views were those of South African writer Nadine Gordimer in an essay titled "Separate."

Much of Gordimer's work, for which the author won the Nobel Prize for literature in 1991, reflects a liberal approach to problems of race and repression in her native land. Her South African sensibilities—the unique wisdom of an enlightened Caucasian opponent and survivor of apartheid—give her an insight that we Americans, white and black, should try to comprehend. She states that while traveling in the United States from the 1950s until a few years ago, she mixed freely among many American blacks, both ordinary and famous, in their homes and in public places. On visits to this country since 1994, however, she has met few American-born blacks.

She meets so few black Americans these days because they "do not want to mix with whites, however much potential compatibility is beckoning to be recognized," she writes. "The old, old answer I think not only survives but seems to have grown in bitterness, for reasons [of economics and opportunity] Americans know best: When you have been so long rejected, your collective consciousness tells you that the open-door, open-arms invitation has come too late. You gain your self-respect by saying 'no.'"

As an example of gaining self-respect by saying "no," Gordimer points to black American playwright August Wilson, winner of two Pulitzers. He wants "black theater for blacks only—black writers, actors, audiences."

Gordimer sees lunacy in Wilson's separatist crusade: "If even the doors of the arts are slammed shut, how shall people find their common humanity? And how to live, in the end, without it? The theater Wilson advocates is Greek tragedy, where wars and violence become the only means of communication, the curse of the gods on humans. Why do self-respect, identity, rest on this ancient and terrible tragedy of white rejection of black?"

Gordimer's answers, comparing conditions in South Africa and the United States, are instructive to anyone sincere about race relations here. Race in South Africa, in fact, shines a bright light on race in America.

In her estimation, the more than three centuries of racist exploitation and oppression of black South Africans under apartheid are unequaled in human history. But despite their perpetual suffering, Gordimer argues, South African blacks "have had their own earth under their feet. Despite neglect in official education, their languages have remained intact as mother tongues. Their names are their own ancestral names.

"Nothing—neither cruel apartheid denigration nor liberal paternalism—has destroyed their identity. They know who they are. In relations with whites, now that everyone is equal before the law, they do not have to say 'no' in order to assert pride of identity or self-respect. It is for the average white to discover, earn and affirm a valid identity in a society with a black majority and non-racial government."

And despite the intransigence of many lifelong racists and the corrosive effects of lingering injustices, many black South Africans are enjoying a large measure of economic empowerment, even in businesses tied to the stock market. Moreover, Gordimer writes, ethnic, political, and cultural bonds are growing among blacks and whites throughout South Africa. She sees a land of vitality and hope, a place where the grand experiment of a "non-racial" society still has a chance to succeed.

Now, compared to South Africa, what about relations between blacks and whites in America? The following observations of Gordimer took on profound meaning for me as I covered the NAACP convention last month in Pittsburgh. For the first time in many years, NAACP members openly supported "separate" public schools for black children. Anger and disillusionment filled the convention center.

What is Gordimer's assessment of black-white relations in America? "It is unfortunate to have to say it: History is against you in the U.S.A.," she writes. "Americans cannot give back to blacks a lost identity; black Americans are reluctant to accept that that identity cannot be found in an avatar of apartheid.

"They are all Americans, and whether the whites like it or not, and whether the blacks like it or not, a common destiny has to be worked out. Alas, Martin Luther King is dead, and you have no Mandela. A common identity is not simple. It's not simple in South Africa either, but . . . we are doing better than the U.S.A."

Unfortunately, I agree. Here in America, the wounds of resentment and hatred may be too deep, the cancer of denial may be too metastasized, and our morality may be too relativistic for us to heal ourselves.

If only we, like South Africans, had a real way to start over. We do not. We have had the big moments in our social history, and the changes have been insufficient. The Emancipation Proclamation, for example, ended slavery, but the harsh legacy of the "Peculiar Institution" endures. And affirmative action, created in modern times to remedy old wrongs, has been rejected by the very beneficiaries of our nation's racist heritage. Our future, therefore, is our past: a labyrinth of personal and institutionalized abuses that, either out of habit or expediency or willfulness, we will visit time and again.

The many and varied uses of an ugly word

OCTOBER 19, 1997

Well, here we go again.

Last time, we African-Americans tried to legitimize a bastardized version of standard formal English exotically dubbed "Ebonics." Now we want to deconstruct how dictionaries—the world's repository of language—define words.

In this most recent mess, a woman named Delphine Abraham, a computer operator in Ypsilanti, Michigan, and another woman named Kathryn Williams, curator of the Museum of African American History in Flint, Michigan, have launched a movement to remove the word "nigger" from *Merriam-Webster's Collegiate Dictionary*. It defines "nigger" as "a black person—usually taken to be offensive."

Abraham, Williams, NAACP President Kweisi Mfume, and others are making the uninformed, outrageous claim that the word's mere existence in *Merriam-Webster's* legitimizes it, perhaps even for normal use. "I can't believe," Abraham said, "that in 1997, you can look up 'nigger' in the dictionary and it says 'a black person.'"

Those who want "nigger" stricken from dictionaries are misguided and should mind their day jobs. Indeed, "nigger" is the worst of racial slurs, but it also has a complex history and multitudinous uses. First used disparagingly in the 16th century to denote a black person, African-Americans use it both pejoratively and lovingly among themselves. Virtually all gangsta rap wraps itself around "nigga."

All that said, I want to use this opportunity to open a linguistic window for the rest of the world, especially the white world, into the rich use of "nigger" in black culture. The various uses of the ugly word reflect, in fact, the ability of black Americans to buffet a hostile environment by creating neologisms, some endearing, from an epithet.

Following is an abridged glossary, culled from *Juba to Jive: A Dictionary of African-American Slang and Black Talk — Words and Phrases from the Hood to the Amen Corner*:

Nigger breaker: a slave driver; an overseer on a plantation.

Niggerdemos: slave variant term for Nicodemus of the Bible.

Nigger driver: a white man hired to oversee and drive black prisoners in picking cotton or some other fieldwork; specifically, the overseer at Parchman Penitentiary, which, as late as 1957, was still run like a brutal plantation.

Nigger flicker: a long-blade knife or a razor carried in the pocket as a weapon of self-defense or attack.

Nigger heaven: the balcony in a theater where black people had to sit if they were to see a film or a performance. The term originated in Harlem.

Nigger in charge, or *"head nigger in charge"*: used ironically to refer to a black boss.

Nigger luck: a term used ironically referring to good luck; putting the best face on a bad, if not tragic, situation.

Nigger night: Saturday night.

Nigger rich: having a pocket roll of singles covered with a $20 bill; maintaining outward signs of wealth without real money.

Nigger rig: any makeshift device or structure of poor quality.

Nigger mess: any messy personal or community affair of African-Americans; something that should be resolved in-house, within the black community or black "family."

Niggamation: used in reference to the practice of speedups on automobile and other industrial assembly lines, where the majority are black, in order to increase productivity without having to pay workers overtime wages. This once-widespread practice often led to serious injuries. The workers said that the companies increased productivity by using black labor, not automation—thus niggamation.

Black Talk offers other interesting contextual uses of the word "nigger" and its variant "nigga":

"Now that brotha, see, he ain like them ol' e-lights, he real, he is shonuff nigga," meaning that this black man is "culturally black and rooted in black-ness and the African-American Experience."

"That party was live; it was wall-to-wall niggas there," meaning many blacks were at the party.

Source magazine uses these descriptions of NBA superstar Charles Bark-ley: "Charles calls [black men who] push and fight '90s niggers. While with the Philadelphia 76ers, Barkley answered the press about a bad shot he had made: 'I'm a '90s nigger. . . . They want their black athletes to be Uncle Toms. I told the white boys you've never heard of a '90s nigger. We do what we want to do.'"

If the editors of *Merriam-Webster's* and other mainline dictionaries strike the word "nigger," then African-American publications—like *Juba to Jive* and *Black Talk*—must drop it, too. No publication, black or white or other-wise, should be permitted to define it. And while we are at it, why not bowd-lerize this slur of slurs from all literature—novels, short stories, plays, po-ems, essays, even newspaper columns?

The folks at *Webster's*, in a statement to the would-be censors, offer an airtight case of logic and sanity: "We have made it clear that the use of this word as a racial slur is abhorrent to us, but it is nonetheless part of the language, and as such, it is our duty as dictionary makers to report on it. To do less would simply mislead people by creating the false impression that racial slurs are no longer part of our culture; and that, tragically, is not the case."

"There were no brothers" on board

MAY 3, 1998

Most white people I know have seen *Titanic*, but I know only a handful of African-Americans who have seen this most expensive film ever. Evidence shows, in fact, that black interest in the movie is far below that of whites. And few black girls—if any—are swooning over Leonardo DiCaprio's "ter-rific" eyes.

Why the differences? The answers are based in history.

When asked about the reactions of blacks to his masterpiece, director James Cameron spoke candidly: "There were no brothers on *Titanic* when it went down, because it was a rich man's ship. So it was like there's this justice to it, this symmetry which you can totally appreciate. One of my regrets on this film is that, you know, there were no African-Americans on *Titanic*, so there was no opportunity to cast them."

The notions of "justice" and "symmetry" that Cameron refers to partly explain why today's blacks and whites react differently to the film, and these notions also explain why blacks and whites living in 1912, when the ship sank, reacted differently to the tragedy.

Because no blacks were among the more than 1,500 passengers and crew who perished, many blacks were jubilant after the *Titanic* went down. Intellectuals such as Booker T. Washington and other middle-class blacks voiced "deep and sincere sympathy" to the loved ones of the victims. Washington even wrote to President Howard Taft expressing his sorrow. W.E.B. Du Bois, editor of *The Crisis*, the NAACP's monthly journal, also wrote sympathetically. But the overwhelming majority of African-Americans, especially those in the South and in the urban ghettos of the Northeast, dismissed these expressions of compassion as the "accommodationism" of Uncle Toms.

The reality was that racial brutality and Jim Crowism were at their zenith when the *Titanic* sank. In fact, 1912, with 61 black men lynched by whites, was a year of horror. Other types of violence—floggings, home burnings, and Klan harassment—made life unbearable for tens of thousands.

America was a "white man's country," and black resentment was greater than it had been at any time since Reconstruction. The sinking of the lily-white *Titanic*, therefore, was, as Cameron suggests, "justice." Many blacks publicly called it divine retribution and recorded the awful news in prose and in verse. One such lyrical invention, called a toast, is a rhythmical oral narrative that often rhymes and can be recited or sung. Often, it is picaresque, profane, and obscene. *Titanic* toasts are always contemptuous of whites.

The black attitude toward the calamity is best captured in toasts featuring Shine, a character who mocks the white man as he receives his comeuppance. Shine—a derogatory term for blacks, especially dark-hued males—is the black man's black man. In action, speech, and temperament, he embodies the full range of black emotion, cunning, and physicality.

Although the details of Shine's exploits differ from one storyteller to the next, the core of the myth—a victim who beats tough odds, those of nature and those of the white man—never changes, as this summary illustrates:

> Shine, the ship's only black, works as a stoker. Slaving below deck, he is the first to learn that the ship is taking on water. The captain does not believe that the vessel is sinking and argues this point with Shine.

Finally seeing water below deck, the captain seeks Shine's help in saving himself. But Shine rejects his bribes: money and sexual relations with his wife and daughter. Seeing that the ship is going down, Shine jumps overboard, demonstrating his superhuman swimming ability. Indeed, when news of the tragedy reaches shore, Shine is already on dry land.

Here is the punch line of a stanza praising Shine's escape:

> When the news got around the world that the great *Titanic* had sunk,
> Shine was in Harlem on 125th Street, damn near drunk.

Another:

> When all them white folks went to Heaven,
> Shine was in Sugar Ray's Bar drinking Seagram's Seven.

The *Titanic* toast, like a William Faulkner story, draws sharp distinctions between whites and blacks. Although the white characters are shown as being powerful and wealthy, they are simultaneously portrayed as being vain, greedy, stupid, stubborn, and immoral, which makes Shine, the ultimate trickster, the superior character.

Songs of the time echo this assessment of race and character. For example, a Leadbelly song describes heavyweight champion Jack Johnson, who had been persecuted by whites for marrying white women, dancing at the news of the *Titanic*:

> When he heard the mighty shock,
> Mighta seen that man doin' the Eagle Rock.
> Fare thee, *Titanic*, fare thee well.

In the same song, Leadbelly rejoices at the irony that, because of racism, blacks were barred from the ship:

> Black man oughta shout for joy
> Never lost a girl or either a boy.

I was the only black in the theater when I saw *Titanic*. And I was not surprised. Sure, I wish that all blacks could transcend the fact that *Titanic* is a "white" film, accept the universality of human loss, and appreciate Cameron's special artistry. But, then again, perhaps I am asking too much of a people whose collective memory of suffering and violence, of being perpetually excluded, still guides their daily lives.

Even though I can let go of the past and approach events and ideas intellectually, I, or anyone else, would be naive to expect most other blacks to suspend the reality of their status of inferiority in American history. We would be naive to ask them to pretend that the *Titanic* is their ship, too.

Black doesn't always equal white

September 6, 1998

Each time I or any other African-American writer points out problems that seem to affect blacks disproportionately, many white people, liberals and conservatives alike, and certain blacks weigh in with what I call white equivalency.

It is a logical fallacy, much like false analogy and ad hominem. From time to time, all of us are guilty of fallacious thinking, but white equivalency is worse than most other breakdowns in logic because it is a judgment that creates false images and draws faulty conclusions.

Here is how white equivalency works: If I write a column showing that teenage pregnancy and out-of-wedlock births are big problems in black culture, I receive letters and telephone calls arguing that whites have the same problems. That's white equivalency.

My answer is yes, but we are talking about black society—only. Introducing a white equivalency makes no sense in this instance because white society, the nation's baseline in most areas, is wealthier, and the families are far better equipped to protect their children from many of the problems associated with such births. And, of course, whether or not they have one, whites have easier access to a safe abortion.

The typical black teen who gets pregnant comes from a family with few bucks and many social problems. By most measures, she will have a tougher time than her white counterpart. Teen pregnancy in black society, in fact, exacts a greater toll on everyone involved than it does in white society. So to compare white teen pregnancy to that of black teens is to commit the fallacy of white equivalency.

Another example of white equivalency occurred after I wrote about black clerks being rude to black customers. Many whites wrote describing how they, too, had been treated rudely by blacks. I explained to some readers that I was not speaking of the general rudeness and incivility that have infected the nation, that I was writing exclusively about a special brand of black-on-black rudeness caused by black self-hatred, as suggested by the woman I interviewed for the column.

Whenever I write about the serious problem of low academic achievement, especially the inability to read, in low-income black neighborhoods, whites chime in that white kids have the same problems. Yes, I reply, but do you not see the differences, that the two scenarios are not equivalent?

Low academic achievement has always plagued black America in unique ways, beginning the moment that learning to read was taboo for slaves, continuing during Jim Crow's separate-but-equal days, and persisting in the age of anti–affirmative action propositions and so-called colorblind college admissions standards. White society has nothing equivalent to the debilitating bias that blacks have faced in education—and never will.

Why do we introduce white equivalency so casually?

Many white liberals do so perhaps to avoid facing the truth that blacks, a group whose battles they have fought and died for, are often their own worst enemies, that blacks and the poor may not be noble victims after all. In their sincere way, white liberals are trying to say that blacks are not so bad because whites do the same things.

White bigots, on the other hand, use white equivalency to argue that, see, blacks are no different from whites and, therefore, do not deserve so-called preferential treatment.

In either case, white equivalency is fallacious.

Many blacks who are defensive about our culture also use this fallacy. Like white liberals, they use it to show that black sexual promiscuity, for example, is no great evil because whites are promiscuous, too. Yes, but sexual promiscuity is one of the biggest reasons that AIDS is decimating our ranks, and we must treat it in a special way.

White equivalency, a form of recrimination, does not make whites and blacks equal, and it does not make their sins comparable. When I was a college teacher, my black students used white equivalency all of the time. When I would tell them, especially males, that they could not afford to miss class or fail to complete an assignment, they would respond with something like this: "Whites miss class, too. You don't jump on them."

My answer? You cannot compare yourselves with whites who, on average, have much more money, attended better high schools, already have a leg up in the job market because they are of the majority group and have relatives and acquaintances with the right contacts. The bottom line, I would say, is that most white students are born with a head start.

One of the most striking examples of white equivalency came the other morning during a National Public Radio segment on Saturday's Million Youth March in New York. Dismissing march organizer Khalid Abdul Muhammad as a charlatan, a black professor said that the antics of the former Nation of Islam spokesman demonstrate the dearth of leadership in black America. David K. Shipler, who is white and the author of *A Country of Strangers: Blacks and Whites in America*, agreed with the professor but said that white America also has a dearth of leadership.

Shipler's argument is faulty. Whites are the majority group and control every facet of U.S. life. The term "white leader" is ridiculous. Blacks, however, the nation's most despised minority group, need dynamic leaders, such as a Martin Luther King or Kweisi Mfume, to galvanize their interests. "Black leader," therefore, makes perfect sense. By putting down white leaders, Shipler was trying to blunt negative criticism of black leaders.

The fallacy of white equivalency, in the hands of policy makers, worries me mainly because we often wind up with legislation that harms blacks. A common misconception these days, one that results from white equivalency, is that instead of affirmative action programs intended for blacks, all programs should be based strictly on class because low-income whites and low-income blacks have the same problems.

Yes, some of the problems are similar or the same. But let us not fool ourselves; black skin and the unique problems that come with it do not have white equivalencies—and never will.

Friends of Bill: why blacks stand by Clinton

OCTOBER 4, 1998

Many white people, especially conservatives, and the majority of the nation's leading pundits are confounded that blacks are standing by President Clinton. Polls consistently show that more blacks than whites approve of the way Clinton is handling his job and view him favorably.

Clinton haters are further dismayed that he is more popular among blacks than either the Reverend Jesse Jackson or Gen. Colin Powell. So strong is support for the president among black leaders in Lumberton, North Carolina, for example, that the local branch of the NAACP has asked members to vote against members of Congress who attack the president, according to the *Raleigh News and Observer*.

As with the O. J. Simpson verdicts, reponses to the Monica Lewinsky phenomenon explain why blacks and whites continue to shout over a gulf of hatred, mistrust, and fear. "Nothing," writes David K. Shipler in his book *A Country of Strangers: Blacks and Whites in America*, "tests the nation, or takes the measure of its decency, quite like the rift between black and white."

Blacks' support of the president is rooted primarily in their perceptions of race and the realities of how they and their forebears have been abused by individuals and by American institutions. Based on his handling of issues important to them, most African-Americans like Clinton and trust him to protect their interests. They see him as an ally in a society hostile to them.

Listen to U.S. Rep. John Lewis (D–Georgia), a black, describing his constituents' desire to protect the president: "People . . . say, 'Take care of the president,'" Lewis told the *New York Times*. "They don't want to see him resign. They don't want to see him impeached. They just want us to leave him alone because there's this deep feeling in the black community that this president has been there for us."

Clinton champions policies, such as affirmative action, that are designed to assist blacks. And the economy, which began to expand on his watch, has boosted black employment, home ownership, entrepreneurship, and opportunities in education.

Few blacks will forget the president's historic trip to Africa, where he apologized for slavery. In addition, the overwhelming majority of blacks laud Clinton's national race initiative, even though many whites, who may never confront the enduring legacy of racism, condemn the effort. Despite a few early missteps, such as the jettisoning of Lani Guinier's nomination as attorney general and the firing of Jocelyn Elders as surgeon general, Clinton has appointed more blacks to Cabinet and other posts than anyone else who has ever resided at 1600 Pennsylvania Avenue. In fact, 13 percent of his appointments are black.

Beyond politics and the economy, many African-Americans see Clinton as a spiritual soul mate. They like his personal style: his savoir-faire and his unpretentiousness in their company. They like the fact that his golfing buddy is a brother, that his personal secretary is a sister, that he invites himself to black churches, that he prays with blacks and sings their songs without using a hymnal. He regularly brings black jazz musicians, rock stars, athletes, children, and business owners to the White House.

For these reasons and others, comedian Chris Rock said that Clinton is "the first black president." The Reverend Joseph Lowery, former head of the Southern Christian Leadership Conference, said that Clinton "has soul." (After all, The prez's instrument of choice is the funky saxophone.)

African-Americans have measured the man's affinity with them. He is egalitarian. He cares about blacks without being patronizing, and he understands that they are genuine underdogs, victims of racism. He understands that, as a member of the majority group, he has a moral obligation to set matters right for those whom his group has abused and still abuses.

And how have blacks fared under recent Republican presidents? Nixon shunned them. Ford did not register either way. Reagan despised blacks. Bush, bowing to instinct and pressure from party wing nuts, ignored them.

Again, Clinton is different. And blacks, who have good reason to distrust a prosecutor, identify with the president's recent plight. Many see him as a victim of powerful forces—independent counsel Kenneth Starr, the GOP-controlled House Judiciary Committee, the Christian right, and other fanatical Republican affiliates.

Consider these comments by two black leaders who believe that Clinton's treatment is unfair. U.S. Rep. Charles Rangel of Harlem: "His support is stronger than ever. The more they beat up on him, the stronger his support will be among the African-American community. African-Americans know what persecution is." Julian Bond, chairman of the NAACP's national board: "Instead of starting with the crime and looking for the man, Kenneth Starr started with the man and looked for the crime. . . . If any president has been persecuted, William Jefferson Clinton has been persecuted. Now I'll agree with you that he has cooperated with his persecution by producing bullets for Ken Starr's gun, but he has been persecuted."

Studies show that, as a group, blacks are more religious than whites, which may explain why they are more willing to forgive the president. "Forgiveness," a black man told the *New York Times*, "has been a [black] survival technique. We couldn't survive with . . . pent-up hatred, hostility and fear, so we've had to forgive and move on." Ironically, many critics of black people's capacity to forgive Clinton are racists who will not hire blacks, lend them money, or rent or sell them property. Clinton's peccadilloes are less reprehensible than the evils these self-righteous whites commit as a natural part of their daily lives.

African-Americans, then, do not need lectures on character and principle from whites about their support of the president. Blacks are standing by their man—a person who has been their genuine friend.

Jefferson's affair opens a door

November 4, 1998

I am mentioning the Thomas Jefferson–Sally Hemings affair for two reasons—one a good reason; the other, selfish. I write not out of malice but in an attempt to be brutally honest about the volatile issue of race at the bottom of this founding father's love affair.

First, the selfish reason for mentioning the affair: When I wrote a column a few months ago stating that circumstantial evidence pretty much confirmed that the nation's most revered president had fathered at least one illegitimate child with a slave, the hate mail came in volumes. One Jefferson scholar weighed in with ad hominem attacks.

To these detractors, I now say: DNA is destiny. And I feel vindicated.

Now, to the good reason for writing about the saga: it gives the nation one of its best chances ever to discuss race civilly and with a sense of general goodwill and national purpose. This controversy can help us stop deceiving ourselves about race. Beyond problems caused by black-white sexuality, race relations (that is, between blacks and whites, not between these two groups and other ethnicities) seem to defy solution.

If Hemings had not been a black slave, a member of an inferior caste, but a white woman of social standing, scholars and political partisans would not have tortured themselves with denials and other forms of legerdemain for these many generations. "The dehumanization of blacks, which began with slavery, haunts us to this very day and distorts historical perspectives," writes Annette Gordon-Reed, an associate professor at New York Law School and the author of *Thomas Jefferson and Sally Hemings: An American Controversy.*

Gordon-Reed is right. I believe, in fact, that very few whites have the intellectual and moral willingness to comprehend, let alone come to terms with, the enduring public and private effects of the more than two centuries that blacks were treated more cruelly than farm animals. Trust me, a black male, when I tell you that the effects of racism can be psychologically and emotionally crippling. Based on racial attitudes nationwide, I dare say that few whites can imagine the private hell of being despised, of being nothing. This condition has sent more blacks to psychiatrists and to jail than anyone can calculate.

At the risk of being premature, I applaud the white residents of Jasper, Texas, who seem to be coming to terms, both intellectually and morally, with their racism. There, white men recently dragged a black man to death behind a truck. After months of introspection—in which blacks and whites have spoken honestly and without defensiveness—many whites are reconciling their pasts and forging wholesome relations with black neighbors they had previously shunned.

The key to racial understanding is personal contact—empathy, vicariousness. In a news article, Jasper resident Nancy Nicholson shared her feelings after engaging in her first honest, public talk about race with blacks. "It was an eye-opener," she said. "I did not know the depth of their sorrow and pain." In response, a black minister, John Hardin, told Nicholson, "I just wish you could live in my shoes for one week and see what we go through."

I have long argued that race can be comprehended only through enlightenment, which comes with personal experience and intimacy. Whites whose grandchildren are mixed-race are on a better footing to enable them to achieve this comprehension than whites who have no such relations. Whites who adopt black children tend to become empathetic. Whites who date or marry blacks tend to "get it."

In other words, people accept those they see as family, through either direct bloodline or ethnic identification. "The Jefferson-Hemings story is really about family more than just about sex, and it has broad implications for all Americans," Gordon-Reed writes. "Now that we are free to consider the story in a fair and open fashion, perhaps we can also bring a new understanding to slavery and race and to our growth as a nation."

Susan Taylor Martin, senior correspondent for the *St. Petersburg Times*, wrote an article in Tuesday's edition about her own discovery that she is a Jefferson descendant. One of the underlying themes of the article is that, because of DNA, Martin now knows that she has at least one black relative.

Will this fact help her reconsider, or consider for the first time, some of her notions about race? She and Jefferson's other white descendants have a golden opportunity to upgrade the nation's conversation on race. For her part, Martin told me that she is excited about having black relatives and "would very much like to meet some of them." I believe her.

Novel provides ammunition for hate

August 18, 1999

Several years ago, when Morris Dees of the Southern Poverty Law Center initiated a letter-writing campaign to dissuade bookstore chains and distributors from stocking William Pierce's novel *The Turner Diaries*, much of America thought the KlanWatch founder was overreacting to the violence of a handful of white supremacists.

Now, with increasing numbers of white males targeting and gunning down members of minority groups, Dees's failed book-banning campaign—although still unreasonable to most Americans, myself included, on First Amendment grounds—is not as unpalatable as it once was. The reason is that *The Turner Diaries* serves as a bible for killers such as Tim McVeigh, Ben Smith, and Buford Furrow, suspected in the L.A. day camp shooting.

Published in 1978 and set in the 1990s, the novel depicts Armageddon between select whites and everyone else—blacks, Jews, government officials, journalists, cops, military personnel. On the "Day of the Rope," tens of thousands of blacks and Jews are exterminated. This also is when the "Organization" eradicates liberalism, feminism, and the other "isms" of compassion.

Amazingly, very few people besides scholars, terrorism experts, and, of course, white extremists have read *The Turner Diaries*. Even more shocking, at least to me, is that so few journalists have read it. The following edited excerpts from the novel should give readers a glimpse of what our home-grown terrorists are reading for inspiration:

> Liberalism is an essentially feminine, submissive world view. Perhaps a better adjective than feminine is infantile. It is the world view of men who do not have the moral toughness, the spiritual strength to stand up and do single combat with life, who cannot adjust to the reality that the world is not a huge, pink-and-blue, padded nursery in which the lions lie down with the lambs and everyone lives happily ever after.

> One day we will have a truly American press in this country, but a lot of editors' throats will have to be cut first.

> "Women's lib" was a form of mass psychosis which broke out during the last three decades of the Old Era. Women affected by it denied their femininity and insisted that they were "people," not "women."

> There is no way a society based on Aryan values and an Aryan outlook can evolve peacefully from a society which has succumbed to Jewish spiritual corruption.

> The [Uncle] "Toms" will eventually get their more militant and resentful brethren back into line, but meanwhile Izzy and Sambo are really at one another's throats, tooth and nail, and it is a joy to behold.

> The hanging of a few of the worst race-criminals in every neighborhood in America will help enormously in straightening out the majority of the population and reorienting their thinking. In fact, it will not only help, but it is absolutely necessary. The people require a strong psychological shock to break old habits of thought.

> Talk of "innocents" has no meaning. We must look at our situation collectively, in a race-wide sense. We must understand that our race is like a cancer patient undergoing drastic surgery in order to save his life. There is no sense in asking whether the tissue being cut out is

"innocent" or not. That is no more reasonable than trying to distinguish the "good" Jews from the bad ones—or, as some of our thicker-skulled "good ol' boys" still insist on trying, separating the "good niggers" from the rest of their race.

We'll go to the uttermost ends of the earth to hunt down the last of Satan's spawn.

After the Organization conquers the world with nuclear weapons, the "Great One" hands down a final edict: "It [is] no longer sufficient to be merely white; in order to eat one [has] to be judged the bearer of especially valuable genes."

After the Oklahoma City bombing, author Pierce, aka Andrew Macdonald, who holds a doctorate in physics and is a former professor, quipped that "someone may have read *The Turner Diaries*."

An understatement, for sure. As head of the Neo-Nazi National Alliance, the biggest and most active of such groups nationwide, Pierce invites at least 100 members who possess what he calls "leadership potential" to a private workshop each year at the Hillboro, West Virginia, headquarters. There, the future stalwarts, who mistake paranoia for patriotism, are trained in the civilized art of hatred.

The main training manual? *The Turner Diaries*. Besides these 100 crazies who are required to read the book each year, many such as McVeigh, Smith, and Furrow discover it in their own way and reenact its graphic mayhem.

Showing women's rights includes black women, too

AUGUST 22, 1999

As the nation's economy hums along and the quality of life for many Americans improves, a disproportionately high number of African-American women and their children remain trapped in dead-end circumstances.

Why?

Sharon Russ, a 38-year-old student at St. Petersburg Junior College, believes she knows a major part of the answer. She also believes she has a few solutions. An avowed feminist who admires abolitionist Sojourner Truth, Russ maintains that African-American women—natural victims of a sexist, race-conscious society—have let themselves become permanently marginalized. "We black women have rights that were never affirmed by the civil rights movement," she said. "We worked side by side with the black man, but when it was over, black women still didn't have equal rights."

This is the message Russ will deliver Thursday, when all area chapters of the League of Women Voters, the National Organization for Women, and the Campus Women's Collective celebrate national Women's Equality Day, which commemorates 80 years of women's right to vote. As one of a handful of African-Americans in NOW locally and nationwide, Russ intends to speak directly to her sisters in low-income environments, whose lives are shaped by drugs, alcohol, pregnancy, and unreliable men.

Her words are unadorned and blunt: "Black men contribute to the oppression of black women by leaving them with a houseful of children and then bragging about it. They need to stop introducing young girls to crack so they can use them. Black men need to take responsibility for their children and become role models."

Russ speaks from personal experience. Born in the Florida Panhandle, she fell in love with the man with whom she had three boys, now 18, 20, and 21. After the union broke up, she vowed that she would not fail her children—or herself. When youngest son Todd, now a senior at Pinellas Park High School, was born with cerebral palsy, Russ dedicated herself to his security. Although the family lived on welfare and was surrounded by drugs and violence, each time they moved Russ would turn their modest dwelling into an oasis.

Today, she is more determined than ever to succeed. "After what I've been through, nothing can stop me from taking charge of my life," she says. Five days a week, she works from 3:00 A.M. to 9:00 A.M. as a sorter at United Parcel Service. After work, she stops at home to shower and then heads to campus, where she takes a full academic load of 14 credits. She also tutors elementary pupils 20 hours a week through a college work-study program. She wants to teach English for a few years before applying to law school.

Her example is a guiding force in the lives of her children. Rodney, the 20-year-old, will attend Florida A&M University this fall. He will study business. Reginald, who won a basketball scholarship, attends Morehouse College in Atlanta. "These boys give 100 percent," Russ says. "They've won awards and are outstanding students. They're miraculous,"

As a child, Russ, like most black women of her generation and earlier, drew inspiration from the strong African-American women in her extended family. Today she is nurtured by the friends and acquaintances in the St. Petersburg chapter of NOW and by other NOW members she meets from around the country.

An obvious question, of course, is why turn to NOW, when very few black women have ever belonged to it or have ever called themselves feminists? For Russ, the answer was a no-brainer. All that she, a black woman, had to do was observe the many strides white women had made through NOW to realize that she, too, had much to gain by joining.

"Why are black women not in NOW to get the same support I have received, which has encouraged and supported me to get a college education?" she asks. "Attending college and belonging to NOW have helped me keep my kids off drugs and out of jail. I have learned to hold my head up.

"Many [black] women on the south side of St. Petersburg and other cities nationwide have lost their way. They're being used by men and by the system. Some women have five or more children by different men. Where does it get these women? What does it get their children? These women need to be taking charge of their lives and their children's future. No one else will. A man is not the answer. Education is. Black women don't need to have a man or have a baby to be somebody. They need to get self-respect."

Russ's black mentors—bell hooks, a noted feminist author, and Mary Willis, a professor at the college she attends—gave her the courage to challenge her old ways of thinking and to take risks. Her dream is that more African-American women nationwide will join NOW so that they can discover their "real womanhood" and forge successful futures.

A double standard on drugs

August 25, 1999

This is a tale of the two ways the Gainesville Police Department enforces narcotics violations. Or, at the very least, it is a tale about the perception of dual enforcement—one for the city's black residents, the other for whites. Unfortunately, what is happening here in Florida's leading college town happens throughout the nation.

During last week's Police Community Committee meeting, angry black residents told members that they are sick and tired of cops' harassment and physical abuse. In attempting to stamp out drug sales, GPD officers have become overzealous, blacks argued. Several young men described being stopped, searched, and detained for no legitimate reasons—other than "standing still while black" or "walking while black" or, as one told me last Sunday, "existing while black."

Many African-Americans said they do not want drugs in their neighborhood, but neither do they want to see young men mistreated simply because their skin is black. "I worry about my son, not because he uses drugs or sells them but because these cops are going to get themselves a black male no matter what," a woman said. "My boy's been harassed three times this year simply because he's black and lives on Fifth Avenue. Why don't they go after some of those rich white kids over on University Avenue doing all those fancy drugs all night at those rave parties?"

Indeed, why not case the rave clubs? This is the same question most other blacks and increasing numbers of whites are asking. Throughout Florida and other southeastern states, Gainesville is known as the "rave capital," where exotic drugs materialize like manna.

"What has astonished officers in Gainesville and elsewhere is the wide-open nature of rave drug use and sales," Florida drug czar James McDonough wrote in the *Gainesville Sun*. "Patrons make no efforts to conceal drug activity, as if this was normal and accepted behavior. Comparing a night on the street to a night in a rave club, one Jacksonville narcotics officer reported he observed far more illegal and dangerous activity in the club." Am I reading McDonough correctly? If cops know that designer and traditional drugs—Ecstasy (XTC), ketamine or Special K, gamma-hydroxybutyric acid (GHB), cocaine, heroin, methamphetamine, marijuana, LSD—are pandemic at rave joints, why are they not hauling away wiped-out white kids?

A recent *Sun* editorial went to the heart of the matter: "As the controversy over raves has slowly unfolded in Gainesville . . . perhaps the most 'unfathomable' thing of all has been the absence of outrage on the part of the city commissioners themselves [at] the reports of drug abuse, drug-induced sexual activity, the presence of 14- and 15-year-olds at raves, people throwing up on public streets and sidewalks and the litter of drug paraphernalia.

"At one meeting, Commissioner John Barrow seemed to shrug it off with the observation that drugs have always been part of the Gainesville scene. At another meeting, he otherwise indicated that the whole flap was no big deal."

These same commissioners believe, however, that drugs—mostly old-fashioned pot and cocaine—are a big deal in the black part of town and that the cops should continue their abusive crackdown, as it were.

Local hospital emergency rooms are not reporting excessive treatment of overdoses among young African-Americans. But ERs are treating huge numbers of white rave goers, most of them young University of Florida students and high schoolers, who have overdosed. (Speaking of students, many white kids come to Gainesville for the exotic drugs.) They do not do XTC at Mom's Kitchen, a popular soul food eatery in the black community. No, they do it downtown, often in full view of the police and rave club owners and, apparently, a few elected officials.

This double standard in the shadow of Florida's flagship university should shame everyone in the state. And everyone—especially parents who send their Cindys and Brendans off to study—should be outraged.

Meanwhile, the black community continues to be demonized as an open-air drug market when, ironically, the real drug mecca is in the city's white business district. But busting well-connected white university students poses more problems than body slamming some black kid. African-Americans are not excusing drugs in their neighborhoods by criticizing law enforcement and the attitude of the commission. They are simply asking for one citywide standard for narcotic violations.

An angry voice of inequitable times

SEPTEMBER 8, 1999

Standing at Malcolm X Boulevard and 118th Street in Harlem during the controversial Million Youth March, I felt and heard the rumbling of the subway far below ground. Dozens of people—black children and older adults, white journalists and tie-dyed revolutionaries, Rastafarian wanna-bes, wary NYPD cops, lawyers and nurses, American and foreign tourists— milled around me.

As the afternoon sun blazed and the subway shook the ground, I sensed a foreboding, something dangerous in the caverns beneath us, a thing that was pulling all of us down into a bottomless pit. When a dreadlocked black teenager walked in front of me carrying a sign reading "Cops, Stop Murdering Black Men," I recalled a sentence in James Baldwin's 1985 book *The Evidence of Things Not Seen:* "A stranger to this planet might find the fact that there are any black people at all still alive in America something to write home about."

These disquieting words came to mind because their meaning was a powerful subtext of Khalid Abdul Muhammad's so-called "black power" message. Muhammad founded and directs the New Black Panther Party. If you remember, Nation of Islam leader Louis Farrakhan ousted Muhammad from the Black Muslim group several years ago for his anti-Semitic remarks on college campuses.

But Muhammad is back. America would be ill-advised to ignore him. For the last two years, he has gone to court, for example, and won the right to hold his youth rally after New York mayor Rudolph Giuliani (whom Muhammad calls a "racist, cantankerous, constipated cracker") refused to grant him permission. Last year, the event attracted more than 6,000 participants. This year, probably because of several weeks of negative press and the personal efforts of black politicians, newspaper columnists, and Jewish leaders to kill it, about 2,000 of the faithful showed up. As one indication of the event's unpopularity in important offices, City Councilman Bill Perkins, a black Democrat representing Harlem, said, "We're praying for peace. And rain."

Well, the rally was peaceful, and rain did not dampen its controversial message: blacks must endure one race-related atrocity after another. In aggressive, insult-laced rhetoric, speakers called for a black militia to protect them from the nation's cops, especially those in Gotham City. Shaunette Daniels, the first speaker, said: "We have long been denied self-determination for black people. We must make sure there are no unarmed black men on these streets. . . . Let me hear you say black power."

Wearing black from collar to toe, Muhammad, his bald head glistening with sweat, served up his usual fare of (among other things) Jew-baiting, Uncle Tom bashing, and black self-reliance. Referring to the mayor as "Adolf" Giuliani, Muhammad said, "You can't tell me to stop calling the white man a devil. It is my religion. Giuliani wants to keep us in line. These crackers crack the whip and the black politicians are buck-dancing and scratching."

Here are more Muhammadisms:

"Black man, go back to your black woman. Rebuild the black family. Give the white man back his dope, his weed, his drugs, his alcohol."

"From this day forward, wake up, clean up, and stand up. We want to be the people looked upon as the light of the world again."

"The so-called Jews are Johnny-come-lately Jews who climbed out of the caves of Europe. We are the real Jews."

The foreboding I sensed—the rumbling below ground—is the cause of Muhammad's madness. An old black woman next to me said: "These white bastards say Khalid is a hatemonger. He's no hatemonger. He's tired of white folks messing over black people. Whites are the hatemongers. White America produced Khalid. He's right in your face, but he's black and beautiful."

During a speech in another part of Harlem shortly after the rally, the Reverend Jesse Jackson—citing crumbling public schools, a Wall Street that refuses to invest in Harlem, widespread police brutality, do-nothing absentee landlords—suggested that Muhammad is a "voice of alienation and despair." Jackson added, "So long as there is alienation and pain, there will be voices of alienation and pain."

No matter how offensive I—and the rest of America—find Muhammad's message, demonizing him and the growing numbers following him will not eradicate the ugly, institutionalized inequities that push black men like Muhammad outside the mainstream. A few days on the streets of Harlem would give any sensitive, honest person another view of Muhammad's outrage.

Activist shouldn't get or want apology

September 15, 1999

This is my first—perhaps last—time writing about the controversy of apologizing or not apologizing to Uhuru leader Omali Yeshitela.

We all know the story: In 1966, Yeshitela (Joe Waller in those days) ripped down the grand staircase mural in St. Petersburg City Hall. It contained caricatures of black troubadours entertaining white picnickers at the beach. Then, Yeshitela said the mural "depicts Negroes in a most despicable, derogatory manner." He, along with other protesters, dragged it through downtown streets. He was arrested, convicted of destroying city property, and served two years in prison. He also was stripped of his civil rights.

No one has asked for my opinion in this matter, but I give it because an important issue bearing on the real meaning of the situation has been ignored. First, Yeshitela deserved to be locked up. Second, he deserved to lose his civil rights. Why? Because he knowingly broke the law. He committed the time-honored act of civil disobedience. Like Henry David Thoreau, Rosa Parks, and Martin Luther King Jr. before him, he challenged what he considered to be a government-sanctioned injustice. He knew that cops would chase him down, cuff him, and toss him in a cell. He got exactly what he wanted. Like other effective black activists of the period, he incited the worst instincts of a bigoted establishment.

Today, he does not deserve an apology. And he should not accept one. An apology would nullify the revolutionary spirit of his action of more than 30 years ago. Those who commit civil disobedience do so with their toothbrushes and combs in their pockets, their eyes staring at imprisonment.

In his tract "Civil Disobedience," Thoreau wrote, "Unjust laws exist; shall we be content to obey them, or shall we endeavor to amend them, and obey them until we have succeeded, or shall we transgress them at once?" Thoreau chose to transgress at once what he perceived to be an unjust poll tax. He proudly went to the hoosegow.

When a weary Rosa Parks refused to relinquish her seat on that hot bus, she thumbed her nose at the sheriff and his jail. As did Martin Luther

King—wearing a wry smile—after refusing to leave the streets of Birmingham, Alabama. Listen to King, writing about the efficacy of civil disobedience, in his "Letter from Birmingham Jail": "Words cannot express the exultation felt by the individual as he finds himself, with hundreds of his fellows, behind prison bars for a cause he knows is just. . . . In no sense do I advocate evading or defying the law, as would the rabid segregationist. That would lead to anarchy. One who breaks an unjust law must do so openly, lovingly, and with a willingness to accept the penalty." From King's book *Why We Can't Wait*: "If a people can produce from its ranks 5 percent who will go voluntarily to jail for a just cause, surely nothing can thwart its ultimate triumph."

Yeshitela is a smart, well-read provocateur, but I wonder if he has read "Civil Disobedience" and "Letter from Birmingham Jail." I agree with him and others that the city should apologize to the black community for the mural to start a long-overdue, communitywide healing process. Neither the city nor any other entity, however, should apologize to Yeshitela personally. He got what was coming to him. I have not spoken with him on this matter, but if he asked me, I would tell him to tell City Council member Bea Griswald to take her old lukewarm apology and, well, save it for a different black cause.

Council member Frank Peterman is right to describe Yeshitela as a "hero." But Peterman, too, misses the point by demanding a personal apology for Yeshitela. Again, it would diminish Yeshitela's legacy. Chief of Staff Don McRae, Alvelita Donaldson, Yeshitela's sister, and other members of a group calling itself the Concerned Citizens Action Committee should accept the council's "general" apology. Then they should do something *substantive* to help St. Petersburg's dysfunctional black community. Why not, say, try to persuade more black parents to take their children's education seriously?

I admire Yeshitela for tearing down the mural and going to prison. Martin Luther King captured the real meaning of such acts. Detractors such as Griswald, who call Yeshitela a criminal for his deed, also should heed King's wisdom: "An individual who breaks a law that conscience tells him is unjust, and who willingly accepts the penalty of imprisonment in order to arouse the conscience of the community over its injustice, is in reality expressing the highest respect for law."

Racism lingers in the shadows of our denials

JANUARY 30, 2000

Finally, the folks who take care of Monticello, Thomas Jefferson's estate in Virginia, have relented before the urgent call of DNA and have all but acknowledged that the nation's third president probably fathered at least one—perhaps all six—of the children of Sally Hemings, one of Jefferson's slaves.

The affair does not bother me. My concern is the matter of denial. For more than 200 years, Jefferson's white relatives and others have tried to bury strong evidence that the president had carnal knowledge of a black concubine. The very idea was so repugnant that the keepers of Jefferson's legacy went into deep denial. Many have remained there and may never emerge.

In psychology, this phenomenon is called a defense mechanism, the process of repression by which an unacceptable idea is made unconscious. Again, in this case, Jefferson's defenders denied an obvious reality that was too painful. Such denials—and the American psyche suffers from many—contribute to many of the nation's enduring social and race problems.

In a now-infamous editorial, the *Florida Times-Union* of Jacksonville, in an attempt to support Gov. Jeb Bush's initiative to end affirmative action in the state, blithely commented that slavery "existed briefly in America" and that "slavery is not unique and its effects are not permanent." Denying the profound, residual effects of slavery may seem fitting for the *Times-Union*, which has an unfortunate reputation for being insensitive to African-Americans. But such denial prevents the editors and writers from seeing the truth, guaranteeing that the paper will continue to have poor relations with an entire segment of Jacksonville's population.

Another symbol of gross denial flies atop South Carolina's statehouse. Many South Carolinians still refuse to acknowledge that the Confederate flag stands for all that was wrong in the South, that the banner was raised to protest federal civil rights legislation of the 1960s that gave blacks rights that white Americans took for granted. Many South Carolinians, moreover, cannot bring themselves to acknowledge that Dixie fought the North to preserve the evil institution of slavery. As long as the Rebel banner flies in Columbia and people continue to deny the crippling effects of slavery, South Carolina will never begin to heal its racial wounds.

In a recent column, *Miami Herald* editorial board member Kathleen Krog wrote about the worldwide propensity for inhumanity as we enter the 21st century. Drawing parallels between the Holocaust, U.S. slavery, and other international atrocities, she urged people to acknowledge the wrongs and not to forget them. "In a sense, the Holocaust is like American slavery," she wrote. "It's the ugliness in our past that just won't go away. Slavery's after-effects still inflict such profound damage—as fresh as the latest class-action discrimination lawsuit—that's it's obvious why this example of man's inhumanity to man won't fade from our cultural consciousness. It remains a deep lode—as much as an unhealed wound—for historians, sociologists, educators, civil-rights activists, clerics, writers, filmmakers, journalists and others with truth and revelations on their minds."

More than half of the white readers who correspond with me accuse me of being a racist because I dare to discuss and acknowledge the continuing effects of race in contemporary life. "You're what's wrong with America," a typical letter commented. "If you and those other race pimp niggers would stop talking about race, we wouldn't have any problems. My grandfather didn't own slaves, and we're sick and tired of hearing about slavery. You weren't a slave so what are you whining about?"

What we do about this kind of troubling denial, I do not know. I do not have the answer. I used to think that education was the answer. Today, however, I am not so sure. Tens of thousands of books, articles, and videos are available that document the horrors that have been committed. Public schools and colleges offer courses in ethnicity and diversity, U.S. and world history, the Holocaust, the Civil War. Yet the denials endure.

In a real sense, denying is another way of forgetting. And we should never forget. Krog commends the nations and organizations that have established war-crime tribunals and reconciliation committees that confront the horrors of the past. While lauding efforts to hunt down criminals and punish them in some instances and forgive them in others, she warns that we fail if we merely remember and acknowledge without taking preventive action: "It is good that we remember and now are more willing to confront our pasts. But knowing and remembering are not enough to protect us from the inhumane instincts that the Holocaust and other heinous atrocities prove exist in every single one of us."

America and the rest of the world will become safe for everyone when we stop denying, when, as Krog says, we resolve "never again, anywhere, and find an effective means to turn those words into action." Acknowledgment is the first step.

The Bush brothers may be far from perfect, but they're not racists

MARCH 19, 2000

In a March 8 speech she delivered at a federal Department of Education seminar promoting diversity, Jane Elliot, a former third-grade teacher from Iowa, described Governors George W. and Jeb Bush as racists. W. is the governor of Texas, and younger brother Jeb is the chief executive of Florida. Their dad, of course, is former President Bush.

Besides calling the Bush Boys racists, Elliot advised her audience, all on the government payroll, not to vote for any Republican political candidates. Wouldn't you know that the Bushes are GOP stalwarts.

Now, before we outright denounce Elliot, we should remember that she has some respectable bona fides on matters of race. She created, for example, the controversial diversity study that separates students based on eye color. I have seen the famous video of the program in which Elliot alternately gives preferential treatment to blue-eyed and brown-eyed students. The results are chilling. Each time I walk away from the images, I worry about humankind's willingness to commit acts of horror based solely on something as God-given, as natural, and as simple as pigment.

But to describe the Bushes as racists is, I think, unfair. I do not know if W. has thoughtfully contemplated any subject enough to be considered extreme in his view—in this case, racist. Indeed, I know he spoke at bigoted Bob Jones University and wavered on the South Carolina Confederate flag issue, but I am smart enough to know that these were purely political moves to stabilize his campaign for the White House.

As for Jeb, well, he also caused a lot of his own problems with race by being flippant when he ran a losing campaign against the late Gov. Lawton Chiles a few years ago. When asked what he would do to improve the plight of black Floridians if elected, Jeb said, "Probably nothing." He was trying to be a wiseacre for fellow Republicans.

Many blacks apparently forgave Jeb and voted for him in the latest gubernatorial election. But he dashed that support when—by executive order—he ended affirmative action as we know it in the Sunshine State. Jeb calls his program to end affirmative action One Florida. Essentially, it does away with giving leg-ups to blacks in state contracting and college admissions.

Despite his "probably nothing" comment, I do not believe that Jeb is a racist today. He may have been one a few years ago, before he ran into that unmovable object called reality, before he met T. Willard Fair, president of the Greater Miami Urban League. I know for a fact that Fair, along with other African-Americans, influenced Jeb in positive ways. They established Florida's first charter school in Miami's predominantly black Liberty City community.

On more than one occasion, I have seen Jeb interact with black parents and children at the school, and I am convinced that the man has learned to care. Yes, Jeb is arrogant, impatient, and has many of the other traits that come with being privileged. But racist? I do not think so.

A black man, California businessman Ward Connerly, forced the governor to implement One Florida, a plan that protects parts of college admissions. As he had done in California and the state of Washington, Connerly entered Florida and began collecting signatures on petitions to place an anti–affirmative action measure on the state ballot. The measure passed in California and Washington. The Florida Supreme Court has yet to rule on the initiative.

Because Connerly's proposal is draconian and divisive, Jeb never wanted the Californian in the state. He still does not want him here. The unfortunate irony is that before Connerly chose Florida as his next plaything, the state did not have an affirmative action problem. No one talked about it. During the past five gubernatorial elections, affirmative action never surfaced as an issue.

Why?

Blacks are not overrunning our professional schools. We are not crowding out white building contractors. We are not taking the jobs of white firefighters and police officers. We are not muscling out qualified white teachers. Florida's affirmative action problem is a figment of the imagination.

When Connerly came knocking, Jeb tried to head off trouble by introducing One Florida. Frankly, I would not want to be in his shoes, even though the majority of white voters—nearly all of them outsiders who brought their dislike of blacks down from the North and Midwest—support the executive order.

Although Jeb has lost the core black vote forever, and W. continues to run farther to the right, I do not believe the brothers hate us. Are they political animals? You bet. But not racists. Elliot and those who agree with her may owe the Bush Boys an apology on this one.

"Black" means tolerating criminality?

MAY 17, 2000

Few people are more contemptible than some self-anointed Keeper of Negritude who attempts to teach other blacks how to be black. This is precisely what happened on May 7, when the *St. Petersburg Times* published a letter by a well-known former head of the local chapter of the NAACP. I was the butt of the blacker-than-thou missive. Here is the man's first sentence: "Just when I was beginning to feel that columnist Bill Maxwell had regained his inborn knowledge of the black experience, he loosed a tirade of criticism against African-Americans."

The "tirade" to which he refers is the subject of my April 30 column praising black residents of Washington, D.C., who turned in a black 16-year-old suspect. The boy allegedly shot seven other black teenagers, one critically, at the National Zoo on April 24. Washington's black police chief, Charles H. Ramsey, also praised the residents for their help. Has Ramsey also failed to regain his "inborn knowledge of the black experience?" And what about the black mayor who also supports the actions of the residents? We should tell him how he has failed to regain his "inborn knowledge of the black experience."

Our Mr. Black Man suggests, of course, that he is the true black and that the D.C. mayor, and police chief, and I are not because we do not believe in letting crime fester among our people. As all such fools and hypocrites do, he argues that, because blacks have been mistreated by the police, we must not cooperate with them when they come for the bad guys destroying our communities.

To the contrary, I agree with writer Stanley Crouch, in the latest issue of *New York* magazine: "The greatest threat to black life and limb is not the police; it's criminals in our community." Only a fool or a shameless hypocrite pandering to popular black opinion or to the affection of certain personalities would say otherwise.

Let me tell you about my mother's neighborhood in the mostly black area of northwest Ft. Lauderdale. Until I personally went to the police, she and her husband, both in their 70s, could not get a full night's sleep. The black dope dealers raised hell from dusk to dawn—chasing cars, yelling, fighting, urinating everywhere, playing loud music, and often firing automatic weapons. My sister and brother have to bring my mother and stepfather to their homes for the old couple to get a respite from the tyranny outside their front door. My stepfather often wants to confront the thugs with his own handgun, but I have advised him against it.

I went to the police. The major in charge of my mother's neighborhood promised that his officers would do something. Next, I went to her congressman, the black city manager, and the heads of the local NAACP and Urban League. "My mother and stepfather deserve some peace of mind in their home and should not be terrorized by their own people," I told these leaders.

Each time I visit home, I go to the police to either praise or condemn their efforts. Lately, I have been condemning them. A younger, bolder, meaner breed of pushers has moved into the area. My mother tells me, though, that things are a bit quieter because I went to the cops.

I will not apologize for removing criminals from the neighborhood where my mother lives, for helping her get a good night's sleep, for removing the stench of urine from her front easement, for eliminating the trash that dealers leave behind. Perhaps I am not black enough for my letter writer, but I am black enough to know that black criminals victimize their own people. And evidence tells me that black people here in St. Petersburg also need to turn in thugs who make life unsavory in many southside neighborhoods.

If we do not help the police, we deserve mayhem and dysfunction. When we refuse to snitch on a home invader, we invite him to repeatedly abuse us and our neighbors. When we turn our backs on drug deals near our homes, we help depress property values in our communities.

Given the claim of my letter writer to authentic blackness (read that as wrongheaded silence), I wonder how many black armed robbers ply their trade because he did not report them? How many black children use drugs because our authentic black brother did not snitch on dealers? I wonder if he knows any illegal gun dealers but would not rat on them?

The black wall of silence threatens black life and limb as much as the gang banger who fires an AR-15 in a drive-by shooting. If tolerating criminality is being truly black, then I never will be truly black. If being truly black means being a fool, I must forego the experience.

Politics: Let Us Just Tell It Straight

Florida's crackers lose a kinsman

DECEMBER 16, 1998

In light of Gov. Lawton Chiles's death and the recent election of Jeb Bush to replace him in January, I am reminded of a news story with the headline "Chiles's native tongue speaks to a new state," published during the 1994 gubernatorial campaign. I realize anew, as the article suggested, that people born in Florida before the 1950s are fast becoming cultural outsiders in this vanishing paradise that we natives call home.

"Gov. Lawton Chiles speaks cracker about as well as any politician who ever roamed Florida's towns and cities in search of votes," the article stated. "The trouble is that Florida is growing more multicultural and diverse by the day . . . diluted by a steady flood of new residents from the eastern half of the United States and Latin America." Our governor-elect, a 45-year-old Texan, speaks fluent Spanish.

Everything is changing, sometimes altering our lives in ways that diminish the natives' sense of who we are. Many natives are mourning the passing of Chiles and, with his death, the virtual disappearance of one of our most colorful traditions: Florida crackerdom.

The term "cracker" has several definitions. Most Floridians prefer the one claiming that the original crackers were white cowboys who cracked whips as they drove cattle across the peninsula. Another version states that crackers were the poor Georgia and north Florida whites who pounded or cracked corn to make grits, flour, and meal. For our purposes, crackers are whites descended from Scotch-Irish frontiersmen in the South, especially in Georgia and north Florida. Unfortunately, because the South is associated with racism, "cracker" has taken on derogatory connotations everywhere, except among those who consider themselves members of the group. Blacks, for example, have always used "cracker" as a racial epithet.

Their greatest chronicler in fiction, Marjorie Kinnan Rawlings, had a love-hate relationship with crackers when she lived among them at Cross Creek. "These people are 'lawless' by an anomaly," she told Maxwell Perkins, her editor. "They are living an entirely natural, and very hard, life, disturbing no one. . . . Yet almost everything they do is illegal. And everything they do is necessary to sustain life." They hunted out of season and fished beyond the limit. They didn't believe in licenses of any kind. The earth was theirs to pluck—without government interference.

This is the same herd from which Gov. Chiles was cut. He was born and reared in Lakeland, where Jim Crow felt right at home. Yet Chiles was no racist. He appointed more African-Americans to office than any other Florida governor. Most natives are not ashamed to say that they miss Chiles's cracker wit and are already thinking of some of his gems nostalgically.

During the first gubernatorial debate in 1994, for example, Bush tried to blame the buildup of national debt during the 1980s on Chiles, who had been chairman of the U.S. Senate Budget Committee. "I know you have a lot of firsthand knowledge about the federal debt," a sarcastic Bush said, having forgotten that his father, George Bush, had been vice president and president during that period—and had never once submitted a balanced budget to Congress.

A Beltway-wise Chiles replied, "Gosh, it seems like there was somebody else above me sending those budgets. Jeb, there's a cracker saying: Never mention rope in a house where there's been a hanging."

Here are other crackerisms that have been cited in this newspaper:

"It's a sorry frog who won't holler in his own pond."

"A cut dog barks."

"Even a blind hog will root out an acorn once in a while."

Chiles spoke his most famous crackerism, which earned him a new nickname, during the final debate on November 1, 1994, at the Tampa Bay Performing Arts Center. The Bush campaign was ahead in the polls by a few percentage points, and his supporters had been crowing.

Warning Bush and doubting journalists that he would pull victory out of the jaws of defeat, Chiles described himself as the embodiment of one of Florida's most cunning and hard-to-capture wild creatures: "The old he-coon walks just before the light of day."

Bush was confused, and so was the overwhelming majority of the audience. Crackers, especially coon hunters who watched the debate on television, laughed. They knew exactly what their brother, that "sly old Lawton," was saying. Who speaks for these crackers now?

What others won't say about presidential candidate George W. Bush

SEPTEMBER 19, 1999

Let's stop dancing around with W. and the D-word. I keep reading and hearing smooth euphemisms about the Republican presidential front-runner. He is "flip," he is "cocky," he is "not a details man," and he is "not a policy wonk."

Give me a break. Let us just tell it straight, Texas-style: W. is dumb.

Most political pundits, however, publicly skirt the issue. With all of his money and his charmed head-start at birth, George W. Bush, son of former President George Herbert Walker Bush, should be well-read. And brilliant.

But he is neither. And some observers even have the gall to excuse W.'s inarticulateness and ignorance of important issues. One of the latest examples comes from none other than *New York Times* columnist Maureen Dowd. This Pulitzer Prize winner, who made a cottage industry of calling Bill Clinton and his wife every nasty name permitted in a family newspaper, merely hints that W. is a dummy. She mentions one of his quintessential Dan Quaylisms—referring to the East Timorese as the "East Timorians." She also quotes him at a Bedford, New Hampshire, elementary school imparting his brand of wisdom to innocent children: "Some people say that I proved that if you get a C average, you can end up being successful in life."

Keep in mind that many of these same children would be frowned upon or taken to the woodshed if they earned a C average. They belong to a new generation of pupils who must overachieve, who are being tested into fits of vomiting and recurring nightmares by the likes of the Lone Star state's education governor.

The plain truth is that W.'s mediocrity may prove that he became "successful in life" because of his name and his family's wealth. Most other guys of "average" intelligence, who fumble their thoughts and wear a smirk, could not dream of becoming governor of any state—let alone becoming U.S. president. (Ronald Reagan being, of course, a notable exception.)

Frank Rich of the *New York Times* comes as close as any other pundit in stating unequivocally that W. might suffer from gray matter deficit syndrome. In a column arguing that W. won the cocaine joust with journalists, Rich writes: "Some voters are less concerned with what drugs, if any, passed through Mr. Bush's brain than with what other traffic, if any, did.

"Though otherwise cooperating with a seven-part *Washington Post* profile this summer, this would-be education president would not permit Andover or Yale to release his grades. Asked by a South Carolina elementary-school kid at a campaign photo op . . . to name his favorite book as a child, Mr. Bush responded, 'I can't remember any specific books.'" Amid all the creakhead cracks on late-night talk shows was David Letterman's chillingly straightforward, "I have the feeling that this guy could turn out to be a colossal boob."

Whenever I hear W. speak, I sense that I am listening to a faux Texas hick. How, for heaven's sake, can a serious presidential candidate publicly confuse "Slovenians" and "Slovakians"? How can he say "Grecian" (formula perhaps?) when he means "Greek"? How, pray tell, can he use "Kosovians" when he should say "Kosovars"?

We have a serious problem here, fellow voters.

I am convinced that W., like Dwight D. Eisenhower in the 1950s, stands at the front of a new cycle of anti-intellectualism in the United States. Eisenhower, a celebrated general of World War II, was known for his conventional mind and clumsy speech. He ran and won against Adlai Stevenson, the "egghead" Democrat whom historian Richard Hofstadter, author of the book *Anti-Intellectualism in American Life*, describes as "a politician of uncommon mind and style."

Like Ike, W. is of conventional mind and sounds as dumb when opening his mouth. W. operates in a party that blames the nation's social problems on the so-called cognitive elite. One wag called this trend a "jihad against gray matter"—an apt allusion. That ofttimes vacant look on W.'s face reminds me of the main character in the movie *Forrest Gump*.

In falling all over W., as polls indicate, is America simply reacting to the sorry escapades of the brainy, oversexed Clinton by celebrating stupidity?

Check out what Tucker Carlson writes about W. in the September issue of *Talk* magazine: "Toward the end of one interview with Bush I decide to test the Larry King Theory—that dumb questions are the most evocative—and ask Bush who his heroes are. Expecting the stock Albert Schweitzer-Aristotle-Mother Teresa phoniness, I am surprised when Bush can't seem to come up with an answer. After thinking for an uncomfortably long moment, he names only one: retired baseball player Nolan Ryan. (In the airport later, I notice that Ryan, a close friend of Bush's, happens to be on the cover of that month's *Texas Monthly*.) When I ask Bush to name something he isn't good at, there is no hesitation at all. 'Sitting down and reading a 500-page book on public policy or philosophy or something,' he says."

I am not making this up, America.

One reason that Bush might not let Yale or Andover release his grades is that, as a rich kid who filled "legacy" slots, he made lousy grades and probably did not belong on either campus. His first grade in English at Phillips Academy was a big fat goose egg. He also struggled in math.

Am I saying that the intellectually challenged are not fit for public office? Nope. We are swamped with legions of them at all levels of public life. Am I saying that such a person should not be president of the world's last superpower? Absolutely.

Do we really want W. Gump at 1600 Pennsylvania Avenue?

GOP blacks make race a matter of convenience

NOVEMBER 7, 1999

"You can run, but you can't hide," some smart person said long ago. I do not know the original context of these words, but I know for sure that they apply to today's black Republicans—especially Messrs. Ward Connerly, Alan Keyes, and Clarence Thomas, who traipse around the country pretending that race does not matter, that their skin color has nothing to do with their success.

Connerly is the California businessman and member of the Board of Regents who persuaded voters in California and the state of Washington to scrap affirmative action in college admissions and in the awarding of government contracts. He is leading a similar effort in Florida. Keyes, a talk show host, is a perennial presidential candidate. Thomas is the one black person on the U.S. Supreme Court.

Each man is the darling of white conservatives. Like the Bible's Simon Peter, each is defined by his denial of his true self, his essential blackness. And like the protagonist of James Weldon Johnson's novel *The Autobiography of an Ex-Coloured Man*, each fancies himself an ex-colored man.

The ugly truth, however, always comes crashing down on these frauds, usually during fits of anger following moments when they feel betrayed by their white admirers or when they are locked in a room with blacks who despise them.

If you recall, Thomas's real colored self broke through—in all of its naked rage—after some Senate Judiciary Committee members aggressively questioned him in 1991 about accusations of sexual misconduct leveled against him by University of Oklahoma law professor Anita Hill. Thomas lost it, calling the content and manner of the interrogation "a high-tech lynching." Why did he use the word "lynching"? Because, under pressure, he became fully conscious of being a black man, of being out of place, of being a member of a group whose history is a chronicle of the gallows—both literally and symbolically. Our would-be justice went on to recount the nation's use of racist "language about the sexual prowess of black men, language about the sex organs of black men and the sizes, et cetera. That kind of language has been used about black men as long as I've been on the face of this earth, and these are charges that play into racist, bigoted stereotypes, and these are the kind of charges that are impossible to wash off."

However, since joining the nation's highest court, Thomas—the designated black justice—has been hostile toward nearly everything in the interest of blacks that has come before him. He is trying his damnedest to be an ex-colored man.

A few weeks ago, while playing up to a group of white Republicans in Florida, Ward Connerly let his real colored soul spring loose. He was angry about comments in an editorial about his Indian, Irish, French, and African-American ancestry. He called the comments "very demeaning of my heritage. . . . I think that's racist. Your damn paper gets away with it because I'm a black."

Is this the same Connerly who paints a color-blind America? Indeed, he is. He also is the same Connerly whose friend, California state legislator Pete Wilson, got him a job in housing and community development in the administration of Gov. Ronald Reagan. And guess how Connerly got rich? Through affirmative action. His land consulting firm is a by-product of affirmative action.

Of course, Connerly told *Palm Beach Post* political editor Brian E. Crowley that his jobs and clients were not the result of affirmative action: "Say I'm a crony of Pete Wilson. Say I'm appointed because I gave him $130,000 for his campaign. But instead, we would rather believe a black person got something because he is black. That stigma is not helpful."

Neither is disingenuously denying the enduring scourge of race in America.

Although Thomas's outburst was fiery and Connerly's self-pitying, Keyes's was zany. Following the recent debate among Republican presidential candidates in New Hampshire, Keyes, the only black person in the GOP hunt for the White House, attacked the media for not taking his campaign seriously: "I often win these debates, and every time I stand before you press folks, you have no questions. I find it kind of amazing. At some point . . . one has to start to wonder. The people of this country have gotten over their racial sickness. I don't know that you folks have. I think that merit means nothing to you because you can't look past race. And I think I'm deadly sick of it."

Needless to say, the journalists shook their heads in wonderment. What Keyes failed to see was that his race is not the reason his campaign is ignored. Journalists do not cover him because few voters see him as a viable candidate. Were he Gen. Colin Powell, who credits his blackness for much of his success, the press would be all over him. But Keyes, a Simon Peter, did what his ilk does best: he played the race card when it was convenient.

These brothers cannot have race both ways. Either race matters, or it does not matter.

In speaking of Connerly, Tony Welch, an African-American and director of communications for the Florida Democratic Party, aptly sums up this whole sorry trend of denial among black Republicans. His comments are worth quoting at length: "Every breath Mr. Connerly breathes as the head of this petition drive is a breath of hypocrisy. You have to ask, who would listen to Mr. Connerly were he white? The answer: nobody. This only works with a black man leading the charge. Connerly was recruited for his current role because of the color of his skin. . . . In every speech, every article, Connerly is affirmative action attacking affirmative action. Occasionally, you'll hear Connerly or Alan Keyes lament that they've been the victims of discrimination.

"It's interesting to note that they're willing to abandon their talk of the colorblind society when discrimination in some form hits them. Then, it's discrimination. It seems to me they wear black just fine when it can do them some good. Professionally, they've carved out a niche for themselves—the black and anti-black. It's good pay. You just have to avoid mirrors."

In the end, Thomas, Connerly, and Keyes can run, but they cannot hide from their coloredness.

Black Republicans are strange indeed

December 8, 1999

By all standards, some creatures are just plain strange, making us do double takes because their compositions or habits or appearances defy our sense of logic and our way of viewing reality. Take the wildebeest, the warthog, the hyena, the brown pelican, the shar-pei. These animals, seemingly wrought by committee, make us laugh or shake our heads.

Another such creature, of the human kind—and perhaps the strangest of all—is the black Republican. Do not laugh. This is a serious matter, given yet another Alan Keyes run—absurd as it may be—for the White House. He is the talk show host who exhibits an obnoxious messianic complex that emerges each time he appears on TV to debate his white counterparts. My grandfather, a smart Pentecostal pastor who died five years ago, would have said that Keyes, along with others like him, is "out there cuttin' up 'round them white folks." This was my gramps' portrayal of black sycophants, whose raison d'être was pleasing their white "superiors."

After each debate, Keyes declares himself the winner and attacks the press for not praising him. He is not praised because he acts too much like a kid pledging a fraternity he instinctively dislikes. Doubling Keyes's misery is his pathetic effort to persuade white Republicans to accept him.

And therein lies the rub: black Republicans fail to understand that white Republicans will never accept them as equals. Although they will not acknowledge the truth, white Republicans, like most other whites, view black Republicans as strange creatures.

Following last week's GOP debate in New Hampshire, *New York Times* columnist Maureen Dowd interviewed Keyes and revealed that the prez wanna-be is an existential mess. He cannot understand why the networks' Sunday morning talk shows ignore him. "He does not seem to accept the fact that it is his own party that dismisses his candidacy as an oddity, useful only in enabling Republicans to make a perverse claim to diversity," Dowd wrote. With few exceptions (Gen. Colin Powell being a notable example), black Republicans are trotted out like unfinished trophies, Pirandello-like proof that the GOP's "big tent" is real in someone's warped mind.

White Republicans feign consternation that most blacks find them contemptible, arguing that those mean old Democrats have been black people's real enemy all along. Keyes and others, such as U.S. Supreme Court justice Clarence Thomas, Oklahoma's Rep. J. C. Watts, and California businessman Ward Connerly, also spout this nonsense. Keyes told Dowd: "The people who invented this system of racism, segregation, sort of American apartheid, were Democrats."

Oh, please.

If Keyes and others are talking about Dixiecrats, they should say so. They certainly are not talking about the millions of white Democrats who joined blacks against Republicans to secure every piece of civil rights legislation.

Blacks who switch to the GOP say they do so because they share Republican values on crime, family, and self-reliance. I do not know a single black person, except for the vicious thugs, who sees any benefits in crime. Blacks have always opposed crime. Most black people, like whites, love their families. Self-reliance? Until urban renewal used expressways to break up many black communities, black businesses thrived and people took care of themselves. Such values are not in the sole possession of Republicans.

African-Americans do not need hypocrites like Keyes, Thomas, and Connerly to lecture them. They certainly do not need the advice of white Republicans.

Some blacks, like General Powell, become Republicans because they see a clear political advantage or because they work for Republicans. Most others, however, are mean-spirited self-loathers who rarely find anything positive to say about fellow blacks. They out-nasty the worst white racist, calling the likes of Jesse Jackson, the NAACP's Kweisi Mfume, and the Urban League's Hugh Price evil men hell-bent on destroying America.

White Republicans love this kind of stuff. They wink and nod each time black Republicans claim that racism is a thing of the past, that whites and blacks are free to compete equally. Black Republicans have fooled themselves into believing that white Republicans are their brethren. And, of course, black Republicans delude themselves into believing that they alone are responsible for their success.

Strange, passing strange.

Dear Jeb: Your attitude needs work

JANUARY 26, 2000

Hello Gov. Jeb Bush,

This is my first e-mail to you. I am making it public because of the stink you instigated last week, the one in which—despite your assertion that you were talking about reporters—you referred to two black legislators staging a sit-in near your office and said, "Kick their asses out."

Profanity does not bother me, Jeb, because I am a marine and a ghetto man-child and have been known to use a few graphic &%#$+!!! myself. I do not even mind your volcanic temper. What does bother me, though, is the attitude in your words.

And let us get one thing straight up front: unlike many other journalists, I like you and wish you well. I respect what you have done for the kids at Liberty City Charter School, and I applaud your dialogue with farm-workers.

That said, back to your attitude. You are a true-blue Republican—a privileged white dude with so many breaks in life that the world literally is your oyster. I mean, your father is a wealthy former United States president. You never worried about anything—the next meal, a roof over your head, home heating oil, a reliable car, money for college, health insurance, a job. You have had it all, Jeb, for just being born.

Like the typical Republican, you are a creature of class. You believe in it, and you live it. You know what I mean by class: the division of society into social ranks and castes. High and low. Attitude, Jeb. One of the problems with you and most other Republicans is that you all lie about class, pretending that it does not matter.

Even worse, many of you delude yourselves into believing that class does not exist in America. You all do not want to talk about class because it reminds you all that the GOP is, as blacks have always said, a bunch of mean-spirited, country-club white boys who still cannot get that noblesse oblige thing right.

When politicians downplay the significance of class, at least two bad things happen. One, they distort reality. Two, they make bad laws. Let me give you an example, Jeb. Your A+ Plan to improve Florida's public schools has a few nice touches. But it also has a terrible flaw that results from your attempt to avoid class.

The flaw is that all schools, no matter how rich or poor, are graded the same. The truth is that poor schools, such as those in Miami's Liberty City, make up the bulk of the failing schools. Why? It is a class thing, Jeb. Kids in Miami's wealthy Kendall community invariably perform much better than those poor ones in Overtown. This is not rocket science, my man. Just dirty reality.

Whenever journalists make this point, you and that Frank Brogan guy accuse us of believing that poor black children cannot learn. I do not know anyone who believes such crap, Jeb. You and Brogan are not telling the truth, and you two know it.

Confidentially, Jeb, I think the A+ Plan may yield some good results if we 'fess up about class and, unapologetically, put more money and resources into our poorer schools. Even better—while the state is rolling in lucre—we need to train many low-income parents how to be effective parents, how to put their children's education first. We are still talking class, Jeb. And attitude.

You and that Brogan act as if only you two care about Florida's schools and children. Well, Jeb, my son attended public school, my daughter graduates in May, and my grandson is in fifth grade. My siblings and I attended public school. We give a damn. And my colleagues here at the *Times*—who have sons, daughters, grandchildren, and great-grandchildren in our schools—care.

Even some of your fellow lawmakers accuse you of having a rotten attitude, calling you a control freak whose body language telegraphs disrespect for other officials, especially those who disagree with you. And, Jeb, your nasty attitude toward the press will not help you and your cause. We are not going away, and you cannot control us. We are doing our job when we watch you. "No comment" and snide remarks (which you are full of) hurt you more than you think, Jeb. Most journalists are college-educated, well-read, well-traveled, hard-boiled professionals. So do not talk down to us or try to push us around. We push back, and we watch governors come and go.

Last point: you may want to lose black sycophants Willie Logan, James Hargrett, and Rudy Bradley. Time will prove that these soul brothers do not have a clue, Jeb.

Well, that is all for now. Any time I think you are getting too big for your britches, I will e-mail you. And I know how much you love e-mail. Until your next "Kick their asses out!" moment—

Your pal, Bill Maxwell

George W.'s evasiveness on flag just won't cut it

FEBRUARY 6, 2000

There he goes again.

Leave it up to George W. Bush to weasel his way out of those ethical jams, especially those involving issues of race. Last month, the South Carolina NAACP asked the Texas governor and Republican presidential candidate to state his position concerning the Confederate flag atop the South Carolina Capitol. His answer? Bush said the people of South Carolina should make their own decision about flying the Confederate flag in Columbia.

No good.

Bush is running for president of the United States, not for South Carolina state representative. He should have more to say about the Confederate banner, a symbol of human subjugation, racism, and death. During a recent stop at CBS's *Face the Nation*, Bush was challenged to identify a moral issue the president should take a stand on even if the issue involves states' rights.

"Bigotry and racism and prejudice," Bush said.

Bush does not have the courage of his convictions. He did not—and has not—taken a stand on the Confederate flag. Although the flag flap is still raging, Bush waltzed into South Carolina the other day and showed that he has trouble standing up to bigotry and racism and prejudice. Are these the kind of sentiments the governor can tolerate?

Here is what happened: Bush—Mr. Compassionate Conservative—spoke at Bob Jones University in Greenville, South Carolina. Bob Jones represents everything that was and is bad about Dixie. Founded in 1927 by the Reverend Bob Jones Sr., an unreconstructed racist, the university in the 1970s admitted blacks for the first time ever, and only after the federal government yanked its tax-exempt status.

The university still maintains a policy prohibiting interracial dating. In fact, such dating is grounds for expulsion. "In defending the ban on interracial dating," according to the *Charlotte (North Carolina) Observer*, "school officials point to the biblical story about the Tower of Babel, where God divided the tower builders by their different languages. Some segregationists have interpreted the story as a warning against mixing races." At a news conference, the *Observer* stated, Bush said that although he opposes the ban on interracial dating, he saw no conflict between his visit and his so-called message of inclusiveness.

So why did Bush speak at this bastion of bigotry and racism and prejudice? "I went there to see 7,000 people," he told the *Observer*. "I went there because I was invited to go."

Let me understand.

If the Ku Klux Klan invites Bush to speak at its national convention, he would go because he was invited? Would he compliment them on their spiffy new hoods and designer sheets? I exaggerate, of course, but where will Bush draw the ethical line in his search for votes? Why is he so craven in the face of such issues?

Many Bush supporters will argue that I and others are making too much out of his noncommittal stands on the flag and Bob Jones University, that these are small matters. I do not think so. If Bush is seriously trying to woo black voters, he is going about it in a dumb way. Blacks will not forget Bush's words and reactions. For many blacks, tolerating racist behavior and philosophy is more contemptible than all of Bill Clinton's sins combined.

Keepers of the Flame

A national family reunion

JULY 20, 1997

A tall, slender African-American woman sat at a table in front of the David L. Lawrence Convention Center reading the *Pittsburgh Courier*, a local black newspaper. Another woman, dressed in traditional African garb, approached and called out, "Verlette! Girl, is that you?"

"Paula?" the woman reading the newspaper screamed.

They embraced, swaying from side to side. They rubbed each other and cried. Eyes closed, they held each other in this manner for more than three minutes.

Observing these friends reunite, I realized that, perhaps unlike any national gathering of any other group, the annual convention of the National Association for the Advancement of Colored People is a cultural phenomenon in every sense of the term. And this, the organization's 88th meeting, was no exception, even though the group faces many serious problems. While journalists understandably were seeking the big political or social story, right in plain view were millions of living vignettes that define the nation's most remarkable homecoming.

Take the family—a mother, father, three teenagers—that parked at the Doubletree Hotel and unloaded 10 pieces of luggage from a GMC Safari sporting Mississippi license plates. The mother carried in both hands potted African violets from home. One son lugged a giant boom box and a plastic bag filled with cassettes; the other bounced a basketball and pretended to make jump shots. The daughter carried a framed poster of hit singer Babyface.

The father, wearing a Million Man March T-shirt, waved and walked over to other men holding placards that read, "We Demand Justice for

Jonny Gammage." Above the words on each sign was a big photo of Gammage, the Syracuse businessman who died in the custody of white police officers in Pittsburgh on October 12, 1995.

This family, like most others, had come to stay for a week, to make the hotel their home, to bond with others like themselves. Controversial boxing promoter Don King, who received one of the NAACP's highest awards before a crowd of more than 4,000, aptly described the familial sense of the gathering: "I look out into this audience and see people who look just like me. That makes me feel good all over." For better or for worse, the crowd roared. Above all, conventioneers came to get a transfusion of a culturally shared experience they cannot find anywhere else.

Outsiders often wonder why blacks tend to act in groups or tenaciously support people and causes that seem to be against their best interest. Why? Because at the center of the black experience, which is framed by the annual convention, is the irrepressible memory of slavery and the generations of tragedy and injustice that have followed. In effect, the convention is testimony to the creativity and resilience of blacks in the United States. Nearly everything at the convention manifests the black experience or intensifies it in some way.

Prayer, for example, opened and closed each plenary session. These were not simple prayers routinely offered, but heartfelt invocations to a God who promises that "the meek shall inherit the earth," as one minister said during the benediction. And gospel songs, themselves the handiwork of toil, fear, and courage, echoed each night throughout the convention center. Several groups, including the Harlem Boys Choir, had practiced all year for a chance to inspire their adopted family, to strike chords from the past while offering visions of the future.

The Reverend Julius C. Hope, national director of religious affairs for the NAACP, recognized the relationship between gospel music and the conferees and helped to organize the Gospel Extravaganza Saturday night. "Throughout history, this is where we come from," he said. "It's important to invoke the spirit of God to guide and lead us in the convention. And so we brought in the Gospel Extravaganza, where we come and unashamedly let the world know that we haven't forgotten where we come from and who made it all possible."

Conventioneers also shared their unique experience in workshops centered on coping with, correcting, or overcoming institutionalized racism in various areas of American life. Topics of the sessions included police brutality, the segregation of public schools, anti–affirmative action measures, and breaking through the glass ceiling. Few if any black people here in Steel

Town for the meeting had escaped being the victim of institutionalized bigotry, a shared experience that breeds a special kinship.

But nothing else captured the spirit of the convention more than the maternal presence of Myrlie Evers-Williams, the chairwoman of Board of Directors. In her personal tragedy—the slaying of her husband, Medgar Evers, field director of the Mississippi NAACP, by a white racist—the conventioneers saw their own plight. Whenever she appeared, people instinctively wanted to stand. They wanted to show respect. And whenever Coretta Scott King, the widow of Martin Luther King Jr., joined Evers-Williams, some people did stand. These widows, bittersweet symbols of the black condition, never went far from each other the second day of the meeting.

And when they locked arm-in-arm and gave a tearful tribute to the late Betty Shabazz, who died from wounds suffered in a fire set by her 12-year-old grandson, a hush fell over the hall of nearly 5,000. After they introduced two of Shabazz's daughters, Gamilah and Ilyasha, many people cried openly.

This was a national family reunion—a spiritual and cultural happening that everyone in the David L. Lawrence Convention Center will long remember. Even the evil specter of the white-robed American Knights of the Ku Klux Klan outside the center during President Clinton's address on Thursday, the last day of the meeting, could not spoil the depth of the experience the conventioneers had shared.

Reassessing the value of desegregation at the national level

JULY 12, 1998

To the approximately 600,000 NAACP faithful around the world, Julian Bond and Kweisi Mfume are the black "dynamic duo." Never before in its 89-year history has the National Association for the Advancement of Colored People, the nation's oldest and most venerable civil rights organization, had such capable leaders in its two top positions at the same time.

Bond accepted the chairmanship of the Board of Directors in February. He replaced Myrlie Evers-Williams, who had served for two years. Mfume became president and chief executive in 1996, replacing Benjamin Chavis, who was ousted in scandal.

For the near future, each man will need to capitalize on the power of his good looks, charisma, and exceptional intellect because, despite the NAACP's promising economic outlook, the organization is at a crossroads on several fronts, including the redefinition of its role in the wake of the nation's new conservative mood.

Ironically, its most serious dilemma, which will surface this week at the annual convention in Atlanta, revolves around school desegregation, the concept that has defined the NAACP and the Legal Defense Fund since 1954. That is when the U.S. Supreme Court—with the NAACP representing black children—outlawed separate-but-equal public school facilities in *Brown vs. Board of Education.*

Years later, in 1971, the court ruled in *Swann vs. Charlotte-Mecklenburg Board of Education* that "forced busing" could be used to achieve racial balance in public schools. The NAACP believed that it had discovered the perfect tool for bringing whites and blacks together in the same schoolhouses. Most blacks and many white liberals believed that the education of black children would radically improve as a result of desegregation. Until then, black children in the South had been victims of de jure and de facto segregation, which meant used books, slim budgets, few materials and resources, and, of course, run-down buildings.

Today, nearly 45 years after *Brown,* some NAACP board members, many state and local directors, and rank-and-file members attending this week's national convention argue that desegregation is no longer viable either as a political tactic or as a social philosophy.

During the weeks leading up to last year's annual convention in Pittsburgh, Evers-Williams promised that the organization would seriously debate whether it should continue to pursue the desegregation of public schools or redirect its efforts into improving the schools that the bulk of black children attend because of where they live. She even told a *New York Times* reporter that she would consider a resolution to reverse the board's traditional stance on desegregation. The day before voting delegates arrived in Pittsburgh, however, she reversed herself, saying the NAACP would never alter its position on integration in the schools.

Mfume joined Evers-Williams at the podium to calm delegates who had expected a forthright debate. He suggested that desegregation is a complex process that requires more than busing and mixing the races in the classroom. He said also that desegregation—or real integration—will occur when segregated housing patterns change and when gaps between the incomes of whites and blacks are closed.

"We can't let ourselves be isolated from the real world," he said. "If we're separated, we can't survive. I understand the lure of separatism. When people are ticked off, they dig in. They pull away from each other. They make generalizations about this group or that group. . . . Separatism doesn't have a functional reality in our pluralistic world."

Mfume and Bond, today's NAACP leaders, must again sort out the group's stance on desegregation and neighborhood schools. Although the two are not publicly talking about the issue in advance of the voting delegates' arrival, as Evers-Williams did last year, conferees who support vouchers and charter schools are saying that they deserve and want some straight answers. After all, recent surveys conducted by the Joint Center for Political and Economic Studies, a Washington think tank, and by other public opinion organizations show that most blacks nationwide support vouchers and neighborhood schools. They certainly are disenchanted with public schools.

Where does Bond, a former Georgia state representative, stand? Remember, he is a civil rights legend who, as a student at Morehouse College, led demonstrations to desegregate public places in Atlanta. And in 1960, the Student Nonviolent Coordinating Committee hired him as its first communications director. "Generally among black Americans," Bond said last year, "there is a feeling that [school integration] has come to naught, that so much energy has been put into it without commensurate results and that white America has been so resistant that you're butting your head against the wall. I think that it's a wrong attitude, but it's an understandable attitude."

Evers-Williams and Mfume shut down the desegregation debate in 1997. This time, though, pro-debate delegates have more ammunition on their side. Increasing numbers of federal judges, for example, are releasing school districts from desegregation orders. Here in Florida, Hillsborough and Pinellas Counties soon expect to receive "unitary" status. A unitary district is either one that never practiced racial segregation or one that, through good-faith compliance with court orders, has remedied—to the extent practicable—the vestiges of such discrimination. While judges are preparing to declare districts unitary, more systems nationwide are establishing charter schools and voucher programs each semester. These trends show no signs of slowing down.

At this year's convention, the group's 89th, the dynamic duo will need to pull out all the stops to silence rank-and-file conferees—most them parents—who want to publicly reevaluate the viability of school desegregation. Sooner or later, the NAACP's top brass must let a real debate take place. Sooner is better than later, many delegates are saying.

Tune in to differences and turn off TV

JULY 14, 1999

Here we go again, another well-intentioned but doomed diversity crusade, replete with threats, textbook oratory, and enough political, social, historical, and mythological allusions to wow an Ivy League doctoral committee on American popular culture in the 1990s.

By now, most Americans know that the NAACP, the nation's oldest civil rights organization, has promised to fight the major television networks over the ethnic makeup of fall offerings. During a rousing speech Monday to nearly 3,000 members attending the 90th annual convention of the National Association for the Advancement of Colored People, the group's president and CEO, Kweisi Mfume, said that of the 26 new prime-time shows slated for the fall on ABC, CBS, NBC, and FOX, not one has a minority-group member in a leading role. "This glaring omission is an outrage and a shameful display by network executives who are either clueless, careless, or both," Mfume said. "When the television-viewing public sits down to watch the new prime-time shows scheduled for this fall lineup, they will see a virtual whitewash in programming."

How does Mfume propose to fix this problem—one that I do not think needs urgent repair and one that diverts precious energy away from more pressing issues? For starters, the NAACP will establish a watchdog arm in Tinseltown to monitor the TV and film industries. Mfume said that if meetings with network and advertising executives do not produce satisfaction, he may call for a boycott of these "highly segregated shows." His most exotic tactic will be pursuing civil action against these industries. Lawyers will base claims on the 1934 Federal Communications Act, which makes the airwaves public property.

Mfume suggested that racism is to blame for the small number of blacks on prime-time TV. He is right—indirectly. Indeed, most advertising and programming bosses are white and they air material that appeals to them. Mfume seems to have forgotten, however, that prime-time TV is showbiz and that showbiz is not about social and cultural crusades. It is about mega bucks. Nielsen ratings. Market share.

The truth is that TV executives are not "clueless" or "careless." They know America. Surveys indicate that black shows (particularly sitcoms) and characters turn off most white viewers. With blacks constituting only 13 percent of the population and with only a tiny part of that number interested in network fare, network moguls do not see a natural need to create black shows. What is in it for them, when blacks flock to cable to see themselves?

Whites prefer upscale, white-oriented shows infused with slick repartee, such as *Seinfeld, Friends,* and *Frasier.* Why would a CBS producer, a businessperson, include a black headliner who turns off white viewers? On the other side, only a handful of African-Americans watch the major white sitcoms. Blacks do not like white stuff. When will the NAACP learn that much of the cultural divide is natural, that what often seems like racism may be, in reality, a matter of being comfortable with those who resemble ourselves and share our special heritage?

Should the NAACP abandon its TV diversity crusade? No. But the organization should not make it an expensive, time-consuming priority.

Why? Nationwide, educators worry that black children, even those in the middle and upper classes, lag far behind their white counterparts academically. Harvard University researcher Ronald Ferguson, for example, tried to learn why middle-class black students at academically acclaimed Shaker Heights High School near Cleveland, while making up 50 percent of the student population, constitute 9 percent of those who graduated in the top fifth of their class but 83 percent of those at the bottom.

Among other factors, Ferguson discovered that black students watch twice as much TV as white students. Obviously, black students do not need to be lured into the silliness, black or white, on prime-time TV. They watch the tube too much already.

Yes, I know the arguments that black children need positive role models and that TV can provide them. But maybe the long hours that black children spend watching TV to learn a lesson of negligible value from a remote role model is a bad trade-off. They need to be taught to stick their faces in books, not TV screens.

I will bet that if the networks do what Mfume wants, African-Americans will regret the long-term, unintended consequences. Our children watch three hours of TV a day. Enough already.

NAACP must keep focus on solving problems of black Americans

July 18, 1999

If the announcements and legal challenges made last week during its 90th annual convention at the Hilton in midtown Manhattan are signs of things to come, the National Association for the Advancement of Colored People is no longer AWOL.

For too long, the nation's oldest and largest civil rights organization was mired in scandal, infighting, and money problems. As a result, it became lethargic, irrelevant, and disconnected from the concerns of the grassroots black population. Worse, it was out of touch with young African-Americans in search of adult leadership.

During its six-day convention in the Big Apple, where more than 14,000 members gathered, the NAACP emerged as a force to be reckoned with on several issues dogging the nation. It promised action, for example, against the easy availability of guns and outlined new efforts to help improve public education. The group also focused on issues specifically affecting blacks, such as racial profiling, police brutality, the lack of ethnic diversity in prime-time television, the disproportionately low number of blacks using the Internet, voter registration, and discrimination in the hospitality industry.

Even with these new battlefronts, however, the NAACP remains ambivalent about its identity and the roles it will play in various areas of American life in the new century. Will it remain essentially a black organization? Or, given the changing faces and weapons on the civil rights battlefield, will the NAACP employ a strategy that willingly embraces other constituencies and ethnic groups?

"In the 1950s and '60s, civil rights had to do with race," David Bositis, a researcher for the Joint Center for Political and Economic Studies, told *USA Today*. "[Civil rights] had to do with black people. And in the 1990s and beyond, you're talking about civil rights which involve a whole variety of different people. . . . You're talking about gays and women and senior citizens."

NAACP top brass, including the chairman of the Board of Directors, Julian Bond, have acknowledged the new reality. "We know that colored people come in all colors in this country," he said during a speech on the first night of the convention. "We know we move forward fastest when we move forward together. Where there are others who share our condition, even if they may not share our history, we intend to make common cause with them." Experts say that the hues on the demographic landscape in 2050 will not resemble those of today, at least not in percentages. Non-Hispanic whites are predicted to make up 52.8 percent of the population, Latinos 24.5 percent, blacks 13.6 percent, Asians 8.2 percent, and American Indians .9 percent.

But not all blacks close to NAACP operations, including Bositis, who studies the nation's changing demographics, believe that the organization can or should become an umbrella for cross-cultural alliances. "The NAACP has too long a history as the premier black organization in the United States," he said. "That doesn't mean the NAACP won't be able to work with other groups in coalition. But the NAACP is a black organization. There's no way it's going to be anything else."

I agree. Too many African-Americans still have not learned that they are the key to their success, that within them—inside their own minds and bodies—lies the real revolution that can transform black life in one generation. During his speech, Bond demonstrated that he understands what I am talking about: "Despite oppressive forces around us, despite the heavy weight of the self-satisfied and the self-haters, despite the coldheartedness of the neoconservative confederacy, a great deal of the solution to our current problems lies within our own control."

Of course Bond is right. The NAACP needs to spend more time on efforts fostering a sense of solving our own problems. It cannot, and should not, become everything to everyone. Like Jewish organizations that focus solely on Jewish problems, the NAACP needs to focus on black problems. After all, is any other viable group on the national level—besides the Nation of Islam—tending exclusively to black problems?

Speaking at the convention, the Reverend Jesse Jackson casually sounded the same coalition-building note when he said that the NAACP's next crusade should be "the battle to provide greater access to capital and economic power" to all Americans. This statement has broad appeal. But like other such comments that floated around the convention floor, it means nothing as long as blacks remain ignorant, for example, of investing and saving.

Whites, Asians, and most other groups do not need the NAACP to teach them how to invest and save.

The organization needs to pull out all the stops to teach blacks how to quit spending themselves into the poorhouse. By buying luxury cars to the tune of $35,000 to $140,000 and other depreciating toys—in an attempt to show that we are "somebody"—we are mortgaging our futures, literally condemning our children to perpetual second-class citizenship. Black America is a conclave of consumers, not investors. Transforming this unproductive trait should be one of the NAACP's focuses—not worrying about white America, which can damned well take care of itself.

The NAACP is no longer absent without leave. Now it needs to find its identity. The time for ambivalence has long passed. Coalition building is admirable, but the NAACP is not prepared to solve the problems of other groups. For this powerful organization, nothing is more important than teaching black Americans that "the solution to our current problems lies within our own control."

Opiate of the Masses

Pope's view of women knocks him off pedestal

NOVEMBER 27, 1994

I went off to college in 1963 believing that knowledge nearly always produces wisdom—the ability to choose the soundest course of action. Then I took a poetry course featuring the works of T. S. Eliot and Ezra Pound. Nothing was the same after that. At first, few things intrigued me more than the symbols and allusions Eliot uses to capture J. Alfred Prufrock's spiritual trauma. Nothing was more intellectually challenging than trying to decipher one of Pound's dense, Latinate cantos. Imagine my astonishment when the professor revealed that these two great poets hated blacks and Jews. Pound had even supported Adolf Hitler and Benito Mussolini. *How could these brilliant men hate their fellow humans so passionately?* I thought. Later, in a journalism course, I was shocked to learn that H. L. Mencken, the *Baltimore Sun* essayist whose work we were studying, also despised blacks and Jews.

By my junior year, I had been disabused of my blind faith in the power of knowledge to lead us from the cave. And now, at age 49, I am still obsessed with the overriding question: what causes so many learned people, especially the icons of civilization past and present, to succumb to the base sentiments and emotions we routinely attribute to the uneducated and the ignorant?

On a lesser scale, why do so many influential thinkers, like Charles Murray of *The Bell Curve* fame, use their knowledge to perpetuate harmful myths and stereotypes? Why do other smart people, like House Speaker-to-be Newt Gingrich, a former university professor with a doctorate in history, use their knowledge to diminish innocent people and warp the truth? Why would Gingrich, for example, offer mandatory prayer in public schools as the enlightened solution to the complex problem of America's deficit of values? Such simpleminded thinking is deeply flawed and often dangerous.

But no contemporary intellectual disappoints me more than Karol Wojtyla, Pope John Paul II. I have just finished his most recent book of essays, *Crossing the Threshold of Hope*. From the first page, the pope, a trained philosopher and a former university professor, reveals a brilliant mind. And his facility in highlighting the philosophies of Descartes, Feuerbach, Kant, Wittgenstein, and others places him among the world's first-rate scholars. His vast knowledge of the documents of the Second Vatican Council gives even non-Catholics a better sense of the Roman Catholic Church's mission to reinvigorate its spirituality and establish its proper place in our chaotic, modern world.

One of the most striking features of the book is the pope's objective discussions of other religions and beliefs. His views affirm his ecumenical quest, portraying him as a progressive leader determined to bring humankind and the divine into an intimate relationship, one that will dignify our earthly existence. I am impressed with his respect for the "religiosity" of Muslims and his assessment of Jews "as [Catholics'] elder brothers in faith." He even compares ancestor worship with the Christian concept of the Communion of Saints. And I was surprised when he did not denounce Cardinal Hans Urs Von Baltassar's position on universal salvation.

Nothing in the book prepared me for John Paul II's flawed thinking on the family, on married sexuality in general, and on women in particular. If I had remembered the Holy See's positions at the recent International Conference on Population and Development in Cairo, however, I would have been ready for the pope's gruff dismissal of women, his rejection of them as serious participants in the church's hierarchy. Even worse, he does not see women as the keepers of their own bodies. He does not see them as adults with authority to make decisions on sexuality and reproduction. To John Paul II, women who use birth control are as guilty as abortionists.

The pope insists on what he calls "responsible parenthood," an unconvincing concept that requires women to conceive for as long as their bodies can hold out. And yet John Paul II offers no substantive way for the Roman Catholic Church itself to resolve the economic crises his concept of parenthood causes. If the pope makes "responsible parenthood" infallible, as many are certain he will, he has the moral obligation to provide an infallible, church-centered solution.

The Reverend Diarmuid Martin, who headed the Holy See's delegation in Cairo, expressed the pope's laudable but unrealistic solution: "Wealthy states must realize that it is only by helping poor countries raise their living standards that they will solve the population problem, not by forcing them to adopt Western attitudes toward abortion and contraception."

Obviously, I still expect too much of intellectuals. I do not understand what makes this brilliant man not see that the best answer to population lies with individual women who must be empowered to make practical choices. No, I am not talking about abortion. Like the pope, I believe that economic development, education, and health care must anchor all efforts to control population. But the pope's concept of "responsible parenthood," if it is to become viable in the real world, also must include responsible birth control. I do not understand what blinds the pope to women's equal status in civilization nor what makes him think that feminism is grounded "in the absence of true respect for women."

Why is his essay on women only a page and a half—the shortest one in the book? Is the otherwise brilliant pontiff a contemporary victim of the supposed inerrancy of ancient Scriptures and church dogma? Can the pope reunite humankind with what he calls "the Last Things"—the innocence, the respect for life, and the love for others that make daily existence worthwhile?

I do not think so, because, according to him, women do not merit the right to cross the threshold of hope he envisions. Such intellectual rigor mortis is compromising the legitimacy of his leadership and debasing his claim to moral authority. In short, Karol Wojtyla's view of women is pernicious—proving that knowledge does not necessarily produce wisdom.

Breaking through the impasse on religion in school

For his own sake, but mostly for the sake of the thousands of young lives in his care, David Mosrie, superintendent of St. Lucie County schools, should bone up on John T. Scopes, the Tennessee schoolteacher convicted and fined in 1925 for teaching Charles Darwin's theory of evolution in defiance of a state law requiring the teaching of creationism.

Mosrie is not in trouble for advocating, as Scopes did, that humankind is descended from monkeys. Nor is his problem, as Scopes's was, the total rejection of creationism in public schools. His dilemma, which has national implications because of the religious right's growing influence on the Republican political agenda, stems from meetings he had with two Christian groups. He allegedly told them, without informing School Board members, that while he believes in the theory of evolution, he also supports the "discussion" of creationism in science classes. Several leading members of the religious groups interpreted Mosrie's use of the term "discussion" as nothing less than tacit approval to "teach" creationism.

At last week's board meeting, Mosrie clarified his position: "I do not now, nor have I ever intended to require creationism [to] be taught as a part of our science curriculum. I still believe it is perfectly appropriate and legal for teachers to permit open classroom discussion of alternate theories, including the possibility of an intelligent creator." While the theory of evolution remains school policy, he does not want to require science teachers to tell students who believe in the biblical creation that their beliefs are wrong. Teachers should use discretion in letting students talk freely.

An exchange between board member Tom Coss and resident Nancy Spalding demonstrates the tenor of the ongoing debate.

Coss: "I have no problem with students knowing more than one theory. I feel students should know that there are two theories. It's America, and if they want to sue me, they can."

Spalding: "That is unthinkable. If that comes up in a science class, the students must be told that there is no scientific validity to creationism."

Unfortunately, such either/or positions reach beyond St. Lucie County. Across the nation, advocates and opponents of religion-related issues such as teaching of creation science and establishing prayer in schools are at a dangerous impasse where only two irreconcilable alternatives are apparent.

But Charles Haynes, visiting professor at the Freedom Forum First Amendment Center at Vanderbilt University, offers a third option that might bring some sanity to such debates: why not teach religion in the schools with scholarship and calm, not with dogma and vituperation? "Most people neither wish to impose religion in the schools nor eliminate religion from the schools," Haynes said recently. "They want programs that give religion an appropriate place while protecting everyone's freedom of conscience."

The occasion for Haynes's comments was the publication of *Finding Common Ground*, a Freedom Forum guidebook for teachers and administrators on how constitutionally to include religion and religious sentiments in public schools. The book's major premise is that we have hurt public education by excluding religion from the curriculum. However, the book argues that we can repair the damage without violating the mandate of church-state separation. Such a course should not proselytize or impose beliefs on students. It should be an academic subject in which all faiths and denominations are studied.

"Omission of facts about religion can give students the false impression that the religious life of humankind is insignificant or unimportant," the book states. "Failure to understand even the basic symbols, practices and concepts of the various religions makes much of history, literature, art and contemporary life unintelligible."

But is such a course possible, or needed, in today's supercharged climate? What must be done first?

Iris M. Yob, a professor at the School of Education at the State University of New York at Geneseo, sought answers to these questions nearly two years ago when she taught an elective called "Religion and the Public Schools." Her 13 students, all working on master's degrees, were full-time teachers in the public schools.

Because Yob had few examples to follow, her task was daunting. "How could I set up the course to model the best of our understanding regarding the fundamental principles of freedom of religion and expression and the principle of separation of church and state?" she writes in November's *Phi Delta Kappa* magazine. "And how could we best scrutinize our cherished beliefs and personal prejudices in an effort to prepare teachers to meet the religious diversity that shapes today's classrooms and the world in which we live?" The centerpiece of the course was showing students how to create a climate of neutrality, objectivity, flexibility, and caring in their classrooms. Discussions were often heated but always instructive. In addition to exploring specific aspects of religions—including secular humanism—students kept a journal in which they explored their personal doubts and affirmations of faith.

Did the course yield insights on whether or not religion should be taught as an academic subject in the nation's public schools? No solid consensus emerged. But everyone agreed that the success or failure of such a course would depend mainly on how well individual teachers handle potentially volatile issues.

Yob said that each student left the class with "a sense that the large, unexplored territory of religious faith is a powerful force in personal and group life and should be better understood by everyone in the interests of effective teaching and learning." In this light, the flap over creationism in St. Lucie County, along with other such controversies, is the result of "religious illiteracy," a condition in which both sides refuse to learn more about their opponents' positions. As with other societal problems, the nation's impasse on religion in the schools can be resolved only with education, hard work, and sincerity.

Baptists' apologies are right

JUNE 25, 1995

For about 10 years, I have been writing about the concept of collateral responsibility. I define it as our moral duty to correct the residual effects of the collective wrongs of earlier generations of our relatives and other people we emulate, those who have shaped our negative behavior toward others or who have bolstered our capacity to condone human cruelty.

For too long, too many whites have shirked their duty to redress the legacy of slavery—America's "original sin." Its perniciousness lingers in our collective psyche and continues to divide the nation. This legacy continues to define too many black people, forcing them to view themselves as outsiders in their own homeland.

But a ray of hope shines from an unexpected source. And those of us who believe in collateral responsibility are cautiously pleased. The 15.6-million-member Southern Baptist Convention, at one time the nation's best-organized and largest group of bigots, apparently has seen the light.

At their recent 150th anniversary in Atlanta, 20,000 conferees approved a resolution on racial reconciliation with African-Americans: "We lament and repudiate historic acts of evil such as slavery from which we continue to reap bitter harvest, and we recognize that the racism which yet plagues our culture today is inextricably tied to the past." The document specifically asks for "forgiveness from our African-American brothers and sisters, acknowledging that our own healing is at stake."

Blacks are justifiably skeptical of this conversion. After all, the Southern Baptist Convention was founded before the Civil War by whites who saw no ethical conflict in worshiping Christ, owning slaves, and going to heaven. Neither have blacks forgotten that this is the same church that opposed the civil rights movement in the 1950s and 1960s, and that had hundreds of thousands of members who supported the Ku Klux Klan's evil agenda.

And, paradoxically, today's Southern Baptist Convention is the same organization that is supporting the Republicans' cynical attack on affirmative action even as it seeks forgiveness for its racist past. Mind you, racism is the mother of affirmative action, and racism still makes affirmative action necessary. If southern Baptists are serious about atoning for their historical sins, how can they also join Republicans in destroying affirmative action—the one federal program that modestly attempts to redress some of the wrongs of discrimination?

Such a contradiction between rhetoric and action makes me, and millions of other blacks, wary of the southern Baptists' facelift. For the church to convince us that it has traveled the road to Damascus, its lay membership and all of its top officials must publicly and earnestly make the case for affirmative action. Sure, we know that with the middle class's hunt for scapegoats to explain its economic troubles and with conservatives' use of race as a wedge issue, no one can make an effective social, legal, or intellectual case for affirmative action. But the Southern Baptist Convention, with its vast reach and clout, could and should make the moral argument for affirmative action. Such a move would be politically unpopular, but morality must be brought back into the debate. Affirmative action is as much a moral issue as abortion. And southern Baptists do not need to send missionaries to, say, Ethiopia. They could deploy a million or more of them throughout the United States to help root out acts of racism.

Ultimately, though, the church's quest for atonement will fail if blacks reject it. The Reverend Gary Frost, second vice president—and the first black officer—of the Southern Baptist Convention, correctly assessed the situation: "One of the challenges is going to be [for] black Christians to forgive, and that may be a greater hurdle than repentance. It's going to be very challenging to us as a people to be able to accept this apology and to begin healing and mending and moving on." For average blacks to forgive, for the "healing" and "mending" and "moving on" to begin, the Southern Baptist Convention must make the moral case for affirmative action.

Even though the church stopped short of using the term "repent"—preferring to use the words "acknowledge" and "lament" instead—I still commend its leaders for the resolution. It is nothing short of a minor miracle because, by assuming collective responsibility for the sins of their forebears, the conferees rewrote the denomination's doctrine which holds that an individual member can only repent for his or her own sins.

But the real irony—and beauty—of the resolution are that it is a belated tribute to Martin Luther King Jr., the Baptist Convention's former nemesis, and King's "Letter from Birmingham Jail." King wrote the letter in response to a statement that was highly critical of his mass demonstrations, published by southern Baptist ministers and ministers of other denominations. Urging his detractors to stop attacking him and the movement, and to accept their collective responsibility for the sins of this white, Christian nation, King wrote: "Individuals may see the moral light and voluntarily give up their unjust posture; but, as Reinhold Niebuhr has reminded us, groups tend to be more immoral than individuals."

Bibles for, and of, the people

September 17, 1995

"Now when the Almighty was first down with His program, He made the heavens and the earth. The earth was a fashion misfit, being so uncool and dark, but the Spirit of the Almighty came down real tough, so that He simply said, 'Lighten up!' And that light was right on time."

Compare the following version with the one above: "In the beginning when God created the heavens and the earth, the earth was a formless void and darkness covered the face of the deep, while a wind from God swept over the face of the waters. Then God said, 'Let there be light'; and there was light."

Obviously, these passages depict the beginning of the Creation. The first comes from the 1993 *Black Bible Chronicles: A Survival Manual for the Streets;* the second, from *The Holy Bible: New Revised Standard Version.*

While critics reject the propriety of the *Bible Chronicles,* P. K. McCary, who revised the Old Testament books of Genesis, Exodus, Leviticus, Numbers, and Deuteronomy, ably explains his purpose: "The *Black Bible Chronicles* is an attempt to put the most important message of life into the language of the streets. This is in keeping with the very origins of the Bible. The New Testament was originally written in Koine Greek, the street language of the people. Subsequently, Martin Luther and others translated the Bible into the language of the people of their day. The *Black Bible Chronicles* stands in this tradition, bringing the Word to our younger generation in contemporary language." As far-out as the *Chronicles* may seem, it is part of a legitimate movement to make the Bible more broadly accessible. After all, we are in the age of "inclusiveness," so obsessed with political correctness that God would have a hard time pleasing most of us.

"So let there be PC Bibles," the new faithful are saying. And publishers are complying, as Bibles roll off the presses like manna. Over the years, 400 translations and revisions too numerous to count have appeared, representing almost every group and lifestyle.

The latest entry, which hits the shelves this week, is called *The New Testament and Psalms, An Inclusive Version.* It surpasses the 1994 *New Testament of the Inclusive Language Bible* and the breezy *Contemporary English Version of the Bible* in being politically correct. God, for example, is depicted as the androgynous "father-mother," and Christ becomes the more incarnate "human one" and "child of God." Dying on the cross, the human one says, "Father-mother, into your hands I commend my spirit."

Other changes are equally interesting. For instance, the 17th-century King James Bible shows Jesus teaching the disciples to pray thusly: "Our Father which art in heaven, Hallowed be thy name. Thy kingdom come. Thy will be done, as in heaven, so in earth." But the new inclusive Scriptures present Jesus saying: "Father-mother, hallowed be your name. May your dominion come."

The new PC Bible, moreover, bowdlerizes most of the familiar King James expressions and customs by neutering references to the sexes, by tidying up politically incorrect references to people with disabilities and people of color, and by empowering women. Wives, for example, should be "committed" instead of "submissive" or "subject" to their spouses. "Black" and "dark" no longer represent evil. And references to the "right hand" of God become the "mighty" hand, so as to respect the feelings of left-handed folk.

Again, the PC Bible's attempt to reflect contemporary attitudes is not new. In the 1950s and 1960s, thousands of southerners delighted in Scriptures called *The Cotton Patch Version of Paul's Epistles* and *The Cotton Patch Version of Luke and Acts: Jesus' Doings and the Happenings.* Sarcastic, earthy, intense, and funny, these slim volumes are the handiwork of the late theologian Clarence Jordan, founder of Koinonia Farm in Americus, Georgia. This pioneering cross-racial agricultural colony, where the seeds of Habitat for Humanity took root, was integral to the civil rights movement.

Here is Jordan re-creating a scene in Acts 14:19, where Jewish agitators persuade a group of locals to stone Paul and get rid of him: "Some good white folks came down from Vicksburg and Natchez, and got the people on their side. They beat the tar out of Paul and then dragged him out of town, leaving him for dead. While the Christians were hovering over him, he got up and reentered the city."

Jordan had a good reason for placing Jesus and the disciples among rednecks, crackers, and poor blacks: "By stripping away the fancy language, the artificial piety, and the barriers of time and distance, this version puts Jesus and his people in the midst of our modern world . . . alongside the rest of us."

Jordan thoroughly enjoyed the Bible, unlike many of the uptight, dolorous revisionists who came before and after him. For instance, the editors of yet another version of the Good Book aimed at blacks, *The Original African Heritage Study Bible*, clearly think too much of themselves and their product: "Afrocentricity, the idea that Africa and persons of African descent must be understood as making contributions to world civilization as proactive subjects within history, is the methodology with which the (Heritage Bible) endeavors to reappraise ancient biblical history."

Are such PC revisions good for the Bible, for religion? I think so. If nothing else, they are fun. Furthermore, inclusiveness is a noble goal, even when misguided. And none of us should worry that God (father-mother) is being discounted. Moses, the cool homeboy in *Black Bible Chronicles*, reassures us that God's omnipotence is safe, that humans cannot disrespect God: "Don't diss the Almighty, brothers. You ain't got the strength to beat Him."

Hallelujah!

Saved, in several ways

JUNE 1, 1997

Author Flannery O'Connor once described the South as "Christ-haunted." I recalled this eerie image a few days ago while reading Rick Bragg's article "A Years-Long Revival Draws the Multitudes" in the *New York Times*. Bragg takes a detailed, sensitive look at the nearly two-year, soul-saving phenomenon at the Assembly of God church in Pensacola, "the largest and longest-running Pentecostal revival in America in almost a century." With Christ haunting every aspect of the service, it attracts 3,000 to 6,000 nearly every night, many of whom fall to the floor struck numb by the "Holy Spirit."

While reading Bragg's portraits of "pilgrims" seeking salvation from "damnation" and "hellfire," I was transported back to life with my grandfather, Robert Albert Bentley, a presiding elder in the House of God, Church of the Living God, the Pillar and Ground of Truth Without Controversy, a black Pentecostal, or Holiness, denomination. I especially recall the events of one night.

My grandfather was pastor of congregations in St. Augustine, Palatka, and Crescent City and routinely conducted or participated in revivals from the slums of Orlando to desolate sharecroppers' plots near the Georgia border. In those days, the House of God was a poor denomination, the church buildings in my grandfather's circuit nothing more than shotgun-styled shacks of unpainted clapboard.

Ah, but how these lowly, tiny structures, with legal seating capacities of no more than 200, would shake and quake during "revival meetings." My grandfather would stand in the pulpit and invite the would-be faithful to "git saved with the Holy Ghost" and "jine" [join] the church. One by one, adults and teenagers would file to the altar, drop to their knees, and begin to "tarry"—repeating the name "Jesus" until they "spoke in tongue." Or did not speak in tongue. This ritual often lasted for hours, with well-wishing congregants urging on the seekers.

The longest tarrying that I witnessed occurred one summer in 1962 in Georgetown, Florida. Service started at 1:00 P.M. with sixteen pilgrims seeking salvation. At 2:00 A.M., three men and four women were still tarrying, saliva pouring from their mouths and their sweat-drenched clothes matted to their bodies. During the entire time, members of the choir took turns singing, and several drummers and pianists came and went. Most of the young children had fallen asleep on the rear pews.

Without warning, those tarrying began to speak in tongue at the same time. "Glory! Praise His holy name!" my grandfather screamed at the top of his lungs. About 100 worshipers remained. They surrounded the newly saved and broke into song and clapping. The bass drum created a hypnotic syncopation, pulling everyone, including my grandfather, into a holy dance, or shout, that lasted for more than an hour.

Then the most troubling thing I have ever seen in church happened. The wife of a visiting preacher was dancing uncontrollably. I marveled at how fast her feet moved and how high she jumped off the floor. I saw her pink bloomers slowly slide down her legs and around her ankles. She neatly stepped out of them and danced more wildly than before. I sat transfixed, unable to take my eyes off the mass of pink fabric heaped on the floor.

When I saw the big silver safety pin gathering a bunch of white elastic, I became embarrassed for the woman. Looking around the building, I saw that all of the adults, except for my grandmother, seemed oblivious to what had happened. The other children were like me: dumbfounded, intrigued, embarrassed.

The underwear just lay there, the entranced congregants stomping and dancing around it. I kept thinking: *Who is going to step on it? Why are they going around it? Do they see it?*

My grandmother, dignified and grim, glided across the floor, scooped up the drawers, and put them in her purse. She went back to her seat, looked me in the eye, winked, and tossed her nose toward the ceiling.

When the service finally ended at about 4:00, I could not keep my eyes off the preacher's wife. Would she retrieve her unmentionables? How would she do it? Would she boldly or discreetly ask? As my grandparents and I drove home to Crescent City, I asked my grandmother about the undergarment.

"The Lord didn't see nothing, so you didn't see nothing," she said. "The Holy Spirit caused it, and the Holy Spirit took care of it. Don't never mention it no more."

"Yes ma'am," I replied, and turned my attention to the shadows of the pines outside my window. The events of that night and the words of my grandmother always have puzzled me—even now.

I have never been strongly religious, but that night gave me lifelong respect for those who are religious and for the enduring power of faith to dignify people such as my grandparents, the Christ-haunted, the poor, and the dispossessed who have the ability to empathize with the suffering and crises in the lives of others. What could have become a source of eternal shame for the preacher's wife did not. To this day, I have never heard anyone in Crescent City or Georgetown discuss that incident. Perhaps my grandmother was right: "The Holy Spirit took care of it."

The black church remains a beacon

SEPTEMBER 24, 1997

We should not let the seemingly unending revelations about the Reverend Henry J. Lyons and others delude us into believing that the black church as an institution is fundamentally flawed.

Despite the sins of its preachers and despite the poor business practices of some congregations, the black church remains the most viable entity in black life. For some Tampa Bay area churchgoers, of course, the church experience, especially Sunday morning, has changed forever because of pastors such as Lyons. But for the overwhelming majority of blacks with whom I have spoken, the church remains and always will remain their shining beacon on the hill. Even more, the church has the singular power to organize black life, to give it meaning when reality may suggest otherwise, to give it purpose when hopelessness is an enticing option.

The reasons for these sentiments—which most whites remain ignorant of or ignore—are grounded in the social, cultural, and intellectual fabric of black history. "The black church has no challenger as the cultural womb of the black community," write C. Eric Lincoln and Lawrence H. Mamiya in their seminal book *The Church in the African American Experience*. "Not only did it give birth to new institutions such as schools, banks, insurance companies and low income housing, it also provided an academy and arena for political activities, and it nurtured young talent for musical, dramatic and artistic development."

For these reasons and others, noted sociologist E. Franklin Frazier refers to the black church as a "nation within a nation."

That it is.

Even though the reputation of another area cleric, the Reverend Wilkins Garrett Jr., has been sullied because of the Lyons controversy and a car accident involving alcohol, the longtime pastor of Mount Zion Progressive Baptist Church in St. Petersburg is an example of what Frazier means. He transformed the church, located in the middle of the area that was hit by violence last fall, into an economic and social action agency that accomplishes more than its federal counterparts.

Most residents in the immediate vicinity of Mount Zion have benefited either directly or indirectly from the church's efforts. In many ways, it has replaced government and has become the sole anchor for the truly disenfranchised, a nation within a nation. I know of several former crack addicts and dealers, for example, who found their way through Garrett, who have become successful leaders and business owners in their own right.

In a less tangible way, the church is an oasis that offers liberty and relief from a hostile environment. "A major aspect of black Christian belief is found in the symbolic importance given to the word 'freedom,'" Lincoln and Mamiya write. "Throughout black history the term 'freedom' has found deep religious resonance in the lives of African-Americans. . . . During slavery it meant release from bondage; after emancipation it meant the right to be educated, to be employed, and to move about freely from place to place. In the twentieth century freedom means social, political, and economic justice."

Whites are rightly confused because large numbers of blacks have come to the defense of Lyons. Again, history is a guide, as it relates to how whites and blacks view the concept of freedom and the church. "For whites freedom has bolstered the value of American individualism," Lincoln and Mamiya write. "But for African-Americans freedom has always been communal . . . black people have seldom been perceived or treated as individuals; they have usually been dealt with as 'representatives' of their 'race,' an external projection."

In other words, many religious blacks—as was shown at the National Baptist Convention's recent meeting in Denver—see an attack on Lyons as an attack on them, too. And the constant barrage of press coverage has only hardened the sense of "us" versus "them" for many conventioneers, even though they believe that Lyons committed the deeds he has been accused of. The sense of communalism and family is stronger in the black church than it is in any other black institution. If this point is lost, then understanding the church is next to impossible.

"Our church is the one thing that we invented by ourselves, for ourselves," said Gerald Hart, a longtime member of a storefront church in north Tampa. "It's the one place where people who look like me are in charge, where we can just be us. I don't like Reverend Lyons, but I want his church to survive for the people's sake."

Churches can lead fight against AIDS

DECEMBER 2, 1998

Tuesday was World AIDS Day. It was not a celebration—at least not one of life. As it should have been, it was a mass memorial, especially in most of the nation's black communities. Let us start with some of the oft-repeated estimates and statistics for the United States:

- Although African-Americans represent only 12 percent of the U.S. population, they account for more than 40 percent of current AIDS cases.
- Today, 300,000 to 500,000 blacks are infected with HIV, the virus that causes AIDS. Most are young. Many live in poor neighborhoods.
- AIDS kills twice as many black males age 25 to 44 as does homicide. AIDS has become the leading cause of death for blacks under age 55, even before cancer and heart disease.
- African-American women constitute two-thirds of all cases of women with HIV reported to the Centers for Disease Control and Prevention.

- More black children are infected with HIV than children of all other races and ethnicities combined.
- By 2000, an African-American woman will be nearly 20 times more likely to have AIDS than a nonblack American woman.

Given this grim portrait, all segments of black society should have mobilized years ago to fight this killer. Slowing the spread of AIDS should be the next civil rights movement. Instead, even as AIDS decimates our ranks, blacks in general are in denial about the race relevance of the disease or are turning their backs on its victims.

The result of such apathy is a self-destructive, institutionalized silence. In a recent article for the *Civil Rights Journal*, Bernice Powell Jackson, executive director of the United Church of Christ Commission for Racial Justice, wrote: "We need the silence to end in our fraternities and sororities and on our college campuses. We need the silence to end in our high schools and in our Sunday schools. We need the silence to end in Laundromats and beauty parlors. We need the silence to end in our homes." Of special concern, however, is the silence from the pulpit. Indeed, the black church has abnegated its responsibilities in dealing with AIDS. Why the focus on the church?

"The church is where the structure is in the African-American community," Julia Walker, a spokeswoman for the New York–based Balm in Gilead, an AIDS information organization, told the *Tampa Tribune* in October. "A drug user may not set foot in a church, but his mother probably does."

Walker and other AIDS workers, such as Mary Stephan of the AIDS Partnership in St. Petersburg, believe that black churches—by disseminating information about services, lifestyle changes, and treatment—can become centers for prevention. "The process can't get rolling until preachers jump on board," Walker told the *Tribune*. "Right now many people in these churches can't have a conversation about AIDS because they're so busy associating it with homosexuality."

Other activists, such as Michael Howard of the Tampa AIDS Network, are equally disappointed with the black church. "A lot of churches have the 'don't ask, don't tell' attitude," he said. "These pastors have a great responsibility. They have an obligation not only to the spiritual needs of their congregations, but to the physical needs, too."

Stephan, whose son died of AIDS, wants black churches in the Tampa Bay area to become actively involved in AIDS prevention. She wants pastors to create environments where churchgoers can freely talk about AIDS. Pastors could, for example, preach about the disease compassionately rather than contemptuously. Stephan wants churches to become AIDS education centers. After all, they have captive audiences. Churchgoers need to know that AIDS is a disease that can be prevented through education, understanding, and caring.

"Pews are filled with people whose lives have been touched by AIDS, who sit silently fearing to share their pain because AIDS is 'not spoken' there," an AIDS Partnership brochure states. "And others are absent from the pews because they feel they can no longer worship with people who ignore their hurt, or, worse, condemn those who are suffering."

The urgency for the involvement of the black church has never been greater, Stephan said. By 2005, according the Centers for Disease Control and Prevention, 60 percent of all AIDS cases in the United States will be among African-Americans. Many of those casualties will occur here in Tampa Bay. The black church, the most powerful institution in black culture, must come out of denial and lead the way toward prevention.

Church finds its calling in children

April 18, 1999

Retired Gen. Colin Powell's smiling face, along with that of a teenage girl, graces the cover of the April 11 issue of *Parade* magazine. The accompanying story discusses the celebration of the 11th annual National Youth Service Day. It is an inspiring article, showing youngsters and adults performing wonderful deeds to make their communities better.

While celebrities such as Powell bring national attention to worthy programs and volunteers, many other projects and workers we never read about—especially older citizens—toil each day, often at great personal expense and effort, to raise the quality of life for their friends and neighbors.

I know of no better example of such selflessness than the congregation of Christ United Methodist Church on Gainesville's predominantly low-income east side. The church has 83 members, with about 30 attending services regularly. In 1997, the Reverend Paul M. Jowett and the administrative board discussed ways to attract new members and persuade those who did not attend to show up more often.

The major obstacle to attracting new members was a matter of demographics. When the church moved to its current location in 1965, the neighborhood was overwhelmingly white and blue-collar. Today, the area is mostly black and poor. But only two of the church's members are black. In addition, while the average age of area residents is 30 years, that of the members is 65. "In other words," a member said, "our church is a bunch of old white people in a younger black community."

A revival the previous year had been a "blessing," the pastor said, but it did not increase membership. Betty Jewett, the pastor's wife, asked, "Why not just do what Jesus said we should do—serve people?"

Less than two years later, that simple question has produced Prime Time, a unique after-school program that is free of charge to the neighborhood's kindergarten and elementary school children. Currently 18 children, all African-American, attend the program each school day from 2:30 to 5:30. It has had as many as 25. None of the children or their parents are members of the church.

"Prime Time is for children from households unable to afford traditional after-school programs," said Betty Wagner, chairwoman of the program's Board of Directors. "Prime Time offers assistance with reading, writing, and arithmetic skills and provides activities that promote the development of creative talents. We want to keep these children from becoming latchkey children. We don't want to see our children roaming the streets."

Diane Loyless, the program's treasurer, expresses a more long-term goal: "By helping them now, we want to deter the children from going the wrong way in later years. So many times in larger families, some children just don't get special attention. Our volunteers work one-on-one with the kids."

Homework is just one part of the activities. The students keep a personal journal and write and publish their own newspaper—called, of course, *Prime Times*. A University of Florida music professor teaches piano lessons, and another professor teaches art. Each week, the children are taken on field trips, visiting places such as museums, hospitals, and the airport. "We take the children to these places because we want them to become complete citizens," the Reverend Jewett said.

Donna Simpson-Brown, a 47-year-old self-employed hairdresser who is often away from home in the afternoon, enrolled two children and two grandchildren in the program from the outset and believes that she made the right decision. "The tutoring is worth a million dollars in itself," she said. "Dominique is on the honor roll. Kaytlyn . . . brought up her grades from Cs to As and Bs. And she is taking piano lessons. She loves it. I definitely see an attitude shift in my children since they've been in Prime Time. They don't want to stay home after school. They want to come here. I don't have to worry about them getting into trouble if I'm not home."

While Jewett and the volunteers believe that Prime Time is a miracle, they also believe that how it became a reality is just as miraculous. After establishing an Advisory Board, Jewett had to raise money for a safe playground, two paid staffers, a van, and supplies.

The first $20 came from a local restaurant where the pastor ate each Sunday. Jewett wrote to a friend in California describing his plan, and the friend, a retired Warner Bros. executive, donated the $4,000 that established a memorial playground for Prime Time students. Since then, many other permanent donors have come aboard. "The most rewarding and blessed part of this whole experience is the way that people want to help if you tell them what you're doing," Jewett said. "They respond. A professor at the university and his wife, for example, have underwritten two children to attend the program for a year."

Jewett says his budget is about $25,000 a year, but the families pay only a $10 registration fee. Everything else is free. "We are struggling," he said, "but we believe that we are doing what we should be doing as representatives of Jesus: helping people."

"Return to sender" sends clear message

May 14, 2000

Jesus, the Christian Messiah, came in the mail to Palm Beach County residents the week before Easter. But the ubiquitous protagonist of the New Testament was sent packing by an overwhelming number of angry would-be converts. I am writing about the event at this late date because the fallout from it has contaminated the national faith scene. Those contemplating a repeat of the effort should cease and desist.

This is what happened: a coalition of 100 local churches, members of an organization called the Jesus Video Project, mailed a film of the life of Jesus to every soul (450,000 of them) in Palm Beach County.

Imagine. Every household—mansion, condominium, house, apartment, trailer—was targeted to receive a film. Such an action may seem benign but only if we forget that approximately 225,000 Jews, many of them practicing, live in the region. More over, the film was mailed during Passover, a high holy time for Jews.

And why did the Christian churches mail the video?

"We did this because God's nature is loving and giving, and we wanted to give the gift of Jesus to everyone in the county so they could view him without all the religion and other trappings," the Reverend Gene Walton of Grace Fellowship in West Palm Beach told the *Palm Beach Post*.

A graduate school chum of mine, now living in Boca Raton, sent me his copy of the film. Made in 1979 and starring British actors, it is 83 minutes long and depicts the life of Jesus from Bethlehem through death and the resurrection. It is an accurate account of the Gospel of Luke. The Orlando-based Campus Crusade for Christ, an evangelical group, owns the rights to the tape and has been distributing it in mass mailings worldwide since the 1980s.

But the $1.2-million south Florida effort mostly backfired when thousands of irate recipients mounted a "return to sender" campaign, dumping the unsolicited videotapes into the laps of local post offices. Rabbi Stephen Pinsky of Temple Beth Torah in Wellington told the *Post* that many residents were so angry that they tied a brick to the tape and wrote "return to sender" on the accompanying postcard, hoping that the Jesus Video Project would have to pay additional shipping charges. "It's not something we need in our homes, especially during Passover," Pinsky said.

Also condemning the mailing, Bishop Anthony O'Connell, head of the Catholic Diocese of Palm Beach County, told the *Post:* "We must stop seeing ourselves as rivals before the one God." One man was so angry, according to the *Post*, that he sarcastically thanked the project, saying he had used the tape to copy a porn movie.

Obviously, not everyone was incensed about receiving the tape. Many people, in fact, welcomed it. Even so, the mass mailing demonstrates the arrogance and insensitivity of Christian evangelicals who, as Bishop O'Connell suggested, believe that God is theirs and theirs alone, that only they will pass through the pearly gates and sit on the right-hand side of St. Peter. The Reverend Harris Campbell, a local preacher, exemplifies such intolerance. Speaking to the *Post* about the mailing, he said, "We're doing this because it's our fundamental belief that unless a person trusts in Christ, they will not be saved."

We may assume, then, that all practicing Jews, for example, are going straight to hell, that the Holocaust was a mere warm-up of what is to come. As a Unitarian Universalist, I must certainly have a seat reserved for me in the burning chamber down below.

I have traveled to every continent and have studied, to some degree, all of the world's major living religions. Although I am not intellectually equipped to explicate each faith and its comparative validity, I know in my own crude way that Christianity is no better than, say, the different brands of Judaism I witnessed in Israel. Or the Islamic sects in Gaza, the West Bank, and northern Africa. Is Christianity holier than Zoroastrianism and Hinduism? As far as I know, the Sikhs of India's Punjab region and the Jains have no reason to follow Christ. Are they all going to accompany me to hell? Why do Christians think that they have a message for the Buddhists I have met in different parts of the world? The Chinese and the Japanese have practiced their religions for centuries and will continue to do so. Why should they listen to Christian proselytizers? If anything, some Christian groups should beg American Indians for forgiveness for the sins committed against them.

My purpose is not to condemn Palm Beach County's evangelical community for its faith. I am simply arguing that Christianity is just one—that's *one*—of the world's living religions. The Navajos' belief in "holy people" and "earth-surface people," for example, makes as much sense as the Christian belief that a woman became pregnant without having intercourse. Or that a man survived in the belly of a whale. Or that a man, by raising a stick in the air, caused the Red Sea to part.

Anyway, instead of bringing people of various faiths together, the mass mailing engendered permanent resentment and pushed many people even further away from Jesus. I like what Jac Wilder VerSteeg, deputy editorial page editor of the *Post* said: "I can't picture a God watching men, women and children die in Hitler's ovens and then deciding to turn up the temperature—and for eternity—because those people didn't trust in Christ. Where is the Christian who can reside happily in heaven while those souls burn in hell?"

Amen.

Arm-twisting religion fuels resistance

May 31, 2000

As expected, my May 14 column about Palm Beach County residents who returned a Jesus video to its sender, the Jesus Video Project, brought an avalanche of letters and e-mail from irate Christians. Based on these correspondences, along with others of the same nature I have received over the years, I must conclude that most Christian newspaper readers who write about the issue of faith are arrogant and downright mean and nasty.

Here is an example of this attitude, part of a letter published in the *St. Petersburg Times* on May 21. Because I think that Palm Beach County residents were justified in returning the tape, the letter writer describes me this way: "Perhaps God will deal with [Maxwell] as he did with another persecutor of Christians, Saul, who became the Apostle Paul."

I, a "persecutor of Christians"? How absurd! If I remember correctly, the high priest of Jerusalem commissioned Saul to travel north to Antioch and

Damascus to arrest any followers of "The Way" he could find. I have no such commission, nor do I want one. Heck, I am no Saul, just a newspaper hack. I do all I can to avoid all contact with evangelical Christians.

The problem is that evangelicals possess the gall to try to ram their dogma down other people's throats. But they cannot abide rejection. They hate being told to "get lost." I would never knock on a stranger's door to proselytize. Nor would I knock on the door of a Christian to persecute him. People who know me know that I mind my own religious business—until, of course, some overzealous do-gooder invades my space.

Am I to believe that the return of an unsolicited video about Christ condemns a person to hellfire? I humbly suspect that God's eternal script for humankind is more complex.

Most of the messages that came to me personally—and not to the editor for publication—carry a subtext of racism: how dare you, Bill Maxwell—a black man—write such words about our Christ! That message is there, oozing between the lines, revealing the contents of the letter writers' hearts. Do not forget that I, along with other blacks, was born in "Christian America"—the same nation that branded us as inferior beasts who lacked a human soul and were therefore deserving of enslavement.

Christianity as an organized religion has to redeem itself on many fronts. Sure, I trust certain individual Christians, care for them, and admire them, but I keep a wary eye on this thing called Christianity. Growing up, I witnessed many atrocities committed by southern Baptists and some Methodists. I know of white preachers who stood in their pulpits and delivered racist sermons. The Southern Baptist Convention, in fact, was founded before the Civil War by whites who saw no ethical conflict in worshiping Christ, owning slaves, and going to heaven no less.

And I have not forgotten that this church opposed the civil rights movement in the 1950s and 1960s, had hundreds of thousands of members who supported the Ku Klux Klan's racial agenda, had hundreds of Klansmen in their pews. How wholeheartedly am I expected to trust an organized group with such a long history of discriminating against me?

My grandfather, a presiding elder in his denomination, worried about the messages that came from many white churches. He often wondered aloud if black and white Christians worshiped the same God. Given that bigots such as George Wallace, Strom Thurmond, Bull Connor, Huey Long, and others professed to be Christians, I was certain that our deities were different.

Like evangelicals today, my grandfather tried to save souls. He and other black preachers would pitch giant tents in cities, vacant lots, and fields statewide and hold revivals. I would accompany him. He always told me that those who want to be saved will find their way to a tent. "God will send them here," he would say. In other words, he and other black preachers provided the venues for salvation—without offending the very souls they wanted to save. He knew that people resist arm-twisting. The evangelicals mailing and hand-delivering today's Jesus video need to learn this simple lesson: because of their aggressive tactics, they are failing to win over the very people they are trying to rescue.

Anyway, a college chum sent me his copy of the Jesus tape. And I watched it. The story is the same one that I have heard since childhood, that I still read in the Gospels, that I was taught in college religion courses, that I see in movies at Christmas and Easter, that I experience each time I go to the Old City of Jerusalem and to Bethlehem—the birthplace of Christ.

Goobers and Good Ol' Boys

Olympic torch brings a chance for hospitality

JULY 16, 1995

Even as the so-called New South prepares to represent the United States of America in front of the world as host of the 1996 Summer Olympics, some of its old intolerances—homophobia, jingoism, racism—are rising to the surface. The Olympic volleyball competition, for example, was moved out of one Georgia county after lawmakers there passed an antigay ordinance. Then another county refused to be the host for Somali athletes because a mob dragged the body of an American soldier through Mogadishu during our failed peacekeeping effort there.

From all indications, the New South is nothing more than a pastel version of its old Gothic self. It is still a tinderbox of contradiction, a place where, sings Louisiana native Hank Williams Jr., "We say grace and we say 'ma'am.' If you ain't into that, we don't give a damn." Williams portrays Dixie as being religious and mannerly. And a recent survey conducted by the University of North Carolina's Institute for Research in Social Science supports this portrayal. The survey shows that southerners, more so than other Americans, instruct their children to address adults as "ma'am" and "sir" and that more southerners attend church and read the Bible.

But while southerners can be nice and religious, they will not hesitate, as Williams's lyrics also suggest, to show outsiders their behinds. This attitude is reflected, for instance, on the bumper sticker that says "We don't care how y'all did it up North," warning expatriated Yankees to stop trying to change how things are done below the Mason-Dixon line.

Why are southerners so defensive, and why do they seem to have an attitude? No single person has all the answers. But folklorist and historian Allan M. Trout has discovered a major clue in what he calls the South's "irrepressible cussedness," a perversity and stubbornness that define the region's esprit. "A streak of inherent cussedness keeps most men from acknowledging defeat," Trout writes. "The combination of adverse circumstances at last reaches the point where the only thing left to do is to grin and bear it. At the moment an overburdened man grins he invariably says something that contains a trace of wisdom and truth."

African-American writer Zora Neale Hurston, a southerner, also grasps the puzzling nature of this cussedness, this unique—although not necessarily good—wisdom and truth that provide the context for southern relationships. One of her characters is especially memorable because he is cussedness personified: "And all the time, there was High John de Conquer playing his tricks of making a way out of no-way. Hitting a straight lick with a crooked stick. Winning the jackpot with no other stake but a laugh. Fighting a mighty battle without outside-showing force, and winning his war from within."

Folklorists, sociologists, and others struggle to make meaning of the New South. Unless they spend serious time with rednecks—those pork-eating, beer-guzzling, working-class white men who embody the contradictory traits the world associates with the South—these academics will never understand this region that H. L. Mencken dismissed as "The Sahara of the Bozart." The redneck, the South's Everyman, is independent and clannish, tough and thin-skinned, loud and menacingly silent, violent and gentle, hardworking and irresponsible, disciplined and wild, realistic and sentimental, honorable and rascally, mean-spirited and bighearted.

More than anything else, though, the biggest contradiction about the redneck is found in his relationship with black people. This relationship colors how these southerners treat other people and will influence how they treat the visiting Olympic athletes. University of Georgia historian F. N. Boney accurately describes the redneck's relationship with blacks: "The redneck's main problem is that he has always been open and candid in his conviction that blacks were inferior to whites. Yet at the same time over the centuries he has blended his culture and his blood with blacks, and in many ways he understands blacks perhaps better than his white detractors do. In his rough, earthy kind of way he may be less a racist than those whites who denounce him so harshly." I am a native southerner, and I, like Boney, believe that most southern rednecks are less racist than most of their detractors in other parts of the country.

As the 1996 Olympic games approach, the South's image is on the line. Politicians may pass more antipeople ordinances, but, ultimately, the athletes of other nations who will compete here, along with the officials accompanying them, will judge the South based on how well local citizens, many of them rednecks, treat them. The South has the best opportunity in many years to show that it, too, has savoir faire, that it can do more than utter perfunctory "ma'ams" and "sirs." Moreover, the occasion can give other parts of the United States a chance to reevaluate their relationship with the South and learn more about the region in general.

Southerners can learn some valuable lessons from their international guests. These are the 1996 Summer Olympics, and the hosts have the awesome responsibility of representing all Americans—especially the best of the South. Now is the time to restrain the homophobia, the jingoism, the racism, the cussedness. Now is the time to make that mythical "southern hospitality" a reality.

More to Civil War history than most understand

July 23, 1995

On June 29, the U.S. Postal Service began selling 20 new Civil War stamps. Many black people are outraged that a federal agency would so commemorate the fratricidal war between the states.

In Richmond, Virginia, following a divisive debate that reopened deep racial wounds, the City Council voted on July 18 to place a bronze statue of black tennis great Arthur Ashe on Monument Avenue—the place honoring Confederate "heroes" who fought to save the South's "Peculiar Institution."

At Harvard University, an alumni committee is feuding about whether to recognize graduates who died fighting for the South during the Civil War. The dispute was sparked by the renovation of Harvard's Memorial Hall, built five years after the Civil War to honor alumni who died for the Union. Although one-third of Harvard graduates who served in the Civil War fought for the South, the deed for the shrine forbids the names of these soldiers from being inscribed there. The names of all other Harvard men who died in subsequent wars, however, are displayed—including one who fought for the Nazis.

These contemporary disputes show that, even though it ended more than 130 years ago, the Civil War still is central to answering the question— "What is America?"—that black historian Benjamin Quarles poses in his landmark book *The Negro in the Civil War.* At some point, all earnest Americans struggle to answer Quarles's question, and we always return to Dixie's "Lost Cause."

"Any understanding of this nation has to be based . . . on an understanding of the Civil War," said Civil War historian and author Shelby Foote in a telephone interview. "It defined us as what we are and it opened us to what we became, good and bad things. And it is very necessary, if you're going to understand the American character in the 20th century, to learn about this enormous catastrophe of the 19th century. It was the crossroads of our being . . . the suffering, the enormous tragedy of the whole thing." If Foote is correct, why do so many of us cringe at the mere mention of the Civil War? Because we, perhaps more so than other people in the West, have a naive view of the past. We dislike and avoid the parts of our history that expose our hypocrisies.

The inhumanity of the Civil War and its aftermath shame us, forcing us to confront honestly the ideals expressed in the great documents—the Constitution, the Declaration of Independence—that we cherish. And, always a nation of optimists, we are fast becoming a tribe of revisionists. We like our history "lite," suited to our sensibilities, tidied up to corroborate the nice images and myths we have created of ourselves and of those we admire. We demand a history filtered through today's ethnic and gender politics, a history that has relevance to the now.

Washington-based journalist Richard Prince, who condemns the Civil War stamps, said that, although the Postal Service's action did not provoke much controversy, "Its symbolism rankles, and not only because it comes amid an affirmative-action backlash, continuing skirmishes over the flying of the Confederate flag, and best-selling books declaring blacks intellectually inferior. It is disturbing because it continues the falsehood that the Union and the Confederacy both represented respectable ideologies."

We demand a history that bears our personal imprimatur or that of our group. It must make us feel good. It must validate us. Listen, for instance, to Shirley Jackson speaking to the Richmond City Council in support of placing the Arthur Ashe statue on Memorial Avenue: "A hero is a hero whether he is a defeated Confederate soldier or a great humanitarian. Mr. Ashe deserves to be on Monument Avenue because he is our hero."

We demand the right to disassociate ourselves from a history that we view as immoral. Robert Shapiro, a Boston attorney leading the Harvard alumni panel, is an example. He said that he does not want anyone to mistake his and the panel's review of the proposal to memorialize the university's southern dead as "an endorsement of either the Confederacy itself or of the policies for which the Confederacy fought."

As a lifetime student of the Civil War who visits battlefields and museums as often as possible, I fear that the historical integrity of this significant event has been lost forever to emotion, cynicism, cultural politics, and ignorance. We are unable to give the war the distance required for us to treat it objectively. We fail to see it as a tragic phenomenon that occurred in time. Most blacks and white liberals will never accept the fact that, although the South's cause was evil, tens of thousands of yeoman farmers fought bravely—not to defend slavery but to protect their families, their homes, and, of course, the land they loved. Were these men wrong to fight? New research indicates that many blacks fought as loyal infantrymen for the South. Trained historians and other mature thinkers genuinely interested in the nation's past treat the Confederacy with respect, letting it and its troops assume their rightful place in time.

To erect the likeness of Arthur Ashe alongside the likenesses of Confederate President Jefferson Davis and Gen. Robert E. Lee trivializes Memorial Avenue's raison d'être and unwittingly misrepresents Ashe's accomplishments. But to memorialize the names of Harvard's Johnny Rebs and to issue Civil War stamps are reasonable ways to acknowledge the Confederacy's real place in history.

Those who would deny these modest recognitions should heed the words of Miguel de Cervantes: "The poet can tell or sing of things not as they were but as they ought to have been, whereas the historian must describe them, not as they ought to have been, but as they were, without exaggerating or hiding the truth in any way."

Black southerners forgive again and again

August 31, 1997

As I watched *George Wallace*, a television film about the quarter-century political career of Alabama's infamous governor, I again became aware of the uniqueness of the South in general and that of black southerners in particular.

Nothing stood out more than the scene at the Dexter Avenue Baptist Church in Montgomery where Martin Luther King had been pastor. There, George Corley Wallace, a crumpled old white man in a wheelchair, begged the all-black congregation to forgive him his racist past and the enormous pain and suffering he had caused a generation of African-Americans. As Archie, Wallace's loyal black servant in the movie, pushed the wheelchair down the aisle toward the exit, black hands reached out to touch the very man who would not be "out-niggered"—the same demagogue who, in his first inaugural address as governor, had shouted: "Segregation now! Segregation forever!"

In the movie, as in real life, the people in the church—representing thousands of other African-Americans nationwide—forgave the genuinely contrite Wallace. This moving scene revealed one of the noblest traits of black southerners: their inscrutable capacity to forgive white people. Somewhere in the South each day, such a tale of white hatred, redemption, and black forgiveness unfolds.

Currently, this black-white dynamic is being played out in Laurens, South Carolina. There, the Reverend David E. Kennedy, pastor of the New Beginnings Baptist Church, and the more than 100 members of this black congregation have forgiven Michael Eugene Burden Jr., a white man.

Burden, as the grand dragon of the South Carolina Ku Klux Klan, first made international news about two years ago when he opened the Redneck Shop and Klan Museum. The shop sold and displayed KKK paraphernalia (including white-hooded Klan uniforms), photographs of lynchings, T-shirts emblazoned with racial epithets, Confederate flags, and emblems and trinkets promoting the National Association for the Advancement of Rednecks. After the shop opened, Kennedy and his congregation led protests and staged many demonstrations denouncing it.

Burden, a white supremacist in every sense of the word, despised black people and loved the Klan. "I was led to believe that [the Klan] was my family," he told a reporter for the Columbia newspaper. "That was my life That was my destiny. And I done the best I could to live up to it. I ate, slept, drank and studied Klan all the time."

Suddenly, however, Burden found his Road to Damascus. He fell in love and married. His new bride, the divorced mother of two children, persuaded him to quit the Klan. As "a wedding present," he gave up his old life. In retaliation, Burden's white partner and former Klan mentor soon evicted him from the apartment above the Redneck Shop. The family was forced to live in Burden's pickup. Local whites who had been his friends and associates turned against him. He was fired from each of the more than 10 jobs he has had since quitting the Klan.

A week after the eviction, Burden bumped into Kennedy on the street. "I know you don't trust me," Burden told the black pastor, according to the *Washington Post*. "But I need to talk to you. I'm hungry, and I got two young'uns and my wife living in my truck." Without hesitation, Kennedy took Burden and his family to a steak house and treated them to lunch. Then he took them to the Welcome Lodge and paid their rent for a week. The grateful Burden went to City Hall and initiated the withdrawal of the Redneck Shop's license.

Burden asked Kennedy if he could come to New Beginnings and apologize to the black community. Before an overflowing gathering, the proud Burden asked for forgiveness.

And how did Kennedy and the church respond?

"I'm proud to say that my whole congregation stood with me 100 percent and forgave Mr. Burden," Kennedy said in a telephone interview. "We're a unique church in the sense that we fight against racism, and we fight hard. But the end we seek is not destruction. The end we seek is righteousness and justice. When we fought against the Klan and Mr. Burden asked for forgiveness, we forgave. That's why I call our church New Beginnings.

"We are forgiving when people ask for forgiving. But we will fight legally and nonviolently. We protest a lot. Every time we see that ugly snake, racism, raising its ugly head, we ask God for the power of Samson, for that head to come off. But we do it through what Martin Luther King called direct action. We do it with a lot of love and nonviolence."

Ironically, though, Kennedy—who has a photograph in his office of an uncle who was lynched by whites—understands that forgiveness, especially when seen as weakness, may give racism a reprieve.

Today, Burden and his family live in a trailer in Laurens's black community. Residents and members of New Beginnings protect their new white neighbors from other angry whites. When Burden, who cannot find steady work, cannot pay for electricity, the congregation takes up a collection. Burden's children are called "nigger lovers" at school.

Kennedy and his parishioners understand.

"We have no tolerance for racism," he said. "And we think that all people, regardless of race, creed, religion, or color, must rise together in a concerted effort to bring about constructive change. And forgiveness is part of the equation."

Southern for beginners

November 23, 1997

> The romantic South of the professional Southerner with its soft sweet
> speech of Dixie is false and to some of us distasteful. The romantic
> South was a literary convention. . . . [But] the speech of our South . . .
> is oh, so sweet to the ears of a Southerner. . . . Let us preserve it.
> —William Cabell Greet

A few days ago, I had the wondrous experience of hearing Republican Sen.
Strom Thurmond of South Carolina speak on television. I say "wondrous"
because to hear this grand ol' segregationist scalawag "tawk" (a method of
speech peculiar to the South, despite decades of television and radio) is to
take a linguistic tour of the nation's most inscrutable region. I am still trying
to figure out what the nearly 95-year-old southerner was saying. His accent
was so thick that the words sounded like a foreign language.

Please understand that I am not writing a treatise on southern dialect,
even though such a document would be valuable. Sure, Yankees and others
could benefit from knowing, for example, that generations of illiteracy, isolation, and a host of other social and cultural forces caused southerners to
speak the way they do. But a newspaper column is not the appropriate forum
for such an exegesis. My goal is less ambitious. While listening to Thurmond hold forth (actually, mumble) on the Senate floor, I realized that millions of snowbirds are flocking to the South for the winter, and tens of
thousands of them will have trouble trying to figure out what the hell we are
saying down here.

What follows is an alphabetically arranged primer of words and expressions to help snowbirds navigate the mysterious shoals of southern dialect.
My main source is Steve Mitchell's book *How to Speak Southern*. You will
notice, by the way, that black and white southerners use many of the same
terms.

Ah: The organ you see with, and a first person pronoun. "Ah think Ah've
got mud in my ah."

Attair: contraction used (the speaker usually pointing) to indicate a specific item desired. "Pass me attair bowl of griyuts [grits], please."

Bad off: (1) In desperate need of. "What you doin' with *Hustler* magazine? Son! You must be bad off." (2) Terribly ill. "Bubba stayed in bed all
weekend with a hangover. He's bad off."

Break bad: To act violently or outrageously. "That durn Willie broke bad
over that ol' pickup. His tail now in jail."

Comin' up a cloud: An approaching storm. "Ain't no need to wash the truck. It's comin' up a cloud."

Commite nigh: To come extremely close to (come mighty nigh). "When Connie Sue saw her ol' man huggin' that stripper, she commite nigh shootin' him."

Cut the fool: To behave in a foolish or goofy manner. "Boy, stop cuttin' the fool and slop them hogs."

Done: (1) Finished. "Is that gal done cookin'?" (2) Already. "Has the train done gone?"

Eat up with: An excessive affliction. "Ol' Larry's plumb eat up with love."

Favor: To resemble. "They say when a married couple git ol', they favor each other."

Fixin': Preparing to. "Ah'm fixin' to fry a mess of catfish."

Go to the bad: To spoil. "Don't eat them collards. They done gone to the bad."

Liable: Likely to. "When Earl gits home, he's liable to be drunk as a skunk."

Like to: Almost. "When Ah seen the preacher in the car with Sister Louise, Ah like to dropped my beer can."

Mind: To obey. "Joey, you mind your mama while Ah'm at the tavern."

Nairn: Not any; not one. "Sorry Ah can't give you a cigarette. I ain't got nairn."

Nome: A kid's negative reply to a woman's question. "Tammy Sue, did you take Jim's slingshot?" "Nome."

Play like: To pretend. "Here he comes. Play like y'all don't see him."

Prolly: Likely. "Jimmy Carter prolly won't run for public office again."

Ratcheer: In a particular spot. "Put that Bud ratcheer on the bar."

Sorry: Shiftless, lazy. "That mechanic so sorry he won't lift a wrench to fix his own mama's pickup."

Toreckly: Later. "Git on out there and cut the yard. Ah'll be along toreckly."

Ugly: Disagreeable, mean, or unpleasant. "Ah know you don't like your brother, but you don't need to be ugly to him."

Wore out: Used up, exhausted. "That ol' mule is plumb wore out."

Zackly: Precisely. "Ah left that hound dog zackly ratcheer."

So if you are a snowbird and plan to mingle 'mongst good old boys, crackers, rednecks, and rural black folk, bring along this primer. I must warn you that it might not help in translating Thurmondese—a piece of work unto itself.

Discrimination on the basis of accent

JUNE 7, 1998

A colleague of mine at the *St. Petersburg Times* and her husband lived in Lansing, Michigan, during the late 1970s. She, a New Yorker, wrote for the *Detroit News*. He, a southerner, was a law student.

They rented an upscale apartment on the river near the governor's mansion. One night while they were shopping, a clerk asked for their address. After the husband gave it, a prosperous-looking man within earshot blurted, "How in the world did you get a place like that with an accent like that?"

In her best New York accent, my colleague dressed down the stranger. "Based on [my husband's] accent, he obviously thought we were hayseeds," she says now. "That was by far the worst example of 'accent bias' [my husband] ever encountered. But so many people made fun of his accent over the years—including some of his classmates—that he and I were very glad to leave the place as soon as law school was over."

What my colleague's husband experienced occurs all too often and in too many places when people—especially northerners—hear the sweet tone of the southern drawl. Misunderstood, castigated, and mimicked, the southern accent can bring ostracism, hurt, anger, and feelings of inferiority that may last a lifetime. Even President Bill Clinton, the most powerful man on earth, is ridiculed as a "Bubba" because of the Dixieland in his voice.

When I was an English professor at the University of Illinois–Chicago, a Mississippian, his drawl as slow as a summer afternoon, was in one of my classes. The first time he participated in a discussion, a hush fell over the room. After he stopped speaking, several students laughed.

"Who is that? Gomer Pyle?" a Bostonian asked, pointing. The southerner was mortified. I felt his pain and clumsily said something perfunctory about a university campus and respect for the cultures of others.

He never missed a day of class. But he never participated in another discussion.

North Carolina native Charles Hadley, a teacher at Queens College in Charlotte and a dialect coach for the movies, has experienced his share of put-downs while working up North. "It's 'Oh, those poor little darling southerners,'" he said in the *Richmond Times-Dispatch*. "I have literally seen people lose jobs because of their southern accents. There's really nothing wrong with having a southern accent—as long as you don't have to use it in business outside the South."

Michael Montgomery, an English and linguistics professor at the University of South Carolina, agrees, arguing that most Americans think nothing of discriminating against dialects and accents. "The message given to people is: If you want to get a job anywhere in the country and increasingly in the South, don't talk like a southerner," he told the *Times-Dispatch*. "We're supposed to live in an enlightened age. They haul you into court for discriminating on the basis of race, gender or creed, but an accent is supposed to indicate your intelligence. . . . Those prejudices and stereotypes are stronger than ever."

Here at the *Times*, southerners whose accents are as thick as homemade molasses surround me. Take Robert Friedman, deputy editor of editorials, for whom I work. A Georgia native, he has a moderately heavy drawl. I am always amused when readers are shocked to learn that this man with a Jewish name and who writes brilliantly is not, as one man said, "your prototypical New York Jew."

Harriet and Mike Abrahm, both native Alabamians who are Jews, have similar encounters. People think that they, too, should be from New York. Harriet, executive director of the Florida West Coast American Jewish Committee, has one of the most beautiful southern accents I have ever heard. Many people discount her intelligence until they realize that they have done exactly what she expects—and also whatever she wants—of them. Mike, a lawyer, loves to litigate against his silk-suited Yankee peers. By underestimating his intelligence, these hotshots suffer the agony of defeat every time. And Mike? He smiles self-deprecatingly all the while.

My boss, Phil Gailey, is a Georgia boy with a thick accent. Often, visitors to the newspaper—the governor, presidential advisers, senators and representatives, bank presidents, big-time lawyers, scientists—are taken aback when Phil demonstrates easy familiarity with difficult subjects.

This element of surprise—the underestimation of the southerner's intelligence—is a recurring theme in the comments of my southern colleagues at the *Times* and elsewhere.

Lucy Morgan, who won the Pulitzer Prize for tough articles exposing a corrupt sheriff and his cronies, has a heavy, musical drawl. As our Tallahassee bureau chief, she has thought long and hard about being treated dismissively. "All of the good ol' boys presume that I have no brain—until it's too late," she says. "Actually, I think it has helped me over the long haul to be underestimated. Some people don't like that, but it's fine with me if people want to think that my brain is as slow as my drawl. . . . Being underestimated is good for reporters in many instances. I suspect that black reporters are often underestimated, too. I tell them to expect it and build on it."

Florida native James Harper, a reporter whose accent booms across the room, agrees with Lucy: "In an adversarial situation, it can be an advantage when people underestimate you. That's an old southern trick used by whites and blacks."

Times editorial writer Sharon Bond, who was born in Georgia and reared in North Carolina, points out yet another burden that comes with having a southern drawl: northerners assume that anyone with the southern accent must be a racist. Even worse, Sharon learned as a college student in New Jersey the awful truth of historian Henry Steele Commager's observation that "every Southerner is held responsible for the entire South."

My good friend Stephen Jackson, an Alabamian who teaches journalism at Stillman College in Tuscaloosa, offers an amusing twist on the southern drawl. Having spent many years in Colombia, Steve speaks fluent Spanish. His problem? "I even speak Spanish with a southern accent," he says. "Vamos, y'all, I always say in Spanish, meaning 'Let's go, you all.' Colombians are very patient with me. They know that I'm a gringo speaking Spanish. Unlike Americans, they are not judging my intelligence by my accent—as far as I can tell."

Of the South, but not a southerner

JUNE 14, 1998

I love the South and, until quite recently, fancied myself a southerner. Now, even though I was born and reared in the South and do not plan to ever leave it, I no longer believe that an African American can be a southerner.

My thinking began to evolve about two years ago shortly after referring to myself as a southerner in a column and receiving letters from white males in South Carolina arguing otherwise. "Sir," one writer commented, "a nigger can't be a southerner. You and your kind have never belonged here. My people committed the sin of bringing your kind to our great region in the first place."

Initially, I was angry but calmed down after viewing the comments intellectually. A student of the Civil War, I was reminded of this issue again in April when Marion Lambert, a member of the Tampa Bay chapter of the Sons of Confederate Veterans, a group of history buffs and Confederate descendants, invited blacks to their annual Confederate Memorial Day celebration. He told the *St. Petersburg Times* that "African-Americans should celebrate this . . . day because they are southerners."

Most blacks scoffed at the invitation and condemned black singer Belinda Womack, who performed at the gathering. The cause of their reaction goes to the heart of the question of whether or not a black can be a southerner. I have asked whites and blacks this question. Liberal whites have said, without apparent reflection, that a black can be a southerner. White conservatives, especially males, have become defensive, but most have said that a black can be a southerner. All but one African-American, a student at the University of North Carolina at Chapel Hill, have agreed.

In politics, is the quintessential southerner a "Pitchfork Ben" Tillman, a George Wallace, a Eugene "Bull" Connor? In literature, a Eudora Welty, a William Styron, a Flannery O'Connor, a William Faulkner? What about enlightened journalists such as Hodding Carter, Ralph McGill, and Eugene Patterson who risked everything to support blacks? In average life, is the redneck our model southerner?

The definitions of a southerner are as varied as the people who address the issue. The southerner has been defined as anyone born in the South, as one reared here, or even as one who adopts the region as home. Some people say that being a southerner, like the South itself, is a state of mind. "A southerner," an 80-year-old white man said, "is anyone, black or white, who loves the land of their southern birth. Southerners love the land in a way that people in other parts of the country do not." A colleague's wife said: "Southerners believe that God is in charge of our world, that family is important, and that we are supposed to help each other. Those beliefs seem to be stronger in the South than in most other regions. Those beliefs don't depend on being a certain color, a certain gender, or being in a particular financial class."

As sincere as the above attempts are, they, like most others, ignore centuries of historical, social, cultural, and political forces that prevent African-Americans from being true southerners. Although their sweat was essential to the economy, African-Americans have never been a natural part of the South. Brought here as slaves, they were declared subhuman—creatures without souls and, therefore, unable to experience Christian redemption. From the outset, they became a segregated pariah class in a region already distinct from the rest of the nation.

"The Negro," David L. Cohen wrote for *Look* magazine in 1955, "did not seek to come to the United States; he was dragged here to satisfy white greed. He alone, of all the racial stocks here, was satisfied to remain in his native home. The others came either to improve their condition economically or spiritually, or because they were run out of town." The African-American, as imported chattel, was the South's original exile, the bastard who could not join the fraternity. Many critics of this position argue that the descendants of black slaves are now bona fide southerners.

But are they?

"To be born with a dark skin is unforgivable in the South," writes Louis E. Austin, "and only the Negro must forever be assigned a place of hatred in the heart of the Southerner. . . . So deep are the roots and so well fertilized have they been by generation after generation of his ancestors that long before he is born, the pattern, the way of life for the white child in the South has already been provided."

At an early age, white children know to despise blacks. Sure, many blacks and whites worked the land together, worshiped the same God, and experienced the same poverty. "Yet, in this region of ironies," writes David R. Goldfield, "the supreme irony was that the two races lived side by side for centuries and knew each other not at all. The sin of race pride had come between them and created an abyss so deep that few held out hope for reconciliation."

Goldfield is right. The races have not reconciled because African-Americans cannot meet the two main tests for being a member of the South's clan: having white skin and accepting the concept of white superiority.

In Ralph Ellison's prize-winning novel, *Invisible Man*, the protagonist encapsulates the black man's predicament in the South: "I am invisible, simply because [white] people refuse to see me. When they approach me they only see my surroundings, themselves, or figments of their imagination—indeed, everything and anything except me."

Further, racial etiquette—the institution dictating that blacks must "stay in their place"—did more than anything else to marginalize former slaves, effectively making them permanent aliens. For too many generations, racial etiquette forced whites and blacks to attend separate schools, drink from separate fountains, eat in separate restaurants, use separate restrooms. The mere labels of "white" and "colored" denoted superiority and inferiority and established a false hierarchy impossible to tear down.

W.E.B. Du Bois understood, as I do, the destructiveness of this hierarchy: "In a world where it means so much to take a man by the hand and sit beside him, to look frankly into his eyes and feel his heart beating with red blood; in a world where a social cigar or a cup of tea together means more than legislative halls and magazine articles and speeches—one can imagine the consequences of the almost utter absence of such social amenities between estranged races."

The late Malcolm X went beyond the question of whether or not a black can be a southerner. He dared to wonder if a black can be an American.

The South no longer matches its myths

SEPTEMBER 27, 1998

Many Americans who do not follow politics closely believe that the South remains a monolithic region largely populated by backwoods, benighted bigots in pickups with gun racks and Confederate emblems who vote for Democrats, and by obsequious blacks living in shotgun shacks who would rather die than vote for a Republican.

Not so, argues Ferrel Guillory, director of the Program on Southern Politics, Media, and Public Life at the University of North Carolina in Chapel Hill. "To look at the South close-up is to see a politics that is anything but one dimensional," he writes in the spring issue of the journal *Southern Cultures*. "The rule of rural Democratic barons has been broken as population and jobs have shifted from the countryside to the city and suburb. Blacks walk into voting booths and hold elective offices from which they were once barred.

"Republicans outnumber Democrats among Southern governors, senators, and representatives. The reality these days is that the South produces a diverse set of officeholders, and that it is possible to be both genuinely Southern and genuinely different in style and ideology.... It is important to understand the currents and cross-currents behind politics in the South, because the region, once so out of sync, now often serves as a leading indicator of national trends and as a wellspring of national power."

Guillory contends that American politics itself has been "southernized," correctly pointing out that national issues such as tax cutting, budget balancing, crime, race, religion, and family values took deep root in the South long before they did in the other regions. And Washington's most powerful leaders—President Bill Clinton, Vice President Al Gore, House Speaker Newt Gingrich, Senate Majority Leader Trent Lott, and House Majority Leader Dick Armey—hail from Arkansas, Tennessee, Georgia, Mississippi, and Texas, respectively.

At the first meeting of the Southern Journalists' Roundtable, a subsidiary of the Program on Southern Politics, Media, and Public Life, Guillory, and other UNC scholars, journalists from around the South, and representatives of the Pew Center on the States discussed the South's emergence as a crucible in U.S. life and how southern journalists can play a major role in helping the rest of the nation understand the complexities of the region.

James H. Johnson Jr., E. Maynard Adams Distinguished Professor and director of the Urban Investment Strategies Center at UNC, argued, for example, that the South's demographics, especially its conflicts, are no longer a matter of black people versus white people. He described an "inequality paradox" in the New South, where mostly American-born blacks are losing jobs to the continuous influx of Hispanics, Africans, Asians, and West Indians into states such as Arkansas, Florida, Georgia, Maryland, and Tennessee. On this front, Johnson said, the South resembles Los Angeles, where minority groups battle among themselves for old and new jobs.

Hispanics, for example, are leaving the traditional port-of-entry centers, such as New York and Miami, and are resettling in small to midsize towns throughout the South. Arkansas and North Carolina, where meat processing plants flourish, attract large numbers of Hispanics. They displace African-Americans who have held these jobs for many years.

Calling this phenomenon "employer-induced conflict," Johnson said that many southern corporations desire newly arrived immigrant labor over native Americans—especially black males. This situation is responsible for deep interethnic and intraethnic divisions. In Atlanta, Africans have displaced American-born blacks in the taxi, hotel, and hospital industries. In Miami-Dade, Broward, and Palm Beach Counties in Florida, West Indians and Hispanics have won jobs that blacks held for generations.

Since the 1980s, Johnson said, "Most of the human conflagrations have been between ethnic groups, not between whites and blacks." Johnson argued also that American blacks, who do not have an entrepreneurial tradition, clearly lose out to Asian and other immigrant cultures that come the United States with well-honed business skills, money, and networks with ties to banks and other lending sources.

Other roundtable presenters described the South as a leader in education reform, especially with regard to charter schools. North Carolina is a leader in this area. Several southern states, such as Florida, have model welfare reform efforts and programs that protect young children. On the downside, the South is also one of the fastest-growing regions of the nation, and with such growth come more zip codes, area codes, and, of course, the social isolation of gated communities and sealed waterfronts.

Dixie, where Confederate Gen. Robert E. Lee surrendered in shame to northern Gen. Ulysses S. Grant 133 years ago at Appomattox, Virginia, is as mainstream as any other part of the nation and through self-examination has become a major player in shaping the issues, trends, and customs important to most Americans. The key now, Guillory said, is to nurture journalists who can "cast trained, experienced eyes across the South's political landscape, seeking not to perpetuate myths but to illuminate reality."

Thank God It's Football

Blacks lose by winning in sports

JANUARY 19, 1997

During last football season, Ft. Lauderdale's mostly black Dillard High School beat mostly white Western High 31–24. My brother and I sat on the Dillard side, where some of our former schoolmates shouted to Dillard players, "You better not let them white boys win!" and "Ain't no white boys gonna beat Dillard!" Based on these and other comments I heard that night, I realized that, far from being a mere game, this homecoming event represented a classic comparison of the races: muscular, speedy blacks against less athletically endowed but intellectually superior whites.

This insight was rekindled a few days ago as I read John Hoberman's new book, *Darwin's Athletes: How Sport Has Damaged Black America and Preserved the Myth of Race*. Hoberman, a professor of Germanic languages at the University of Texas at Austin, argues that the nation's obsession with black athletic prowess has evolved into a destructive force in black society and plays a worrisome role in race relations in general. Because blacks traditionally have been excluded from other areas of success, sports stars have become our role models, our "race heroes." We have given our most gifted athletes messianic status, a conferment that prevents us from confronting the realities beneath the illusions.

One of the biggest illusions of black athleticism, Hoberman writes, is the belief that the high numbers of successful blacks in most sports indicate that sports have become a deracialized utopia where blacks are equal to their white teammates, thus making America itself more egalitarian. Nothing could be further from the truth, he contends. The specter of rich, flamboyant, black superjocks constantly in the public eye does not indicate real success but, on the contrary, contributes to deepening racial divisions and the further degradation of black athletes and black life per se.

How? During the 19th century and the early 20th century, sports were proof of white superiority, authority, and entitlement in Western civilization. Today, paradoxically, instead of elevating blacks to a level of respectability, our dominance in many sports has become a sign of our inferiority. Our extraordinary physicality has come to mean that we are incapable of intellectual achievement and other significant mental activity that the nation values.

Who cares that we brothers can jump higher, run faster, slam-dunk with more ferocity, catch passes more gracefully, and steal more bases? Aside from their entertainment value, these skills have no application in contemporary life. Whites, in effect, do not sweat relinquishing dominance in sports to us. "Therefore, there is nothing liberating about black athletic achievement—not for African-Americans generally, and certainly not for the athletes, regardless of how much money they make," writes black scholar Gerald Early, reviewing *Darwin's Athletes* in the latest issue of the *Wilson Quarterly*. "The old racial myth—of blacks depoliticized, trivialized, reduced to the Freudian primitive in the white mind—remains intact."

White America sees black male athletes as oversexed, undisciplined savages and violent criminals. These stereotypes fuel "scientific" theorizing that blacks are less intelligent and less ethical than whites. And Lord knows, we have enough superstars—boxer Mike Tyson and Dallas Cowboys players Michael Irvin and Erik Williams—who give weight to "the growing black-pathology business" and a host of cynical myths associated with black superjockdom.

But these and other problems pale beside the anti-intellectualism that our sports fixation has spawned across black America, an anti-intellectualism that encourages tens of thousands of young black males to shun academic achievement. Wealth and fame from athletics are so valued that being "smart" is uncool.

Hoberman condemns black intellectuals for railing against other forms of cultural enslavement while remaining mute on sports fixation. He argues that "some black writers see stylish black athleticism as a kind of cultural avant-garde." Nelson George, for example, calls black athleticism a "black athletic aesthetic" and "music put into physical motion." Hoberman continues: "When Michael Eric Dyson writes of Michael Jordan's 'herculean cultural heroism,' he is making the athlete an artist by placing him in the vanguard of modern black self-expression. At a time when a flamboyant black athletic style is widely seen as opposed to a more sedate white one, the celebration of black athleticism as culture is an implicit act of resistance directed at white cultural standards."

And with black superstars spewing Ebonics on television—"We wasn't worried" or "I don't think he seen me" or "When we hits the field, we one team"—race-conscious authors such as Dinesh D'Sousa and Charles Murray salivate. For them, black English, or Ebonics, confirms the biological inferiority of the "muscular Negro," a creature who, as part of the Darwinian struggle of survival, cannot compete with "civilized whites in a modern society."

Hoberman has written with courage and wisdom. Readers will either love him or hate him. But no one can peruse his pages without being disabused of many illusions about sports and their corrosive effects on black America. While reading *Darwin's Athletes*, I recalled the words that a Dillard student yelled to a Western student: "You all got the brains, but we won the game." The white student from Western shrugged and kept on walking toward the exit gate.

In the grip of football fever

August 26, 1998

That time of the year is upon us. The nights are cooling, marching bands and cheerleaders are practicing, and a general excitement is in the air. In case you have been in Russia and do not know what time it is, you need to know that college and high school football season is here.

Northerners, midwesterners, and westerners love football, but they do not love it as much as southerners. Down here in Dixie, we go dad-blamed crazy about the game. "Football mania" is the only term that accurately describes the mass psychosis that grips southern towns such as Athens, Auburn, Baton Rouge, Clemson, Columbia, Gainesville, Knoxville, Little Rock, Oxford, Tallahassee, and Tampa.

Tampa? Yes, Tampa—home of the University of South Florida Bulls. More on the Bulls shortly.

Football occupies the southern mind 13 months out of the year. Hunting and stock car racing only serve as momentary distractions. In many small towns—such as Chiefland, High Springs, Live Oak, Newberry, and Williston, in Florida—the level of community pride is directly tied to the number of wins and losses the local football team amasses each season. In short, pigskin prowess is a matter of southern honor.

Florida football fans are truly fortunate. We are a football haven. Each of our three major football programs has been national champion at least once during the past 10 years. This year, the Associated Press has the Florida State University Seminoles and the University of Florida Gators ranked 2 and 3. Along with their counterparts in Texas, Florida high schools attract college scouts like stink attracts flies. If a coach in Michigan wants a scatback, he knows to go, for example, to Glades Central in Belle Glade. The South sends more football players to college teams and to the National Football League than other parts of the nation. Many men in the South, especially black fathers, start grooming their sons early for football careers.

Scholars have long recorded the South's obsession with the gridiron. In his article "Geography of Sports," Oklahoma State University professor John F. Rooney Jr. writes that "football mania is still intensifying throughout the South. . . . Though football is a national game, the ability to play it well is inordinately concentrated in the South." Many social critics cast a wary eye at this obsession. They believe, argues University of Iowa professor Benjamin K. Hunnicut, that the game, like many other popular pastimes, reflects regional values and characteristics that crave so-called blood sports and materialistic games.

Here in Dixie, the well-known initials TGIF have a double meaning: Thank God It's Friday and Thank God It's Football. James M. Gifford of Appalachian State University says that "Friday night in the autumn is the time for a major southern ritual occasion. Football is the center of a complex cultural event involving more than players on the field." Football is, in fact, an instrument of psychic survival in the Old Confederacy.

Now, back to Tampa and USF.

College football fever has even invaded the land of Santo Trafficante, the Tampa Bay Bucs, and cigars. The Bulls are heading into their second season as a Division I-AA independent. During its first season, the team scored an impressive 5–6 record, with a near-upset of Georgia Southern, the perennial Division I-AA powerhouse. The Bulls' first game—an 80–3 skunking of Kentucky Wesleyan—still has the sports world scratching its head. The team also sold 22,000 season tickets, the most ever for an inaugural season in I-AA.

"I doubt whether there's ever been a more successful launch of a football program than the launch of the program at South Florida," said Michael Slive, commissioner of Conference USA, the conference that the team may join in 2001.

The team is already paying for itself, with bucks left over. Why? Because USF fans, like those at other southern campuses, are rabid, loyal college football fans. In fact, we are just seeing the beginning of USF pigskin mania. And all of those naysayers, who whined for years that football would come at the expense of academics, should shut up and buy season tickets. The Bulls are here to stay.

I would be remiss if I did not acknowledge one of the real sources of the team's phenomenal success: head coach Jim Leavitt, a first-class act if there ever was one. His style is exactly what a start-up program needed.

Level the paying field for athletes

AUGUST 1, 1999

Those who run big-time college football—presidents, coaches, boosters, athletic clubs, foundations, politicians—need to come clean about the corruption in the institution and the abuse of young men who hit the gridiron each autumn Saturday to butt heads.

The time has come to end the pretense that players on Division I-A teams—such as Notre Dame, University of Florida, Alabama, UCLA, Nebraska, Michigan, Auburn, Ohio State, Penn State, and Florida State—are *student*-athletes, regular kids lugging their book bags to and from class. Fine-tuned, chiseled, testosterone-soaked, and egocentric, these young men are not *student*-athletes.

They are *athlete*-students.

The sooner everyone understands this distinction and acts on it honestly, the better off the I-A scene will be for everyone involved, especially for the athletes and their families.

We need to start treating college football players like real paraprofessionals deserving of the benefits and protections that come with such employment. I am not alone in proposing this change, which was brought into sharp relief last week with articles about William "Tank" Black, an NFL Players Association agent. The association handed Black the harshest punishment ever given an agent for rules violations. His certification was revoked for three years, and he must pay a $25,000 fine when he reapplies for certification.

What Black is accused of doing is nothing more than standard operating procedure among many agents. In May, the NFLPA lodged a complaint against him and his company, Professional Management, Inc., alleging eight violations that include gifts of cash and cars to football standouts at the University of South Carolina, Louisiana State, and Florida before the athletes' NCAA eligibility had expired.

At least four players at the University of Florida have been directly linked to Black and PMI. In his NFLPA affidavit, former Florida linebacker Johnny Rutledge depicts the shadow world of *athlete*-students and agents. Here are salient excerpts from the affidavit (Black denied the accusations):

"Beginning in 1997, my junior year, I began receiving money from Alfred Twitty, who worked for Tank Black and his company PMI in Columbia, S.C. I initially received $200 per month, but in the summer of 1997 I asked for more. Twitty told me then that the usual amount for players like me was $600 per month. I thereafter received $600 per month through December of 1998. On occasion, I would get more than $600, like in December for Christmas and during my birthday month when I got $1,000 in cash.

"Twitty began asking me about what car I wanted during my junior year, when it was possible I would consider turning pro. I decided to play my senior year instead. During my last season in 1998, Twitty again asked me what car I wanted. I eventually told him in December of 1998 that I wanted a Mercedes Benz S420.

"I understood while I was receiving cash from Twitty that it was being provided by Tank Black. I met Tank Black in Tampa in the summer of 1998 at an event arranged by Twitty. Present were myself, Jevon Kearse, Fred Taylor and others from Tank's agency. At that time, Tank asked me, 'Is Tweet taking care of you?' I answered in the affirmative. And he told me that if I ever needed anything, I should contact Tweet.

"I also talked with Tank during the balance of 1998 when he would call me by telephone and ask how I was doing. On one such call, I told him I needed money to buy furniture. Soon thereafter, Twitty came with the cash (about $700), and Reggie McGrew and I used it to purchase furniture for our apartment.

"I was aware that Jevon Kearse and Reggie McGrew were also receiving monthly cash payments from Twitty. On occasion, the entire amount for all three of us would be delivered to one of us. . . .

"I knew all along that it was expected by Twitty and Tank Black that I would sign with PMI when I turned pro. I informed them late in the 1998 season that I would do so. The day I signed with PMI—January 4, 1999—I got the car I told Twitty that I wanted, which was a 1999 Mercedes S420 with all of the equipment I had said I wanted."

Rutledge's experience is not unique. Nationwide, hundreds of other football superstars have similar stories. Agents' raison d'être is to make as much money as they can, and many will resort to any measures to sign players who will give them maximum bargaining power with NFL teams.

Money and expensive gifts are the best ways to attract players. The dire circumstances of most players make them easy targets for fat wallets. Many I-A football players come from medium- to low-income families. They cannot buy luxuries, and many cannot afford the simplest of things—pizza, decent furniture for their apartments—or extras like a car. They see other students living the good life. The catch-22 is that unlike regular students, *athlete*-students on scholarship are prohibited from working. They cannot earn legitimate money if they want to.

There is more: even if they were permitted to work, they would not have time to do so because, along with taking full class loads, they practice two to three hours Monday through Friday. Game day is devoted to the game. If they travel out of town to play, the entire weekend is devoted to the sport.

Meanwhile, their universities—and their coaches—are raking in millions of dollars on their backs and from their sweat. The entire student body benefits from the sport. When I was a graduate student at the University of Florida in the early 1980s, for example, proceeds from Gator games literally bankrolled summer school. The money was a godsend because budgets were tight.

Football is a plantation. Slavery. The players are "meat on the hoof," as Gary Shaw called them in his book of the same title.

Football is big business. Period. The National Collegiate Athletic Association needs to establish a uniform system to pay *athlete*-students what they deserve. If nothing is done, the system will continue to corrupt players and their universities.

Please do not tell me that these players are students before they are athletes. Nonsense. They have one purpose on a major campus: to play football and generate lucre for their schools.

I do not know how to devise a system of fair monetary compensation for these *athlete*-student paraprofessionals. But I know that it can be done.

Most universities have competent business colleges. A committee of economics teachers, along with other experts, from select schools should immediately start to work on a solution—one that has clean money and other fair compensations as its focus.

One player's not enough to spoil game

OCTOBER 24, 1999

Although many pseudomoralists, especially newspaper pundits, have trashed Peter Warrick, the legal problems of this 21-year-old football standout are not the whole story. Warrick—the Florida State University wide receiver who was busted, along with teammate Laveranues Coles, for sweet-talking a Dillard's department store worker into selling $412.38 worth of designer clothes for $21.40—is but a speck on the national landscape of big-time college football.

After some hold-your-breath finagling among Warrick's lawyer, the university, and the state attorney's office, the felony grand theft charge against the Heisman hopeful was changed to a misdemeanor petty theft charge, thereby clearing the way for him to rejoin the nation's top-ranked team in time to suit up against conference rival Clemson on Saturday. Warrick will serve one year of probation with no jail time, pay $579 in restitution and $295 in court costs, stay out of Dillard's, spend 30 days in a work program, and donate the discounted clothes to the Children's Home Society.

These are the kind of developments that give Division I-A football an ugly name. But college football—especially winning programs—has an important, positive side that we in the media rarely write about, and the thousands of Peter Warricks are the heart and soul of that positive side.

In a recent article about Kansas State University's successful football program, *Chronicle of Higher Education* sportswriter Welch Suggs gets to the heart of the matter: "According to conventional wisdom, a winning football team—much more than any other sport, even basketball—has immense payoff for an entire university. Winning teams make alumni, fans, board members, donors, students, and prospective students happy, and so the university prospers when its team does. Donations go up, applications go up, and the money pours in from fans, bowl payouts, and television contracts."

Florida, my home state, has embraced college football completely. All sports insiders marvel, for example, that the University of South Florida's team is a major contender in Division I-AA in its third season of existence. Just last week, the Bulls whipped 6th-ranked Illinois State and moved up to number 17 in the polls. In 2001, the Bulls will join Division I-A, a phenomenal move for a start-up program.

Dividends from such success are clear. Because USF is on the central Gulf Coast, the joke used to be: "Where in south Florida is the University of Florida?" That joke is no more. Now, thanks to football, folks know Florida's second-largest university is in Tampa.

Formerly a commuter campus without a yearbook, USF is getting sustained national attention for the first time. Profiles touting the university's student enrollment, international diversity, faculty, courses, degrees, and local amenities have appeared in prestigious news venues such as the *Washington Post*, the *Atlanta Journal-Constitution*, *USA Today*, the *Chronicle of Higher Education*, *Sports Illustrated*, and on major network and cable shows. Even during the school's first year of football in 1997, Director of Media Relations Todd Simmons said, "Without doubt, our football program made all this possible. We can now leverage the publicity in ways that benefit us."

One immediate benefit is that alumni now have reason to return to campus often. They are bonding like never before, and, of course, many are writing bigger checks—more often. In addition to enticing alumni back to campus, the team is attracting some of Florida's brightest students, and it is causing out-of-staters to give USF and the Tampa Bay region a closer look.

Administrators at other Florida universities have heard the triumphant news from Tampa and have contracted pigskin fever. Florida Atlantic in Boca Raton will field its first football team in 2001. Its head coach, Howard Schnellenberger, is a proven winner. He helped Don Shula coach the 1972 Miami Dolphins to a 17–0 season, and he took the University of Miami Hurricanes to a national championship in 1979.

A few miles down the road from FAU, Miami's Florida International University has initiated the process of bringing football to the 27-year-old campus. Officials will ask the Florida Board of Regents, during the next three months, to approve their plan for a team. "This is a society in which football is considered part of the collegiate experience," Paul Gallagher, FIU's senior vice president for business and finance, told the *Miami Herald*. "Kids want to get an education, obviously, but they also want to have a life. . . . Football does something for a university nothing else does." Predictably, many FIU faculty scorn football. FIU president Modesto Maidique, with former Miami Dolphins quarterback Don Strock as his point man in Tallahassee, believes, however, that the regents will let the gold-and-blue-clad Golden Eagles hit the gridiron in 2001.

Meanwhile, in another part of the nation where football is king, University of Oklahoma President David Boren echoes the sentiments of his counterparts at Florida Atlantic, Florida International, and South Florida. "Football is not just football," he said in the *Chronicle*. "It's wrapped up in the spirit and self-consciousness of the state."

Strictly in terms of football, Seminoles fans had good reason to wring their hands over the fate of Warrick. His loss would have been the university's loss. And, like it or not, his loss would have been the state of Florida's loss. We have a winning tradition. We are a place that produces national champions.

Warrick's exceptional athleticism reflects Florida's winning esprit de corps. Like it or not, Warrick's lawyer, John Kenny, said it all in describing the sentence handed down the day before the Clemson game: "It was a fair resolution for the state, a fair resolution for Peter Warrick, and a fair resolution for the university. And we know it's a fair resolution for our fans."

The game in black and white

FEBRUARY 6, 2000

At long last, someone has the guts to tell it like it is. Actually, Jimmy the Greek, late of ABC News, told it like it is years ago and was canned. The "it" is the fact that African-American athletes as a group are naturally superior to white and other athletes—or so claims former NBC and ABC journalist and Emmy Award–winning producer Jon Entine in his book *Taboo: Why Black Athletes Dominate Sports and Why We're Afraid to Talk About It.*

In 400 pages of easy-to-read prose, Entine uses the most recent findings in evolution and genetic science, including the heralded Human Genome Project, to explain why blacks run faster, jump higher, and last longer, and why, for example, the best running backs, wide receivers, and cornerbacks are black. Although *Taboo* will delight racists and mortify those such as Stephen Jay Gould and Richard Lewontin, who argue that race does not exist, Entine has done the world a great service by breaking the silence on a topic that makes nearly everyone run for cover. Racists will be disappointed, though, that Entine refuses to link physical prowess and intellectual ability.

Anyone who watches sports even casually has at one time or another wondered why blacks dominate. Is the reason environment? Or is it physiology? While acknowledging the importance of environmental factors, Entine pulls no punches in arguing why blacks, descendants of West and East Africa, are endowed with superior athleticism. "There is extensive and persuasive evidence that elite black athletes have phenotypic advantage—a distinctive skeletal system and musculature, metabolic structures, and other characteristics forged over tens of thousands of years of evolution," he argues. "Preliminary research suggests that different phenotypes are at least partially encoded in the genes—conferring genotypic differences, which may result in an advantage in some sports."

What gives Jerry Rice and Michael Jordan the advantages of power, quickness, and explosiveness? We are not talking about *impressions* of advantages, as in some sports, but about quantifiable advantages.

For answers, Entine turns to research: "Blacks with a West African ancestry generally have: relatively less subcutaneous fat on arms and legs and proportionally more lean body and muscle mass, broader shoulders, larger quadriceps, and bigger, more developed musculature in general; smaller chest cavities; a higher center of gravity . . . faster patellar tendon reflex; greater body density . . . modest but significantly higher levels of plasma testosterone . . . which is anabolic, theoretically contributing to greater muscle mass, lower fat, and the ability to perform at a higher level of intensity with quicker recovery; a higher percentage of fast-twitch muscles and more anaerobic enzymes, which can translate into more explosive energy."

In addition to being an analysis of performance research, *Taboo* is a powerful history of African-Americans in sports itself. The reader is taken on a journey from the highlands of Kenya to the sandlots of southern California to the Olympic Games in Atlanta. Familiar faces—Jackie Robinson, Wilma Rudolph, Jack Johnson, Arthur Ashe—are given human context.

Entine tosses out the canard that a lack of opportunity in other fields accounts for black athleticism. Only outsiders believe such nonsense, he argues. Most athletes, even whites, believe blacks are naturally dominant and dismiss the sociological arguments. "I work camps in the summertime with white kids," NBA forward Christian Laettner told Entine. "The white kids are still trying as hard as they've ever tried. They're probably trying now harder. The players who tend to be really athletic and really good once you get to the higher levels, more and more it seems to be the black group. That's just the way it is."

And from Lebanese-born Rony Seikaly: "The black players are superior. No doubt. I go to Lebanon in the summer, and we have pickup games, and there's this one eighteen-year-old Nigerian playing in the Lebanese league who can touch his head to the rim. It's amazing, [blacks'] athletic ability. They're built, they're buffed. We work out to get a body like that, and they come out just naturally gifted."

Thanks to Entine, the genie is out the bottle, and the debate about race and athleticism will never be the same.

Coach helps his players score on field and in life

MARCH 12, 2000

To Theophilus Danzy, the 69-year-old head coach at private, historically black Stillman College, football is no mere game. While acknowledging that such a view of the sport has become cliché, he has proof that the gridiron, with the right adult leaders on the sidelines, is the ideal venue for building character.

Why did football return to Stillman in 1999 after a 50-year hiatus? After all, the school, affiliated with the Presbyterian Church, has an average student population of about 1,000, and it is continually strapped for money. "When President Earnest McNealy announced that the school was bringing back football, I asked why," said Danzy, who had been retired since 1990. "I said, 'God dog, that's a big chore.' Then I realized that our president has a mission."

In addition to boosting alumni interest in the 124-year-old campus and encouraging more giving, McNealy wanted to increase the number of males on campus. During most recent years, the college has been roughly 65 percent to 70 percent female, and McNealy believed that football would help reverse that trend.

He was right. "It is safe to say we probably have 200 male students who would not be here otherwise," he told the *Tuscaloosa News*.

Incredibly, 300 students tried out for the squad, with more than 100 biting the dust early on and others failing the cut. McNealy and the coaches expect football to have a domino effect, believing that even males who do not want to play football will want to be on an all-black campus that has the sport.

The next task was to find the right coach. "I selected a coach that I thought would bring the same types of values to the table that are at this institution already," McNealy told the *News*. Most of those values are manifested throughout the tiny campus, and the head coach must be in sync. "If [athletes] don't do their work, they will go home," McNealy said. "If they don't behave, they go home. We fully expect our students to go to class. We fully expect them to graduate." Violence is not tolerated, and even profanity is cause for expulsion. One player recently overheard cursing, for example, was kicked out of school.

"So far," McNealy told the *News*, "our football players are among the most controlled students on campus."

Give most of the credit to Danzy, the straight-talking fatherlike figure who acknowledges that he is "very firm." Beneath that firmness, however, are a vision and a willingness to save troubled young black males. When McNealy asked Danzy to be Stillman's first contemporary football coach, Danzy saw a chance to renew efforts he had started in 1958, when he took his first coaching job. "I had been reading that one in every three black males couldn't vote because they were in jail or in some other kind of situation where voting was taken away from them," he said. "I told myself the best way for me to help is to step in here at Stillman. I had been successful every place I worked."

He can rattle off the names of many current and former NFL African-American players whom he turned around and put on the right path, especially at Alcorn State University in Mississippi. But he takes most pride in the ordinary ones who are making a difference. "Everywhere I go, I see them in places where I have recruited hundreds of kids," Danzy said. "I see successful professionals who, when I first got them, their teachers said they would never make it. And now many are assistant principals, business executives, attorneys, teachers, some even pastors. I feel that I have succeeded when they go back into the community they came from and produce, when they become functioning citizens. Football is a great sport for producing these kind of results."

The coach knows student success is a two-way street. On an office bulletin board, for example, he has written the words "grade sign-off sheet." The note reminds him to regularly monitor—complete with signatures—the players' course grades.

"I have to make sure they're doing their part, that they are studying," he said, taking a telephone call from a prospective linebacker in Mississippi. "They must do their part academically. They just can't sit around and wait. But my job is to set up mechanisms and tools to make sure the kids function well."

As a Division III program, Stillman cannot offer athletic scholarships or establish endowments. Players must find financial aid, loans, and other assistance to attend Stillman. In other words, they have to have a burning desire to attend the school and play football.

"Not having scholarships makes coaching doubly hard," Danzy said. "You sell the young men the concept that you want to get them an education. You sell that concept real, real hard. It is very hard to retain many of these young men. They have faced many negative forces and still face them, and it is tougher than ever before. Regardless of football, you want to make sure they get an education. Even if a kid stays here two or three years, he is elevated. He is a better person."

Danzy said too many high schools and colleges exploit black athleticism and discard it—and the player. He believes the historically black campus is best for those with troubled pasts. Unlike traditional campuses with thousands of students, which also may have special programs for minority athletes, the typical black campus is a network of caring. "Black schools have more net to catch the troubled kid," Danzy said. "I have no problem in saying that this thing is separate, segregation. You take care of yours. When you cease to take care of yours, then things go awry."

Florida natives Michael Cunningham, 21, Jermaine Blakely, 21, and Antwan Blatch, 19, each the first in his immediate family to attend college, appreciate their coach's philosophy and credit it, along with their parents, for their success. Each is determined to earn a degree and become a professional after football. Each knows that he is at Stillman because of football.

How does Danzy consistently inspire most of his players, many from the inner city, to work hard and stay on the straight and narrow?

"I try to see farther than they're looking," he said. "I try to cultivate them in a way that will bring them into society and show them the value of doing a good job. Simply, I want to build character among young black men."

Bill Maxwell has written a twice-weekly syndicated column for the *St. Petersburg Times* for the past seven years. His columns appear in 200 newspapers worldwide and have received many writing awards, including the Florida Press Club's plaque for general excellence in commentary (twice) and the Community Champion Award from the American Trial Lawyers Association. From 1988 to 1994 he wrote for the *New York Times* Regional Newspaper Group. During and before that period he taught journalism and English for eighteen years, at the University of Illinois (Chicago), Governor's State University (Park Forest, Illinois), Northern Illinois University (DeKalb), Santa Fe Community College (Gainesville, Florida), Broward Community College (Pembroke Pines, Florida), Indian River Community College (Fort Pierce, Florida), Florida Keys Community College (Key West), and in the Florida prison program at Lake City Community College.